S0-BIR-291

City of Friends

City of Friends

A Portrait of the Gay and Lesbian Community in America

Simon LeVay and Elisabeth Nonas

The MIT Press
Cambridge, Massachusetts
London, England

This book was set in Palatino by the MIT Press.

Printed on recycled paper and bound in the United States of America.

Library of Congress Cataloging-in-Publication Data

LeVay, Simon.
City of friends : a portrait of the gay and lesbian community in America / Simon LeVay and Elisabeth Nonas.
p. cm.
Includes bibliographical references and index.
ISBN 0-262-12194-8 (hc : alk. paper)
1. Gay communities—United States. 2. Lesbian communities—United States. 3. Gay men—United States—Social conditions. 4. Lesbians—United States—Social conditions. I. Nonas, Elisabeth, 1949- . II. Title.
HQ76.2.U5L46 1995
306.76'0973—dc20

95-34824
CIP

Contents

I dream'd in a dream I saw a city invincible to the attacks of the whole of the rest of the earth,
I dream'd that was the new city of Friends,
Nothing was greater there than the quality of robust love, it led the rest,
It was seen every hour in the actions of the men of that city,
And in all their looks and words.

—Walt Whitman

Preface

As ever-growing numbers of lesbians and gay men raise their voices in the many spaces of American life, they are laying claim to the same citizenship as all other men and women, while at the same time attempting to reclaim their own ancient heritage and culture. This balancing act, difficult enough for members of any minority, is made doubly hard for gays and lesbians by the accident of their birth: for whatever the actual circumstances that predispose to homosexuality, the appearance is that of a random seeding, as if some mischievous spirit had left queer changelings in the cribs of honest burghers.

Indeed, the gay person's life unfolds with all the mysterious illogic of a fairy tale. Stumbling between perplexed elders and too-knowing playmates, the child asks questions that are answered only with riddles or silence, while inner whisperings hint at distant adventure. One day, after many a winter, a gnome offers the growing youth the key to the Door of Self-knowledge, which swings creakily open, revealing shelf after shelf of becobwebbed tomes...

We are that gnome, and this book the library—condensed, to be sure, to suit today's shorter attention span. The content, though, is the same. It is a survey of what it means to be gay or lesbian: where gays and lesbians come from in history and in individual development; what are their common interests, needs, and aspirations; and a portrait of the gay community as a seething coalition of groups and subgroups that resolve ultimately into the splendid uniqueness of the gay individual.

In an ideal world this book would not be necessary, because all this material—introductory as it must necessarily be—would be instilled by parents, schools, and the media long before a young person even became aware of her or his own sexual orientation. It would be common knowledge. But in the real world this knowledge is withheld, even from those whose own heritage it should be.

Because we ourselves went through this process of self-discovery years ago, when it was considerably more daunting than it is today, we wish to help smooth the path for another generation of lesbians and bisexuals and gay men. But it is not only gays and lesbians for whom this book is intended. All men and women have a close involvement with the gay community. If not gay or lesbian themselves, then they are the parents, children, brothers, sisters, spouses, exes, friends, enemies, employers, employees, doctors, patients, teachers, students, entertainers, audience, pastors, or parishioners of lesbians and gay men. This book is offered as a guide to them too.

Understanding something about gay people means understanding something about diversity: that diversity does not mean simply a collection of separate identities, but also the interpenetration and mutual enrichment of different cultures. Being gay or lesbian is excellent, but it also may mean lacking the direct experience of heterosexuality. We have nevertheless learned something of heterosexuality through culture, and we would like to return the favor.

Both of us have been involved over the past three years with the Institute of Gay and Lesbian Education in West Hollywood (Simon LeVay as a cofounder, Elisabeth Nonas as a faculty member). This experience has helped us understand the need for a book of this kind, and it has also greatly enriched our own understanding of the gay and lesbian community. We are most grateful to the students and faculty of the institute who have shared their knowledge and ideas with us. This book could not have happened without them.

Innumerable individuals have aided us in the preparation of this book, by agreeing to be interviewed or by supplying pertinent written materials. We especially wish to thank the following: Shella Aguilar (and the Los Angeles Asian Pacific Islander Sisters), Luis Alfaro, Ruth Barrett, Bishop Carl Bean, Alison Bechdel, Malcolm Boyd, Colleen Brady, Kaucyila Brooke, Lisa Channer, Kate Clinton, Jane Cottis, Barbara Grier, Harmony Hammond, Dorsie Hathaway, Margaret Holub, Loraine Hutchins, Louis Jacinto, Guy Jones, Peter Katsufrakis, Jonathan David Katz, Gregory King, John Knoebel, Maureen Gallery Kovacs, Bruce Lehman, Harriet Leve, Leon Lodge, Jeffrey Majors, Greg Merrill, Joseph Neisen, Connie Norman, Adam Novsam, Catherine Opie, Jesus Ornelas, Jan Oxenberg, Angela Pattatucci, Elizabeth Pincus, Martha Richards, Ron Rogge, Eric Scheir, Hank Stack, Deanna Stevenson, Terry Tauger, Sherry Thomas, Virginia Uribe, Watts Wacker (of Yankelovich Partners, Inc.), Nancy Walker, Katy Wallace, William Waybourn, Winston Wilde, Morgaine Wilder, Alistair Williamson, Beth Zemsky, and the women of Mendocino County.

We also thank Judith Branzburg, Peter Katsufrakis, Amy Ryan, Laurie Saunders, Keith Wisot, and three anonymous reviewers for reading portions of the manuscript and suggesting improvements.

We thank Fiona Stevens and Melissa Vaughn of The MIT Press for their extensive advice and encouragement throughout the project.

Finally, Elisabeth Nonas wishes to thank Judith Branzburg, Amy Ryan, Leslie Belzberg, and Barbara Zaszlow for their great support and friendship during the completion of this project.

I Origins

Although the major focus of this book is the gay and lesbian community in the contemporary United States, we begin with a broader survey of homosexuality and history. We start, in chapter 1, by considering the meanings of the words that will be recurring throughout the book—"lesbian," "gay," "gender," and so on. Chapter 2 depicts the various modes of homosexuality that have existed at different times and places around the world, modes that also exist in our own culture. In chapter 3, we sketch the main lines of development of the lesbian and gay community in the United States, with particular emphasis on the gay rights movement that began in the 1950s. We complete our survey of gay origins in chapter 4 by taking a look at what science has to say about the factors that influence a person's sexual orientation.

1
Meanings

This book is about lesbians and gay men; its main focus is the culture they have established in the contemporary United States. But who is "lesbian" or "gay"? What do the words mean? We need to start by considering some definitions.

All definitions are fuzzy around the edges, and nowhere is that more true than when we are trying to categorize human beings. Words like "deaf people," "Americans," or "doctors" seem at first glance pretty clear-cut. But just how deaf is "deaf"? Are "Americans" citizens of the United States, of North America, or of both Americas? Do "doctors" include only M.D.'s, or also O.D.'s, Ph.D.'s, and J.D.'s? Using different definitions of these words can lead to estimates of the numbers of Americans, deaf people, and doctors that differ by several-fold. It's the same with "gay" and "lesbian."

Before we attempt even a provisional definition, we need to look at some more basic terms that describe human sexuality, like *sex, sexual behavior, sexual orientation,* and *gender*. Then we can construct a working definition of "gay" and "lesbian" out of terms we have already defined.

Sex

The word "sex" describes the attempt to categorize people into two classes, women and men, on the basis of physical characteristics. We can further refine the distinction by naming the kind of physical characteristics we are talking about—for example, the number and appearance of a person's chromosomes, or the anatomical organization of a person's genitalia.

No matter which characteristic we use, however, not everyone will fall unambiguously into the category of females or the category of males.

Chromosomal sex refers to whether a person has the sex chromosomes typical of a man (one X and one Y) or of a woman (two X's). Most people can be classified unambiguously by this criterion. But there are people with unusual combinations of sex chromosomes, for example, two X's and one Y, or one X and no Y. Furthermore, the pattern of sex chromosomes does not always predict a person's sex as defined by anatomy, because what really matters is not the chromosomes but the sex-defining genes *on* the chromosomes, and these can differ even between individuals who have the same complement of chromosomes.

Anatomical sex refers to whether a person possesses the internal genitalia, external genitalia, and secondary sexual characteristics typical of a man or a woman. Among these characteristics, the external genitalia are most commonly used to assign sex. Individuals with a vagina, labial folds, and clitoris are generally called female, and those with a penis and scrotum, male. There are individuals, however, whose genitalia are intermediate between the "male" and "female" pattern. These people are "intersexes." How many intersexes there are depends on how rigorously one defines words like "penis" and "clitoris." The tendency in contemporary Western culture is to assign anatomically intersexed babies to the category of "male" or "female," and to perform reconstructive surgery as necessary to make the baby correspond to the assigned category. Some people have argued that we should be more tolerant of anatomical variations in the genitalia, and that we should allow these intersexed children to grow up and make their own decisions about their bodies and their sex when they are ready to do so.

Sexual Behavior

Some sexual acts are more commonly performed by one sex than the other. For example, taking the insertive role in sexual intercourse (whether vaginal or anal) is male-typical behavior, while taking the receptive role is female-typical behavior. The fact that receptive intercourse is atypical for men does not mean that it is pathological or wrong when men exhibit it, only that it is less common. The same goes for insertive intercourse by women. There are some men and women who have a strong, lifelong preference for sex-atypical sexual behavior.

Of course, there are plenty of human sexual behaviors that are not differentiated between the sexes: pelvic thrusting during intercourse, for example, and oral sex of various kinds. There are also behaviors that appear to be sex-differentiated, if one looks narrowly at contemporary American practice, but that are seen to be far more flexible if one looks at a wide variety of cultures. An example would be the relative positions of men and women during heterosexual intercourse.

Sexual Orientation

Sexual orientation is a dimension of personality that describes whether a person feels sexual attraction predominantly toward people of the same anatomical sex (*homosexual*), of both sexes (*bisexual*), or of the other anatomical sex (*heterosexual*). Note that we say *anatomical* sex. Thus a man who is attracted to other men who are feminine in manner, dress, etc., is still homosexual, according to this definition, so long as he is aware that they are anatomically men.

It should also be noted that we use the word *predominantly* in qualifying the direction of sexual attraction. There are probably very few people who have not felt, at some time or another, some sexual attraction to both men and women. Where the division between homosexual (or heterosexual) and bisexual should be placed is arbitrary, because sexual orientation is a continuum. But if the word homosexual is to retain any usefulness, it must be defined broadly enough to allow *some* opposite-sex attraction.

A person's sexual orientation is not necessarily a fixed, lifelong attribute. Sexual orientation can change: for example, a woman may be predominantly attracted to men for many years, and perhaps have a happy marriage and children during that time, and then become increasingly aware of same-sex attraction in her thirties, forties, or later. This does not mean that she was concealing or repressing her homosexuality during the earlier period. To argue that she was "really" homosexual all the time would be to change the definition of sexual orientation into something murky and inaccessible. The same would be true even if there were some marker (in her genes or her brain, for example) that could to be used to predict that she would ultimately become homosexual. But equally, if that woman deliberately chose to conceal a predominant same-sex attraction, or not to act on it, out of shame or a desire to have a conventional family, then she *was* homosexual, even before she came out of the closet.

Gender

The word "gender," as we use it, refers to the constellation of self-images, personality traits, and behaviors that are sexually differentiated. Within this constellation one can make a broad distinction between a person's purely subjective feeling of which sex he or she is (*gender identity*), the collection of cognitive and personality traits that are sexually differentiated (which does not have a recognized name to describe it, but which is often included within gender identity), and the sexually differentiated behaviors that a person shows when interacting with other people (*gender role*).

One of the problems with the word "gender" is that is has become closely associated with the notion that this constellation of images and behaviors is the consequence of environment, socialization, or culture. Indeed there are those who define the words "sex" and "gender" to refer specifically to the "biological" and "environmental" aspects of sexual differentiation respectively. The fact is, though, that anatomical differences can come about through environmental mechanisms (drugs influencing fetal development, effects of nutrition, sex-change surgery, etc.). Equally, sexually differentiated personality and behavioral traits may have at least in part a genetic or other non-environmental, biological basis. For example, sex differences in toy preference, aggressiveness, and visuospatial skills are all at least partly brought about through differences in prenatal hormone levels, which are themselves partially under genetic control. For many aspects of what is called "gender," we simply do not know what the relative contributions of genes, nongenetic biological factors, and the environment may be. It therefore seems unwise to make a distinction that presupposes one type of causal mechanism.[1]

Because of this confusion of meaning, an earlier book written by one of us (Simon LeVay's *The Sexual Brain*) avoided the use of the word "gender" altogether. In planning this book we decided that the use of the word was necessary. We do emphasize, however, that our use of the word makes no assumptions about how gender identity or gender role develop.

Commonly, the words "masculine" and "feminine" are used when categorizing by gender. These words too have become loaded with associations and value judgments, for example, that men "should" show masculine behavior. Again, we use the words in this book, but we stress that we do so merely to describe what is actually observed, not to say what is appropriate for men or women to feel or do. Furthermore, the spectrum of gender has many separate dimensions; words like masculine and feminine are most useful when the traits they are being used to describe are clearly defined.

Gay and Lesbian

We use the noun "lesbian" to refer to a homosexual woman, and the noun "gay" or the phrase "gay man" to refer to a homosexual man. We use the adjective "lesbian" to mean homosexual, but only with reference to women. We use the adjective "gay" to mean homosexual, or pertaining to homosexual people, without regard to sex. If we were fully consistent in this matter we would never use the phrase "gay and lesbian," because "gay" would be sufficient. However, we do use both words on those occasions when we are referring to people ("lesbian and gay politicians"), out of respect for the separate identities of lesbians and gay men. We use the single word "gay" when describing other things ("gay rights," "gay ghettos," etc.). In this we are following common though not unanimous usage.

Since we defined as homosexual all those people who are sexually attracted predominantly to other people of the same sex as themselves, it will be apparent that we are calling many people gay or lesbian who do not call *themselves* gay or lesbian. For example, a closeted homosexual woman will not call herself lesbian, but our definition includes her, because it does not require that a woman be open about her homosexuality. Some Latino men who prefer sex with men, but only take the insertive role in anal intercourse, will not call themselves gay, but our definition includes them because it does not take account of what kind of sex acts, if any, are engaged in. Pre-operative female-to-male transsexuals who are sexually attracted to women may not call themselves lesbians, but our definition includes them too, since it is the anatomical sex of both parties that counts in our definition, not their gender identity.

In calling all these people gay or lesbian—some of whom might reject the label—we are flouting a trend toward self-assignment or peer-recognition as the criterion for categorizing human beings. Why do we feel the need to do this? Why don't we say "Those of you who consider yourselves gay or lesbian raise your hands, and we'll write a book about you"?

The answer, simply put, is that too many people would abandon the category if we gave them the chance. Certainly, we would be left with a core group of people who would be gay or lesbian by almost everyone's agreement. But equally, almost everyone would claim that we had left out a whole lot of people that we should have included, even if they could not agree on *which* people these were. Therefore we take a stand with a broad but clearly stated definition, one that we believe joins people who share at least one important aspect of their nature.

Having said this, we emphasize that gays and lesbians, as we have defined them, are not all the same. On the contrary, one of the major themes of this book is the enormous diversity among them. In chapter 2, for example, we describe several quite different patterns of homosexuality that have recurred in a wide variety of cultures. In later chapters we discuss differences in ethnicity, living arrangements, political and religious beliefs, and so on, and how these differences affect the experience of being gay or lesbian. We expect that most people who read this book to the end will have a greatly strengthened sense of the diversity within our community. That was certainly our experience in writing it.

Yet, through all this diversity there are common threads that link people in unexpected ways. This is the other theme of the book. If one stands back and, respectfully, ignores for one moment the names and meanings that people attach to their own sexuality, it may be possible to see a unity that otherwise would escape recognition. When we point out, as we do in the next chapter, a similarity between same-sex behavior among youths in the forests of New Guinea and among boarding-school children in Britain, we are claiming to see something that is invisible to either of the two cultures themselves; invisible, not just because each culture is unaware of the other's existence, but because the two cultures have attached mutually contradictory meanings to the same behavior.

Coming closer to home, we can see common threads that link many, though not all gays and lesbians in contemporary America. One theme is gender nonconformity. We will argue that gender nonconformity exists, not just in transsexuals, where it is defining, or in drag queens and bull dykes, where it is obvious, but also, in a subtler fashion, in many "conventional" lesbians and gay men who might deny being gender nonconformist at all. We believe it influences, although to greatly varying degrees, their childhood development, their sexual style, their ways of interacting with society, and their art. Another common thread is the discrimination and stigmatization to which so many lesbians and gay men are exposed, a history of oppression that inflicts characteristic wounds, but that also provokes characteristic positive responses. Oppression, whether we like it or not, is a strong unifying theme in our community.

In the course of the book we mention hundreds of individuals by name, with the stated or implicit assumption that they are or were gay or lesbian. We considered whether we should we spell out the evidence for each person's homosexuality. The issue is not a very significant one when we are talking about current representatives of gay and lesbian organizations: if they're not gay, then for our purposes they might as well be. But what about William Shakespeare? What about Emma Goldman? In the case of Shakespeare, calling him gay depends on a reading of his sonnets that even some gay critics, such as W. H. Auden, have disagreed with. In the case of Goldman, calling her lesbian depends on a collection of letters that say a lot more about the woman who loved her than Goldman's own feelings.

We decided not to attempt a justification for every case. Besides requiring extensive annotation, such an approach is ultimately degrading to gays and lesbians. Why should the sexual orientation of a lesbian or gay man require proof, but not that of a heterosexual person? We take the view that if there is sufficient evidence (from homoerotic material in his or her writing, from other indications of intimacy toward people of the same sex that goes well beyond the norms for the culture that person lived in, from self-identification, or from known facts about that person's life) that a person shared what we are calling the experience of homosexuality, then we are entitled to include that person in a book like ours, which defines homosexuality very broadly. We can understand that scholars who find no reference to sex acts, or to the desire to perform them, in the historical record may be inclined to take refuge in concepts like "homosociality," "romantic friendship" and the like. But historically, people did not write about sex acts, especially same-sex acts. Our sentiments are more with the nonscholarly but still useful approach of writers like Martin Greif, author of *The Gay Book of Days: An Evocatively Illustrated Who's Who of Who Is, Was, May Have Been, Probably Was, and Almost Certainly Seems to*

Have Been Gay During the Past 5,000 Years.[2] In other words, common sense and intuition may get us closer to a broad truth about lesbian and gay people than any amount of scholarly analysis, even if the cost is an occasional blunder.

One sometimes hears it said that "lesbians" and "gay men" did not exist until these words, along with the word "homosexuality" itself, came into common use toward the end of the last century. Before then, it has been argued, there was same-sex behavior (in the case of male-male behavior it was often called "sodomy") but no identity to the people who practiced or desired to practice it.

We have only limited sympathy with this point of view. Certainly there is a far clearer notion of "homosexual people" in the United States today than there was 150 years ago, and this clearer notion has dramatically influenced the lives of lesbians and gay men, both for better and for worse. But even today many Americans, perhaps as many as half the entire population, believe that homosexuality is simply a set of behaviors that anyone could show (if they didn't know better). Denial of the identity of lesbians and gay men is central to efforts, for example by the Christian Coalition, to deny gays and lesbians protection from discrimination. And conversely, there clearly were people, long before the nineteenth century, who sensed that they were different from other people by virtue of their sexual orientation, and who attempted, often successfully, to find and establish some kind of community with other people similar to themselves.

More fundamentally, we believe that it is an error to refuse an identity to a group of people simply because that group was misunderstood or ignored, or its existence was denied, even by members of the group themselves. To do so, in our view, is to confuse the "discourse" about a thing with the thing itself. Homosexuality is not something that happens by cogitation or by talking with one's neighbor, any more than heterosexuality is. The question of its nature and its causes is different from the question of what people have historically thought about its nature and causes.

However carefully we attempt to define our terms, there will always remain some fuzziness and uncertainty in words like "gay" and "lesbian." There are women, in particular, who interpret the word "lesbian" more broadly than we do. Adrienne Rich, for example, has written of the "lesbian continuum," meaning the whole range of women-identified experience that is not limited to conscious same-sex genital desires.[3] It may be true (even if this risks echoing stereotypes) that the division between sexual and nonsexual intimacy is less sharp for women than for men, at least in our present culture. If so, then the word "lesbian" cannot be defined as precisely as "gay male," however hard we try.

Some of these issues may become clearer in the course of the following chapters. We revisit the question of the identity of gay and lesbian people, and the nature of the community and culture they have established, at the end of the book. For now, we will go with our working definitions and see where they lead us.

2
A Global View

People's ideas about homosexuality are based primarily on their experience of themselves (if they are homosexual) and their lesbian and gay acquaintances, and their knowledge of the contemporary gay and lesbian community in the United States. But it is important to be able to put this "local" knowledge into a broader perspective. Do lesbians and gay men exist in all cultures, and did they exist in all periods of history? Have there been different kinds of homosexuality at different times and places? Have there been differences in the way homosexual people are perceived or treated? For that matter, does anything corresponding to homosexuality exist among nonhuman animals? The answers to these questions are important, not in order to justify or to stigmatize homosexuality, but because they can help us to understand the position of gays and lesbians in nature and society, and to develop a vision of the community's future, a vision unconstricted by our immediate experience.

What we find is that there are several kinds of homosexuality that recur in widely scattered cultures. In one kind, homosexuality is associated with a very marked gender nonconformity. Women and men who exhibit this kind of homosexuality (typified by the "amazons" and "berdaches" of Native American cultures) couple with more conventional individuals of the same sex as themselves. Another kind of homosexuality (we call it "straight homosexuality") is shown by those more conventional individuals who couple with amazon- or berdache-like people. The relationships thus established are sometimes called "transgenderal" because they are between two people who, though they are of the same sex, nevertheless differ at least partially in gender. A third kind of homosexuality is "age-disparate": this is shown by individuals who, at least at some phase in their lives, are attracted specifically to people of the same sex who are either younger or older than themselves. Couplings between such people are sometimes called "transgenerational"; we do not use that term here because many of these relationships involve age differences of only a few years, not the twenty or thirty years of a full generation. Finally, there are people who are attracted to others who are like themselves in sex, gender, and age. We call this phenomenon "companionate homosexuality."

Amazons and Berdaches

Strongly gender-variant women have been recognized in many different cultures. The ancient Greek historian Herodotus told of the Amazons, a Scythian race of female warriors who supposedly removed one breast to improve their skill with the bow. Mythical though the Amazons perhaps were, the word amazon came to be used to refer generally to tall, powerful females (including the queen in chess).[1] The Amazon river of Brazil was so named because of the abundance of such women encountered in this region by the early explorers. In his book *The Spirit and the Flesh*, anthropologist Walter Williams cites a sixteenth-century account concerning the Tupinamba Indians of northeast Brazil:

> There are some Indian women who determine to remain chaste: these have no commerce [sex] with men in any manner, nor would they consent to it even if refusal meant death. They give up all the duties of women and imitate men, and follow men's pursuits as if they were not women. They wear the hair cut in the same way as the men, and go to war with bows and arrows and pursue game, always in company with men; each has a woman to serve her, to whom she says she is married, and they treat each other and speak with each other as man and wife.[2]

Whether these women were really as totally gender-reversed as this account suggests is open to question. Closer study[3] of amazons in native North American cultures—who went by names such as *kwe'rhame* (Yuma), *warrhameh* (Cocopa), and *hwame* (Mohave)—suggests that many of these women took on roles that were partly masculine and partly feminine, the end product of which might be described as a third gender. Furthermore, certain aspects of the way they were treated by society—especially the common notion that amazons were more spiritual than conventional women—does not reflect a simple shift along a feminine-masculine dimension, but rather to a position outside of the regular conception of gender. Paula Gunn Allen has recounted how the Lakota *koskalaka* ("young man" or "woman who doesn't want to marry") was accorded a spiritual power bordering on black magic or sorcery. She could be united to another woman in a ceremonial dance in which a rope was twined between them to form a "rope baby."[4]

How did women become amazons? Generally, they were already markedly gender nonconformist in childhood, for example in desiring to engage in rough-and-tumble play or hunting with boys, and in rejecting dolls and refusing to help with women's chores. It was believed that such a girl had gone through a change of "spirit," perhaps as a result of a dream she had had while still in her mother's womb. Parents might encourage or discourage these gender-nonconformist traits, but there was little sense that the parents had "caused" the girl to become an amazon.[5] In some groups, such as the Mohave, a girl who was a potential hwame took part in a ritual trial or transition rite which, if successfully undergone, cemented her hwame status. She then took a new, masculine name and was entitled to marry a (nonhwame) woman, with whom she had sexual relations. She would be accepted as the father of any children her wife had.

Gender-variant males were also noticed by the early explorers of the New World. These men aroused strong antipathy on the part of the Europeans. The explorer Balboa, for example, on his way across the Isthmus of Panama, encountered some Native American men dressed as women. "Balboa learnt that they were sodomites," wrote a contemporary historian, "and threw the king and forty others to be eaten by his dogs, a fine action of an honorable and Catholic Spaniard."[6] Balboa's (and the historian's) attitude was nearly universal. Speaking of "Joyas" (male Indians of Southern California who took women's roles and married conventional men), an eighteenth-century priest wrote:

> Many Joyas can be seen in the area of Santa Barbara Channel; around there, almost every village has two or three. But we place our trust in God and expect that these accursed people will disappear with the growth of the missions. The abominable vice will be eliminated to the extent that the Catholic faith and all the other virtues are firmly implanted there, for the glory of God and the benefit of these poor ignorants.[7]

Just as there are native American terms for amazons, so there exist terms to describe men who take on a female or intermediate social role: *winkte* (Lakota for "become a woman"), *mexoga* (Omaha for "instructed by the moon"—the moon being a female spirit), *nadle* (Navajo for "one who is transformed"), and so on. Collectively, anthropologists refer to them as *berdaches*. Berdaches typically wore women's attire, or some combination of male and female attire, and participated in women's activities such as gathering or growing food, food preparation, looking after children, basket-weaving, and so on, while avoiding hunting and warfare. They were sometimes sexually inactive, but more usually they had sexual relations with non-berdache men. In these contacts the berdache would commonly take the receptive role in anal or oral intercourse, and would avoid (or was supposed to avoid) the involvement of his own penis in sexual acts. Quite often, berdaches were in long-term domestic partnerships with men, and these had the same status as heterosexual partnerships.

The surprising thing about berdaches, from our point of view, is the respect and social status they were accorded in many (though not all) Native American cultures. The basis of this status was the notion that berdaches had both a male and female spirit, and therefore were more blessed than individuals who had the spirit of only one sex. This allowed them to mediate between men and women, and also between the physical and spiritual world. Contemporary Native Americans sometime refer to both berdaches and amazons as "two-spirit people." Berdache-like figures were prominent in the creation myths of some American Indian cultures. Berdaches were often shamans (ceremonial magicians and healers), or were consulted by shamans. They often had control over the property of their extended family, and could influence tribal politics to the benefit of their own relatives. For this and other reasons, families that counted a berdache among their members often considered themselves fortunate and elevated in status.

Like amazons, berdaches generally displayed markedly gender-nonconformist traits in childhood: they might associate with girls or prefer to help with food preparation rather than take part in play-fighting and exploration. On this basis a boy was recognized as a potential berdache by his family. At some point in later childhood the boy would make the choice of berdache status in a ritualized trial. For example, the boy might be placed in a brushwood enclosure, with a bow and arrow on one side of him and a basket on the other. The brushwood was then set on fire. If, in escaping the flames, the boy seized the bow and arrow, he was assigned the male role in adult life, while if he took the basket he was assigned berdache status.

This developmental process suggests that berdaches and amazons may have been innately gender-variant individuals. There is considerable evidence from contemporary scientific studies that sex-specific childhood behavior is influenced by biological factors operating before birth, and furthermore that children who are markedly gender nonconformist in childhood have an increased likelihood of becoming homosexual adults (see chapter 4). If berdaches and amazons are indeed biologically gender-variant individuals, one might expect to find such people in other cultures besides the native cultures of America.[8] In fact, berdache-like men have been described in widely distributed regions of the world. The record for women is far more sparse, but that may well reflect the general lack of attention paid to women in traditional anthropology, especially where sexual matters were concerned.

In northern India there exists a class of gender-variant individuals known as *hijras*, that has been studied by Serena Nanda (see Further Reading). Like the berdaches, hijras are usually born as anatomical males, although some of them are intersexes with ambiguous genitalia. They dress as women and form a distinct cult devoted to the Hindu mother goddess Bahuchara Mata, whose temple is at Ahmedabad in the state of Gujarat. Their main social role is to perform ceremonial blessings at marriages and at the birth of male children; in these ceremonies they sing and dance in an exaggeratedly feminine, even lascivious style. Some hijras form long-term relationships with nonhijra men, and many work as prostitutes. In either case they generally take the receptive role in anal intercourse. Unlike the berdaches, the hijras usually undergo an emasculation operation, which involves the removal of the penis and scrotum, without construction of a vagina. The operation is performed in secret by a specially trained hijra known as a *dai ma* (midwife) and is accompanied by elaborate rituals that emphasize the significance of the event as a rebirth.

Although the physical emasculation of hijras might seem to place them in a radically different category from the berdaches, it should be born in mind that berdaches did avoid the use of their penis in sex. Besides its spiritual significance, emasculation has the worldly advantage of providing indisputable evidence of membership in the cult. Performance of ritual blessings is an important source of income for hijras, and they have to compete with impostors who dress as women and mimic the hijras' rituals. Exposure of the mutilated genitals is the ultimate proof of authenticity. Furthermore, there exists another cult-based group in southern India—the *jogappas*—who are similar to the hijras in most respects but who do not undergo emasculation. The hijra practice of emasculation is undoubtedly influenced by the tradition of eunuchs in the medieval Moslem world, which included northern India.

Yet another similar group are the *mahu* of Polynesia. The mahu are individuals with male (or occasionally intersexed) genitalia who dress as women or in a mixture of male and female clothing, and who take on a mixture of male and female roles. They are (or were, on the islands that have been strongly Westernized) accorded high status and take part in religious ceremonies, especially as dancers and chanters in the *hula* or other ceremonies of spiritual significance. One and only one person has mahu status in each village, though there may be "backups" ready to step into the mahu's position when necessary. Mahus have sex with nonmahu men, taking the receptive role in oral or intercrural (between the thighs) intercourse.[9]

Comparable people exist or existed in Africa and Arabia. The Lango people of East Africa and the Tanala people of Madagascar both recognized a class of sex-variant men who were traditionally entitled to become one of the wives of conventional men. These individuals, called *sarombavy* by the Tanala, displayed feminine traits from early childhood.[10] In Oman, an Islamic state on the Arabian side of the Persian Gulf, there still exists a class of sex-variant men known as *xanith* ("effeminate") who are permitted to occupy an intermediate position between male and female in this rigidly sex-segregated society; they often work as prostitutes serving conventional men, like many of the hijras of India. They retain masculine names and the legal rights of men, but they do women's work and are allowed a social familiarity with women that other men are not permitted. Their clothing is a hybrid of men's and women's styles, and their hair is cut to a length intermediate between the short hair of men and the long hair of women.[11]

Does contemporary Western culture have its amazons and berdaches? The answer is both yes and no. Yes, in the sense that individuals with similar characteristics exist among us as among the non-Western cultures. Somewhat like amazons are "bull dykes"—lesbian women with mannish features and mannerisms, who dress like men and exhibit forceful, even aggressive personalities—and female-to-male transsexuals. Somewhat like the berdaches and hijras are "drag queens," male-to-female transvestites and male-to-female transsexuals. This is not to deny the real differences between and even within these categories, but to emphasize the features that are shared by many of them and that link them to berdaches and amazons: the display (or even parody) of the manners and dress of the other sex, sexual attraction to conventional individuals of the same sex, the frequent (though not universal) preference for a sex-atypical role in sexual intercourse, and an atypical gender identity.

In another sense, nothing like berdaches or amazons exists in contemporary America. Bull dykes and drag queens are not accorded a special, respected, or honored status among us. They are not believed to be especially spiritual or blessed, nor do they confer status on the families that they come from. It would be more accurate to describe them as disconnected from society as a whole, and even to a degree from mainstream "gay" and "lesbian" society, although they may flourish in a smaller society of their own making. Yet, even in our own society there are hints of a connection between gender variance and spirituality, a connection that we will explore toward the end of this book.

"Straight" Homosexuality

So far, we have described a kind of homosexuality marked by a constellation of gender-variant traits, a clear rejection of the norms ascribed to the individual's sex, and an aversion to sexual activity with members of the other sex. The people who exhibit this kind of homosexuality—berdaches, amazons, and their equivalents in other cultures—generally seek as sexual partners conventional or "straight-acting" members of their own sex. But who are these partners? How "conventional" are they? Are they homosexual at all?

In many non-Western cultures, these partners are not viewed as a class of people distinct from those who engage in conventional heterosexual relations. Often the men who married berdaches had previously been in heterosexual relationships, and they might return to a heterosexual marriage if the marriage with the berdache came to an end. The same may be true of women who married amazons. On the other hand there were also men with a definite preference for berdaches, possibly because of the practical benefits associated with this status, but also perhaps because they had an intrinsic sexual attraction toward androgynous or effeminate males. Whether or not the partners of berdaches and amazons were intrinsically different from conventional husbands and wives, it is clear that they were not considered so. No significance was attached to such a preference, and no special words were used to describe it.

On the Polynesian islands, many men who have sex with mahus also have sex with women, and they do not consider the difference to be very significant. "It's just like doing it with a woman," one man told an interviewer, "but his way of doing it is better than with a woman, as you just take it easy while he does it to you."[12] Some men who have sex with mahus also have sex with nonmahu men.

Similarly, the men who have sex with hijra prostitutes in India are not seen as different in any important way from those who have sex with female prostitutes. Asked about this, one hijra explained:

> These men who come to us, they may be married or unmarried.... They have no desire to go to a man, they come to us for the sake of going to a girl. They prefer us to their wives. See, there's many a customer whose wife has already had three or four children and he still longs for sex, which his lawful wife won't be able to provide. But the hijras can do this from the back, from behind. These people are attracted to the hijras because they get the satisfaction from the back or a satisfaction from between the thighs.... Each one's tastes differ among people.... It is God's way; because we have to make a living, he made people like this so we can earn.[13]

The hijra's account diminishes the significance of the choice of hijra or woman as sex partner, while at the same time accepting that God created men with diverse sexual tastes.

In ancient Rome, especially during the early empire, a similar attitude seems to have prevailed. Homosexuality was fairly well tolerated, and while it was recognized that conventional masculine men could differ in their sexual preference, little significance was attached to these differences. This attitude is expressed in a fragment of poetry from that period cited by John Boswell in his book *Christianity, Social Tolerance, and Homosexuality.* The poet alludes to the bisexual exploits of the Greek god Zeus:

Zeus came as an eagle to god-like Ganymede, as a swan came he to the fair-haired mother of Helen.
So there is no comparison between the two things; one person likes one, another likes the other; I like both.[14]

In our own culture, individuals who are generally conventional in their sexual personality and social role, but have sexual relations with markedly sex-variant partners of their own anatomical sex, are not always clearly distinguished from heterosexual people. For example, a man who has sex with a male prostitute of conventional appearance may be labeled as gay, while a man who has sex with a male transvestite prostitute may not be. Even the type of sexual behavior performed can influence the judgment: a man who takes the (sex-typical) insertive role in anal or oral intercourse may not be labeled gay (or consider himself gay), while the man who takes the (sex-atypical) receptive role very likely will be. This distinction is especially apparent in some Latin American societies, as well as in prisons and other sex-segregated environments.

Nevertheless, our society often does categorize the sexual partners of berdache- and amazon-like figures as gay or lesbian. The term homosexuality is generally used to mean sexual attraction to people of the same anatomical sex, regardless of their other characteristics. Sodomy statutes in the United States have generally made no distinction between the culpability of the insertive and the receptive partners in anal intercourse. Lesbian- and gay-rights activists, as well as their opponents, do not usually attempt to obtain or deny different rights for strongly sex-variant and more conventional lesbians or gay men.

It is natural enough to place the kind of homosexuality we are describing here near the boundary between homosexuality and heterosexuality. In the case of men who have sex with emasculated hijras, indeed, it does not even fit our definition of homosexuality, as laid out in chapter 1. Even in the other cases, a man who desires to have sex with a psychologically unmasculine man is clearly less different from a heterosexual man than one who is attracted to men with conventionally masculine gender identity and gender role. That is why we call the phenomenon "straight" homosexuality.

Transgenderal homosexual liaisons between relatively sex-typical and markedly sex-variant individuals (both male and female) seem to occur widely throughout the world. What varies from culture to culture is the extent to which these relationships are recognized, named, tolerated, sanctified, scorned, or forbidden. The respect they were traditionally given in many Native American cultures had three major causes. First, the high status of women in these cultures meant that men were not seen as degrading themselves if they exhibited a female or nonmasculine personality and social role. Second, permissive attitudes in matters of sex, marriage, parenting, and family life, such as existed in Native American cultures, fostered a tolerance of unusual relationships. Last, the important role of sex-variant individuals in the mythology of these cultures was a mechanism by which this tolerance was institutionalized and communicated over many generations. In India also, sex variance plays a substantial role in mythology and tradition, but this benign influence is counteracted by the generally low status of women in Indian society. Thus the hijras are scorned and shunned by many Indians because of their rejection of masculinity, even though their ceremonial role is generally acknowledged and valued.

Our own society has been dominated by a patriarchal religion in whose traditions sexual variance is barely represented. Sexual expression in general has been severely restricted and codified, and women in our society have not until recently been accorded a status comparable to that of men. For all these reasons sexual relationships between men, regardless of the gender identity of the two partners, have generally been despised and forbidden, while those between women have been shunned or ignored.

One way in which transgenderal homosexual relationships have been able to escape punishment or stigmatization is by deception; that is, by the transgendered partner's passing as a member of the other sex. Many such cases no doubt have gone undiscovered, but others have come to light by one means or another. A celebrated example was the case of "Murray Hall," a New York woman active in city politics in the last decades of the nineteenth century.[15] She was a member of the General Committee of Tammany Hall, married two conventional women, drank, smoked, and gambled with city officials, and voted regularly in primary and general elections long before women were legally permitted to do so. Luckily for Hall, her female anatomy was not discovered until after her death. Of course, there were probably complex motivations in cases like Hall's: we cannot say to what extent her actions sprang from a transgendered identity in the sense that we use the word today, how much from a conscious plan to conceal a lesbian relationship, and how much from a desire to break through the social barriers that all women were subject to at that time.

Age-Disparate Homosexuality

In some cultures, homosexual relationships between males of differing ages have been common and accepted. Ancient Greece is the best-known example. In Athens of the classical period (the fifth and fourth centuries B.C.), as well as during the following Hellenistic period when Athens was under Macedonian rule, adult men commonly courted and developed close homosexual bonds with boys or youths. A typical relationship might begin when the man (who might well be married) took a fancy to a youth working out at the gymnasium, an all-male institution where athletic activities were carried out in the nude. He would attempt to engage the youth in conversation and to get to know him, and eventually would make a courtship offering: a cockerel was the traditional gift. Acceptance of the gift signified the youth's acquiescence. It seems that the youths were typically early to midteens: in vase paintings they are shown as shorter than adults and lacking facial hair; there is a literary reference suggesting that the age of first appearance of facial hair is the most desirable. To judge from vase paintings, the usual kind of sexual intercourse in these relationships was intercrural, with the older man as the inserter. It is possible that the depiction of intercrural rather than anal intercourse was an artists' convention, since there are references to anal intercourse between men and boys in Greek comedies. However, heterosexual anal intercourse *was* frequently depicted on vases.

Although these age-disparate relationships might last a number of years, they were not viewed as permanent. When the youth reached adulthood the relationship would be expected to terminate. As one poetic fragment put it, the poet will love his boyfriend "so long as his cheek is hairless."[16] Sometimes the junior partner was old enough to bear arms: the celebrated sixth-century lovers Harmodios and Aristogeiton jointly assassinated the tyrant Hipparchos. In exceptional cases these relationships persisted for long periods. A particularly well known example was the relationship between Pausanias and Agathon, both of whom are portrayed by Plato as participants in *The Symposium*. Agathon, the younger partner, was famous for his beauty as a teenager. As an adult he shaved or closely trimmed his facial hair (an unusual practice among the Greeks) and was considered to be effeminate in dress and manner. On this account he was ridiculed unmercifully in the comedies of Aristophanes: much of the ridicule revolved around the suggestion that he was the receptive partner in anal intercourse—a degrading role for a man. In spite of this mockery, the relationship between these two men is believed to have lasted at least twelve years and possibly twenty years or more. It is worth realizing that Pausanias's speech in *The Symposium*, which ardently praised and defended homosexuality, and which is often cited as representative of Greek attitudes in general, was put into the mouth of someone who was clearly "atypical" in his sexuality, in that he maintained a long-term relationship with another grown man.

What was the meaning of these age-disparate relationships to the participants, as well as to society as a whole? First, of course, there was the sexual and affectional bond between the lovers. This bond, however, was asymmetrical. The younger partner was supposed not to be sexually excited or to come to orgasm during sexual intercourse, if we are to believe Plato and Xenophon. The latter wrote: "Also, the boy does not share in the man's pleasure in intercourse, as a woman does; cold sober, he looks upon the other [who is] drunk with sexual desire."[17]

At an emotional level, the relationship was clearly between unequals, the older man having a dominant, possessive, or didactic role, while the youth was the protégé who stood to gain materially and educationally from the relationship. This is in no way to devalue this kind of relationship or to deny its emotional significance to both partners, but to emphasize how different it was from the more equal type of homosexual relationship to be discussed later.

Social attitudes to these relationships were somewhat paradoxical. On one side, little if any stigma was attached to a man who took up with a boy or youth. On the other hand, there are many references indicating that the boy's role *was* stigmatized. Parents attempted to prevent their sons from becoming involved sexually with an adult man, and a teenager who took such a role could be exposed to ridicule later in life. If the younger partner took money from the older he was considered a prostitute and could be permanently deprived of many of the rights of citizenship.

This asymmetry is reminiscent of the "double standard" in our own society, whereby a man who has nonmarital sex with women has traditionally been viewed more favorably than a woman who does the same thing with men. Indeed, there is a connection between sexism in classical Greece and attitudes toward the two partners in male age-disparate homosexuality. Greek women were treated like property: they were largely excluded from participation in public life, and whether married or unmarried they were rigorously "protected" from male advances. It was a near-impossibility for a man to develop a sexual (or even a nonsexual) relationship with a free-born woman, except by marrying. Certainly he could meet prostitutes, courtesans, and foreigners, but such liaisons were unlikely to offer more than purely physical gratification. Thus teenage boys, whose physical androgyny and inferior status made them more "womanlike" than adult men, offered an attractive alternative. The idea that these boys were debasing themselves by taking a "feminine" role was never far from the surface.

Although the seclusion of women may have contributed to the prevalence of age-disparate homosexuality in ancient Greece, we do not mean to suggest that Greek homosexuality was entirely a social construction. Far from it: it is clear that there were men who were attracted (perhaps by nature) to youths, and others who did not form such relationships or did so only for lack of heterosexual outlet. That the Greeks were aware of this is implicit in the famous passage in *The Symposium,* put into the mouth of Aristophanes, which explains the origin of heterosexuality and homosexuality in an extemporized creation myth. The original creatures, he said, were male, female, and androgynous. In punishment for their wrongdoings Zeus cut them each into two halves: "Each of us ..." he went on,

> is always looking for his other half. Men who are a half of that original being which was called androgynous are lovers of women; adulterers are generally of this breed. Adulterous women who lust after men have the same origin. Women who are a section of the original female do not care for men, but have female attachments; the female companions are of this sort. But they who are a half of the male seek men, and while they are young, being slices of the original man, they hang about men and embrace them, and they are themselves the best of boys and youths, because they have the most manly nature. Some indeed assert that they are shameless, but this is not true, for they do not act thus from any want of shame, but because they are valiant and manly.... When they reach manhood they are lovers of youths, and are not naturally inclined to marry or beget children—if at all, they do so only in obedience to the law.[18]

Whatever the credibility of this account, the reader is assumed to know that there are two distinct classes of men, homosexual and heterosexual, and the same for women. Aristophanes is represented as favoring a "genetic" explanation for these differences.

The reference to lesbian women in the foregoing passage is one of the few such references in the literature of classical Greece. In fact the word translated as "female companions" (*hetairistriai*) is not found elsewhere in the entire body of extant Greek writings, yet since Plato used it one may assume that the word and its meaning were understood. Much later (in the first century A.D) the historian Plutarch, writing about life in Sparta during the classical period, stated that "women of good repute were in love with girls." This implies the existence of age-disparate female homosexuality in Sparta at least. Because women were much more respected in Sparta than in Athens, it may be that such relationships were publicly known and talked about in Sparta, while in Athens they were ignored.

The most famous Greek lesbian was of course the poet Sappho, who lived on the island of Lesbos during the sixth century B.C., that is, before the classical period. Unfortunately her poetry survives only in a few tantalizing fragments, but they are enough to suggest a person given to the most intense feelings:

> Whenever I look at you briefly, then it is no longer in my power to speak. My tongue is fixed in silence, and straightaway a subtle fire has run under my skin, and with my eyes I see nothing, and my ears hum, and cold sweat possesses me, and trembling seizes all of me, and I am paler than grass, and I seem to myself within a little of being dead. But all is to be endured.[19]

Few details are known about lesbianism on Lesbos. Sappho had a circle of female pupils, which suggests the possibility of age-disparate homosexuality within a didactic environment, rather similar to the male homosexuality of Plato's Athens.

There are very few depictions of lesbian sexuality on Greek vases. One of the clearest examples shows two women of approximately the same height and appearance, but one woman crouches and manually stimulates the genitalia of the other, who stands holding a chalice. The depiction seems to imply a dominant/subordinate relationship involving a difference in age or social status, but this may say more about the (male) vase painter's attitudes than about the actual nature of lesbian relationships.

Another country that had a long tradition of age-disparate male homosexuality, very like that of classical Greece, was Japan. For at least 500 years before the westernization of Japan, man-youth sexual relationships were common and often celebrated. The relationship might be between an adult monk and a *chigo*, an early to midteenage boy from an aristocratic family who was sent to a monastery for his education. It might be between a samurai knight and a mid-to-late teenage youth who was a candidate for samurai status. Or it might be between a merchant and an actor in the kabuki theater. The relationship might be anything from a frankly commercial arrangement to a highly romanticized love affair culminating in a double suicide. At any event, the relationship was supposed always to end when the younger partner reached the age of nineteen and underwent the ritual head shaving that symbolized adult status.[20]

In Native Australian cultures it was common for young adult men, prior to marriage, to take a ten- to twelve-year-old boy as a wife for a few years. The relationship would dissolve when the older partner married a woman and the younger underwent initiation into adulthood.[21]

A present-day non-Western culture that emphasizes age-disparate male homosexuality is that of the Sambia people of the Eastern Highlands of New Guinea. In this culture, which has been studied by Gilbert Herdt (see Further Reading), boys are removed from their families at seven to ten years of age, and housed collectively in a cult house until their late teens. There they are denied virtually all contact with girls or women. Ritualized oral intercourse takes place between the older and younger boys in the group, the younger boys taking the receptive role. The boys are taught that ingesting semen confers the male spirit and is a necessary part of growing up. After leaving the cult house the young men usually marry women and carry on a conventional heterosexual existence, although some male adults return to the cult house to take part in oral sex with boys. In some other ethnic groups of New Guinea, anal rather than oral intercourse is practiced between the older and younger boys.[22]

The institution in Western culture that most closely parallels the Sambia cult house is that of the British "public school." These schools, actually private boarding schools, traditionally educated the children of the privileged classes in a disciplined all-male or all-female environment in which older students wielded considerable authority over the younger ones. Homosexual liaisons between older and younger pupils were common. The great majority of Britons who attended public schools as children nevertheless became predominantly or exclusively heterosexual as adults.[23]

Unlike the Sambia people, the British attached no ritual significance to these age-disparate teenage relationships; they were not to be spoken of, and if they did come to light they were grounds for corporal punishment or even expulsion from school. But stripping away the superstition in one case and the hypocrisy in the other, we are left with a common reality: the need for sexual outlet and emotional attachment in a harsh, single-sex environment.

In our own society age-disparate homosexuality is an important aspect of gay and lesbian culture, but it is an aspect ringed with ambivalence. Our society equates youth and beauty, so it is seen as "natural" for a mature adult to be sexually attracted to a younger person, whether male or female. Having a youthful, attractive partner may be seen as positive and status-enhancing, and the younger person may also be admired by his or her peers for possessing a loving, good-looking, rich, or respected older partner. At the same time, though, such a relationship may be seen as improperly violating an equally "natural" attribute of sexual relationships—that they be approximately age-matched. Furthermore, when the age-disparate relationship involves an adult and a minor, other real or perceived "violations" come into play: of the law, of the innocence of childhood, of parents' property rights over their children, of the moral responsibility of teachers, and so on.

Perhaps most seriously, the younger partner may be seen as trading the "proper" ingredients in a sexual relationship—true love and physical attraction—for purely practical advantages, thus bringing him- or herself down toward the social status of a prostitute. These violations loom twice as large when the relationship is between two people of the same sex. The disrespect paid to age-disparate relationships in gay male culture is particularly evident in the freedom gay men feel to court the younger partner in such a relationship. Age-matched gay couples, by contrast, are accorded some psychological space—a hint at least of the sanctity of marriage.

Companionate Homosexuality

The relationships described so far have been marked by differences between the two partners: differences in masculinity-femininity, in age, or in both. To some extent these relationships mimic heterosexual relationships, in which the difference in the anatomical sex of the two partners is often accompanied by other real or perceived differences that help to define a role for each partner. But there are also lesbian and gay relationships in which the two partners are, on the surface at least, quite similar to each other. The partners are not "he and she" or "senior and junior," but companions.

Companionate homosexuality may well have existed in all cultures and periods of history, but it is hard to document, because such relationships tended to blend into the general fabric of society in a way that masked their sexual nature. Today we make a clear (perhaps too clear) distinction between "friends" and "lovers": lovers are supposed to have bodily contact leading to orgasm, while friends are not. Making such a distinction for historical periods is extraordinarily difficult, for several reasons. First, there is generally no information as to whether a particular relationship was a sexual one or not. Even where there is, the meaning of words changes over time. Shakespeare, for example, often used the word "lover" where no sexual bond was intended. The meaning of acts too can change: today, for example, sleeping together is almost synonymous with sex, but prior to this century beds were commonly shared, even by complete strangers.

Most important, the meaning of relationships themselves may change. If we look back to America of the nineteenth century and before, we find records of many relationships between two people of the same sex that were described as "romantic friendships" or "sentimental attachments": the two women, or less commonly the two men, might openly exchange vows of love, praise each other's physical and moral beauty, and spend hours entwined in each others' arms, and yet there was no general perception that the relationship was a sexual one.

In the introduction to her book *Odd Girls and Twilight Lovers*, Lillian Faderman cites an 1843 newspaper account of two women who lived together in Vermont:

> In their youthful days, they took each other as companions for life, and this union, no less sacred to them than the tie of marriage, has subsisted, in uninterrupted harmony, for 40 years, during which they have shared each others' occupations and pleasures and works of charity while in health, and watched over each other tenderly in sickness.... They slept on the same pillow and had a common purse, and adopted each others relations, and ... I would tell you of their dwelling, encircled with roses, ... and I would speak of the friendly attentions which their neighbors, people of kind hearts and simple manners, seem to take pleasure in bestowing upon them.[24]

The two women and their rustic neighbors seem to have lived in an Age of Innocence from which the writer, perhaps, was just beginning to awaken. Looking back, we cannot tell whether this or the many other romantic friendships were indeed sexual in the narrow sense of the word. Some doubtless were so, some would have been if a sense of propriety had not prevented it, and some very likely were not. For this reason, writers who discuss same-sex relationships in history often speak of "homosociality," the bonding between persons of the same sex that is visible to the world and preserved in the historical record. Unfortunately, the term "homosociality" often papers over a real chasm between individuals who are sexually attracted to their own sex and those who are not.

The two Vermont women were unusual in being able to stay together for a lifetime. More commonly the relationship terminated when, under the compulsion of custom and economic necessity, one or both of the partners married. Thus female romantic friendships before the middle of the last century tended to be between young people. In the latter part of the nineteenth century the increasing educational opportunities for women, and the possibility for financial independence that went with them, allowed many women to resist pressure to marry men. As a result there emerged a new institution, the "Boston marriage," formed by a couple of college-educated women, who were often engaged in teaching or in the early women's movement. No doubt many of these marriages were lesbian in every sense of the word. But until the first years of the twentieth century they were not recognized as such. Only with the rise of psychology and sexology did public attention focus on the question of what actually took place in people's bedrooms. This attention was ultimately beneficial, since it was a necessary step toward the ultimate self-identification and self-awareness of lesbians and gay men, but in the short term it was harmful in that it forced homosexual relationships underground. The process of reemergence from this underground existence is described in chapter 3.

It might be thought that men would have been much freer, in most cultures and historical periods, to form companionate homosexual relationships than were women. So why do we so seldom read of male Victorian couples settling down in cottages in Vermont? Of two Native American men marrying, unless one of them were a berdache and the other not? Or of a sexual relationship between two Japanese samurai, unless they were of differing ages? Even in the early Roman empire, a period of great liberality toward male homosexuality, most gay relationships were of the age-disparate or berdache/straight types. The former is exemplified by the relationship between the Emperor Hadrian and the Bithynian youth Antinous, who was deified after his accidental drowning; the latter by the marriage of the "Empress" Elagabalus (who crossdressed and preferred the receptive role in anal intercourse) to Zoticus, an athlete from Smyrna.

There are several possible reasons for the rarity of companionate male homosexuality in the historical record. First, even in "gay-friendly" cultures there may have been hostility toward male-male relationships that did not mimic male-female relationships; that is, that was not formed by two partners who could be distinguished as "man" and "woman" by virtue of a clear difference in age, "masculinity," social status, or other indicators. Another social constraint may be a practical one: the need for both a "man" and a "woman" in a family. For example, two men in traditional Native American cultures would have had difficulty maintaining a marriage unless one of them were a berdache and one of them a conventional male, because so many of the necessary tasks of life were sex-differentiated.

Beyond the social pressure, though, may be an intrinsic propensity for men to form sexual relationships marked by some clear difference between the two partners. This seems to be true even in the "anything goes" atmosphere of contemporary gay American culture. Looking through the personal advertisements in gay male magazines, for example, one cannot fail to be struck by how many of them specify a difference in age, sexual behavior ("top"/"bottom"), race, or other characteristics between the advertiser and the sought-after partner. One could speculate that the desire for difference in (nonreproductive) homosexual relationships is an instinctive mechanism that, in an evolutionary sense, can be traced back to two necessities of reproductive behavior: the search for individuals of the opposite sex, and (in social species) the avoidance of inbreeding.

Of course, companionate male homosexuality does exist, and probably always has existed, even if it has not been the predominant mode of homosexual expression. Relatively common are companionate gay relationships between adolescents or young adults. Martin Duberman has unearthed letters from 1826 documenting such a liaison between James Hammond and Thomas Withers, who later became pillars of the white heterosexual establishment in South Carolina. At the age of twenty-two Withers wrote to the nineteen-year-old Hammond:

> I feel some inclination to learn whether you yet sleep in your Shirt-tail, and whether you yet have the extravagant delight of poking and punching a writhing Bedfellow with your long fleshen pole—the exquisite touches of which I have often had the honor of feeling? Let me say unto thee that unless thou changest former habits in this particular, thou wilt be represented by every future Chum as a nuisance. And, I pronounce it, with good reason too. Sir, you roughen the downy Slumbers of your Bedfellow—by such hostile—furious lunges as you are in the habit of making at him—when he is least prepared for defence against the crushing force of a Battering Ram....[25]

Note, however, the suggestion that Hammond was the "top" in the relationship: that is, the more sexually aggressive and possibly the insertive partner. The suggestion is furthered by Withers's accusation, in another letter, that Hammond was "charging over the pine barrens of your locality, braying, like an ass, at every she-male you can discover."

One country that has had a long tradition of male-male "romantic friendship" is Germany, where it was called *Freundesliebe* ("love between friends"). In the eighteenth and early nineteenth centuries male couples all over Germany declared their love for each other in sentimental poetry or prose, as in the following passage from a letter from the novelist Jean Paul to his friend, the philosopher Friedrich Heinrich Jacobi: "My dear Heinrich, do tell me once again when the opportunity occurs that you love me. Like the young girl I want to hear that repeated, if not trillions then millions of times...." And from Jacobi to Jean Paul: "I feel that exactly the same as you, that a friend should love his friend as the woman loves the man, the lover the loved one."[26]

In the nineteenth century this kind of affection gradually shifted to the family: husbands and wives were for the first time expected to be linked by an emotional bond. *Freundesliebe* became suspect, and was partly replaced by the *Bruderbund*, the fraternal bond that linked men in more manly associations such as outdoor activities, war, and so on. As incorporated into

Nazi ideology, the *Bruderbund* became violently homophobic, but it had a more gay-friendly echo in the *Gemeinschaft der Eigenen* ("Community of Free Spirits"). This organization, founded in 1903 by the anarchist Adolph Brand, rejected the "third sex" theory of homosexuality (see chapter 4) and promoted companionate homosexuality between masculine men. Even here, though, there was more than a hint of a desire for age-disparate relationships: the pairs of naked youths whose photographs graced the pages of Brand's magazine were as much lust objects for Brand's adult readers as exemplars of companionate teenage homosexuality.

Companionate homosexual relationships between adult men seem to be more common in present-day America than in most other cultures that we know about. It may be that such relationships are nurtured by the newly flourishing gay community: conventional-looking couples who have been together for many years are regularly singled out for a round of applause at gay events, and they are often offered as role models in a gay world that is criticized for its supposed devotion to one-night stands and weird sex. General social and economic factors may also play a role: universal education, washing machines, and fast food have made the distinct roles of "husband" and "wife" unnecessary, and a middle-aged male couple with two incomes and no children can enjoy a lifestyle well above the common lot. Finally, the AIDS epidemic may have contributed to the stability of companionate relationships by discouraging casual sex.

Animal Homosexuality

We can gain an even broader view of homosexuality by studying it among nonhuman animals. It turns out that homosexual behavior, like heterosexual behavior, shows extraordinary diversity throughout the animal kingdom. Rather than attempt to document this diversity, we simply want to make the point that there are parallels in the animal kingdom to the different kinds of homosexuality that exist among humans.

First, there are animals that somewhat resemble "berdaches" or "amazons"; that is, their readiness to engage in same-sex behavior is part of a constellation of sex-atypical or sex-ambiguous traits. Some female rats, for example, are more willing than others to engage in sexual behavior with females, and less willing to have sex with males. These rats display mounting behavior (the male-typical pattern) more readily than other females, and they are less likely to display lordosis (the inverse arching of the back that is a female-typical sexual behavior in rats). They also are more aggressive and more exploratory than other females (two traits that are typically more developed in male rats than in females). This grouping of sex-atypical traits is due, at least in part, to exposure of these females to testosterone during fetal life. The testosterone comes, not from the female fetus itself, nor from its mother, but from male fetuses located near the female within the same uterus.[27]

There are also animals who are not sex-variant, except in their preference for same-sex intercourse. A good example occurs in sheep. Mounting of rams (male sheep) by other rams is very common among wild sheep populations. Scientists at the U.S. Sheep Experiment Station in Dubois, Idaho, studied the phenomenon among domestic sheep.[28] They found that, of 94 rams tested, 8 refused to mount ewes (female sheep) but did readily mount rams. They usually mounted a small group of rams, so-called "receivers," who were unusually willing to be mounted. The mounters never displayed any female-typical traits or behaviors except for their apparent sexual attraction to "receiver" rams. Thus the mounters exhibited something akin to what we have described as "straight" homosexuality in humans. It has recently been reported that the male-oriented rams differ from heterosexual rams in certain aspects of brain organization that may be related to their choice of male sex partners (see chapter 4).

Age-disparate homosexuality occurs very commonly among animals, usually between males. In many species of monkeys, for example, adult males mount juvenile males or lower-ranking adult males; penetration is usually intercrural from the rear. Besides its sexual function, this behavior plays a role in the establishment and maintenance of dominance hierarchies. Perhaps there is an echo of this in human age-disparate homosexuality: it is not uncommon for men who are attracted to youths to seek partners of a lower socioeconomic status (Oscar Wilde's passion for working-class youths is a famous example). Also, the themes of dominance and submission are a recognized part of gay male culture.

Companionate homosexuality is exemplified by the "lesbian" relationships that have been observed among several species of North American seagulls (Western, California, ring-billed, and herring gulls) as well as among Caspian terns and snow geese. The female-female pairs (which can be as many as 10 percent of all the pairs in a breeding colony) were initially discovered among Western gulls by George Hunt and Molly Warner of the University of California at Irvine.[29] The two females court each other, copulate, build a nest together, and share the labor of incubating the eggs and (if the eggs are fertile) raising the chicks. Of course, sex between two female birds cannot produce offspring. The presence of fertile eggs in some of these "lesbian" nests indicates that one or both of the females has copulated with a male outside the nest—just as some lesbian women do if they wish to raise children.

The occurrence of companionate homosexuality among these birds may be related to the lack of differentiated sex roles in these species. Male and female gulls look the same and act the same: they share equally in parenting tasks, and even copulation is more "equal" than with mammals, since neither sex has a penis: the two birds simply bring the openings of their urogenital ducts together. Thus engaging in a homosexual relationship does not require a radical change in behavior by either partner. Again, we can draw a parallel with homosexuality in humans; as suggested above, the blurring of sex roles in contemporary society may facilitate coupling between two people of the same sex.

Besides homosexuality that occurs naturally in animals, it can also be induced in a laboratory setting by relatively simple procedures. For example, a single injection of testosterone before or around the time of birth can predispose female rats to same-sex behavior in adulthood. In fruit flies (*Drosophila*) an artificially induced genetic mutation can cause males to court other males.[30] If a large number of these mutant males are placed in a bottle, they form long chains that weave around the inside of the glass, as each fly makes sexual advances to the fly in front of it. The sight is reminiscent of the chains of sexually joined humans organized for the amusement of the Roman emperor Tiberius.[31]

Of course, we do not intend to suggest that there are "gay" and "lesbian" animals just like their human counterparts. Human sexuality, whether straight or gay, has many facets, some of which are uniquely human. But the striking parallels that do exist between aspects of homosexuality in human and nonhuman animals suggest that we should not search for its roots entirely in the complexities of human culture: homosexuality, like heterosexuality, is at least in part the product of forces that can exist in any species.

Conclusions

By taking a look at homosexuality as it has been expressed at different times and in different places, we see that similar themes tend to recur, although with many variations, in widely scattered cultures. We see that sexual attraction to one's own sex is just one aspect of sexual variance. In some individuals—the berdaches and amazons of this world—homosexuality is linked with many other variant traits. These individuals present a picture that is consistent with the notion of homosexuality as a kind of "intermediate sexuality." The term "third sex" that used to be a popular way of referring to homosexuality seems appropriate in describing people of this kind. In other individuals, homosexuality is not accompanied by a cluster of other sex-atypical traits. Indeed, even the homosexuality of many of these individuals has some "straight" coloring: the attraction to gender-atypical individuals or (in the case of men) to youths can be seen in this light, as can the bisexuality often encountered in such people.

Some biologically oriented psychologists visualize the sexual part of our mind as consisting of a collection of traits, each of which has differentiated toward a male-typical, female-typical, or intermediate endpoint during the sexual differentiation of the brain.[32] The individual traits may be explicitly sexual (for example, our gender identity and our sexual orientation) or they may be aspects of nonsexual cognition that nevertheless typically are developed to a different extent in the two sexes (for example, our spatial and verbal skills). The collection of traits in any individual need not all develop to the same endpoint in the male-female continuum. But there is a tendency for them to be linked, at least in a statistical sense, because there are global factors influencing brain development, such as the levels of circulating sex hormones during fetal life. The result is diversity in human sexuality, but not a random diversity: rather, a tendency for a particular individual's collection of sex-linked traits to lie somewhere near each other on the male-female continuum.

We think this conception of sexual development can help to account for the patterns of homosexual and sex-atypical expression across cultures. The "types" of homosexual people that have been described in this chapter are, of course, somewhat arbitrary. There is in reality a continuum: there are women who are heterosexual and in every other respect female-typical, and there are women who are in almost every respect male-typical (some female-to-male transsexuals fulfill this description). Most women fall somewhere along the continuum between these two extremes. Similarly, most men fall somewhere along the reverse continuum. Even lesbians and gay men who are quite conventional in their general personality and behavior generally have some traits that could be described as sex-atypical beyond their sexual orientation: a childhood history of mild gender nonconformity, perhaps, an unusual profile of cognitive skills, or a preference for a sex-atypical role in sexual intercourse. We believe that this shift in the constellation of traits away from the sex-typical endpoints, highly variable though it may be, is nevertheless a major contributor to the group identity of gays and lesbians and to the development of gay and lesbian culture.

But biology is just the beginning of the story. Environment and experience greatly influence our sexual development after birth, especially the actual sexual behavior that we are allowed to show as adults, the kinds of relationships we establish, the way we see ourselves and are seen by others, and the communities we form. In the following chapters we investigate how the particular history and circumstances of lesbians and gay men in the United States have generated a community and culture that is unique to this time and place.

Further Reading

Boswell, John. *Christianity, Social Tolerance and Homosexuality: Gay People in Western Europe from the Beginning of the Christian Era to the Fourteenth Century*. Chicago: University of Chicago Press, 1980.

Dover, K. J. *Greek Homosexuality*. Cambridge, MA: Harvard University Press, 1978.

Herdt, Gilbert H. *Guardians of the Flutes: Idioms of Masculinity*. New York: Columbia University Press, 1981.

Nanda, Serena. *Neither Man Nor Woman—The Hijras of India*. Belmont, CA: Wadsworth, 1990.

Williams, Walter L. *The Spirit and the Flesh: Sexual Diversity in American Indian Culture*. Boston: Beacon Press, 1986.

3
History

The Depths

At the midpoint of the twentieth century, the life of a gay or lesbian American was one of internal exile. Secrecy, isolation, and denial; self-hatred and self-destruction: these were the common themes of gay existence. Under the triple burden of unjust law, uncaring religion, and inflexible custom it was a struggle just to live; to live with pride was an impossibility. It is the purpose of this chapter to describe that time of degradation, and afterward to deduce the most important circumstances by which lesbians and gay men rescued themselves from oppression; a revolution that will ever be remembered, and whose work is still in progress.

Many lesbians and gay men have provided personal accounts of life in the years after World War II. Some of these accounts portray vividly the consequences of exposure as a "pervert," "deviate," or "homosexual." A woman who was working with an American relief organization in West Germany after the war described her experience:

> I shall never forget the pride I felt, that day in Germany when I was told I had been chosen to represent our Relief Unit at a conference in another city some 500 miles away.... As I sat down with them in the conference room I suddenly became aware of an uneasiness in their manner and a tension in the atmosphere. I felt with cold dread the discussion would not be concerned with German Refugees, but rather, in some unpleasant fashion, with me.... I was told that my record from the Psychiatric Clinic had been brought to the attention of

the State Department. Since my problems had been of a homosexual nature, the State Department demanded my immediate expulsion from Germany. Reservations had been made for me on the plane that very night for the United States.... I was stunned and confused. The whole situation seemed like an evil dream. My plans for the future, my feelings of worthwhile accomplishment, and the work which had come to mean so much to me, were brought to an abrupt and cruel end....[1]

Bars that catered to lesbians or gay men were subject to constant police harassment during the 1950s and beyond. This harassment took two forms. First, undercover agents posing as homosexuals attended the bars to gather evidence that might be used to revoke the bars' licenses. Same-sex kissing or dancing, suggestive talk, or inappropriate dress were all grounds for revocation. The other technique was the police raid. Arriving in force late on Friday night, accompanied by dogs, the police would push the patrons against a wall and strip-search them, then throw them into paddy wagons for the trip to the police station, where they would be held overnight or charged and released. The charges were usually vague in the extreme: disorderly conduct, frequenting a house of ill-repute, impersonating a person of the other sex, and so on. Very often the charges were thrown out, but by that time the damage was done: local newspapers had published the names of the people charged, and their jobs, marriages, and positions in society were all at risk. The harassment of gay bars was a far greater impediment to lesbian and gay life than it would be today, because at that time there were so few other opportunities for meeting gay people, unless one belonged to certain privileged cliques.

Homophobia permeated every aspect of life. Sodomy statutes were in force in every state. While these statutes did not ban every act of same-sex love (the definition of sodomy varied from state to state), their effects were broader than their language might indicate. Even in states whose sodomy statutes were not actively enforced, they served as the underpinning for all kinds of legal oppression of gays and lesbians (see chapter 15).

Employers, led by the federal government, readily dismissed employees who admitted being gay or lesbian, or became known as such as a result of a bar raid or through other means. Nearly five thousand men and women were dismissed from federal employment (including the armed services) for homosexuality between 1947 and 1950.[2]

The medical and psychotherapeutic professions were unanimous in labeling homosexuality a disease, and ruthless in their attempts to extirpate it. Lesbians and gay men who were subjected to "talking cures" were the lucky ones: they might spend a lot of money and end up feeling terrible about themselves, but at least they had the opportunity to recover from the experience (Martin Duberman's book *Cures*[3] tells one such story). The same could not be said for gay men subjected to castration or prefrontal lobotomy. Luckily, these procedures were carried out on relatively small numbers of men, most of whom were prisoners or confined to mental hospitals. Other forms of "therapy" that were used much more widely included aversion therapy (using electroshock or nausea-inducing chemicals) and hormone treatments.[4] Medical assaults on gay men in this period were by no means limited to the United States. In Britain, for example, computer pioneer Alan Turing committed suicide in 1954 after undergoing court-ordered estrogen treatment, while in West Germany brain surgery on gay men (including operations on the hypothalamus) continued into the 1970s.

If lesbians and gay men somehow made it through this gauntlet of legal and medical abuse, organized religion attempted to head them off with the threat of hellfire. Not a single major branch of the Christian religion, nor any other of the major organized religions of the United States, condoned homosexuality in the 1950s. If spiritual warnings did not suffice, some churches turned to physical methods. At Brigham Young University, for example, the school every young Mormon aspires to attend, gay students were subject to aggressive "therapies" of various kinds. As late as the mid-1970s, electroshocks severe enough to cause burns were used on gay BYU students.[5]

In spite of all this, the middle of the twentieth century was a period, like any other, when lesbians and gay men somehow found each other and generated at least an elementary sense of community. This has been particularly well documented by Elizabeth Lapovsky Kennedy and Madeline D. Davis, who reconstructed a picture of working-class lesbian life in midcentury Buffalo, New York, by interviewing old lesbians still living in the area (see Further Reading). One of the features of this culture was the establishment of rigid gender roles (butch and femme) defined by dress and behavior.

For a privileged few, the resort village of Cherry Grove on Fire Island, New York, offered a location—perhaps the only one in the country at that time—where gays and lesbians could freely be themselves. Visited primarily by affluent white gay men, many of them connected with the New York theater scene, Cherry Grove was a summer refuge from the suffocating closet that was gay New York. Like a secret gay country club, it survived in that inhospitable era thanks to a confederacy of exclusion, in which not just straight people but also downscale or nonwhite gays were simply left in ignorance of its existence.[6]

The Seeds of Change

Although the early postwar years were such a difficult time to be lesbian or gay, many seeds of positive change had already been sown. These included long-term trends favoring gay rights, as well as a series of events and group actions that precipitated more rapid evolution.

One historical trend of great importance has been a gradual change in the basis of public morality, from a system based in religious dogma to one concerned with human rights. This trend can be traced back to the Italian Renaissance or earlier, but for us the Bill of Rights, and its gradually broadening interpretation by succeeding generations of jurists, has been its clearest outward manifestation. The trend toward individual rights has worked in favor of lesbians and gays by undermining the ethical basis for discrimination. Although the U.S. Supreme Court has yet to make any definitive ruling in favor of gay rights, it seems a historical inevitability that it will one day do so.

Another important long-term trend has been the rise of science and technology. Charles Darwin's discovery of evolution by natural selection may have diminished Man's place in the cosmos, but it diminished God's place even further; the result was a strengthening of humanism. Biology and psychology provided the basis for the objectification and naming of homosexuality and homosexual people. Discoveries in physics and chemistry were the ultimate forces behind the industrial revolution, and hence to the enormous growth of cities and the possibilities for gay culture that went with them.

Looking to the distant past, one finds evidence of lesbian and gay life both in pre-Columbian America (see chapter 2) and in the traditions of the European countries whose citizens migrated to North America.[7] In eighteenth-century London, for example, taverns called "molly-houses" catered to groups of effeminate men, who acted out ceremonies such as mock marriages or mock births, and who sometimes went dancing in women's clothes.[8] There seems to be some similarity between these groups and the "vogueing" or drag ball culture of contemporary New York (see chapter 11).

Long before 1950 there were institutions in America that (unwittingly) fostered gay and lesbian life. The women's colleges founded in the second half of the nineteenth century, as mentioned in chapter 2, were the breeding grounds for hundreds of "Boston marriages." The YMCA was founded in 1851 to promote healthy living and Bible study, but by the turn of the century it had become the focus of gay male life in many cities: an undercover investigation of a YMCA in Newport, Rhode Island, in 1919 revealed that it was "the headquarters of all cocksuckers," where gay men met, ate, partied, and had sex.[9]

Before World War II, a few places in America had become centers of a bohemian counterculture, where homosexuality was much more accepted than elsewhere in the country. Most famous was New York's Harlem during the 1920s, which not only sustained a vibrant black culture but, with its music, dance, bootleg liquor, and scandalous goings-on, attracted droves of upscale whites.[10] One gay-friendly speakeasy, the Clam House on 133rd Street, was famous for its pianist-singer Gladys Bentley, an enormous tuxedo-clad lesbian who invented obscene lyrics for popular songs, and who showed her contempt for convention by actually marrying her partner in a civil ceremony. (Marriage licenses for same-sex couples could be obtained by a variety of subterfuges). Sex of any description could be had in the "buffet flats"—apartments taken over by a group of paying customers for a night of revels. There were also extravagant costume balls, held in hotels, which often climaxed in drag beauty contests.

There had even been occasional flickers of political action before 1950. In 1915, the Russian-born anarchist Emma Goldman defended gays and lesbians in public lectures.[11] In 1924 the Society for Human Rights was founded by Henry Gerber, a Chicago postal worker, and a group of his friends. Modeled after a German organization of the same name that had been founded five years earlier, the society's aim was to reform the Illinois sodomy laws. Within a few months Gerber was arrested for sending "obscene materials" (the first issue of the society's newsletter) through the mails. Gerber's case was dismissed but he lost his job as a result of the publicity. This later became a standard pattern of punishment for both gay men and lesbians: convictions or imprisonment were rarely needed to complete a person's social degradation, once the word was out.

Although gay political action was rudimentary before 1950, other disadvantaged groups had made significant advances. In 1920, after a seventy-year struggle, women's right to vote was secured by passage of the Nineteenth Amendment. This was the event that made possible the women's movement of the 1960s and 1970s. African-Americans had made few political gains since the Civil Rights Acts of the Reconstruction era, but the groundwork for change had been laid by the urbanization of many blacks, a flowering of black culture in the interwar years, and an increasing movement to end segregation. In 1948 President Truman signed an executive order ending racial segregation in the armed forces. This action was a prelude to the landmark Supreme Court decision in 1954 that declared racial segregation in schools to be "inherently unequal." Jewish Americans were also extremely active in the postwar years: they were heavily involved in the creation and development of the State of Israel, and in 1948 Brandeis University was founded to foster Jewish culture and counter anti-Semitism at home. All these developments were seen by a few politically aware gays and lesbians as examples of what could be achieved for their own community.

The two world wars were of the greatest importance in gay and lesbian history. Although countless gays and lesbians must have died in the wars, they also provided opportunities for same-sex association on an unprecedented scale. World War II especially did wonders for lesbian pride. "The battalion I was in was probably about 97% lesbian," recalled WAC Sergeant Jonnie Phelps in the documentary film *Before Stonewall* (see Further Reading).

We were all over the place. And one day I got called in to my commanding general's office, and it happened to be Eisenhower at the time, and he said "It's come to my attention that there may be some lesbians in the WAC battalion. I'm giving you an order to ferret those lesbians out, we're going to get rid of them." And I looked at him and I looked at his secretary standing next to me, and I said "Well, sir, if the General pleases, sir, I'll be happy to do this investigation for you, but you have to know that the first name on the list will be mine." And he was kind of taken aback, and then this woman standing next to me said "Sir, if the general pleases, you must be aware that Sgt. Phelps' name may be second, but mine will be first." And then I looked at him and I said "Sir, you're right, there are lesbians in the WAC battalion. And if the General is prepared to replace all the file clerks, all the section commanders, all the drivers, every woman in the WAC detachment"—there were about nine-hundred and eighty-something of us—"then I'll be happy to make that list…." And he said "Forget the order!" It was a good battalion to be in.

But the effect of the wars was not just to allow homosexual men and women to get together. The wars mixed and fermented American society, breaking down small-town attitudes and exposing the average American, whether gay or straight, to human diversity well beyond his or her previous experience. Many gay and lesbian enlistees ended up living in the great port cities—New York and San Francisco especially—where the returning transports unloaded them. Even those who never left their home towns were affected by their wartime work experience and by the advances in mass communications that the wars brought with them.

There were a few books published before 1950 that exposed homosexuality to public gaze. One of these was *The Well of Loneliness* by the British lesbian novelist Radclyffe Hall.[12] The novel, depressing and apologetic though it was, represented both a literary milestone and a political statement urging a more sympathetic approach to the "problem" of homosexuality. The book was banned on its original publication in England in 1928. Later that same year it was published in the United States; over 20,000 copies were sold in the first three weeks. The following year the book was ruled obscene by a New York Court, but the ruling was reversed by a higher court a few weeks later. The attendant publicity did much to swell the book's fame. For many lesbians, and even for many gay men, who grew up in the 1930s and 1940s, *The Well of Loneliness* was what first made them aware that they were not the only homosexuals in the world.

A book of a very different color, but even more important for the development of the gay community, was *Sexual Behavior in the Human Male* by Alfred C. Kinsey, Wardell B. Pomeroy, and Clyde E. Martin, which caused a sensation on its appearance in 1948.[13] With financial support from the Rockefeller Foundation, Kinsey and his colleagues at Indiana University had interviewed 5,300 men about their sexual history, habits, and desires. Out of the great mass of statistical data in the book, two items seized the public's attention with extraordinary force. First, the authors calculated that 37 percent of the male population had had at least one homosexual contact to the point of orgasm after the beginning of adolescence. As if the statistic needed more vivid expression, the authors pointed out that "this is more than one male in three of the persons one may meet as he passes along a city street." Indeed, the finding gave lonely gay men every reason to scan the faces of passers-by with a new interest and a new hope. In addition, Kinsey reported that 10 percent of men are more or less exclusively homosexual for at least three years between the ages of sixteen and fifty-five. This figure was later seized on by gay rights activists and taken to mean that one in ten men are gay. In fact, however, Kinsey stated that only 4 percent of the male population are exclusively homosexual throughout their lives. (The incidence of homosexuality is discussed further in chapter 5.)

The Kinsey Report forced the American public to acknowledge that homosexual desire and homosexual behavior were commonplace. While gay men gloated, ministers and politicians expressed shock and moral outrage in innumerable speeches and sermons. Closeted gays and lesbians in public life got a chance to vent their internalized homophobia. The anthropologist Margaret Mead joined a chorus of voices denouncing Kinsey. He should never have made his findings public, she declared, because they were undermining the resolve of young people to lead conventional sex lives.[14] The conservative backlash destroyed Kinsey. In 1952 Assistant Secretary of State Dean Rusk was appointed head of the Rockefeller Foundation, and he soon put an end to the foundation's funding of Kinsey's work. Although Kinsey was able to publish the companion volume on female sexuality in 1953,[15] his work was brought to a grinding halt, and he died, a broken man, in 1956.

The New Dawn

In July 1950 Harry Hay, a former Hollywood actor and Communist Party member who lived in Los Angeles, drafted a prospectus for a gay rights organization. The document began:

Preliminary Concepts ... copyrighted by Eann MacDonald
July 7th, 1950

International Bachelors Fraternal Orders for Peace and Social Dignity
sometimes referred to as Bachelors Anonymous

"Eann MacDonald" was a pseudonym used professionally by Hay. The document described the current oppression of homosexuals, and called for an action group to rectify the situation. It continued:

> We, the androgynes of the world, have formed this responsible corporate body to demonstrate by our efforts that our physiological and psychological handicaps need be no deterrent in integrating 10% of the world's population towards the constructive social progress of mankind.[16]

The 10 percent figure acknowledged the influence of the Kinsey Report (apparently, a first draft of the prospectus was written two years earlier, shortly after the publication of Kinsey's book). The use of the word "androgyne," as well as the reference to physiology, suggests that Hay's thinking was influenced by the prewar German gay movement led by Magnus Hirschfeld, a movement that was based on the "third-sex" theory of homosexuality (see chapter 4). Hay himself has stated that he had no knowledge of gay organizations prior to his own, but the record indicates otherwise.[17]

Hay and his lover Rudi Gernreich, who was then at the beginning of an illustrious career as a fashion designer, circulated the prospectus among acquaintances in Los Angeles. They were joined by three men, Bob Hull, Chuck Rowland, and Dale Jennings, and in the next year by two others, Konrad Stevens and James Gruber. Their organization was named the Mattachine Society, and it began to put on private or semi-public meetings for discussion of gay issues. The organization was cloaked in secrecy, partly because of the danger of exposure, but probably also because several of the founding members had been members of the Communist Party, and thus had been inculcated with a cloak-and-dagger mentality. Because of this secrecy, the Mattachine Society in its first years was politically ineffective, even though its founders had made the important conceptual step of defining gays and lesbians as an oppressed minority. The society functioned mainly as a bolster to the psychological well-being of its members and visitors. It did, however, score a legal success in 1952. Dale Jennings had been arrested on a lewd-conduct charge by means of police entrapment. The society organized a campaign on his behalf and hired a lawyer to fight the case. After the jury divided on the verdict, the charges were dismissed.

In the first two years of its existence the Mattachine Society formed several secondary discussion groups in Los Angeles as well as in the San Francisco Bay Area. In 1953, however, dissension arose over the secrecy issue, and a faction led by Hal Call engineered the resignation of Hay, Rowland, and the other founding members. The new Mattachine, based primarily in San Francisco, was indeed a more open organization. It helped people arrested at police busts of gay bars, it put out a magazine, the *Mattachine Review*, and it helped publicize gay causes in a variety of ways. Chapters were formed in New York and other places. But the society gradually lost the fire of its founders. In 1961 the national Mattachine organization dissolved, and the local branches went their own ways or went out of business. A splinter group of the Los Angeles Mattachine Society, known as ONE Incorporated, was for some years the most radical element in the gay movement.[18] Founded by Dorr Legg and Jim Kepner, it published the influential *ONE Magazine*. After the U.S. Post Office declared the magazine obscene, ONE sued and, in 1957, was vindicated by the U.S. Supreme Court.

The Mattachine Society was open to men and women, but it was dominated by gay men. In 1955 a group of lesbians in San Francisco, including Del Martin and Phyllis Lyon, founded the Daughters of Bilitis,[19] an organization open only to women. The DOB's aims were to educate lesbians, help them "adjust to society," break down prejudice, participate in research on homosexuality, and propose changes in the law. They put out a magazine, *The Ladder*, and spun off a number of branches in different cities, including New York. Apparently the DOB was bankrolled by a prominent but closeted lesbian whose identity is still unknown.[20]

The Daughters of Bilitis generally kept a low profile; there were members who advocated political action, but by and large the DOB functioned as a social and consciousness-raising organization. As with the Mattachine Society, there was always a hint of acknowledgment that there was something wrong with homosexuals: the DOB were willing to listen to therapists who lectured them about "cures," and they did not admit minors lest they be accused of corrupting youth. It would be many years before the gay and lesbian community firmly grasped the concept that it was heterosexuals, not gays and lesbians, who needed to "adjust." Yet the two groups did wonders for the psychological well-being of their members, and of the many others they reached through their magazines. Even more important, they demonstrated that homosexuals could be organized, an idea that had been widely scoffed at in 1950. The founders of the Mattachine Society and the Daughters of Bilitis deserve an honored place in gay and lesbian history.

While these organizations were getting started, the political life of the country took a rightward lurch as Republican senator Joseph McCarthy initiated his witch-hunts of political deviates. Homosexuals, according to McCarthy, ranked second only to communists as threats to the political and moral integrity of the nation. The purge started at the State Department, but in 1953 President Eisenhower signed an executive order by which all homosexuals in federal employment were to be investigated and dismissed without legal recourse. Soon, the entirety of public life was affected. Tests for college admission and for many fields of employment attempted to ferret out deviant men and women. Newspapers and magazines denounced the perverts lurking in every school and business, ready to lure new recruits. The Daughters of Bilitis was penetrated by informers who handed over their membership lists to the FBI. Even the American Civil Liberties Union refused to act against the hate campaign, stating in 1957 that "it is not within the province of the Union to evaluate the social validity of the laws aimed at the suppression or elimination of homosexuals."[21]

By the mid-1950s, the fires of bigotry were beginning to burn out. In 1957 a little-known psychologist, Evelyn Hooker, published a study that asserted that homosexuality was compatible with complete psychological health.[22] She had found that a series of experts were unable to distinguish gay from straight men by their performance in a battery of tests (such as the Rorschach ink-blot test) that were supposed to give an indication of mental health. Today this finding may seen unremarkable. But in the 1950s the notion that homosexuality was a serious mental disease was the consensus in the medical and psychological professions. Hooker's work was not only intellectually original; it also took considerable personal courage to pursue this line of investigation. Hooker, who is heterosexual, has recounted how her motivation to do this work arose out of her friendship with a gay couple in San Francisco in the 1940s.[23]

Yet another significant event occurred in 1957. Losing patience with the refusal of some states to comply with the 1954 Supreme Court ruling in *Brown vs. Board of Education*, President Eisenhower sent federal troops to Little Rock, Arkansas, to enforce the racial integration of schools there. The struggle to integrate schools went on for many years—in fact it still continues—but the events in Little Rock marked a watershed in which the federal government first committed itself fully to the protection of civil rights throughout the nation.

The turmoil of the civil rights struggle—the bus boycotts, the lunch counter sit-ins, and the marches—and the sweeping legislative victories of the 1960s, were not lost on homosexual men and women, many of whom participated in those dramatic events. Prominent among them was the pacifist Bayard Rustin, who was a close aide to Martin Luther King, Jr., and an organizer of the 1963 March on Washington. A white participant in the civil rights struggle, Episcopal priest Malcolm Boyd later became one of the first ordained Episcopalians to come out of the closet.

The Daughters of Bilitis and Hal Call's Mattachine Society were too demure for these changing times, and other, more vocal organizations began to supplant them. In 1961 Frank Kameny, an astronomer who had been dismissed from U.S. government employment for homosexuality in 1957, organized a gay group in Washington. It also took the Mattachine name, although it was in reality a completely independent group, since the national Mattachine had dissolved. Kameny was one of the first gay leaders to emphasize that homosexuality was something healthy and valuable, an idea that eventually became encapsulated in his revolutionary slogan "Gay is Good!" The Washington Mattachine began protesting discrimination in the federal government, an activity that won them the attention of Congress as well as close surveillance by the FBI.[24] In 1963 fifteen activists picketed the White House. Of the three women participants, one was Judy Grahn, who twenty-one years later published a famous celebration of gay culture, *Another Mother Tongue*.[25] Kameny and other gay and lesbian activists in New York formed an umbrella organization called ECHO (East Coast Homophile Organizations). In 1965 ECHO began picketing government agencies, and in October of that year ECHO staged an even bigger demonstration at the White House: all of thirty-five men and women took part, dressed for the day in the most conventional of suits and skirts. They marched up and down with placards demanding equality in federal employment.

One demonstration outside the State Department evoked a characteristic response from the secretary of state, who was conducting a news conference inside the building: "I understand that we're being picketed by homosexuals," he said with a sneer. "The policy of the Department is that we do not employ homosexuals knowingly, and that if we discover homosexuals in our Department we discharge them." The secretary was Dean Rusk, fresh from his stint at the Rockefeller Foundation.[26]

Nowhere was social ferment greater than in San Francisco.[27] By the late 1950s, writers like Jack Kerouac, Lawrence Ferlinghetti, and Allen Ginsburg were making the city a center of resistance to conformity. In 1958 Ginsburg's *Howl*, a book of poetry that explicitly celebrated male homosexuality, stirred up a firestorm of controversy. Ferlinghetti, whose City Lights bookstore stocked the book, was charged with selling obscene literature. In the following year the homosexual activity in the city became an issue in the mayoral campaign, and there followed a backlash in which the police harassment of gays and lesbians was greatly increased. Many gay bars were closed down and many others were raided. Gay cruising areas were closely monitored, and the number of arrests skyrocketed. The crackdown continued through 1961. Responding to the oppression, a drag entertainer at the notorious Black Cat bar, Jose Sarria, ran for city supervisor. The first openly gay man to run for public office, he collected 5,600 votes. Sarria's action awakened San Francisco's gay community to the possibility of political action. In 1962 several owners of gay bars formed the Tavern Guild to resist the bar raids, and in 1964 the Society for Individual Rights was founded. The SIR was active both at a political and a social level. It campaigned for gay-friendly candidates for office, opened the first gay community center, and offered testing for venereal disease.

On the evening of January 1, 1965, a costume ball was held at California Hall to raise funds for the Council on Religion and the Homosexual, a new group of ministers, some associated with the Glide Memorial Methodist Church, who were concerned with the welfare of gays and lesbians in the city. The dance was brutally busted by the police, but in the ensuing trial the defendants, who were represented by the ACLU, won a dismissal of charges. The case won considerable sympathy for the homosexual community, and led to the birth of another crop of gay and lesbian organizations. San Francisco became more and more recognized as the center of gay life in the United States, a magnet that attracted gays and lesbians from the heartland by the thousands.

The actual number of people active in gay politics during the 1960s was minuscule. Even the SIR had less than a thousand members in 1968. Generally the attention of gays and lesbians, like that of the country as a whole, was focused on other issues—the civil rights campaign, the Vietnam War, and the beginning of the women's movement. But as the suburbanite morality of the 1950s decayed, attitudes toward gays and lesbians began to improve. After all, the 1960s was the decade of the sexual revolution, when most sex between men and women lost even the notion of a connection with procreation. In this atmosphere, gay and lesbian relationships seemed less foreign than in earlier times. Even without major political activity, therefore, gays and lesbians made significant gains. In 1961 the state of Illinois eliminated its sodomy statute. For the first time, some Americans could legally practice homosexual intercourse. Other states slowly followed suit, so that by 1983 twenty-five states no longer had sodomy statutes. Most of these victories did not happen as the result of specific political campaigns. They usually came about as part of the "housecleaning" of dead-letter legislation that states undertake from time to time. The importance of the legal changes was not so much to free gays and lesbians from police intrusion into their bedrooms as to remove the justification for oppression in other fields of life.

Gradually, mainstream America began to pay attention to the lesbians and gay men in their midst. Articles about them, usually negative in the extreme, began to appear in newspapers and magazines. An 1966 essay in *Time* magazine[28] concluded with the following words:

> [Homosexuality] is a pathetic little second-rate substitute for reality, a pitiable flight from life. As such it deserves fairness, compassion, understanding and when possible, treatment. But it deserves no encouragement, no glamorization, no rationalization, no fake status as minority martyrdom, no sophistry about simple differences in taste—and above all, no pretense that it is anything but a pernicious sickness.

It might be wondered how, after Evelyn Hooker's work, such a pathological image of homosexuality could be maintained. But psychiatrists were in no agreement about her findings, and psychoanalysts were still adamant that homosexuality was a neurosis caused, for the most part, by defective parenting. Irving Bieber, who organized a federally funded study of gay men in analysis, reported in 1962 that "not one of the fathers [of the gay men] could be regarded as reasonably 'normal' parents." He went on to claim that with a minimum of 350 hours of analysis, gay men stood a 47 percent chance of becoming heterosexual. "[I]n our judgment," he concluded, "a heterosexual shift is a possibility for all homosexuals who are strongly motivated to change."[29] It was Bieber and others like him who permitted newspaper editors to parade their homophobia under a guise of medical concern.

Unfriendly though the media generally were, they could not mention the homosexuals' fledgling organizations without inadvertently driving more gays and lesbians into them. In 1968 an umbrella group, the North American Conference of Homophile Organizations, promulgated a charter that demanded an end, not just to the sodomy laws, but to discrimination on the basis of sexual orientation in public and private employment as well as in other fields. The gay rights movement was becoming more and more explicitly a battle for civil rights, like that which had been fought by African-Americans. Only the mass demonstrations and the martyred leader were missing.

Stonewall and After

In the small hours of the morning of June 28, 1969, a riot broke out outside the Stonewall Inn, a bar on Christopher Street in New York's Greenwich Village. The Stonewall was a sleazy Mafia-controlled establishment that catered to gay men, transvestites, and transsexuals, many of whom were Puerto Rican. Two hundred patrons had been evicted from the bar in a fairly routine police raid, but instead of going home they remained in the street outside, pelting the police with coins and cobblestones and helping those who were arrested to escape from the paddy wagon. The police took refuge inside the bar, which was then set on fire. Riot police arrived and a pitched battle took place, in which several policemen and demonstrators were hurt. The rioting and demonstrations went on for several days.

The Stonewall rebellion (subject of a book by Martin Duberman—see Further Reading) marked a turning point in the struggle for gay rights. Although the initial melee was no more than an act of exasperation against the police, by the second night the event had already taken on a decidedly political flavor. "Gay Power" was the slogan as politically active gays of many backgrounds joined the drag queens who had started the disturbance. A demonstration took place the following Friday (July 4) at Independence Hall in Philadelphia. In the ensuing months new organizations like the Gay Activists Alliance put on further protests, some of them provoked by other bar raids. The following June marches took place in both New York and Los Angeles to mark the anniversary of Stonewall. The event became the annual Gay Pride March, and spread to more and more cities.

Parallel with this increase in gay activism, another movement was also on the march. This was feminism. The interactions between Women's Lib and Gay Lib were deep and complex. Both movements were a response to oppression by heterosexual men. But to gay men, it was the heterosexuality of their oppressors that mattered, while to women, it was their maleness. To which ranks did lesbians belong? Many of them answered this question by abandoning the use of the word "gay" to describe themselves and joining the women's organizations. Their reception was mixed. In 1971 a resolution was passed by the National Organization of Women explicitly stating that lesbians were a valued element in the organization. Yet to some lesbians it seemed that acceptance carried with it a price tag: a tacit agreement to soft-pedal their own special concerns as lesbians in favor of those of women as a whole.

Lesbians played a leading role in NOW and many other women's groups, helping to raise the status of women in all fields of life. The net effect of these achievements was to make it far easier for a woman, or a female couple, to lead a fulfilling life independent of men. Yet the women's movement also helped gay men. As the status of women rose, so automatically did that of gay men. This coupling of fates is a consequence of the coupling of homophobia and sexism: male homosexuality is often seen as a rejection of masculinity, but such a rejection is only a debasement to the extent that masculinity ranks above femininity. The women's movement brought about a marked narrowing of that difference in rank.

Besides giving lesbians new visibility and status, the women's movement also brought more women to lesbianism. Lesbianism became a choice, a political statement, the ultimate in liberation from the male yoke. It also became egalitarian: gone were the butch/femme roles of yesteryear.

All this left gay men a little confused. The "ladies' auxiliary of the gay movement"[30] had decamped, leaving them the sole guardians of feminine virtues. By a series of forced marches, gay men hurried to take a new ultramasculine position, expressed not only in a more aggressive sexuality but also in appearance (muscles, short hair, and mustache), style of dress (bomber jackets and boots), and manner of speech (curt). The "clone" was born. Those who could not keep up, the incurably limp-wristed drag queens, were consigned to the garbage heap of gay society.[31]

Thus the 1970s was a period of relative separation between lesbians and gay men. Lesbians identified with women—perhaps it would be more accurate to say that they identified women with themselves. Gay men identified with men: not with real, heterosexual, homophobic men, of course, but with some celluloid vision of how men ought to be: manly, clean-cut, go-getting, yet spiced with enough sensitivity and humor to temper the more jarring flavors of masculinity. Gays and lesbians fought out their own private battle of the sexes. Gay men were generally made to feel unwelcome in lesbian bars, and vice versa. Contacts were maintained to some extent within the political organizations, but much less in the cultural sphere.

Within gay male culture in the 1970s, sex dominated everything. Public resistance to gay bars, sex clubs and bathhouses declined greatly during the decade, especially in the cities with the largest gay populations: San Francisco, Los Angeles, and

New York. Even outdoor sex was a much safer proposition than earlier: in San Francisco, certain rustic corners of the city became gay safari parks where police harassment was minimal. Altogether, the opportunities for sexual contact between gay men were probably as rich as at any time since the early days of the Roman empire. Already by 1969/70, when Alan Bell and Martin Weinberg carried out a survey of gay men and lesbians in the San Francisco Bay Area,[32] the statistics were remarkable. Of the gay white males they interviewed, 43 percent said that they had had over five hundred different homosexual partners, and 28 percent said they had had a thousand partners or more. Black gay men were only a little way behind. By contrast, more than half of the lesbians polled said they had had fewer than ten sexual partners.

At the beginning of the decade, the sex life of most gay men was still fairly conservative. One of Bell and Weinberg's "ethnographers" closed his report on a leather bar with the following words:

> The sound of revving cycles and their exhaust filtered through the bar throughout the evening. What a crowd! But as raucous as the place is, it is friendly. The rough-looking attire and costumes are incongruent with the warm and friendly persons I've met there. The S and M connotation of the leather crowd is pretty much a myth.[33]

As the 1970s progressed, however, not only did the quantity of organized gay sex increase vastly, but its flavor also became more astringent. Anonymous group sex, rimming (oral-anal contact), fist-fucking, S/M scenes, and drug use became the order of the day at the scores of bathhouses and sex clubs in New York, San Francisco, and other large cities. Along with this came the inevitable epidemics—syphilis, gonorrhea, hepatitis, and intestinal parasites—as well as alcoholism and drug addiction. But by and large there was the sense that all these problems could be fixed with a jab of penicillin or a couple of weeks' R & R.

The emphasis on sex as the focus of gay life did nothing for the political advancement of gays and lesbians, even though, for many gay men at least, their sex life *was* a political statement. The heterosexual public saw little of these goings-on. Instead, what they saw was a growing community of more or less conventionally living gays and lesbians who were a little more open about their identity than had been their predecessors. Whole tracts of real estate, especially in San Francisco, were "homosexualized," that is, renovated and decorated as only gay men know how. It became much more common for lesbians and gay men to be "out" at work. During the decade, polls showed that an increasing fraction of the population thought they knew at least one lesbian or gay man, and attitudes toward gay rights gradually improved.

Perhaps the most dramatic sign of the changing times was the decision of the American Psychiatric Association, in 1973, to delete homosexuality as a category of mental illness from the *Diagnostic and Statistical Manual of Psychiatric Disorders*. This decision came as a result of increasing pressure from gays and lesbians, especially Frank Kameny and Barbara Gittings. Within the psychiatric profession, the impetus for change came largely from UCLA psychiatrists Judd Marmor and Richard Green, as well as from a small number of openly gay psychiatrists such as Boston University's Richard Pillard. The opposition was led by psychoanalysts Irving Bieber and Charles Socarides. (Socarides remains adamant even today that homosexuality is a serious mental disorder.) The American Psychological Association quickly followed the psychiatrists' lead, but the American Psychoanalytic Association did not follow suit until much later.

The improving attitudes toward gays and lesbians in the early 1970s led a number of cities to pass ordinances that protected gays and lesbians from discrimination in such areas as employment and housing. Not uncommonly these ordinances were enacted in states that still had sodomy statutes. The reason for this discrepancy was that tolerance toward homosexuality was (and still is) most widespread in cities. The more conservative suburban and rural populations tended to oppose liberalization of the state sodomy laws. By 1977 about forty cities had enacted some kind of protection for gays and lesbians. In January of that year Miami was added to the list.

The victory in Miami proved to be a hollow one, because it inspired a backlash of enormous proportions. Singer Anita Bryant and her Save Our Children movement led an emotional campaign against the ordinance, and in June it was repealed by an overwhelming majority of Dade County voters. The revolt spread: gay rights ordinances were repealed in several other cities across the country, and by 1978 gays and lesbians on the West Coast were under siege: in Seattle, an initiative to repeal the city's gay rights ordinance was put on the ballot, and in California John Briggs introduced Proposition 6, which proposed banning gays and lesbians from teaching in the California public school system. In all these antigay campaigns, Christian fundamentalists played an important and highly visible role.

Sensing that they had their backs to the ocean, gays and lesbians on the West Coast put up a tremendous battle against the two initiatives. At the June Gay Pride parade in San Francisco, an estimated 375,000 marchers focused their demands on this one issue. They were addressed by Supervisor Harvey Milk, who five months earlier had become the nation's first openly gay city official:

> My name is Harvey Milk—and I want to recruit you. I want to recruit you for the fight to preserve your democracy from the John Briggs and the Anita Bryants who are trying to constitutionalize bigotry.
>
> We are not going to allow that to happen: we are not going to sit back in silence as 300,000[34] of our gay brothers and sisters did in Nazi Germany. We are not going to allow our rights to be taken away and then march with bowed heads into the gas chambers. On this anniversary of Stonewall I ask my gay sisters and brothers to make this commitment to fight: for themselves, for their freedom, for their country....
>
> The blacks did not win their rights by sitting quietly in the back of the bus. They got off!
>
> Gay people, we will not win our rights by staying quietly in our closets.... We are coming out! We are coming out to fight the lies, the

myths, the distortions! We are coming out to tell the truth about gays!...[35]

In September, polls showed the Briggs initiative passing by a two-to-one margin. But the tide was changing, thanks to a massive grassroots campaign by gays and lesbians and their sympathizers. In addition, scores of prominent Americans, most of whom had never said a good word about gays and lesbians before, came out against the initiative. These included former governor Ronald Reagan, former president Gerald Ford, and (at the last moment) President Jimmy Carter. Many churches, school boards, and unions also came out in opposition to the measure. On election day the Briggs initiative was rejected by a landslide: millions of Californians had changed their minds on the topic within the final weeks. The Seattle measure was also defeated, thanks to a campaign that portrayed the measure as an attack on the public's right to privacy.

The New Right had been dealt a crushing defeat. But the rejoicing was short-lived: on November 27, 1978, Harvey Milk and San Francisco Mayor George Moscone were assassinated by Supervisor Dan White. White represented the conservative blue-collar population of San Francisco; his district was the only one in the city that had voted in favor of the Briggs initiative. He had resigned shortly before election day in protest against the supervisors' low salaries, but then changed his mind. Milk had persuaded Moscone not to reappoint him. Enraged by this rebuff, White shot Moscone and Milk in their city hall offices.

The gay community's grief at Milk's death turned to fury six months later (May 21, 1979) when White was acquitted of murder and convicted only of voluntary manslaughter for the two deaths. Particularly galling was the triviality of White's defense: he had been rendered mentally unstable, a psychiatrist testified on his behalf, by his addiction to junk food. A demonstration at city hall degenerated into a riot in which several police cars were torched and the doors and windows of city hall were smashed. Later that night, the police retaliated with a riot of their own: a group of them, acting without orders, stormed a gay bar in the Castro and clubbed everyone in sight. The night as a whole resulted in about 160 people requiring hospitalization: about 60 of these were police officers, and most of the remainder were gay men.[36]

While San Francisco was undergoing these paroxysmal events, the country as a whole was, ever so slowly, becoming more comfortable with homosexuality. The topic was being dealt with more explicitly in mainstream films, plays, and books. Arthur Hiller's 1982 film *Making Love*, for example, featured a male couple who, in defiance of previous convention, actually lived happily ever after.

But gay and lesbian role models were scarcely to be found during the 1970s, whether in the arts, sports, politics, or the professions. All too often, public figures who were gay or lesbian moved in a complacent world of privilege. Their sexual orientation might be known within a wide circle of acquaintances, but they could rely on the discretion of the media not to make it public knowledge. They had little sense of community with less fortunate lesbians and gay men, and hence little motivation to risk their ratings or their image for an unpopular cause. A notable exception was David Kopay, an NFL running back who came out in 1975 at the end of his playing career. His book, *The Dave Kopay Story* (with Perry Young), was a best-seller that did much to combat the "sissy-boy" stereotype of male homosexuality. In fact, it buttressed the reverse, macho stereotype that gay men were then trying to project.

Of the lesbian and gay activists of that period, some came from the ranks of those who had suffered deep personal injustice—people like Leonard Matlovich and Vernon "Copy" Berg, who had been discharged from the armed forces for their homosexuality and who responded by bringing lawsuits against the Pentagon. Others had been educated in activism by their experiences in the antiwar, civil rights, or women's movements. But there was also a new generation of activists who grew up much more comfortable with their homosexuality than was possible for any of their predecessors, and who, inspired by Stonewall, sought ways to incorporate their love for the gay community into their professional lives. One such person was Vito Russo, a film historian who spent the 1970s researching the connection between homosexuality and the cinema. The resulting book, *The Celluloid Closet* (1981), was a devastating indictment of many decades of Hollywood homophobia. Another was writer Jill Johnston; her articles in the *Village Voice* and her 1973 book *Lesbian Nation*[37] became central texts of lesbian feminism.

Through people like these, gay and lesbian activism was slowly diffusing out of the strictly political arena into every corner of American life. But still, activism was not popular within the gay and lesbian communities. Many gay men were too busy leading lives of furious self-indulgence, lives that were portrayed with ruthless accuracy in Larry Kramer's 1978 novel *Faggots;* or else they were absorbed in careers, careers that occupied a separate compartment in their lives from their identity as gay men. Perhaps a larger fraction of lesbian women were consciously engaged in more constructive lives, but often their efforts were, at least nominally, on behalf of the community of women: women's health collectives, women's publishing houses, women's bands, and so on. The "women" in the names of these organizations had originally, as mentioned earlier, meant all women, because lesbian-feminists identified with all women, but as the decade progressed it became more and more a euphemism for "lesbian," a code phrase like the many others—"for human rights," "for understanding," "lambda," and so on—that have been used to label homosexual organizations. Unfortunately, the use of such labels may have reduced the organizations' political effectiveness, because the public did not always know what constituency they represented.

Five months before his death Harvey Milk had called for a March on Washington for gay rights. That march took place in October 1979. Between 75,000 and 100,000 gays and lesbians from all over the country demanded an end to discrimination and oppression. From a public relations point of view the march was a failure: as one of us (Simon LeVay) recalls, the marchers walked through deserted streets, and the event was generally ignored by the media. But it showed that gays and lesbians could be mobilized on a national scale, something that would have been inconceivable only ten years earlier. And it paved the way for the larger, more effective marches that came later.

The Plague Years

In 1979 and 1980 a handful of gay men in New York, San Francisco, and Los Angeles came down with one or more of a bizarre assortment of ailments: fungal infections of the mouth and throat, Kaposi's sarcoma (a previously rare form of cancer presenting as purplish patches in the skin), swollen lymph nodes, diarrhea, and pneumonia due to infection with the protozoon *Pneumocystis carinii.*

At first these cases were nothing more than baffling rarities. But by 1981 they were enough of them to make it clear that a new and deadly disease had appeared in the United States. Several features of the disease suggested that at its core lay a profound disruption of the immune system, but the cause of this disruption—whether an infection, a toxic drug reaction, or some environmental factor—was a mystery. In 1982 the disease was officially given a name: the acquired immune deficiency syndrome, or AIDS.

During 1983, researchers at the Institut Pasteur in Paris succeeded in identifying the cause of the disease, a virus that later was given the name human immunodeficiency virus, or HIV. This discovery led quickly to the development of a test to detect the presence of antibodies to HIV in blood. The test could be used to screen blood intended for transfusions, and to identify asymptomatic, HIV-infected individuals. The discovery of HIV, and the elucidation of its mode of action, led eventually to the development of a class of drugs, the so-called reverse transcriptase inhibitors such as AZT, that at least temporarily slow the progression of the disease. In addition, the discovery of the mode of transmission led to the knowledge of how to avoid infection.

In spite of these remarkable scientific successes, the first decade of the AIDS era was a time of ever-increasing human suffering. The numbers of the victims climbed inexorably: hundreds by the end of 1982, thousands by 1984, over one hundred thousand by the end of the decade, and the majority of these were gay men. Furthermore, as the means to combat the disease improved, so the disease itself showed new and uglier faces. Tuberculosis, lymphoma, blindness, and dementia lay in wait for those who survived the initial skirmishes with pneumonia and Kaposi's sarcoma.

People's attitudes to AIDS were intimately tied up with their attitudes to homosexuality. Some Christian fundamentalists hailed the epidemic as God's punishment for sinning homosexuals. If there were a few "innocent victims"—those who acquired the disease though blood transfusions, perhaps, or while they were in their mothers' wombs—that just demonstrated the mysteriousness of God's ways, or the impossibility of complete precision in any program of earthly retribution.

A much more common attitude, though, was one of avoidance. The gay identity of those who became ill was the talisman that protected heterosexuals from the fear of becoming ill themselves, and hence removed their motivation to do anything about the disease. It was not homophobia, in the sense of fear or hatred of homosexuals, but a simple ignorance about gay people that allowed the majority of Americans to place them, conceptually, on another planet where the disease could safely be allowed to burn itself out.

Even gay men were capable of the same distancing and denial. Many of them actively resisted efforts to educate the community about safe-sex practices, fought to keep bathhouses open, and generally downplayed the seriousness of the situation. All this has been amply documented in *And the Band Played On*, Randy Shilts's history of the early years of the epidemic (see Further Reading).

Among those who did take the epidemic seriously, one man stands out: New York novelist and playwright Larry Kramer. Kramer became alarmed about the disease in mid-1981, and helped raise funds for research into its causes and treatment. Early in 1982 he helped found Gay Men's Health Crisis, the country's first AIDS service organization. Among other innovative services, GMHC invented the "Buddy" program, which matches volunteers to people with AIDS on a one-to-one basis (see chapter 14).

In 1983 Kramer wrote an article for the *New York Native* entitled "1,112 and Counting," which was the first comprehensive portrait of the AIDS crisis. The article laid bare not just the disease itself, but the conspiracy of silence that surrounded it. He attacked the news media, including the gay press, for ignoring the situation. He attacked local and federal government for their failure to act. And he attacked gay men who placed sex higher than life itself. In retrospect the article seems moderate enough, given the crisis situation, but it enraged many leaders in the gay community. To them, everything was thought of in terms of "rights": gay men's "right" to have sex, their "right" to go to bathhouses, their "right" to donate blood, and so on. The American Association of Physicians for Human Rights, for example (another of those "coded" titles; it has recently been renamed the Gay and Lesbian Medical Association), put out a statement that said, in part, "We object strongly to the attempts by some members of the blood products and banking community to identify gay men by questionnaire and exclude them from blood donation. These attempts are an unnecessary invasion of individual privacy and grossly misrepresent the issues to the American people."[38]

Kramer's article made him many enemies, but it also marked the true beginning of AIDS activism. Reprinted in gay papers across the country, it awoke many rank-and-file members of the community to the seriousness of the situation and the necessity for action. Kramer himself left GMHC, which he considered to be focused too narrowly on AIDS relief, and devoted himself to writing a play, *The Normal Heart*, which dramatized AIDS not only as individual suffering but also as a political struggle. It was a major success on its premiere in New York in 1985. In 1987 Kramer cofounded the AIDS Coalition To Unleash Power. ACT UP, which now has chapters across the country, has organized numerous highly publicized actions to further its demands for increased spending on AIDS research, treatment, and relief, and for an end to bigotry and discrimination against those with the disease or carrying the virus (see chapter 14).

Although Kramer's own work against AIDS has been unique in its variety, effectiveness, and long duration, the real story of the 1980s was the gradual engagement of the rank-and-file members of the gay and lesbian communities in the widening battle against the disease. As AIDS spread, so more and more people arrived at a personal confrontation with the virus. Either they were infected or fell sick themselves, or they were forced to witness the ravages of the disease among their lovers and friends. These individual experiences, combined with knowledge about the magnitude of the crisis and the evident inadequacy of the country's response to it, drove them one by one to action on behalf of their embattled community. They organized food banks and laundry services for those who were ill; they founded hospices for the dying; they started support groups for the sick, the infected, the caregivers, and the bereaved; they raised funds for research, relief, and political action; they promoted safer sex practices, especially the use of condoms; they campaigned for greater federal expenditures on research, treatment, and education; they fought for the legal rights of HIV-infected persons; they publicly expressed their grief and anger in articles, books, plays, films, dance, music, art, and photography. Community service centers and AIDS projects in big cities became corporations with multimillion-dollar budgets, scores of employees, and hundreds or thousands of volunteers.

It was not only gay men who did all these things. Lesbians also became involved on a vast scale. They became active at every level, as individual caregivers, as volunteers, as directors of service organizations and political action groups. That they did this is remarkable, given that they might easily have maintained the separatist stance that had characterized much of the lesbian community at the beginning of the epidemic. After all, the disease spread as fast as it did primarily because of the promiscuity of gay men, a trait that lesbians did not share. Nevertheless, they did become involved, and in the process lesbian separatism greatly diminished. By the end of the 1980s, the majority of homosexual organizations, whether AIDS-related or not, were co-gender groups that sought, if not always successfully, to give equal voice to the concerns of their lesbian and gay male members.

The AIDS epidemic forced gay men out of the closet. Most obvious were the famous gay men, starting with Rock Hudson in 1985, whose homosexuality became public knowledge when they became ill or died. But each illness, each death, however anonymous, spread the word. All too many parents found out about their sons' illness and their sons' homosexuality on the same day. Many gay men who fell ill in San Francisco or Los Angeles or New York returned to their home towns to die, forcing the consciousness of their homosexuality on thousands of small towns and rural communities.

But not just gay men with AIDS were outed. The disease motivated lesbians and healthy gay men to out themselves too. Being openly gay or lesbian began to be seen as a necessary part of one's involvement in the community, and a necessary step in the achievement of full mental health. Of course, this was often a tentative, incomplete process, and one that even today all too few gays and lesbians have embarked on. A person might be out to one parent but not the other, at play but not at work, and so on. But the net effect was that, for the first time in American history, gays and lesbians became commonplace items in the social landscape—in offices, at churches, on playing fields, at parties, on talk shows, and at family reunions. There remained only a few corners of American society—the armed forces in particular—where homosexuality was absolutely taboo, and even in these corners the winds of change were beginning to stir up the dust.

As the 1980s came to an end, it was obvious that, as concerned the image of the gay community, the AIDS epidemic was having quite the opposite effect from that which had originally been feared. Though AIDS was, and still is, an unmitigated tragedy for hundreds of thousands of individuals directly affected by it, the disease has also catalyzed an improvement in the visibility and image of gays and lesbians in society that otherwise might have taken many decades to be accomplished. Gone are the proposals to quarantine people with AIDS, gone is the biblical invective, gone, by and large, is the open abuse of gay people by public figures. Not that homophobia is a thing of the past, of course, but now it must be cloaked in at least some semblance of rationality.

The tangible results of this improving climate are everywhere to be seen. By 1995, nine states and over seventy-five cities had some form of codified civil rights protection for gays and lesbians, generally consisting at a minimum of a law or ordinance prohibiting discrimination against gays and lesbians in employment. Some cities and corporations recognize same-sex domestic partnerships for insurance and other purposes, protect HIV-infected people from discrimination, make conscious efforts to hire gays and lesbians, and so on. At the federal level, openly gay and lesbian people are increasingly being seen in high-level Washington appointments, and federal agencies such as the FBI have reversed their long-standing ban on the employment of homosexuals.

Of course, there have also been setbacks and reverses. Perhaps the biggest setback in the 1980s was the 1986 decision of the U.S. Supreme Court in *Bowers v. Hardwick*, which upheld the constitutionality of sodomy statutes (see chapter 15). The decision, which was reached by the narrowest of margins (five to four), represented a lost opportunity to assert a fundamental right to freedom of sexual expression, a right that could have been the basis of many other legal advances for gays and lesbians. As Justice Blackmun wrote in his dissenting opinion:

> Only the most willful blindness could obscure the fact that sexual intimacy is "a sensitive, key relationship of human existence, central to family life, community welfare, and the development of human personality".... The fact that individuals define themselves in a signifi-

> cant way through their intimate sexual relationships with others suggests, in a Nation as diverse as ours, that there may be many "right" ways of conducting those relationships, and that much of the richness of a relationship will come from the freedom an individual has to *choose* the form and nature of these intensely personal bonds ... what the Court [in this case] ... has refused to recognize is the fundamental interest all individuals have in controlling the nature of their intimate associations with others ... the issue raised by this case touches the heart of what makes individuals what they are.

There have also been numerous efforts, some successful, to repeal gay rights laws around the country. Perhaps the most well known was "Amendment 2," passed by the voters of Colorado in 1992, which repealed all local gay rights ordinances. The amendment was subsequently ruled unconstitutional by the district court in Colorado on the grounds that it "violates the fundamental right of an identifiable group to participate in the political process." The ruling was upheld by the Colorado Supreme Court in 1994. The case is headed for the Supreme Court in 1995. Until such time as the U.S. Supreme Court takes an unequivocal stand on the issue of gay rights, this country's fragmented legal system will permit many local communities to incorporate homophobia into law. A year after the Colorado vote, for example, a similar measure was passed by the voters of Cincinnati. It was subsequently ruled unconstitutional by a federal district court, and the case is currently under appeal.

In 1992 gay rights activists focused their attention on one issue above all: gays and lesbians in the military. During the presidential campaign of that year, Democratic candidate Bill Clinton courted the gay and lesbian vote by promising to end the military ban on homosexuals. Since the Republicans were having a particularly homophobic year, the issue seemed a clear-cut one for the community. In fact, gays and lesbians not only voted for Clinton in droves, they also were very active in his campaign. After he came into office, however, Clinton decided against issuing an immediate executive order to enact the new policy. The initiative was then stolen by Georgia senator Sam Nunn, whose Armed Services Committee conducted lengthy hearings on the issue. Nunn managed to stir up a little spasm of homophobia in the country, and Clinton caved in. On July 19, 1993, he announced a policy whereby lesbians and gay men could still be discharged from military service for their homosexuality. The only concessions were that recruits were no longer to be questioned about their sexual orientation, and that investigations of service personnel should only take place if there was credible evidence that they were gay. The new policy was seen as a cowardly retreat from Clinton's campaign promise: most gays and lesbians felt that they had been tricked into supporting his candidacy, and he was denounced in bitter speeches and demonstrations across the country. By 1995, the adminstration's policy had been challenged in a number of legal cases, including a test case (*Able v. U.S.A.*—see chapter 15) brought by the ACLU and the community's own legal organization, Lambda Legal Defense. It seems likely that the legality of the current policy will be decided by the U.S. Supreme Court.

One of the ironies of the "gays in the military" debate is that it focused almost exclusively on gay men, although in fact lesbian women in the services are much more affected by the issue. It is likely, although there are no statistics on the matter, that lesbians are overrepresented in the military, compared with gay men. Between 1980 and 1990, 23 percent of all discharges for homosexuality were of women, even though women constituted only 10 percent of armed forces personnel.

The AIDS epidemic has shown that the gay and lesbian community has the ability to form effective socially and politically active organizations. But the size of these organizations is still relatively small. Somewhere between 500,000 and 1 million gays and lesbians took part in the 1993 March on Washington, an occasion that generated far more national attention than any of the previous marches. But few of the marchers joined or contributed to a national gay and lesbian organization, and when they went home the political energy they generated was allowed to dissipate. Even the largest national gay and lesbian organization, the Human Rights Campaign Fund, with its

80,000 members, pales into insignificance when compared with organizations that represent other sectors of our society (for example, the American Association of Retired Persons, with its 33 million members) or that actively oppose gay rights (such as the Christian Coalition, with between 600,000 and 1 million members).

Recounting the history of a community in broad outline, as we have attempted to do, tends to convey a sense of unity and continuity that may be deceptive. In the following chapters we try to correct this impression by looking at some of the diversity in the lives led by lesbian and gay Americans today.

Further Reading

Duberman, Martin. *Stonewall*. New York: Dutton, 1993.

Duberman, Martin, Martha Vicinus, and George Chauncey, Jr., eds. *Hidden from History: Reclaiming the Gay and Lesbian Past*. New York: Meridian Books, 1989.

Faderman, Lillian. *Odd Girls and Twilight Lovers: A History of Lesbian Life in Twentieth-Century America*. New York: Columbia University Press, 1991.

Katz, Jonathan N. *Gay American History: Lesbians and Gay Men in the U.S.A.* New York: Meridian, 1992.

Kennedy, Elizabeth Lapovsky, and Madeline D. Davis. *Boots of Leather, Slippers of Gold: The History of a Lesbian Community*. New York: Routledge, 1983.

Marcus, Eric. *Making History: The Struggle for Gay and Lesbian Equal Rights, 1945-1990*. New York: HarperCollins, 1992.

Schiller, Greta, director. *Before Stonewall: The Making of a Gay and Lesbian Community* (documentary film, 1986).

Shilts, Randy. *The Mayor of Castro Street: The Life and Times of Harvey Milk*. New York: St. Martin's Press, 1982.

Shilts, Randy. *And the Band Played On: Politics, People, and the AIDS Epidemic*. New York: St. Martin's Press, 1987.

Timmons, Stuart. *The Trouble with Harry Hay: Founder of the Modern Gay Movement*. Boston: Alyson Publications, 1990.

4 Science

What decides a person's sexual orientation? In this chapter we review some of the ways people have attempted to answer this question in the past, and then take a look at current research into the matter, research that uses the tools of genetics, neurobiology, and cognitive psychology.

The History of Ideas

In the nineteenth century there was little notion of sexual orientation as an attribute of personality. Rather, heterosexuality was regarded as the natural human condition, requiring no explanation, while homosexuality was viewed as sinful or criminal behavior that anyone might indulge in, rather in the same way as anyone might commit thefts if they were not restrained by the law and moral teachings. This attitude may be traced back to the teaching of Saint Paul, specifically the biblical passage (Romans 1:26) where he wrote:

> For this cause God gave them up unto vile affections: for even their women did change the natural use into that which is against nature: and likewise also the men, leaving the natural use of the woman, burnt in their lust one toward another; men with men working that which is unseemly....

Even in the nineteenth century there were voices dissenting against this view, most especially in Germany. Karl Heinrich Ulrichs (1825–1895) was a lawyer who took it into his head to become the first gay activist.[1] Besides campaigning for gay rights, at great personal cost, he argued that gays and lesbians were intrinsically different from heterosexual people. For them, he declared, homosexual behavior *was* natural, because their minds had developed differently from the minds of heterosexuals. In this he appealed to an earlier, pre-Christian tradition, made explicit for example in Plato's *Symposium*, which viewed homosexual and heterosexual individuals as intrinsically different and equally "natural" (see chapter 2).

Ulrichs's ideas were perpetuated in the early twentieth century in the notion of the "third sex." This was the idea, most explicit in the writings of the sexologist and gay rights activist Magnus Hirschfeld (1868–1935), that gays and lesbians occupy an intermediate position between men and women.[2] Gay men, according to the third-sex theory, are more feminine than other men, lesbian women more masculine than other women. Staking out a territory in this intermediate zone between the sexes, gays and lesbians in Berlin and other European cities developed a distinct culture, best known to Americans through the stories of Christopher Isherwood.

The third-sex theory fell a victim to two forces. The first was Sigmund Freud, whose theories of sexual development dominated the twentieth century. Freud maintained that male homosexuality is a state of arrested sexual development; specifically, a failure to break an intense sexual attraction that a young boy feels toward his mother.[3] This failure could result from several causes, but Freud laid special stress on the way parents treated their young children: a mother who was too dominating or possessive, or a father who was distant or hostile, made the young child's separation from his mother, and his development as a separate individual, more difficult. Homosexuality was the end-product of this failure, according to Freud, because the man who as a child failed to complete the separation process seeks constantly to reenact it in his sexual relationships. Not a terribly logical theory, perhaps: it would seem more likely to direct men's sexual attention to women than to other men. But Freud proposed that in these adult reenactments the gay man takes his mother's role, and seeks out other men who represent himself in his infancy. Freud's ideas about homosexuality in women did not amount to a coherent theory, but in his one detailed case study of a lesbian he attributed her sexual orientation to a number of causes, including envy of her brother's penis, rivalry with her mother for her father's love, as well as to constitutional factors.[4]

Whatever the merits of Freud's theories, they have been enormously important in molding society's views about homosexuality. To some extent his theories benefited gays and lesbians, because they acknowledged the existence of homosexuality as a stable personality state, and portrayed this state as arising from factors beyond the affected individual's control. This tended to turn the focus away from the conception of homosexuality as a crime or a sin. But Freud's ideas, especially as developed by his followers in the United States, strengthened the view of homosexuality as a *sickness*, and a sickness that could be cured by appropriate treatment. By helping the gay man to become aware of his childhood conflicts, the thinking went, one could allow him to complete the normal process of psychosexual development and become heterosexual. This approach, which rarely if ever succeeded in its aim, caused much more anguish than benefit to the people it was supposed to help.[5]

There was a second force that caused the third-sex theory to lose ground, especially in the 1960s and 1970s. This was a change of attitude within the gay community itself. As the women's liberation movement developed, lesbian women took a major part in the struggle for women's rights, and in doing so identified more strongly than before with the entire community of women. Gay men also began to become politically active, and a new "masculine," even "macho" image of gay men became the ideal, so much so that the flamboyant drag queens, and other gay men who exhibited "feminine" traits, became an embarrassment to the gay community (see chapter 3). Those years, the 1970s especially, were a time when there was little cooperation or social contact between lesbians and gay men, as both groups emphasized their affiliation with their own biological sex. And even to think about the origins of homosexuality became unacceptable to many gays and lesbians, as if to do so was to acknowledge its pathological nature.

Over the last ten years or so the pendulum has begun to swing back again toward open discussion of the issue, and specifically toward biological ideas reminiscent of the third-sex theory. In this respect the evolution of views about sexual orientation have followed views about differences between the sexes. At the height of the women's liberation movement many writers—Germaine Greer, for example, in *The Female Eunuch*—denied the existence of any intrinsic mental or brain differences between the sexes. Any differences that might exist were culturally imposed: by the kinds of toys parents gave their sons and daughters, for example. But more recently both men and women have become more comfortable with acknowledging the existence of innate personality differences between the sexes, and the scientific evidence for such differences—even in such matters as children's toy preferences—has become very strong. The sexual differentiation of the human brain has become the subject of intense study by neurobiologists, molecular biologists, and cognitive psychologists.

In the realm of sexual orientation there has been a similar trend. Less obsessed with proving that they are "regular human beings," lesbians and gay men have come to acknowledge and value what distinguishes them from heterosexual people. Drag queens and "Dykes on Bikes" are no longer considered the embarrassment at gay pride parades that they used to be. Instead they are more likely to be welcomed as part of the diversity within the gay and lesbian community. This diversity defies stereotyping, but "gender-atypical" traits are acknowledged to be an important part of it. Accompanying this change has been an increasing belief that one's sexual orientation is innate. It is very common nowadays—almost the rule, in fact—to hear gay men assert that they were "born gay."[6] Lesbians, on the other hand, are considerably more diverse in their beliefs on the subject.[7]

Scientific research has supported and strengthened this trend. The scientific findings are still very incomplete, but significant advances have been made both in biology and psychology. The progress in biology includes the demonstration of a genetic component to sexual orientation and the discovery of differences in brain structure between gay and straight men. In psychology, there has been considerable work on mental differences between homosexual and heterosexual men and women that go beyond matters of sexuality. In addition, it has become clear that some young children already show personality traits that anticipate their sexual orientation as adults.

Genetics

That genes play a role in determining a person's sexual orientation has been suspected for many years. For one thing, homosexuality runs in families. A study that showed this particularly clearly was published by Richard Pillard and James Weinrich of Boston University in 1986.[8] They recruited gay men, as well as a comparison group of heterosexual men, and asked them about the sexual orientation of their brothers and sisters. In most cases they also confirmed the sexual orientation of these relatives by direct interview. It turned out that about 22 percent of the brothers of the gay men were also gay or bisexual, compared with 4 percent of the brothers of the straight men. Similar statistics have been gathered on women[9]: from 12 percent to 35 percent of the sisters of lesbians are themselves lesbian (the figures vary according to the exact criteria used), compared with 2 percent to 14 percent of the sisters of heterosexual women.

This clustering of lesbians and gay men in families could have several explanations. Maybe the parents in these families had a special talent for making their children homosexual. Maybe the children grew up in homes that were exposed to high levels of electromagnetic radiation. The possibilities are endless. But the simplest explanation is that the parents carry genes predisposing to homosexuality, and that they pass on these genes to several of their children.

To test this idea more directly, Richard Pillard and Michael Bailey (of Northwestern University) studied the sexual orientation of twins.[10] There are of course two kinds of twins:

monozygotic or "identical" twins, whose entire sets of genes are the same, and dizygotic or "fraternal" twins, who have about half their genes in common, just like regular brothers and sisters. Bailey and Pillard found that, if a twin is gay, the chances of his or her co-twin also being gay depend very much on whether the twins are identical or fraternal. For identical male twins, the chances are about 50 percent, while for fraternal twins, the chances are about 25 percent. A similar pattern is seen in women: the identical twin sister of a lesbian woman has about a 48 percent chance of being lesbian, while a fraternal twin has about a 16 percent chance.[11] These figures suggest that genes exert a strong though not all-powerful influence on sexual orientation in both men and women. Similar data have been published by Fred Whitam and his colleagues at Arizona State University; in fact the statistics in the Arizona study speak even more strongly for a genetic effect.[12]

An even more intriguing observation was made by a group of scientists at the National Cancer Institute, led by molecular geneticist Dean Hamer.[13] They studied families in which there were at least two gay brothers. When they inquired into the sexual orientation of the more distant relatives of these brothers, they were surprised to find that the majority of the male relatives who were themselves gay were related to the brothers through the female line. For example, gay uncles were much more likely to be the brothers' maternal uncles than their paternal uncles, while gay cousins were more likely to be the sons of the brothers' maternal aunts than any of the three other kinds of cousin. This "sex-linked" pattern of inheritance suggested that a gene influencing sexual orientation in men might be located on the X chromosome, the sex chromosome that men always inherit from their mothers. (Similar inheritance patterns are seen for anomalous color vision and certain bleeding disorders.) In the simplest interpretation, the gene would come in two forms, one form predisposing its owner toward homosexuality, the other predisposing toward heterosexuality.

Hamer and his colleagues went on to search for the actual location of the suspected gene on the X chromosome. Genes are strung out along chromosomes like beads on a string; the X chromosome may carry a thousand or so genes, so finding a particular gene's location is no small task, especially when, as in this case, nothing is known about the gene's chemical identity (i.e., its DNA coding sequence). But in recent years techniques have been developed to tackle just such a challenge. An understanding of these techniques depends on an appreciation of some basic facts about genetics. First, any particular chromosome in an individual—the X chromosome in this case—is actually a composite derived from fragments of the two equivalent chromosomes in one of that individual's parents—the mother's two X chromosomes in this case. Let us suppose that the mother carries the "gay" version of the gene on one of her X chromosomes (we'll call it the "X*g* chromosome") and the "straight" version on the other (the "X*s* chromosome"). Then on average half of her sons will carry the "gay" version and will have some genetic predisposition to be gay. These brothers will have inherited not only the "gay" gene from the mother's "X*g*" chromosome, but also a long stretch of nearby DNA, all part of a fragment of the same chromosome. Thus, if there were some recognizable genetic landmark close to the location of the gene influencing sexual orientation, the brothers would be likely to inherit the same landmark. The brothers who did not inherit the "gay" gene, on the other hand, would have no heightened probability (above chance levels) of inheriting the same landmark.

As part of the Human Genome Project, many such landmarks, known as "linkage markers," have been established. They are short stretches of DNA that are variable, that is, they come in a number of slightly different chemical forms that can be distinguished by enzymatic tests. Hamer's group examined all the markers on the X chromosome in pairs of gay brothers. They found that a cluster of markers near one end of the chromosome, in a region with the technical name of "Xq28," had a greater-than-chance likelihood of being identical in each member of the pair, indicating that the two brothers in each pair had inherited DNA in this region from the same maternal X chromosome, presumably the "X*g*" chromosome. Since the pairs of brothers had been selected on the basis of their both being gay, it is very likely that a gene influencing sexual orientation lies somewhere within the Xq28 region.

The linkage analysis procedure used by Hamer's group is called the "expressing sib-pair method," because it depends on the analysis of only pairs of siblings who show ("express") the trait being studied. Siblings who are not gay are not studied. This is an advantage because individuals who state that they are not gay may be concealing their homosexuality, or they may become homosexual later, whereas individuals who say they are gay are likely to be telling the truth, and less commonly change their sexual orientation later. The technique is very powerful in locating a gene for a trait, such as sexual orientation, which is only partly under genetic control. Hamer's data, however, say little about how strong the influence of this particular gene is. To answer this question, it will be necessary to actually identify the individual gene, something that may be achieved in a few years' time. If and when that is done, it will also be possible to ask how, where (in what part of the body or brain), and at what period of pre- or postnatal life the gene exerts its effect.

It seems that sexual orientation in men and women is influenced by different genes. Having a gay brother has little if any influence on whether a woman is likely to be lesbian, and vice versa. The gene in the Xq28 region may therefore not play a significant role in influencing sexual orientation in women. But somewhere, on some chromosome, genes having this effect must exist. Hamer's group, in particular his colleague Angela Pattatucci, are actively searching for such genes in women.

Brain Organization

In thinking about the biological basis of sexual orientation, one focuses naturally on two organs—the brain and the gonads (the testes in men, ovaries in women). As the seat of our mental life, the brain must carry some kind of representation of our sexual orientation, along with every other aspect of our individual personalities. Furthermore, this representation must be *structural* in the broad sense of the word. One does not have to be continuously thinking about sex in order to maintain a stable sexual orientation; in fact, one's sexual orientation will stay the same even if one's brain's activity is temporarily brought to a complete standstill. Therefore the representation of sexual orientation must consist of stable anatomical or chemical features of the brain, not just a pattern of electrical activity. But the brain has so much structure—10 billion nerve cells and 10 trillion synapses (connections between nerve cells)—that searching for the representation of sexual orientation by looking at random for differences between the brains of homosexual and heterosexual people would have little chance of success.

This is where the gonads come in. The brain, like the rest of the body, is sexually differentiated: its structure, its chemistry, and its function are different in men and women. These differences—most of them quite subtle—come about because of the hormones secreted by the gonads during development. During the prenatal life of male fetuses, high levels of testosterone in the bloodstream, secreted by the testes, influence the brain to develop in the male direction. In female fetuses, blood levels of testosterone are low, permitting the brain to develop in the female direction. The ovaries do not secrete significant amounts of hormones during prenatal life or during childhood, but the ovarian hormones—estrogen and progesterone—do influence the female brain at puberty and thereafter.

One of the most striking sex differences is in a small region at the base of the brain called the hypothalamus. The hypothalamus is an "ancient" structure: it exists in all vertebrates, including those, like fishes, that have no cerebral cortex. It plays an important role in the regulation of functions that are basic to our survival: eating, drinking, control of temperature, metabolism and growth, and sexuality. In 1978 Roger Gorski, working at UCLA, was studying the structure of the rat's hypothalamus, specifically the region at the front of the hypothalamus where it is believed that "male-typical" sex behavior is regulated. He noticed that a particular group of nerve cells in this zone was several times larger in male rats than in females. He and his colleagues went on to show that this size difference was indeed brought about by differences in testosterone levels during development.[14] More recently workers in Gorski's lab, headed by his student Laura Allen, found an equivalent structure in the human brain. As a matter of fact they found two such structures, near to each other. The structures have the technical names of INAH2 and INAH3 ("INAH" stands for "interstitial nucleus of the anterior hypothalamus"; "interstitial" means "lying in the clefts between other structures" and "nucleus," in neuroanatomy, means a recognizable cluster of nerve cells). Both of them are larger, on average, in men than in women, but the size difference is more consistent in INAH3 than in INAH2.[15]

One of us (Simon LeVay), then a neuroscientist at the Salk Institute in San Diego, decided to test whether these hypothalamic structures differ not only with sex but also with sexual orientation. He predicted that INAH3 or INAH2 would be smaller in gay men than in straight men, and larger in lesbian women than in straight women. After all, homosexual individuals are clearly "sex-atypical" in the direction of their sexual attraction; if this part of the brain has anything to do with such attraction, it would not be surprising for its structure also to be sex-atypical in lesbians and gay men.

In men, LeVay confirmed his hypothesis.[16] INAH3 was about three times larger in the heterosexual men than in the gay men in his study. In fact, there was no significant difference between the size of INAH3 in the gay men and the women in the study. As far as differences between lesbian and heterosexual women were concerned, however, the study was a failure: LeVay simply was not able to obtain brain tissue from women whose sexual orientation was known.[17]

The main significance of LeVay's study was in showing that human sexual orientation really can be studied with biological methods; that it is not solely the province of psychologists and anthropologists, as many people had previously believed. In this respect LeVay's findings and Hamer's molecular genetic work are in complete agreement. But any interpretation beyond that is a matter of speculation. In particular, it is not yet certain that the size differences in INAH3 exist prior to the age of sexual feelings and sexual behavior. One must admit the possibility of a quite different explanation for LeVay's findings, namely that the small size of INAH3 in gay men is in some sense a *result* of homosexuality rather than a *cause* of it. Although the latter explanation would conflict with the results of the research in rats, we have to remember that humans are not rats. We live much longer lives, for example, so that there may be more time for experience and behavior to influence our brain structure in adulthood. The findings so far are just exciting hints that biology will eventually unravel the mystery of sexual orientation.

LeVay's finding on the hypothalamus is not the only neuroanatomical finding concerning sexual orientation. In 1992 Allen and Gorski reported on another structure that differs in size between gay and straight men.[18] This is the anterior commissure, a small bundle of nerve fibers that interconnects the left and right hemispheres of the cerebral cortex. The anterior commissure is on average larger in women than men. In gay men, however, Allen and Gorski reported that the anterior commissure is significantly larger than either in straight men or in women. After allowing for differences in overall brain size, the anterior commissure turned out to be about the same size in women as in gay men. Here again, then, we have an example of a sex-differentiated brain structure that is sex-atypical in gay men. A third neuroanatomical difference was reported in 1994 by a group of investigators at McMaster University in Hamilton, Ontario.[19] They measured the corpus callosum, the largest bundle of fibers interconnecting the two hemispheres. The measurements were made in living gay and heterosexual men by means of magnetic resonance imaging (MRI). Previous studies have reported that the corpus callosum, or some parts of it, are sexually dimorphic, although the matter has been a subject of controversy. The McMaster group reported that a part of the corpus callosum (the so-called isthmus) was significantly larger in the gay men than in the heterosexual men. The data, however, were marginal in terms of their statistical significance, and so far have been published only in preliminary form.

The use of techniques that permit brain structure to be imaged in living people, such as MRI, offers the prospect of major advances in our understanding of the brain basis of sexual orientation. For one thing, studying healthy living people eliminates the possibility that the differences observed might be an effect of disease. It also means that women can be studied as easily as men. Finally, it allows one to take a detailed sex history, and thus to distinguish between different kinds of homosexuality and to investigate other important psychological and biological variables. Unfortunately, the hypothalamic nucleus INAH3 is well below the limit of resolution of even the best currently available techniques.

Another potentially valuable avenue for research is the basis of sexual orientation in animals. As discussed in chapter 2, homosexual behavior is seen in a wide variety of species. Studying why particular animals show same-sex or opposite-sex preference might give clues to the same question in humans. A particularly promising example is offered by the "homosexual" male sheep described in chapter 2. Because these sheep differ from heterosexual sheep only in the sex of their preferred partner, and not in their sexual behavior (mounting) or others traits, they offer the chance to study the basis of partner preference. In fact, the group of researchers who originally described these homosexual sheep recently reported a difference in the chemical organization of their brains compared with those of heterosexual animals.[20] They measured the levels of estrogen receptors (the molecules that mediate the effects of estrogen) in a brain region called the amygdala, which (among other functions) processes sensory information responsible for sexual arousal. They found that estrogen receptors in the homosexual rams were present at the same concentration as in ewes, and at significantly lower concentrations than found in heterosexual rams. The reason for this difference, and what role it may play in determining the animals' sexual orientation, is at present unclear. Nevertheless, the finding illustrates that experimental animals can be used to probe the mechanisms of sexual orientation in a manner that, for ethical reasons, would be impossible in humans.

Cognitive Psychology

There are also numerous studies in the realm of cognitive and behavioral psychology that bear on the question of a biological basis for sexual orientation. We mention just a couple of these here.

Men (and male animals generally) tend to perform better than women or female animals in tasks involving extrapersonal space (i.e., space beyond one's immediate reach). In animals, this sex difference has been shown to result from the effects of sex hormones on the developing brain.[21] In humans the sex difference stands out clearly in a task like throwing a ball at a target. Men generally do this more accurately than women; the male superiority is independent of sports experience or arm strength, and it exists already in very young children, before the sports experience of boys and girls begins to differ.[22] Jeff Hall and Doreen Kimura (of the University of Western Ontario) compared the performance of gay and straight men, and lesbian and heterosexual women, on a throwing task.[23] They found that gay men performed significantly worse than the heterosexual men, and about the same as the heterosexual women, while the lesbian women outperformed the heterosexual women and the gay men. (The lesbians' superior performance was only of borderline statistical significance, on account of the small number of lesbians studied). Again, the differences could not be accounted for by differences in sports experience or arm strength or size. In Hall and Kimura's view, their finding supports the notion that the prenatal differentiation of the brain proceeds differently in fetuses who later become homosexual than in fetuses who become heterosexual. They do not argue that the brains are fully sex-reversed in homosexual people: there are some tasks that show differences between the sexes but no differences between homosexual and heterosexual people.

Women tend to outperform men in some verbal tasks, especially in tests of verbal fluency such as giving the names of as many animals as possible in a short period.[24] According to Cheryl McCormick and Sandra Witelson of McMaster University, the performance of gay men in such tasks is better than that of heterosexual men, though not as good as heterosexual women (they did not test lesbians).[25] McCormick and Witelson also interpret their results as supporting the notion that sexual orientation is linked to the sexual differentiation of the brain that occurs during prenatal life.

Further interesting differences have been reported with respect to handedness. Gays and lesbians, like heterosexuals, are more likely to be right-handed than left-handed. However, the fraction of gays and lesbians who are left-handed or mixed-handed is higher than that of heterosexual people, according to McCormick and her colleagues.[26] The increased left-handedness among gays and lesbians seems not to be the effect of socialization, because it is least evident for the one behavior, writing, where instruction may play a role.

Functional asymmetries, of which handedness is an example, may reflect asymmetry in prenatal development. Generally speaking, the right side of the body seems to be favored somewhat during development. As an easily measurable example of this, researchers have studied fingerprints. The pattern of dermal ridges that make up the fingerprints are fully established by about sixteen weeks of fetal life. In most people, there are more ridges on the fingers of the right hand than the left hand, but this rightward bias is more marked in men than in women; that is, if one looks specifically at the minority of people who have a leftward bias, the majority of them are women. The reason for this sex difference is not known with certainty but it is believed to reflect an influence of sex hormones on bodily development during fetal life. Recently, Hall and Kimura made a comparison of fingerprint patterns in gay and heterosexual men.[27] They found that the incidence of leftward bias was significantly higher among gay men than among heterosexual men. Again, they interpret the findings to suggest that sexual orientation is linked to biological processes occurring during fetal life. (Hall and Kimura emphasize that fingerprints cannot be used to tell a person's sexual orientation, because the differences only emerge from statistical analysis of considerable numbers of subjects.) So far, no published study has compared the fingerprint patterns of lesbians and heterosexual women.

Childhood Development

A number of studies have attempted to discover what lesbians and gay men are like as children. The problem, of course, is that at the time they are children, their future sexual orientation is not known. There are two ways to get around this problem. The first is to study the issue *retrospectively,* that is, by asking lesbians and gay men about their recollections of their childhood. The second is to study the issue *prospectively,* that is, by studying the personalities of children and then waiting to see which ones become homosexual and which heterosexual.

Retrospective studies[28] are generally in agreement that adult lesbians and gay men tend to report their childhood personality and behavior as being more gender nonconformist than heterosexual adults do. There is a lot of diversity and variability—some homosexual adults recall totally conventional childhoods, and some straight adults recall very gender-nonconformist childhoods—but by and large gay men tend to recall not liking play-fighting or team sports, preferring reading, perhaps being considered sissies, and so on, while lesbians tend to recollect being active and adventurous, being considered tomboys, and so on. This tendency toward childhood gender nonconformity is true not just for the United States but for a wide variety of cultures, as has been shown for example by Frederick Whitam, a sociologist at Arizona State University.[29] The mothers of gay men also recall their sons as having been more gender nonconformist than do the mothers of straight men (regardless of whether they know that their sons are gay), but the recollections of mothers of lesbian daughters are more equivocal.[30]

Childhood gender nonconformity was also referred to in chapter 2 as a characteristic of a certain kind of homosexuality (gender-variant homosexuality) in native American societies. Interestingly, many of the retrospective studies report that the gender nonconformity of pre-homosexual children tends to become less apparent after puberty.

The retrospective studies are always open to the criticism that gays and lesbians may "reinvent" their childhoods to match their perceived self-identities as adults (Radclyffe Hall, for example, author of the lesbian classic *The Well of Loneliness*, is said to have had her childhood photographs retouched to eliminate her long hair). This is where the prospective studies are so useful. Unfortunately there are only two such studies, both restricted to males. The better known of these is the work of UCLA psychiatrist (and lawyer) Richard Green, summarized in his 1987 book *The Sissy-Boy Syndrome* (see Further Reading).[31] Green studied a considerable number of boys who were markedly gender nonconformist—so much so that their parents brought them to a psychiatrist for possible treatment. Typically they refused to engage in rough-and-tumble play, enjoyed putting on girls' clothes, liked to play with girls, and even expressed a wish to be girls. Eventually, about 80 percent of these boys became gay or bisexual adults. None of Green's "control" group of conventional, gender-conformist boys became gay or bisexual. According to Green, the relationship between gender nonconformity in childhood and homosexuality or bisexuality in adulthood is tighter than any other known relationship between childhood and adult behaviors or personality. (Many transsexuals also have a childhood history of marked gender nonconformity; they did not show up in Green's study simply because transsexuality is considerably rarer than "garden-variety" homosexuality.)

These developmental studies suggest that homosexuality does not, as some people imagine, simply appear out of the blue at adolescence or later; it has strong antecedents in childhood. Indeed, it is not uncommon for gays and lesbians to assert that they were aware of same-sex attraction even in early childhood. Do these studies point to an even earlier time, that is, to prenatal life? Not directly, of course. But there are other studies suggesting that gender-differentiated behavior in childhood is influenced by prenatal events. For example, Sheri Berenbaum and Melissa Hines (psychologists at Chicago Medical School and UCLA) have devised a test of sex-specific play of young children.[32] They place the child in the center of a circle of toys, which might include trucks, baking implements, dolls, and so on, and note the amount of time the child spends with each toy. Children who have been exposed to a sex-atypical hormonal milieu before birth—for example girls with congenital adrenal hyperplasia, who as fetuses are exposed to high levels of masculinizing hormones—tend to make sex-atypical choices in this situation. These differences are already evident by two years of age. (The test used by Berenbaum and Hines is strikingly similar to the trials used in native American cultures to identify berdaches and amazons, in which the child has to choose between, say, a bow and arrow and cooking implements [see chapter 2].) This line of research is also supported by research in monkeys, which has shown that manipulation of a monkey's hormonal environment as a fetus can influence its sex-specific behaviors as a juvenile.[33]

Conclusions

In this chapter we have mentioned evidence for genetic differences between homosexual and heterosexual people, for differences in brain structure and cognitive functioning, and for differences in childhood personality and behavior. Can we fit these pieces of the puzzle together to form any kind of comprehensive explanation of why one person becomes gay and another straight?

The short answer to this question is no. The pieces we have do not fit together directly, but through some missing pieces whose nature we can at present only speculate about. In particular, we do not yet know how the gene on the X chromosome, and the other genes still to be discovered, actually function. What proteins do these genes code for? When do they operate during development, and where do they operate? It would be tempting to speculate that somehow they influence the development of brain regions like the hypothalamus, perhaps by affecting the way the hypothalamus responds to sex hormones during its early growth. But we don't understand development well enough to make this prediction with any confidence. Usually, when people try to guess how genes work before they are actually identified, the guesses turn out to be way off target: we simply don't have a broad enough understanding of developmental biology at this point to be able to make such predictions with any confidence. That's why the further exploration of the molecular genetic avenue, opened up by Hamer and his colleagues, is likely to be so informative.

It is only fair to conclude a chapter like this by emphasizing that there are those who reject biological models of sexual orientation altogether, who minimize their significance, or who consider this whole line of study demeaning or threatening to gays and lesbians. The idea that sexual orientation develops out of a web of interpersonal interactions in childhood, adolescence, or later life still has enthusiastic adherents, even among some lesbians and gay men.[34] The main problem with psychodynamic, social constructionist, and other nonbiological ideas is not that they are inherently implausible, but that so few testable hypotheses have come out of them. Human biology, on the other hand, is an exploding field in which new techniques become available every year. Yesterday's theories are today's experiments and tomorrow's body of knowledge (or tomorrow's laughingstock). For that reason alone the excitement is with the biology. It may not be until the current revolution in biology has run its course that we will be able to see clearly what is left over: whether mere crumbs from the table, or the main feast.

Further Reading

Bell, A. P., M. S. Weinberg, and S. K. Hammersmith. *Sexual Preference: Its Development in Men and Women.* Bloomington: Indiana University Press, 1981.

Freud, Sigmund. *Three Essays on the Theory of Sexuality.* Translated by James Strachey. New York: Basic Books, 1975.

Green, Richard. *The Sissy-Boy Syndrome and the Development of Homosexuality.* New Haven: Yale University Press, 1987.

Hamer, Dean, and Peter Copeland. *The Science of Desire: The Search for the Gay Gene and the Biology of Behavior.* New York: Simon and Schuster, 1994.

Isay, Richard A. *Being Homosexual.* New York: Farrar, Straus, and Giroux, 1989.

Kimura, Doreen. "Sex Differences in the Brain." *Scientific American* (September 1992), pp. 119-125.

LeVay, Simon. *The Sexual Brain.* Cambridge, MA: MIT Press, 1993.

II Communities

In the following seven chapters, we attempt to portray in broad strokes the gay and lesbian community as it exists in the United States today. Community, or communities? Actually, it is both. One can look at the entire homosexual population of the country and find certain things that tend to distinguish gays and lesbians from the heterosexual majority and that form the underpinnings of a community that embraces all homosexual people. That is the main focus of chapter 5. But when one looks more closely, one finds important groupings within the overall community. These groupings may be based on the variety of places where gays and lesbians live—in the countryside, in small towns, in cities, and so on. Such locality-based groups are explored in chapters 6, 7, and 8. Or, as discussed in chapter 9, groupings may consist of minorities within a minority—these groupings include minorities defined by ethnicity, age, or other characteristics. In chapter 10, we take a look at four groups defined by sexual mode—bisexuals, leatherfolk, transsexuals, and boy-loving men. Finally (chapter 11), we pick more or less at random a few examples of groups (professional, hobby, and sports) based on common interests.

5

Numbers

In this chapter we consider the entire community of lesbians and gay men in this country, with a view to understanding whether there are characteristics that really do bind all homosexual people in our society and distinguish them from heterosexual people. In making statements about the entire community, we run the risk of echoing fictitious stereotypes. We therefore restrict ourselves for the most part to "hard" data—that is, data obtained from surveys that use statistically valid sampling techniques. Although this approach may be rather dry, it at least has some claim to dependability. In the following chapters, which focus on subgroups within the overall community, we attempt to add human faces to our group portrait.

Incidence

What fraction of the U.S. population is gay or lesbian? The figure one hears most commonly in the gay community is 10 percent. Several gay and lesbian organizations, books and periodicals use this figure in their names,[1] an indication that it is seen as important to gay and lesbian self-esteem.

The 10 percent figure is derived from the Kinsey studies of forty to fifty years ago (see chapter 3). What Kinsey actually reported was that 10 percent of men were more or less exclusively homosexual for at least three years of their adult lives. In Kinsey's data, only about 4 percent of men and about 2 percent of women were exclusively homosexual throughout their adult lives. Furthermore, Kinsey's sampling and interviewing procedures would not be considered scientifically valid today.

More recent studies have consistently produced figures lower than 10 percent. Randomized surveys conducted by the National Opinion Research Center (NORC) in 1988 and 1991 found that only about 2 percent of men and women had engaged in any same-sex sexual activity during the year prior to interview.[2] A large-scale NORC survey performed in 1992 and published in 1994 reported that 2.8 percent of the men and 1.4 percent of the women identified as homosexual or bisexual, but 6 percent of the men and 5.5 percent of the women acknowledged some degree of same-sex attraction.[3] The 1991 National Survey of Men, which studied a statistically representative sample of men aged twenty to thirty-nine, reported that only 2 percent of the men had any same-sex activity during the previous ten years.[4] An NIH-funded study of 717 men found that 2 percent of them identified as exclusively or nearly exclusively homosexual.[5] A national exit poll of 14,000 voters at the 1992 presidential election by the *Los Angeles Times* revealed that 4 percent of the male voters identified as gay and 2 percent of the female voters identified as lesbian.[6] The recent study that yielded the highest proportion of gays and lesbians was a 1993 market research study by Yankelovich Partners Inc., in which 5.7 percent of the respondents identified as "gay/homosexual/lesbian," with little difference between the sexes.[7] Part of the reason for the high incidence of homosexuality reported in this survey may be the fact that there was no "bisexual" option among the interview items. All in all, it would seem that gay men constitute somewhere between 2 percent and 5 percent of the male population, while the numbers of lesbians are probably lower, perhaps around 2 percent.

These data are roughly similar to findings in other countries. In Britain, a national probability sample of nearly 20,000 men and women revealed that 1 percent of the men and 0.5 percent of the women were primarily or only attracted to others of the same sex, while another 4 percent were bisexual to some degree.[8] A French national survey reported that 1.1 percent of the men and 0.3 percent of the women surveyed had had same-sex intercourse during the previous year.[9] In a Dutch study, 3.6 percent of the men and 0.3 percent of the women reported having had only same-sex intercourse during the previous year.[10] In the Philippines (both rural and urban areas) studies indicate that about 1 percent of the men and a smaller percentage of the women are homosexual.[11]

There is no reason to suspect that the incidence of homosexuality has changed dramatically over the years. Nearly one hundred years ago the sexologist Magnus Hirschfeld sent questionnaires to 8,000 male students and metalworkers in Germany. Among the students who replied, 1.5 percent identified as homosexual and 4.5 percent as bisexual; among the metalworkers, the numbers were 1.2 percent and 3.2 percent.[12] Reliable data for more distant periods are lacking.[13]

It does seem that the reported incidence of bisexuality has decreased over the last few decades. In early surveys, such as Hirschfeld's and Kinsey's, more people were bisexual in feelings or behavior than were exclusively homosexual. Recent studies have produced the opposite result, with more people at the homosexual extreme than sitting in the middle of the scale. The apparent decrease in bisexuality has been more marked for men than for women, and is more marked when sexual feelings rather than sexual behavior are measured.[14] We emphasize that we are not attempting to deny the existence of bisexuality in contemporary culture. The issue is discussed further in chapter 10.

Residence

Gays and lesbians are everywhere, but their distribution across the country does not precisely replicate that of heterosexual people. For a start, they are more likely to be found in large cities. According to the Yankelovich survey, 27 percent of lesbians and gay men, but only 18 percent of heterosexuals, live in metropolitan areas with populations over 3 million, and 61 percent (versus 45 percent) live in cities with populations over 1 million. As a consequence, the fraction of the population of very large cities that is gay or lesbian is much larger than in nonmetropolitan or rural areas. According to the 1992 NORC study, this urban bias is considerably more marked for gay men than for lesbians. That study reported that men identifying as gay or bisexual form 9 percent of the population of the central districts of the country's twelve largest cities, 4 percent of the population of smaller cities, 3.5 percent of the population of suburbs and only 1 percent of the rural and small-town population. The corresponding figures for women were 2.7 percent, 1.9 percent, 1.6 percent and an unmeasurable percentage. (But rural lesbians do exist—see chapters 6 and 8.)

Gays and lesbians are less likely than heterosexuals to live in the South: 25 percent of all gay Americans, versus 35 percent of heterosexuals, live there.[15] While they are of course very numerous in the big coastal cities, only one large sector of the country, the North Central United States, can boast a significant overrepresentation of gay people (32 percent of gay people vs. 23 percent of heterosexuals live there). In addition to the actual differences between urban and rural areas, there are differences of visibility: according to a readership survey by *The Advocate,* a leading gay and lesbian newsmagazine, gay men at least are significantly more likely to be closeted in rural areas and small towns than in big cities.[16]

The larger numbers of gays and lesbians in cities could have two explanations: either people who are brought up in cities are more likely to become gay, or gay people move to cities. There is little evidence to support the first possibility, but plenty to support the second. Migration of young gays and lesbians to big cities began on a large scale immediately after World War II, and has continued unabated since. Indeed, such migration is almost a standard component of the gay person's coming-out process, documented in hundreds of biographies. It is often as much a psychological as a physical journey, distancing the gay person from his or her family of origin and bringing him or her into greater intimacy with other gay people.

The really intense concentrations of gay people within metropolitan areas, such as the Castro district in San Francisco and Greenwich Village in New York, tend to be dominated by gay men. Lesbians, like gay men, gravitate to metropolitan areas, but, as indicated above, more lesbians than gay men seem to live outside of the central districts. In order to substantiate this difference between the sexes, we analyzed data on the residences of subscribers to *The Advocate*, who are almost entirely gay, lesbian, or bisexual. *The Advocate* provided us with printouts of the number of male and female subscribers in every zip code in two states, New York and Illinois.[17] In New York state, we found that one-half of all the male subscribers lived in just thirty-one zip codes. To encompass half of the female subscribers, by contrast, it was necessary to go to eighty-two zip codes. In Illinois, the equivalent numbers were twenty-one zip codes (male) and thirty-four zip codes (female). Clearly, the women are much more dispersed than the men. Of course, what is true of *Advocate* subscribers, who tend to be relatively affluent and well educated, is not necessarily true of the entire gay and lesbian population.

Age also may influence place of residence: although objective data are lacking, it is probable that younger gays and lesbians are more likely to live in the gay-identified districts than older ones. This may be because older gays and lesbians are more closeted, or because they have passed through a period of strong gay identification and now desire to be more generally integrated into society, or to live quietly with their partners.

Ethnicity, Religion, Education, and Politics

Gays and lesbians are found among all racial or ethnic groups in this country. It is not certain, however, that they are equally common in all groups. For example, there is some evidence suggesting that male homosexuality may be disproportionately common among Latinos. In the National Survey of Men, Latinos reported engaging in exclusively homosexual activity at a rate nearly three times higher than non-Latinos. In the Yankelovich survey Latinos (men and women combined) were about 60 percent more likely to identify as homosexual than non-Latinos, although the difference was not significant because of the small sample size. It seems unlikely that these differences result simply from a greater willingness on the part of Latinos to admit to being gay, since if anything homosexuality is more stigmatized among Latinos than among non-Latinos. Still, it will require studies that focus specifically on minorities before these and other potential ethnic differences can be verified.

Considering that some branches of organized religion have been strongly opposed to homosexuality over the years, it is surprising to find that gays and lesbians belong to the various major faiths and denominations in about the same proportions as other Americans. In the Yankelovich survey, only the Baptists had less than their share of gay members. This may relate to the low proportion of gays and lesbians living in the South. It seems that when gays and lesbians migrate away from the South, they also tend to abandon the Baptist church. The same is probably true, however, for many nongay people who leave the South; it does not necessarily mean that gays and lesbians leave the Baptist church specifically because of its antigay stance. The Roman Catholic church, which is hardly better disposed toward homosexuality than are the southern Baptists, has its fair share of gays and lesbians: about a quarter of all gays and lesbians in the United States are Catholic, as against 22 percent of heterosexuals. Furthermore, gays and lesbians are no more likely to be nonreligious than heterosexuals. Of course, national surveys sample too coarsely to study membership of small gay-identified or gay-friendly churches and synagogues. Still, it would seem that religious attitudes toward homosexuality do not greatly influence gays' and lesbians' choice of religious denomination. As with other sexual matters, many people seem able to establish an area of privacy around their sexual orientation that is impervious to official religious proscriptions (see also chapter 19).

Several surveys have reported that gays and lesbians tend to be better educated than straight people. In the Yankelovich survey 49 percent of gays and lesbians had some college education, against 37 percent of heterosexuals. Fourteen percent of gays and lesbians had postgraduate education, versus only 7 percent of heterosexuals. The National Survey of Men reported a similar finding. One has to be cautious in interpreting this result, because, according to the *Advocate* survey, college-educated gay men are far more likely to be out of the closet than others, and the same is very likely true for lesbians. But if this were the explanation for the apparent higher educational level of gays and lesbians, there would have to be a very large group of non–college-educated gay people among the interviewees who concealed their homosexuality. This seems unlikely, for the Yankelovich survey at least, since that survey found such a high overall incidence of admitted homosexuality among its interviewees.

If the education difference is real, we face at least two alternatives in attempting to explain it. According to some psychologists, lesbian and gay teenagers are often driven into an "overachiever" mode by the stresses of belonging to a stigmatized group. The hypothesis is plausible enough, although one could equally well explain *under*achievement by this kind of environmental argument. Another possibility is that gays and lesbians have innate mental characteristics that cause them to do better in school, on average, than heterosexuals. In partial support of this hypothesis are a number of studies (none of them fully convincing) reporting that homosexuality is associated with higher than average I.Q.[18] In addition, there are studies reporting that gay men outperform straight men in a variety of verbal tasks, and this difference has been interpreted to result from differences in prenatal brain development.[19] Thus it is conceivable that gays and lesbians are simply better endowed with mental abilities important for success in the educational system. Obviously, one cannot choose between these hypotheses on the basis of the evidence presently available; we just wish to point out that, while almost anything about gay people *can* be explained as a consequence of homophobia and oppression, other explanations are also possible.

In recent years the Democratic Party has espoused far more gay-friendly policies than the Republican Party, and it is usually assumed that gays and lesbians tend to be Democrats. Surveys that report selectively on the more affluent, better-educated, and politically engaged sector of the gay and lesbian community do indeed support this assumption. Among those responding to the 1994 *Advocate* survey, for example, 66 percent were Democrats and only 10 percent were Republicans. The scientifically sampled Yankelovich survey, in contrast, found that the party affiliation of lesbians and gay men was no different from that of heterosexuals (45 percent Democrat, 27 percent Republican, and 21 percent Independent). Among gays and lesbians questioned in exit polls at the 1992 election, however, two-thirds said they were Democrats and less than one-fifth said they were Republicans.[20] If both the exit polls and the Yankelovich survey are correct, gay and lesbian Republicans must have stayed at home in droves in 1992. It seems that, in politics as in religion, *affiliation* is not markedly influenced by sexual orientation, but *behavior* may be.

Occupation and Income

Statistical data on occupation and income are available from two sources. One is the Yankelovich survey, and the other is an analysis of the National Opinion Research Center's data by Lee Badgett of the University of Maryland.[21] The two studies are in agreement on the major points. About the same fraction of gays and lesbians are employed (62 percent in the Yankelovich survey) as of heterosexuals. Gays and lesbians are, however, significantly more likely to be self-employed than heterosexuals (18 percent versus 11 percent). Badgett's study found gay men to be overrepresented in white-collar (particularly technical and professional) employment, and underrepresented in blue-collar employment, while for lesbians it is the other way around: they are overrepresented in blue-collar occupations, compared with straight women.

There are no reliable figures on the actual jobs held by gays and lesbians. There are plenty of stereotypes, of course: of gay men as florists, nurses, interior designers, and dancers, and of lesbians as truck drivers, soldiers, and organizational leaders. It is quite possible that the stereotypes are true in a limited sense: these occupations may well attract more than their share of gay men or lesbians (The overrepresentation of gay men in the arts is touched on again in chapter 18; the possible overrepresentation of lesbians in the military is referred to in chapters 3 and 15). But the stereotypical occupations probably account for only a very small fraction of the gays and lesbians in the country. There are thriving gay and lesbian organizations in all the professions, in many industries and businesses and other walks of life. There certainly are some occupations where gays and lesbians seem very underrepresented, such as the uniformed services, politics (see data in chapter 16), professional sports, and entertainment, but these are exactly the occupations where gays and lesbians are most likely to be closeted. It will take a much larger survey than has so far been undertaken to determine whether gay people really do gravitate to certain walks of life.

Some of the most interesting data to emerge from the surveys concerns income. Contrary to the results of earlier, nonrandomized surveys, which had projected an image of gay men as unusually affluent, the Yankelovich survey found that gay men had personal and household incomes slightly *below* those of heterosexual men. The difference in means was not significant, but there were significantly more gay men than heterosexual men with incomes under $25,000, and significantly fewer gay men with incomes between $25,000 and $50,000. Badgett's study, which matched gays and nongays for educational level and other factors, found an even bigger, and significant, difference: gay men earned 10–26 percent less than straight men. Lesbians, in the Yankelovich survey, had average personal and household incomes that were the same as those of heterosexual women. In Badgett's study, their incomes were slightly but not significantly lower than those of matched straight women. As one might have predicted, the personal incomes of gay men were much higher than those of lesbians (means of $21,500 and $13,300 according to the Yankelovich study), but the household incomes of gays and lesbians were surprisingly similar ($37,400 and $34,800), and after correction for differences in household size they were almost identical (about $12,500 per household member). Thus if one makes the assumption that household members form an economic unit, the data speak against the commonly held belief that gay men have more disposable income than lesbians.[22]

Two demographic features of gays and lesbians, their higher educational level and their tendency to live in large cities, are generally associated with higher earnings. Yet gays and lesbians earn the same as or less than heterosexuals. There must therefore be countervailing factors that keep down their incomes. These factors may well include discrimination against them by employers, as argued by Badgett. It is also possible (to put a more positive spin on the matter) that in choosing their careers gays and lesbians tend to focus on the intangible rewards of work, such as creativity and service, to the detriment of their paychecks.

Marital Status and Children

Reliable statistical data on the living arrangements of lesbians and gay men are scanty. The Yankelovich survey asked about marital status, but without clearly indicating whether the word "married" could be applied to people in same-sex partnerships. Significantly fewer lesbians and gay men described themselves as "currently married" (42 percent) than did heterosexuals (54 percent), and significantly more said that they had never been married (44 percent vs. 26 percent). Still, if we make the assumption that "married" was interpreted as referring only to legalized, opposite-sex unions, then 42 percent is a remarkably high fraction of the gay and lesbian population. It would be interesting to know what fraction of these people are old-fashioned closeted homosexuals, and what fraction are married for more positive reasons.

Lesbians are almost as likely to be mothers[23] as are heterosexual women (67 percent vs. 72 percent in the Yankelovich survey; the difference is not significant), but whether there are differences in the average number of biological children is not known. These data open to question the usual assumption that female homosexuality in our society is associated with lowered reproduction. They also are relevant to lesbian health issues, such as the question of a heightened incidence of breast cancer among lesbians, for one of the factors that is believed to predispose lesbians to breast cancer is nonmaternity (see chapter 12). Lesbians and straight women are also about equally likely to have children under 18 living with them (about one-third of them do).

Gay men, on the other hand, are markedly less likely to be fathers than straight men: only 27 percent of gay men are fathers, versus 60 percent of straight men. This is one of the most marked differences between gay and straight men (and between gay men and lesbians) that has been described, outside of the realm of sexual practices. It could be that, in our present culture at least, opposite-sex attraction is important for male reproduction, but not for female reproduction. But there are other possibilities: the women in the Yankelovich survey may have included more bisexuals, or more individuals who came to identify as homosexual after an earlier period of heterosexuality, during which they became parents. As a probable consequence of this difference in parenting, gay men are much less likely to have children in their households than lesbians (15 percent vs. 32 percent).

Attitudes

The most interesting results from the Yankelovich survey relate to the attitudes of lesbians and gay men on a variety of topics. These results are not broken down between lesbians and gay men, and are rather broad, even "fuzzy," in nature. But the fact that significant differences between the homosexual and heterosexual population were recorded in several topics suggests that gay people are not as blended into the larger society as some of the other demographic data might indicate.

One key area of difference found in the survey was that gays and lesbians are significantly more focused on themselves than are heterosexuals. They are more concerned with physical appearance, physical fitness, and keeping up with fashion, and they much more commonly (43 percent versus 23 percent) state a need for spiritual identification and self-understanding.

Another difference is a greater perceived need to associate with similar people. This does not just mean other gays and lesbians, but also with people of similar identity in terms of ethnicity, shared values, and so on. In spite of this need to "belong," gays and lesbians express more sympathy with disadvantaged or stigmatized groups other than their own, compared with heterosexuals. It is particularly interesting that gays and lesbians, who often experience conflicts with their parents over their sexuality, nevertheless are significantly more likely than heterosexuals to agree with the statement that "age and experience are a benefit to society." This is not to say, of course, that gays and lesbians are totally free from "ageism" (see chapter 9).

A third difference has to do with curiosity, creativity, and fantasy. Gays and lesbians place greater emphasis on individual creativity, are more into fantasy, escape, and novelty, and are more likely to seek out new experiences, especially in the area of entertainment, shopping, food, vacations, and so forth. Compared with heterosexuals, they are restless consumers of life.

Somewhat in contradiction to the difference just mentioned is another trend among gays and lesbians—a greater perceived need for control, and a need to eliminate inessentials. Gays and lesbians are more likely to feel under stress, and to believe that the stress in their lives is increasing. This increase in stress is felt equally in money matters, employment, in their relationships with their parents, and in their personal lives. They are more likely than heterosexuals to be seeking ways to reduce stress, for example by taking leisure vacations, by taking tranquilizers and sleeping pills, by taking measures to secure their homes and possessions, or by avoiding activities perceived as risky.

Finally, and no doubt linked with the previous item, is a greater expressed cynicism and mistrust among lesbians and gay men. They are more likely to believe that large corporations and the government are their enemy, and that there are people actively seeking to harm them.

Of the differences between the attitudes of heterosexual and gay people that we have just mentioned, none are enormous in magnitude, even though they are all statistically significant. Still, it is remarkable that they stand out at all in a randomized, national sample. Some of the differences, such as the greater mistrust and sense of stress, are easy to link causally with gay people's stigmatized position in society. Other differences, such as those related to creativity, inner-directedness, and so on, might be related to stigmatization, or might have other explanations. At any event, the finding of attitudinal trends of this kind in the entire gay and lesbian population should be a spur to more refined analysis of attitudes, and their causes, in subgroups of the population: gay male versus lesbian, closeted versus open, and among different ethnic groups.

6
Localities

We now turn from global statements about American gays and lesbians to a discussion of smaller communities within the overall population. We start by discussing communities that are physical localities—places in the United States where gays and/or lesbians are especially numerous, visible, or close-knit.

Rural Communities

There are probably not many locations in this country where lesbians are numerically preponderant, or where they set the predominant tone of the place. Of the locations where they do so, most are small rural communities where lesbians have congregated over a period of years to establish a safe and mutually supportive environment. One of these communities is the subject of a separate sketch in chapter 8. There are places like this scattered across the country, places where lesbians live out lives of their own creation, insulated to a considerable degree from the heterosexual world and even from national lesbian or gay politics and culture.

Often, small communities of lesbians or gay men are embedded in a rural culture where attitudes toward homosexuality are many decades behind the times. An example of the conflicts that can arise is provided by the case of Wanda and Brenda Henson, two lesbians who purchased a former pig farm in Ovett, Mississippi (population 200) in July 1993. Their aim was to turn it into Camp Sister Spirit, a feminist retreat and education center. Before this community could even come into existence a conflict erupted with local residents, and it escalated to the point that the Hensons received death threats and even warning shots across their property lines. The matter became a focus of national media attention and political action (see chapter 16).

Given the tensions that can arise, it is no wonder that rural gays and lesbians tend to keep a low profile. One tiny hamlet in Massachusetts, for example, has regularly sent half its population to Boston or Washington for gay pride events, but it is indistinguishable, to a casual visitor, from scores of equally picturesque New England villages that are populated by heterosexuals. Searching for gay America by driving around the countryside in a car is a futile undertaking, because it is an America without maps, signposts, or street names. But with the right contacts, as Neil Miller, Darrell Yates Rist, and others have documented (see Further Reading), rural and small-town America reveals just as rich a tapestry of gay and lesbian life as do the big cities.

Northampton

One fair-sized community where lesbians are both numerous and influential is Northampton, a town of about 35,000 in western Massachusetts, about fifteen miles north of Springfield on the Connecticut River. Northampton is the home of a women's college, Smith, that was founded in 1872. Another women's college, Mt. Holyoke (founded in 1837), lies just across the river in South Hadley. The role of women's colleges in fostering intimate and durable relationships between women in the nineteenth century—the so-called Boston marriages[1]—has been mentioned in chapter 3. One of America's most well-known lesbian writers, the poet Emily Dickinson, lived a short distance away in Amherst; her house is now a museum. Thus there are ample historical associations that establish the locality as important to lesbians as well as to feminists.

Smith College has maintained its dedication to women's education. Mary Maples Dunn, the college's president until 1994, supported the concept that single-sex education offers particular advantages tor women. Furthermore, the contributions of lesbians to women's education and culture are publicly acknowledged, even if the college has to walk a narrow path between embracing its lesbian members and avoiding being labeled a "lesbian school."[2] A few courses at Smith focus explicitly on lesbians; many more cover lesbian issues in the context of general women's studies. There are openly lesbian faculty and there is a lesbian and bisexual students' group. Well-known lesbian thinkers, writers, and artists from around the world visit to give public lectures or lead seminars. Still, it is said that lesbians who have not yet obtained tenure tend to be less open about their sexuality than they might otherwise be.

The lesbian presence in Northampton extends well beyond the college gates. There are many lesbians living in Northampton who are or were associated with Mt. Holyoke or the University of Massachusetts at Amherst. Quite aside from the academic community, there are numerous thriving social and cultural institutions in the town that are run by or for lesbians, or which give unusual attention to lesbians' concerns. The minister for the Unitarian Society, for example, is a heterosexual woman, Victoria Safford, but she has many lesbians in her congregation and she performs numerous lesbian commitment ceremonies as well as baby dedications for lesbians. Her sermons tend to be less about God and more about the moral and social questions that progressive women are likely to be concerned with.

Another Northampton institution is the Sleeveless Theater, a women's theater that concentrates on political comedy. Of the four women who run the theater, two (Kate Nugent and K. D. Halpin) are heterosexual. The other two, Lisa Channer and Maureen Futtner, are a lesbian couple, both twenty-nine, who have been together since 1985. They were married by Victoria Safford in September 1994. Channer told us that the theater was founded in 1989 in response to the U.S. Supreme Court decision in that year that permitted states to limit access to abortion. Their first play, "Womb for Rent," was a "pro-choice comedy." Their current production is a one-woman play titled "The Virgin Trip," in which Futtner explores her Catholic upbringing and identity. They took the production to Ireland after its run at their resident stage, the Northampton Center for the Arts. Channer was very positive about Northampton. "I don't know many other places where we could exist," she said. "The gay and straight communities are one: there's no polarization, no ghetto."

Other lesbian-run businesses in Northampton include two bookstores, Lunaria and Pride's, several restaurants, including the North Star and Bela's vegetarian restaurant, and various coffeehouses.

Northampton has two openly homosexual people on its town council, a gay man and a lesbian, Clair Higgins. Smith College, but not the town of Northampton, has domestic partnership arrangements that permit lesbian partners of Smith faculty to be covered by the college's health insurance policy. The Kaiser health-maintenance organization has added a special program for lesbians having babies, and the Family Planning Council of Western Massachusetts has initiated a lesbian health survey that focuses on breast cancer; it offers free or low-price mammograms and counseling. There are also programs specifically for gay and lesbian teenagers and old people.

Numerous social and athletic groups—a softball league, hiking, camping, and bicycling clubs, potlucks, writers' groups, and so on—cater to lesbians specifically or have many openly lesbian members. There is also an annual lesbian festival in July (1994 was its fifth year), which draws musicians, entertainers, and craftspeople from around the country.

Although lesbians in Northampton tend to be politically liberal or leftist lesbian-feminists, they are certainly not all of a kind. For example, one hears the words "gay woman," "lesbian," and "dyke" used to identify subspecies of women-loving women in the town. The "gay women" are probably the least political; they may be businesswomen, for example. The "lesbians" are the more feminist-identified, while the "dykes" are the more radical lesbian-identified women, including the members of the local chapters of Queer Nation and Lesbian Avengers (see chapter 16).

There are also generational differences such as one sees elsewhere: the older women tend to be relatively gender-neutral in appearance, while some of the younger ones make a point of adopting "butch" (masculine) or "femme" (feminine) fashions and mannerisms. While the butch-femme distinction could be seen as a return to the gender roles taken by lesbians in the prefeminist years, there is a playful, fashion-conscious aspect to the current butch-femme scene, at least in Northampton, that may not have been present earlier. It is also said that butch-femme distinctions, as currently practiced, are less predictive of the sexual roles women play or even of the kind of relationships they enter into: two butch women, for example, may form a couple, whereas earlier a butch lesbian would be unlikely to have declared an attraction to another butch.

All in all, Northampton seems to be an extraordinarily congenial place for lesbians, especially for those lesbians who identify strongly with the entire community of women. Of course, for all its culture, Northampton is still a small, largely white New England town. If it escapes some of the problems of urban America (such as gay-bashing), it may also miss some of the diversity. In addition, the feminism that colors Northampton life, and the intellectual ferment generated by the colleges, may to some extent cause the *sexual* aspects of lesbian life to be downplayed. The lesbians of Northampton are no sexless bluestockings, but neither are they pushing the envelope of lesbian eroticism. Rather than being the lesbian answer to West Hollywood or Greenwich Village, Northampton is a thriving social experiment on its own terms: a place where the benefits of single-sex education have been successfully extended to single-sex life.

Urban Centers

The most visible foci of gay life in the United States are of course the urban districts where gays and lesbians live or congregate—the "gay ghettos." One of these, West Hollywood, is portrayed in some detail in chapter 7. It is worth stressing here, however, that the various gay ghettos are not all alike. In some places, like West Hollywood and the Castro district of San Francisco, the gay area is residential as well as a center of social life. In other cities, the gay district is mostly defined by the location of gay bars and other nightspots, and gay people themselves may actually reside at dispersed locations. In yet another format, the gay and straight bars and restaurants are largely intermixed to form a single social focus to the city; this is the case in New Orleans's French Quarter, for example.

Historically, the gay ghettos were centered around the bar scene, and partly for that reason were dominated by gay men. Bars are still very important, but over the last ten or twenty years many other institutions have taken root in the ghettos: coffeehouses and restaurants, gay-owned businesses of all descriptions, churches and temples, service organizations, political groups, and even local governments (West Hollywood, for example, became self-governing in 1984). Some of the ghettos are mini-cities where one can work, play, pray, and sleep around without ever leaving the neighborhood. For this reason more lesbians live or work in the gay ghettos than in the past, even if they still are greatly outnumbered by men.[3] They are specially visible in the service and other nonprofit organizations, but lesbian-owned businesses are becoming increasingly evident, and lesbians form a noticeably larger fraction of people on the street, even during the bar hours, than they did a few years ago.

One hallmark of gay male life that seems to be rubbing off on urban lesbians is sexual adventurousness. Indeed, while many gay men have been toning down their wilder excesses in the face of the AIDS epidemic, some lesbians—the "sexual radicals"—have been gearing up to outdo them. In the mid-1980s lesbian sex magazines, such as *On Our Backs* and *Bad Attitude*, appeared. Pornographic videos are now being made by and for lesbians.[4] Lesbian sex clubs, where anonymous and group sex is permitted, have opened in a few cities, or else gay male sex clubs have initiated women's nights. Numerous books and articles explore the far reaches of lesbian sexuality,[5] and the more conventional lesbian sex acts of yesteryear are sometimes dismissed with one word: "vanilla." Lesbian sadomasochistic sex, once decried as a pathological carryover from heterosexual life, now has its advocates and practitioners,[6] and lesbian-owned companies market specialized sex toys. What fraction of lesbians participate in the new sex scene is hard to say—perhaps not many. But the attention paid to it is useful in emphasizing something about lesbianism that has often been ignored by lesbian feminists: the fact that it has to do with sex.

Resorts

Another kind of gay locality is the gay resort—places, often by the sea, where gays and lesbians like to vacation. Some of these have relatively few year-round residents—Provincetown, Massachusetts, and Fire Island, New York, are examples. But even Provincetown has enough of a permanent gay and lesbian population to have spurred a domestic-partnership ordinance, something that Northampton has yet to achieve. Other resorts are cities with substantial gay and lesbian populations, which are nevertheless greatly added to by seasonal visitors: examples are Laguna Beach and Palm Springs, California, and Pensacola and Key West, Florida. As with the gay ghettos, the lesbian presence at the resorts is far more noticeable now than a few years ago.

Fire Island has for many years been the preferred weekend getaway spot for gay men and smaller numbers of lesbians escaping the Manhattan summer. The history of one of the small towns on the island has been told by Esther Newton in her book *Cherry Grove, Fire Island* (see Further Reading). In the 1950s, Cherry Grove was a primitive oasis of gay and lesbian freedom in an otherwise oppressive culture. Gradually, with improved facilities and transportation, the upscale whites who had been the mainstay of Fire Island life were supplemented by a more mixed ethnic and socioeconomic population, nearly all of whom, however, were men. The increasing gay presence led to increased police surveillance and arrests, but this ended in 1968, thanks in large part to a gay rights campaign orchestrated by the New York Mattachine Society. In spite of this successful action, Fire Island largely turned its back on the post-Stonewall gay liberation movement, and instead turned itself into an escapist fantasyland. The gay life there in the 1970s—the enormous parties, the cruising, the drugs, and the never-ending sex—was caustically portrayed in novels like Larry Kramer's *Faggots* and Andrew Holleran's *Dancer from the Dance* (see chapter 18). In the 1980s, Fire Island took a double hit, first from AIDS, then from the recession, and property values and rental prices dropped precipitously. But in the 1990s it has made a comeback, fueled in part by large numbers of lesbians, who have attempted to reclaim parts of the Meat Rack (the traditional cruising area adjacent to Cherry Grove's boardwalk) for such purposes as picnicking and dog walking.

There are also offshore gay and lesbian resorts—cruise ships and land-based vacations in the Caribbean, Mexico, and elsewhere. Kevin Moissier, chairman of RSVP Gay Vacations, has been a pioneer in this field. Moissier organized his first gay cruise in 1986, chartering a ship from another cruise line. In 1991 RSVP purchased its own ship, the *SeaSpirit*, which now cruises the Mediterranean, the Atlantic, and the Pacific. Another company, Atlantis, rents entire Club Med villages for a week at a time, creating instant gay enclaves on remote tropical coasts. Although some women participate in these trips, the real lesbian action is with Olivia Cruises, an offshoot of Olivia Records. It rents cruise ships and Club Med villages in the Caribbean and Mexico. An expedition to reclaim the island of Lesbos would seem the logical next step, and in fact another company, Greek Island Connection, is planning to organize a women's trip to that destination in 1995.

It might seem that all-gay cruises and all-gay travel destinations represent the ultimate in the self-isolation of gays and lesbians: taking the ghetto along on vacation seems to nullify the very purpose of travel. No doubt security-consciousness and fear of the unknown, noted as common gay personality traits in chapter 5, contribute to the popularity of these vacations. It is also appears, however, that a large fraction of the gays and lesbians who take these trips are suburban or small-town residents who are not strongly identified with the gay and lesbian community. According to Olivia Cruises President Judy Dlugacz, many of their customers are not fully out of the closet.[7] Their vacation may represent a trip *to* the ghetto, rather than away from it.

Further Reading

Miller, Neil. *In Search of Gay America: Women and Men in a Time of Change.* Boston: Atlantic Monthly Press, 1989.

Newton, Esther. *Cherry Grove, Fire Island: Sixty Years in America's First Gay and Lesbian Town.* Boston: Beacon Press, 1993.

Rist, Darell Yates. *Heartlands: A Gay Man's Odyssey across America.* New York: Dutton, 1992.

7
A Gay Ghetto

West Hollywood was formed from the leavings of other cities, and it has an odd, misshapen outline, like dough the pastry-cutter left behind. A bulbous western section is connected by a tenuous isthmus to an irregular eastern panhandle. With perverse flair the "Creative City," as West Hollywood styles itself, made its unbalanced shape into its logo, flaunted on billboards and city hall stationery. But the overall impression of West Hollywood is linear. Santa Monica Boulevard, the city's main street, stretches for three miles from its western to its eastern border, and everything of note is located on the Boulevard or is measured from it.

Along the Boulevard one soon notices a gradient of affluence and respectability. The western end, closer to the ocean, still receives whatever cooling breezes have passed over the mansions of Beverly Hills, while the eastern end merges imperceptibly into the overheated slums of Hollywood. A stroll along the Boulevard reveals the social spectrum within a gay ghetto, from the proper and upwardly mobile to the darkly nonconformist.

For its first mile from the Beverly Hills border the Boulevard is unusually wide: its two carriageways are separated by a broad median, where once the Red Car trolley ran on its way to the beach. Along the center of this grassy strip closely spaced poles carry flags of every color, with every so often a rainbow flag, the emblem of gay pride. In June, when the Gay Pride march makes its way along the Boulevard, every flag is a rainbow.

One of the first landmarks on the Boulevard, on its north side, is the Pavilions supermarket. Entering the store for the first time, a visitor is struck by several things: the high prices, the extravagant variety and quality of the items available, and the large number of well-built men who good-humoredly cruise each other in the aisles or vie with Beverly Hills matrons for the finest produce. If gay men's fondness for shopping, cooking, and sex are three stereotypes, the stereotypes are alive and well at Pavilions.

Beyond the supermarket begins "Boystown," a four-block-long stretch of bars, coffeehouses, restaurants, and other stores that forms the major focus of the city's gay life. Sleepy by day, Boystown begins to stir as the sun goes down. Toward midnight, especially on a Friday or Saturday night, the bars and coffeehouses become so full as to spill patrons out onto the street, where they mill about and fraternize with the throngs of passersby.

The participants in this scene are overwhelmingly gay men, but in other respects they are strikingly diverse. Considering that the Los Angeles area is largely a mosaic of ethnically isolated neighborhoods, the mixture on the Boulevard on a Friday night is astonishing: every skin tone known to nature is represented, along with some produced only by art. In age too the crowd is quite diverse. Men in their twenties and thirties predominate, of course, but older men are also well represented. So are teenagers, who hang out in the Six Gallery coffeehouse, some of them attracted more by the wayward atmosphere of the Boulevard than by any actual homosexual inclination.

The men at this end of the Boulevard are more or less "buff": their bodies are well toned and tanned at the nearby gymnasiums, and the balmy climate allows them ample exposure. They are generally clean-shaven and short-haired, and fashionably if casually dressed. The collision of homosexuality and Hollywood has produced an extraordinary concern with bodily appearance, looks, and clothing on the Boulevard: the inhabitants of the Castro, the gay center of San Francisco, look positively nerdy in comparison.

In spite of appearances, the scene at the western end of Santa Monica Boulevard is tame and civilized, dominated by the bourgeois principles of the mostly white professional men who live in the neighborhood. No sex occurs in the bars there, and precious little drunkenness. Many sexual assignations are made there, no doubt, but they are governed by an unwritten code that requires, for example, two men to know each other's names and some minimal details about each other's lives before heading off to one of their apartments. In fact, many of the men who spend hours dancing or standing around at Micky's, Rage, Revolver, and the other bars are not in the sexual marketplace at all: already coupled, or averse to casual sex, they are there simply because it is the place to be on a Friday night, the place to be wholly, unreservedly gay after a week's grind in the halls of heterosexual America.

The sidestreets of Boystown are lined with apartment and condominium buildings that house thousands of gay men, as well as significant numbers of lesbian women and some straight people too. The buildings are unmistakably Southern California: often they are constructed in courtyard style around a pool, Jacuzzi, and barbecue, all set amid a jungle of palms and hibiscus. Thanks to a city ordinance that requires developers to sponsor public art, many of these buildings flaunt quirky sculptures on their front steps. Plaster spaghetti is festooned around the balustrade of one building, while another sports an enormous three-armed log dangling from a wooden gallows.

"I'm from Lincoln, Nebraska," a young white man who lives in one of one of these buildings tells a visitor.

I grew up in a German Lutheran family. I realized I was gay when I was thirteen. I didn't feel very good about it for years. I was very naive. But I applied to colleges in big cities where I would be accepted as gay. I went to CalTech, in Pasadena. Every weekend I would drive to West Hollywood and go to the bars. I would just stand there in the bar. I didn't have a very good body at the time, so mostly I was ignored, but at least I was around homosexuals.

Now I'm twenty-six. I do genetic research at UCLA. And, yeah, last year I was the biology consultant for *Jurassic Park*. I helped them design the laboratory sets, although they didn't go along with anything I suggested, and I ordered the equipment and dressed the set as if three or four people were doing experiments, filled the refrigerators with bottles that had, you know, colored liquids in them, and put fake labels on them. And I got to be in the film too, playing a scientist. No, it wasn't my being gay that made me get into that; all the graduate students in my lab would have loved to do it.

Music has always been a big part of my life—maybe *that* has to do with being gay. I sing in a choir at All Saints Episcopal Church in Pasadena. It's not a "gay choir," but out of the men, all but two are gay. The church also runs an AIDS service center, and I'm a "Buddy." I'm on my second.... I had one pass away eight months ago. My Buddy now has KS lesions all over, on his face and head, and internally, and it's very painful for him to walk, and he has MAI and that's often lethal so it has him really scared, it makes him really fatigued. He's very different from me, we didn't just click and become best friends, I'm more like a therapist. Sometimes he's in the shittiest mood you can possibly imagine. He needs someone to just talk about it with and vent his anger and work through those emotions, but it's exhausting—and I have to just be there with him and not let it affect me. I've never had to deal with a life-threatening illness myself, but I've been in places where I was that unhappy, and that upset, and I had friends who came and were there and gave me support, and I'm eternally grateful for them, and it feels good to be able to turn around and do that for someone else.

West Hollywood? Well, I like to flirt, and it's nice to be able to walk down to the store and flirt with guys and not, you know, have to hold yourself back or think "Wait, maybe this guy's straight." West Hollywood is a bit like Nebraska, actually, yes, like a village. The people I see at the gym are the people I see at the market and the video store. It makes me feel part of the community to see the same faces and know people's names. But there's also a down side to that. I don't think it's healthy, necessarily, to completely isolate yourself from the rest of the world. I don't think that someone, you know, who cuts hair at a salon in West Hollywood, goes out to the clubs in West Hollywood, does a lot of drinking and drugs, only has friends in West Hollywood and lets that be their entire life, I don't think that's ... for me at least, it's not vibrant and living enough.

I'm still looking for a partner. If I just wanted a boyfriend or someone to go around with, I could have one. But I want someone who I'm really in love with, someone to raise children with and spend the rest of my life with. I'm willing to wait for … for Mr. Right, I guess, even though that's such a cliché. Children? Yes, I would really like to raise and nurture a new little soul, in a healthy loving environment, because I think a lot of children are born and raised in very unhealthy environments. And so, just to do my part to make the world a better place I'd like to try to raise a child with as much love as I could possibly muster.

On the next street, an African-American young man also has both positive and negative feelings about the city.

I love West Hollywood. To me it's safe. I like to be able to walk. I like the idea of parking my car Friday after work and not driving again 'till Monday morning. Everything's here. There's a sense of community. People are the same—they're different but they're the same. You have all ends of the spectrum but everyone's together in a community, and that's what I really like.

Generally I've been treated fine, as a Black person here. But I've had instances. At Pavilions, a store detective followed me all round the store, and outside. He stopped me in the middle of the parking lot, and started poking at me and saying "I saw you take the Marlboro Reds, just give them back and it'll be OK." He looked in my bag, started touching me all around. Then he said "OK, you can go." He didn't apologize. I also got stopped by three police cars on Larrabee, by the video place. What did I do to deserve a three-car arrest? I was Black. They had a description of the man they were looking for—six-foot-three. I'm only five-foot-five. And they frisk me, arms in the air, with everyone walking by looking. I was very upset.

No, I'm not in a relationship right now. But everyone I go out with, there's always the question in the back of my mind, Would this be a person to spend—not necessarily a lifetime—but years, a relationship? If they're not relationship-oriented, then I'm pretty much out of the picture. I don't deal with a lot of trash.

The intersection of Santa Monica and San Vicente Boulevards, in the very center of Boystown, could be considered the political heart of the gay community in Southern California. Numerous assemblies and demonstrations have taken place here. On a night in July 1993, after President Clinton had announced his "compromise" on gays in the military (they could serve so long as they didn't tell anyone they were gay), hundreds of people gathered to hear lesbian and gay community leaders express their anger and frustration. Los Angeles City Council member Jackie Goldberg, School Board member Jeff Horton, West Hollywood cofounder and long-time activist Morris Kight, gay rights lawyer Jon Davidson, and many others denounced Clinton's decision as a betrayal of the community he had promised to support, and vowed to continue the struggle in the courts, in Congress, in the media, and in the streets. Fired by this rhetoric, the crowd marched off to besiege a Beverly Hills hotel where Hillary Rodham Clinton was rumored to be staying the night. If she was there, she did not step out to greet the incensed demonstrators, who eventually dispersed peacefully.

Squeezed among the bars in the heart of Boystown is A Different Light, a bookstore that specializes in lesbian and gay books and periodicals. Whether one wants the latest radical lesbian manifesto, a gay novel, or just some old-fashioned meat-rack pornography, this is the place to come. Once or twice a week authors and poets discuss or recite their works in a cramped space at the back of the store, their listeners a motley group of knowledgeable devotees and confused walk-ins. For those whose attention span does not extend to books and poetry recitals, the Don't Panic! tee-shirt store, a few doors away, is the place to go. Here the philosophy and politics of the community are distilled into phrases of five words or less: "Nobody Knows I'm Lesbian," "It's a Brain Thing," "Support Our Gay Troops," "2QT2BSTR8"—the tee-shirt messages come and go with the ebb and tide of the community's interests.

A few steps down a side street is a building that houses three institutions that provide the city with some measure of academic life. These are two libraries—the International Gay and Lesbian Archives and the June Mazer Lesbian Collection—and the Institute of Gay and Lesbian Education, a new adult-education school where both of us teach.

The Institute, founded in 1992, offers a variety of courses, workshops, and other events. Two especially popular courses are devoted to the psychology of gay men and lesbian women.

There are also courses on gay and lesbian fiction writing, cinema, literature, religion, ethics, and even biology. Among the outings organized by the Institute has been a boat trip to Anacapa Island, home of the lesbian seagulls discovered by ecologists George and Molly Hunt in the 1970s (see chapter 2). On another occasion the Institute visited the Getty Museum in Malibu to learn about attitudes toward sexuality through the ages. A symposium on Sexual Orientation and the Law was an opportunity to educate lawyers on constitutional and legal issues affecting gays and lesbians in employment, housing, parenting, immigration, and many other areas. Although diverse in its offerings, the Institute has a single aim: to further the understanding of gay and lesbian identity, both among gays and lesbians themselves and throughout society as a whole.

Walking eastward along the Boulevard, one comes soon to a building that, in scale and splendor, dwarfs everything else on the street. The Pacific Design Center, home to numerous showrooms that cater to the interior design trade, actually consists of two buildings: one, clad entirely in green glass, is shaped like the lower half of an immense dodecahedron, while the other, in solid blue, provides a long, arcade-like backdrop to the first. Hurting badly from the recession, the Center has had trouble meeting the mortgage payments on its magnificent home. It nevertheless represents both an outstanding architectural landmark and a tribute to a profession gay men have made particularly their own.

A few steps further bring us to a nondescript single-story minimall that houses a sushi restaurant, a copy shop, and Little Frieda's—a lesbian coffeehouse. On the roof of the minimall, rearing fifty feet or so into the sky, are two enormous billboards that carry pictures of attractive, healthy-looking men. They advertise the AIDS clinics of rival medical services: Pacific Oaks woos the westbound traffic, Century City Hospital the eastbound. They are a reminder that AIDS is not just a disease here, it is a large part of the culture and the economy too.

After a few minutes' further walk we reach West Hollywood City Hall—actually, the city rents space above a row of small shops. The elected City Council members are part-time, unpaid officials; the bulk of the work is done by their deputies and the other staff. Deanna Stevenson, deputy to Mayor Abbe Land, is at her desk. She tells us that about one-third of the city's 36,000 residents identify as gay or lesbian, with the gay men outnumbering the lesbians by seven to one. "Yes, we lesbians are in a minority," she said,

> but West Hollywood is a congenial place for any progressive person to live, whether heterosexual or gay or lesbian. Of course, the nightlife is mostly male. There is lesbian nightlife, but it's not so profound an experience, there's just not so much of it. I don't think that bars play a central role in lesbian culture, at least for older lesbians. For myself at least, I've never found bars in my whole life to be a place where I really intersect that much with other women, even when I was young. That's not the place where I would look for lesbian culture. There are other ways. The [L.A. Gay and Lesbian Community Services] Center, for example, has a lot of women involved, a lot of women's programs. The City of West Hollywood specifically funds the lesbian programs there. And now we're doing Lesbian Visibility Week—this is the third year. It's in July. It's an amalgam of cultural programming, workshops that address current needs, psychological needs, discussions about relationships, sexuality, there's a leather section, there's Dykes and their Dogs, there's music, there's businesswomen's awards. Of course it's not necessarily West Hollywood lesbians who attend these events—they come from everywhere, because this kind of program really doesn't exist anywhere else.
>
> The main thing that West Hollywood has achieved is an environment where people feel free to be themselves. We have a nondiscrimination policy that includes sexual orientation of course. If we get a complaint—let's say it's a business who's perceived to be antigay—we'll send someone out to talk with the owner of that business, to explain our policy. Sometimes the residents who are straight feel that we do too much to enhance the gay lifestyle. We don't perceive it that way. On the whole, people live incredibly amicably, side by side.
>
> When the city was incorporated, ten years ago, a lot of people thought West Hollywood would become a hotbed of gay politics, a training ground. Well, we haven't been turning out gay politicians that go to Sacramento or Washington, not yet anyway. You have to have a broader base than just being gay or lesbian, to get elected. But

we are influential in setting an example in our policies, especially with regard to domestic partnership. If the State adopts a domestic partnership policy, it will be thanks to us to a considerable extent—because of our example, and because we have had people in our office working on the State Bills.[1]

West Hollywood is a center for the entertainment industry—film-making and music-making—and it has many well-known theaters. We have an Arts Advisory Council, which I help to staff. I'm enormously excited about the potential for what this city can be in the arts, because we already have the arts around us, but we're going to gather up the forces of these art-making institutions. We're going to hold our first Arts Festival in the fall, probably in conjunction with the tenth anniversary of cityhood.

AIDS? Well, we have the highest per capita incidence of AIDS in the county. There have been over one thousand deaths, and we probably have about eight hundred people living with AIDS or HIV in West Hollywood right now. The city provides money for meals, through Project Angel Food, we fund AIDS programs at the Center, we are opening an HIV drop-in center, we run an adult day health-care program, which is a program for people in the last stages of AIDS, or who really need to be in a place during the day, and we fund housing for people with AIDS. We spend about one-and-a-half million dollars a year on gay and lesbian programs, and a very large part of that is AIDS-related programs.

Across from city hall are two large gymnasia, the Sports Connection and the Athletic Club. Behind the plate-glass windows rows of bodybuilders pit their glistening, near-naked bodies against Nautilus, Hammerstrength, and StairMaster. Squeezed incongruously between the two gymnasia is The Palms, West Hollywood's only lesbian bar. More discreetly fronted than the flamboyant men's bars down the street, The Palms can be hard to find. There are never lines of lesbians outside, waiting to get into weekly beer busts, but inside it can be as lively as any bar in West Hollywood.

Beyond city hall and the gymnasia, a mile from the Beverly Hills line, Santa Monica Boulevard takes a slight rightward bend. At the same time it loses its median strip and narrows down to a more typical Los Angeles thoroughfare. From here on, the gay community shares the Boulevard with other inhabitants of West Hollywood, especially with the large Russian Jewish population. On storefronts the Cyrillic and Roman alphabets vie for the attention of passersby, but the two communities might as well be on different planets, for all the interaction there is between them.

Just beyond the bend in the Boulevard, above an automobile repair shop, are the offices of *Frontiers*, "Southern California's Gay Biweekly." A lively and up-to-date rag covering everything from gay politics to social chat, it is best known for its "Yellow Pages." These are forty or fifty pages of personal advertisements, divided by the nicest of distinctions into nine categories of male-to-male liaison: "Roommates," "Relationships," "Romance," "Want to Meet," "Hardcore," "Sex Dates," "Raunch/S&M," "Models," and "Masseurs." The analysis of these advertisements could provide the material for several excellent Ph.D.'s, packed as they are with the most explicit information about the physical and mental attributes of the advertisers and the men they are looking for, along with detailed descriptions of the activities that are proposed to take place between them. If nothing else, the sheer volume of these advertisements suggests that many gay men have difficulty fulfilling their sexual or emotional needs, even in a gay Garden of Eden like West Hollywood.

A few blocks further down the street, also located in upstairs offices, is Christopher Street West, a gay and lesbian charitable organization that puts on the annual Gay Pride Parade and Festival. The parade, which takes place at the end of June, is a huge affair, featuring every aspect of gay and lesbian life. Somber AIDS activists, flamboyant drag queens, leather-clad Dykes on Bikes, lawyers and politicians in suits, and muscle-boys in next to nothing—the marchers exemplify the diversity of the community as well as its solidarity. For a young gay man or lesbian woman recently arrived from middle America, the parade can be an experience of overwhelming emotional significance.

The other major festive occasion on the Boulevard is Halloween. If the June festival mixes fun with a measure of dull rectitude, Halloween in West Hollywood is all shameless self-indulgence, all glitter, faux pearls, and faux bosoms. Of course, West Hollywood sees plenty of exotically dressed folks on a regular working day, so it takes a special effort to be truly outrageous at Halloween.

Just beyond Christopher Street West's offices we come to the junction of Fairfax Avenue, two miles from the Beverly Hills line. From here on, Santa Monica Boulevard takes on a gradually more impoverished and unsavory appearance. As twilight approaches, the sense of security that West Hollywood generally offers becomes tempered with uneasiness. Fewer businesses are open, fewer people are out and about, and of those who are, some represent the fringes of society. At Plummer Park, an undistinguished patch of green on the north side of the street, we may be confronted by a homeless drunk relieving himself at the curb. If we are men, we may be mistaken for hustlers or johns, for male prostitution is a major street activity at the east end of the city. Perched on the backs of bus-stop benches, or strolling in small groups, the hustlers make an appealing, even romantic impression, combining as they do good looks, extreme youth, and a bohemian lifestyle. But their life is not very romantic.

At La Brea Boulevard, three miles from the start of our walk, West Hollywood ends. But, late though it is, let's venture one block further, and turn down a deserted, ill-lit sidestreet. An unmarked door at the back of a parking lot is the entrance to The Zone, a business that in spirit if not in fact is West Hollywood's final outpost. Reverse discrimination is in full force at The Zone: a man at the entry asks us whether we are gay, and only an emphatic "Yes," accompanied by a sizable membership fee, gets us in.

The Zone occupies a warehouselike building whose windows have been blocked off. Once past the cashier, our first impression is of complete blackness, but after a while we begin to make out a maze of plywood passageways and empty rooms. Barely discernible, men wander in ones and twos from room to room, gathering in expectant groups that as rapidly dissolve. After a while, our anxiety begins to give way to boredom. But finally, in one of the darkest corners, something is definitely happening. We join the fringes of a tight knot of men, whose participants are straining for a view of what is going on within. At the nucleus of the group a man, perhaps younger or better looking than the others, stands with his jeans down to his ankles. He is being serviced by a kneeling man in front of him, as well by another man who stands behind him. Hands reach out from the darkness to touch some part of his anatomy, like the hands of cripples straining to touch the statue of a saint. But before long he reaches his climax and, his appetite slaked, he brushes off his devotees and pushes his way out of the throng. The group dissolves and its members go in search of another encounter. We take a taxi back to civilization.

There is no typical gay man in West Hollywood, nor is there a typical gay ghetto. What exists here is the product of a particular time and place and the assembly of ten thousand individuals. But, drawn together by sexual desire, gay men find that more than sex unites them. Style, sleaze, and all, West Hollywood exudes a civic pride, a togetherness, an exuberance, based on the conviction that gayness is the central attribute of gay people's nature, an attribute that reaches into every corner of their daily lives.

8

Country Lesbians

In the early 1960s many young people filtered out of the cities and into the country, seeking to get in touch with their roots, or to establish a new mode of communal living. Some of them found a haven among the mist-shrouded redwoods of California's North Coast, especially in the area around the old lumbering town of Mendocino, a hundred or so winding miles north of San Francisco along the Coast Highway.

Originally the movement was male-dominated. Most of the first wave of lesbians came with boyfriends or husbands. Some considered themselves bisexual, but most of them had never thought to question their heterosexuality. With the rise of feminism, women started consciousness-raising groups and soon were falling in love with each other.

Fairly typical was Joan's experience. In 1971 she moved with her husband from a conservative Republican suburb of Los Angeles to the outskirts of Fort Bragg. A friend asked Joan to accompany her to a consciousness-raising group because she was intimidated by some of the women (only three of whom were lesbians at the time). Joan went, and listened to fourteen women talking about feminism. They were so articulate, speaking this practically foreign language. Joan hadn't heard any of this before and she was appalled. "Isn't anybody here happily married?" she asked. She attended one more meeting before quitting the group. Still, something had been sparked in her, and in the course of the next year she realized her own attraction to women, fell in love, and came out as a lesbian.

Joan was not the only one to do this. All this talking and soul-baring led eventually to sexual exploration. At the time many feminists across the country were carrying their politics to their beds by sleeping with women. The women's movement gave birth to many "political lesbians," but also introduced many lesbians to their true selves. Another result of the movement in Mendocino County was the conversion of many heterosexual or mixed communes into exclusively lesbian spaces.

Pam has lived in the area since she arrived in 1968 with her two-year-old daughter. She helped establish Table Mountain commune, a mixed community that existed until about 1986. Kids were born and grew up there. Pam started a school on the land, originally just preschool, but eventually it expanded to become a private school (kindergarten through eighth grade) that served the greater community, especially the children of parents who chose not to deal with "the system." She had great success working with children the traditional school system had given up on.

Pam, who is fifty-four, says Table Mountain was a stable commune with a strong sense of family, especially joyous around holidays such as Passover, Thanksgiving, and Christmas. But most other lesbians living communally led a very gypsy lifestyle, traveling between communes, hitching rides, moving from state to state. Many at some point spent time at OWL (Oregon Women's Land) Farm. And through the communal grapevine word spread of the women's communities near Mendocino, and lesbians started arriving in droves.

Flame, forty-four, has lived "in community" for more than twenty years. In the 1970s, disillusioned by the system, she dropped out of school where she was training to be a social worker and went to live in the woods in southern Oregon. A few years later she moved to a "redneck hippie commune, a real gun-loving, beer-drinking group." She was brought out by a "city gal" there, but left to become a fruit tramp for a few years, picking fruit in Oregon, Washington, or wherever the harvest took her. The Oregon lesbian community gave her her first sense of tribe.

This sense of belonging, of being part of a group trying to build something bigger than just a place to live, was a crucial element in every woman's journey to this area. Communes were about living different lives, alternatives to the rigid codes people had grown up with. To live communally, people had to shed their preconceived notions of community and society. Some people even shed their names, choosing new ones inspired by dreams, meditations, or the landscape. Flame, Red Wing, and Sunlight spoke with us about their choices.

"For most people," said Red Wing, who is forty, "it's been about being more connected to the things that are important to them." She changed her name when she first moved to California about seventeen years ago. In a dream she turned into a red-winged blackbird and flew away. Sunlight's name came to her in a meditation. She was sitting on a rock in the sun and heard a voice whisper "Sunlight." She'd been looking for a new name, and believed that's what she was being given.

Flame has changed her name more than once. For her, it goes along with changing identity. Born Susan, she changed her name to Acorn when she came out as a lesbian. "Changing my name was in support of changing my being," she said. She chose a nature name because she felt she was living more with the earth at that time. "I was a little bundle of potential, hence Acorn." In 1989 Kim, a friend from the community, died in a motorcycle accident. Acorn felt she had gained a different perspective on death as well as life. She believed so strongly she was no longer Acorn that she used Susan again for about five days. "But in that time my whole being sprang into a new dimension, a different elemental nature. Hanging out with my woodstove and meditating, I became Flame."

Many lesbians in the late 1960s and 1970s were separatists. Women's land was open to women only. Women found the communes or other country women through ads in magazines like *Country Women*, *Amazon Quarterly*, and *WomanSpirit*. Meadow, forty-nine, who had been living in Willits, about two and a half hours northeast, attended the 1975 Country Women Festival held near Mendocino. It was an amazing event, she said, the epitome of what these women loved about living on the land and learning to be self-sufficient. Workshops covered everything a person needed to know to live on the land: sheep shearing; chain-saw use, maintenance, repair, and sharpening; wood chopping; cabin building; car repair. Other topics included such extracurricular subjects as nonmonogamy and masturbation. Meadow emphasized that all the workshops were led by women who were experienced in each topic; no one was brought in from outside. Flame said: "My sense of lesbian community includes the learning of new skills, especially living rurally. We were born again into the power of women."

That power was palpable to outsiders. Sydelle, fifty-one, moved to the area in 1975 with her four-year-old son. She didn't connect with the lesbian community until she rented a cabin on land owned by lesbians. What drew her to them was a "tremendous life force, an appetite and a zest."

Sunlight, seventy, told us that she's still pretty much a separatist, though less militant than she used to be. When she came out in 1971, the women's movement and gay liberation were just taking off. She was "formed as a lesbian feminist," and those are the tenets she's internalized. Her choice is still to live with women, but she's not hostile to men. That seemed to be the case for the other lesbians too. Most of the women here live essentially lesbian-only lives. They interact with men out in the world, at work, but not much socially.

Though lesbians tried to make everything work as a community, a lot of communes eventually broke up, just as they did all over the country. Too many different viewpoints and ways of accomplishing goals, most of the women say today. But, Flame emphasized, "We learned a lot from our chaos, too." And they brought their skills to the places they eventually settled.

Red Wing agreed that open women's land, though it had a lot of positives, was too much struggle. "Too many different needs and ideas and ideals," she says. Also it was hard to deal with the constant flux of moving around from commune to commune. The four women who formed Red Wing's commune now live independently, though still on the same land. They want to relate still as family, but not as land partners, and are in the process of getting together bylaws and agreements about what will happen to the land should one of them die.

Not just Red Wing's living situation but her career has changed over time. For thirteen years she worked at Corners of the Mouth, a health food cooperative (and informal meeting place for lesbians) in Mendocino. But the week after Kim's fatal accident, Red Wing applied to a nursing program, and she has been a registered nurse since 1992. Though she sees much that is positive in Western medicine, she is looking for ways to incorporate nontraditional healing methods and ideas into health care. She ultimately wants to get her nurse practitioner's license and open a practice. One of her specialties would be caring for the dying, "being a midwife to the transition from body back to spirit."

New jobs or fields of interest have taken others away from the land. One by-product of this mainstreaming is that some women who had always been out of the closet have gone back in. After years of being open about their homosexuality, suddenly lesbians felt they had to be careful about whom they came out to, because they were dependent again on traditional society for their livelihoods.

Though they're no longer living in communes, the lesbians who did live in them still maintain a strong connection with each other and with the land. Sherry, now the director of the Library Foundation of San Francisco, feels "incredibly connected" to the landscape even though she hasn't lived full-time in Mendocino County since 1978. She still finds it the most beautiful place on earth, and she believes the community there possesses a generosity of spirit and an ability to surmount any differences that arise. Many of the women we talked with stressed that in the country people are dependent on their neighbors, straight or gay, conservative or liberal. Because of this need they have to learn to get along.

Laurel said that, because there's a relatively small number of lesbians in the area, they often know a great deal about a potential partner before they become involved. "You can see four single women at a party, and know that one has trouble with commitment, another with codependency, and something about each of the others." But, because of the restricted numbers, women can't afford to limit themselves. "You get involved anyway—almost as if you get to pick which area of your own life you'd like to work on."

A phenomenon of Mendocino living, especially among the old-timers, is that couples don't always live together. Several of the women we spoke to were in long-term relationships—ten years, thirteen years—yet still lived apart from their lovers. We were given three explanations for this: both women may own land and neither wants to give it up to move in with the other; the cabin on the land is often too small for more than one person, beyond the honeymoon stage at least; and people here need plenty of physical and psychological space—that's why they came to the country in the first place.

Flame used to make her living doing odd jobs, mostly wood splitting for local stores, inns, and some individuals. In the summer of 1992 she was diagnosed with breast cancer. After the lump was removed, she chose not to have a mastectomy, chemotherapy, or radiation but to do alternative therapy. After a wonderful ten months, pain in her ribs sent her back to the doctor. Her cancer had spread to her bones and her liver. For many months she was quite ill, unable to do anything unassisted. Just a few weeks before our visit she was being watched by a support team of women who signed up to stay with her in around-the-clock shifts. Yet when we arrived at Deep Dish Ranch, Flame was sitting up in a chair, convinced that her liver and bone cancers were gone, and eager to talk about her community and her history.

"The biggest sources of my healing have come from my community," she told us. Without insurance (which wouldn't have covered her alternative treatments anyway), she was in need of both physical and financial support. She received an abundance of both: financial donations (a benefit raffle was held, and a large women's community in Santa Fe also organized fundraisers for her), physical tending, and gifts of food.

Flame lives on land with Meadow and Sunlight, both of whom joined in our discussion of community. Meadow is an official caregiver, paid minimum wage by the county to give hospice care to Flame. But the woman who took charge of Flame's community support was Pam, who was also there that day. Meadow and Flame had been lovers for two years when Flame first came to the area. Today they are family.

Seeing Flame's frail body, it was hard to believe her capable of the physically strenuous work she used to do. She curled into an overstuffed chair that only emphasized her weakness. Her complexion was pale, with no trace of the healthy glow of someone who works outdoors. On a bulletin board hung on the back of a door in the kitchen were detailed instructions for the support women: time of treatments; procedure for turning off the phone machine when Flame was resting; explanations of her need for quiet and calm. The next month's schedule of caregivers was also tacked to the board, all but a few slots filled in.

In spite of her weakened state, Flame wanted very much to talk. "I want to sing the praises of community.... I wish anyone could experience this.... I've received so much love and sharing and caring. I feel very honored to be experiencing this in my life. And it's a great challenge, and I love a challenge." This has been a "humbling experience for me to be able to receive so much from so many people." She talks of inner growth, spiritual growth—all of which she credits her community for giving her.

As we were leaving, Flame went off for her afternoon nap. A group of friends who call themselves Overbakers Anonymous delivered a batch of muffins just out of the oven. Pam was working out dates for Sunlight to care for Flame. The caregiving went on.

Community support extends beyond physical care. Of course there are the usual friendships and parties and shoulders to cry on that one might find in any lesbian community, but also things that city lesbians would never think of doing. Four women wanted to go to the 1993 March on Washington, so they held an open-to-the-public gay pride dance to raise money for their trip. In essence, the community sent these four to the march. Thirteen other lesbians from the area also went. These women didn't just go to the march, have a wonderful time, and stop there. They wanted to bring the spirit and pride of that weekend back with them, so they organized a contingent to march in the annual Fourth of July parade in Mendocino.

Many lesbians thought long and hard before deciding to join the parade. Homophobia in Mendocino County is very subtle. Liberal residents are happy coexisting with lesbians as long as no one talks about sexuality—a kind of voluntary "don't ask/don't tell" policy. But after the March on Washington, lesbians believed it was important that people understand the contribution lesbians make to the greater community.

"You have to understand," Joan explained, "this is a very small-town affair. Marchers include local merchants and organizations. The floats are home-made. Spectators include tourists, but most are locals from surrounding towns, not just the liberals of Mendocino but the Ft. Bragg crowd as well." And the lesbian contingent was the biggest, most colorful, and loudest in the parade. Many of the women had never come out so publicly before. Red Wing wore her uniform and a stethoscope draped around her neck. She carried a sign reading "Lesbians provide your health care." A teacher's sign read "Lesbians teach your children." (Someone suggested that marchers wear white, but, given the rebellious streak of the community, dress varied.)

One hundred people—mostly lesbians, but some gay men and some supportive heterosexuals—marched proudly under the Women of Mendocino Bay (WOMB) banner, throwing candy into the crowd. One mother shrieked and knocked the candy out of her children's hands, but that was the most blatant incident of homophobia aside from a few catcalls which, the participants say, came from tourists, not locals.

The exact year and reason WOMB came into being is disputed. Some say it dates back to the early 1970s, when the organization was called Witches of Mendocino Bay. Others say it was formed to organize protests at the offshore-oil hearings in 1986. At any event, it was certainly thriving by the following year, when it organized a series of women-only events, a concert by Holly Near, and a dance. At the time the activities were designed more for networking than socializing; one of the group's main objectives was to organize a job bank. At the time, a lesbian-owned hot-tub facility sponsored a women's night on Wednesdays. When that business closed, area women wanted to have a women's center, a place to sit and talk, check out books, have coffee, and host entertainment. Realizing that the community couldn't financially support such a venture, WOMB began to sponsor dances so that lesbians could have a safe space to come together. That's when Laurel got involved. The first events drew between fifty and seventy-five women from as far away as Willits and Ukiah. Now WOMB boasts a mailing list of 350. In addition to dances, WOMB sponsors a game night, video nights, and a barbecue during the women's softball tournament. They also publish a bimonthly newsletter, *WOMB with a View*. It contains editorials, local news, highlights of national lesbian news, a regular column on spirituality, articles and local ads, announcements of events, a letters column, and a listing of resources for gay youth.

No public lesbian or gay space exists in Mendocino County, so most socializing is done on a more personal scale. Potlucks are a standard feature of country living, says Sunlight. Lesbians here say that they could be busy every night of the week with some activity. There's a book group that meets monthly. A salon originally formed to discuss Joan Nestle's *The Persistent Desire: A Femme-Butch Reader* has continued past that issue, spending three sessions (one a month) discussing community, and expanding now into other topics. The Women's Chorus of Mendocino is a most popular organization. A lesbian and straight mix, it features four directors, each with a different repertoire, and a waiting list of 120. There's also a lesbian dance class (fondly referred to as Butch Ballet), plus an active twelve-step community—groups, that is, that meet to support recovery from alcohol or other dependencies.

Unlike an urban population, there isn't much gay or lesbian youth in the area, though Laurel, a career educator at the local high school and college, does speak at area schools on the subject, and the Jewish community sponsors a countywide sensitivity training and counseling program for gay adolescents. In fact, the entire population tends to be on the middle-aged side, people in their late-thirties and up. Rabbi Margaret Holub, thirty-six, attributes this to a one-generation migration to the area. She says she rarely meets people in their thirties, whether in the lesbian or heterosexual communities. The entire community is aging.

Old women are the most invisible of any group, according to Sunlight, though she believes things are a little better in the Mendocino area, possibly because baby boomers are themselves aging and facing the issue. But she has felt ageism from the lesbian community. On one hand, younger women tend to exclude old women as sexual partners. On the other, they treat old women as role models. To Sunlight that means being isolated and not considered a part of the community. She belongs to a group of five old lesbians—they call themselves old "to reclaim the word as something good, not to be hidden"—who meet once a month for a potluck and conversation. They have much to offer, said Sunlight. "The older we've gotten the better we feel. I'm more peaceful now, happier than I've ever been."

Spiritual issues are never far from the minds of these country lesbians. Flame attributed her improved health to the spiritual care she received. She does healing visualizations every day, alone and with anywhere from three to a dozen other women. That she had just begun to want some time alone was proof to her and to some of her caretakers of the curative powers of prayer.

Country women's spirituality is very connected to the earth. Though most of the women were raised in some traditional religion, they have shed those systems to embrace a nontraditional mix of pre-Christian, earth-based, and Native American rituals and beliefs. Meadow, raised Episcopalian in rural Florida, says now that her love of the pomp of church ceremonies was an early manifestation of her pagan spirit. As soon as she came out as a lesbian she began looking for a new way to express her spirituality. When she lived in New York City in the 1960s and worked at a traditional junior-executive job, she participated in women's circles (nature-oriented spiritual groups) held in warehouses in the West Village. Today she writes the spirituality column for the WOMB newsletter, and attends circles celebrating the high pagan holidays: the summer and winter solstices, and the spring and fall equinoxes.

The women who participate in these rituals share a belief in the spirit inherent in everything. The circles are a way of celebrating and acknowledging the seasons, the gifts of the earth, women's wishes and desires. The winter solstice occurs on the shortest day and longest night of the year. Women (these rituals are open to women only, lesbian or not) gather to celebrate the dark time, empty themselves of the past year, and wait to be reborn. Winter is a time of latency for the earth, and the circle maintains an all-night vigil, standing or sitting on the floor. It is a conscious entry into the time of sleeping and darkness. They tell stories, chant, and dance. They pray for world peace. Each circle has a "road leader" who is responsible for the ceremony on a particular occasion. She maintains the energy of the group and directs the rituals. In the last few years, though, everyone has become a little less strict and rigorous about the rituals. According to Sunlight, some circles last only until midnight, and members are allowed to sit on chairs if they're more comfortable. And, because so many of the participants now have traditional jobs, circles are often held on the Saturday prior to the actual holy day.

Even those like Sydelle, who don't actively participate in any spiritual or religious ceremonies, nevertheless see spirituality as the glue that holds the community together. A self-described "cultural Jew," she has no active religious background and feels no spiritual pull. She has sat in on a circle occasionally, and likes the sense of bonding that participation gives her. And though she is "not at ease in the world of prayer," she does believe that the sacredness of the land unites this community, gay and straight, by turning a connection to the land and spiritual beliefs into community action.

Even traditional religion is practiced with a twist in Mendocino. The leadership and most active members of the Jewish community are women. Rabbi Margaret Holub, who is not lesbian, performs a monthly new-moon ritual, *Rosh Hodesh*, for women only. She has also performed a commitment ceremony for a lesbian couple, neither of whom is Jewish, and has sat in the solstice and equinox circles.

Ceril does outreach work in the Jewish community to teens in rural Northern California and Mendocino County. Out for over fifteen years, she identifies "more as a Jew than a lesbian." She and her partner, Sydelle, once had a long argument about their community. In the middle of it, they realized that each meant a different community—Ceril was talking about the Jewish community, Sydelle about lesbians.

And yet no matter what the definition of community, for just about everyone here the bond is with the land, a spiritual and physical tie that is impossible to ignore. For the land is the main attraction here—the majestic redwoods, the sweeping ocean views, the fields and meadows. Even indoors one can't help but be made aware of it, not just by looking out the window, but by the sense of country in the omnipresent wood-burning stoves, and the attention paid to keeping the fires going.

As we concluded our talk on the topic of spirituality, Joan laughingly declared, "I'm a pagan Buddhist." That was typical of the mix of spiritual traditions the lesbians in Mendocino County celebrate, and of the general independent streak that resists traditional definitions and categories.

Meadow said, "There's a lot of ritual in people's lives they don't realize is ritual. We all have an altar in our homes even if we don't call it that." She and her land partners, Flame and Sunlight, "basically live our life as ritual."

This intense connection to the land accounts for so many things, from name changes to the willingness to work two jobs just to be able to stay in the area. From it comes the purpose of this particular lesbian community. Years after communal living, these women are still thinking about the nature of community, questioning and exploring, searching for new ways to build on what they have learned.

9 Minorities

Gays and lesbians who belong to ethnic or other minorities may grow up within cultures that have different attitudes toward homosexuality than does white America. Generally speaking, ethnic minority cultures are marked by more negative attitudes toward gays and lesbians, and by a greater tendency to identify homosexuality with extreme gender nonconformity. This identification can make it harder for gay and lesbian adolescents to recognize themselves as homosexual, let alone be open about their sexuality to their peers or families.

Minority gays and lesbians may feel doubly or even multiply stigmatized, not just by mainstream society but by gays and lesbians who do not share their minority status. A poem entitled "Rejection" by Dragonsani Renteria, who is director of the Deaf Gay and Lesbian Center in San Francisco, describes this experience in an extreme form:

Society rejects me for being Deaf.
The Deaf community reject me for being a Lesbian.
The Lesbian community reject me for not being able to hear them.
The Deaf-Lesbian community reject me for being into S&M.
The S&M community reject me for being Deaf.
Society rejects me for being Chicana.
The Hispanic community reject me for being Deaf.
Patriarchal society rejects me for being a woman.
I am rejected and oppressed,
Even by those who cry out readily
Against rejection, oppression and discrimination.
When will it end?[1]

Another Bay Area lesbian leader, Abby Abinanti, a California court commissioner and the first California Indian to take the bar, expressed a similar frustration in an interview with Lillian Faderman.[2] Her complaint was not so much about stigmatization as simply the sense of always being something of a stranger among any group:

> When I went to Eureka, to my Yurok tribe, I felt as though I was somewhat accepted but they were not always ready for me as a queer, so I had to keep that part hidden a little. It felt easier for me to live in San Francisco than at home. But when I was in San Francisco, in a lesbian group, I felt they couldn't understand the Indian part of me. They're different from what I'm used to: different values, different approaches, a different sense of humor. They didn't know about those families back home I grew up with, the disputes, the importance of questions like "How's the fishing?" There was no place where all of me was validated.

Minority gays and lesbians who do succeed in identifying themselves face a choice of life paths. One choice is to remain within their own heterosexually dominated minority culture. Another is to assimilate into the white-dominated gay culture. A third is to search out and associate with gay and lesbian members of their own minority. Obviously these paths can combine or overlap in various ways. But it is the third avenue that is of particular interest to us here, because it establishes a set of subcommunities within the gay and lesbian population that are defined not by locality but by ethnicity or other minority status, and which to some extent have developed their own cultures.

American Indians

Nowhere are life choices more complex than among lesbian and gay American Indians. One the one hand, the tradition of berdaches and amazons, discussed as a historical phenomenon in chapter 2, does persist to some degree in contemporary Native American culture. This has been documented both by gay white men who have immersed themselves in Native American life, such as anthropologist Walter Williams and gay rights pioneer Harry Hay, and by lesbian or gay Native Americans such as the poet Paula Gunn Allen.[3] The berdache/amazon tradition is a source of pride and identification for many gay and lesbian American Indians.

On the other hand, the influence of Christianity and European culture has been to weaken or even eliminate the respect paid to berdache-like individuals, even on the reservations. Traditional words that identify berdaches, such as the Lakota *winkte*, are now sometimes used as terms of abuse equivalent to "fag," and violence against gay men is not uncommon. In addition, the berdache tradition encompasses only gender-variant homosexuality, not age-disparate or companionate homosexuality (see chapter 2), and it imposes certain expectations about sexual role, for example that the modern gay male Indian will desire only to take the receptive role in anal intercourse. Thus, as Williams and also Will Roscoe[4] have emphasized, the invocation of the berdache/amazon tradition has not been an automatic passport to security and acceptance on the reservations. For many gay or lesbian Indians, therefore, the search for identity has led them to the cities and immersion in the gay cultures there, just as it has for so many non-Indians.

In 1975 Randy Burns (Paiute) and Barbara Cameron (Lakota) founded Gay American Indians (GAI) in San Francisco. The organization provided assistance to new arrivals in the city and worked to increase the visibility of gays and lesbians within the American Indian community in the Bay Area. It is now a national organization with several hundred members. It publishes the writings of gay and lesbian American Indian authors and poets, and cooperates with other similar organizations in the United States and Canada in organizing international meetings of gay and lesbian Native Americans. Both Williams and Roscoe have remarked on the unique atmosphere at the events organized by GAI: rather than being purely gatherings of gays and lesbians, they include nongays, elders, and children who socialize comfortably with the gay people, as if the GAI have succeeded in reestablishing the extended family and its traditionally positive attitudes toward the berdaches and amazons, but in the more modern context of urban homosexuality. This has happened primarily though a conscious effort on the part of GAI leaders to work with and for the larger American Indian community, especially in representing its interests in the halls of government.

Although the visibility of gay and lesbian American Indians is greatest in the cities, there has been a certain improvement in the circumstances of gays and lesbians on the reservations in recent years. This has been caused, according to Williams, by two factors: first, a general movement to reassert traditional Indian values over European ones, and second, the influence of gay and lesbian activists, including Indians who have returned to the reservations and who lead a relatively open gay life there.

Latinos

The Latino[5] community in the United States is of course far larger and more diverse than that of American Indians. Racially it includes natives of both Americas, Europeans, and Africans as well as any and all degrees of mixture of these. In terms of the direction of immigration it includes three major groups, Mexican-Americans (Chicanos), who live predominantly in the Southwest, Cuban-Americans, the majority of whom live in Florida, and Puerto Ricans, most of whom live in the New York area. There are also substantial numbers of Latino immigrants from Central and South America. Latinos include first-generation immigrants as well as the descendants of people who colonized the country centuries ago. Its mother tongues include not only Spanish but English, Portuguese, and other languages.

Gay and lesbian Latinos reflect this diversity: it is almost as dangerous to make a generalization about them as it is to make one about the entire homosexual population of this country. But, reflecting the statistics of the community they belong to, lesbian and gay Latinos are likely to be younger, less educated, and less affluent than gay whites. They are also much more likely to identify as Catholics.

Attitudes toward sex in Latino and especially in Chicano cultures tend to focus on the macho man and his exploits with women. As Carla Trujillo[6] and others have discussed, lesbian women are often perceived as a threat to male dominance, because they refuse to have sex with men or bear their children, or because they work to raise the consciousness of Latino women in general and thus threaten the established order. Women's interest in sex is largely negated, and Latino women who are recent immigrants may lack even basic knowledge of their sexual anatomy or physiology.[7] Male homosexuality, when associated with gender nonconformity or a preference for the receptive role in anal sex, is probably stigmatized even more than it is among whites, but masculine men who take the insertive role in anal sex with men may escape stigmatization. This may be partly because of the "dominant" nature of insertive sex, and also because *heterosexual* anal sex is very common among Latinos.[8] Some Latinos can even participate in *receptive* anal sex and escape the stigma of homosexuality; the Cuban-American writer Reinaldo Arenas described how a heterosexually identified Cuban man asked Arenas to penetrate him on several occasions, saying afterward: "I don't do it for the pleasure; I just need a prostatic massage, which is most important to maintain a healthy equilibrium."[9]

Several factors mitigate the effects of homophobia in Latino culture. First among them is the strong sense of family unity. Louis Jacinto, cofounder of Gay and Lesbian Latinos Unidos (GLLU) in Los Angeles, told us: "No matter what you do as a child, your parents won't kick you out. You could murder, you could even be lesbian or gay and they won't kick you out. But they would probably rather have you be a murderer than be lesbian or gay." In addition, the generally larger family size, and the apparently higher rate of homosexuality in the Hispanic population (see chapter 5), mean that a gay or lesbian Latino teenager is less likely to be the only gay person in the family than is the case for Anglos. Finally, there have been heterosexual Latino leaders, most notably the Chicano labor organizer Cesar Chavez, who have spoken up for the acceptance of gays and lesbians by Latino society.

The relationship between gay and lesbian Latinos and the white gay and lesbian community is an ambiguous one. On the one side, Latinos and whites seem to mix freely in the gay ghettos, especially in New York and Los Angeles. On the other, there is often a sense among Latino gay men, especially those who are politically engaged, that whites may be only interested in them as sex partners, not as associates in other fields of life. "If a white man wants to start a relationship with me, I check to see if he has any Latino friends," said Jacinto.

Most cities with large Latino populations have organizations similar to GLLU, which are forums for social and intellectual exchange among mostly middle-class, English-speaking Latinos. Another example is Gay and Lesbian Hispanics Unidos of Houston, founded in 1978. These organizations often provide leadership and political training for a community that is underinvolved in politics (in Los Angeles, for example, Latinos form 30 percent of the population but only 10 percent of the registered voters). They provide counseling and education, and sometimes operate AIDS service organizations directed at Latinos, such as GLLU's AIDS agency Bienestar. The national gay and lesbian Latino organization, LLEGO, is described in chapter 16. There is also a more radical organization, La Red, which was founded in Mexico City in the late 1980s to combat gay-bashing there. It has several chapters in the United States that provide outreach to gay and lesbian immigrants and draw attention to gay and lesbian Latino concerns through the disruption of community meetings and similar actions, somewhat in the style of Queer Nation (see chapter 16).

Among the openly gay Latinos who have made notable contributions to the gay rights movement are Jose Sarria, who ran for the San Francisco Board of Supervisors in 1961 (see chapter 3), and the Puerto Ricans, including Rey "Sylvia Lee" Rivera,[10] who took a leading role in the Stonewall Rebellion. Among current leaders are Letitia Gomez, the executive director of LLEGO and a forceful advocate for lesbian and gay Latinos, and Mario

Solís-Marich, who cofounded LLEGO and several other Latino organizations and currently sits on the HIV Planning Council for Los Angeles County.

Two very influential Chicana lesbians are Cherrie Moraga and Gloria Anzaldúa. Their 1983 book *This Bridge Called My Back* (see Further Reading) was an inspiration to Latina lesbians and to many Latino gay men too. More recently they have taken somewhat different paths: Anzaldúa emphasizes the place of Latina lesbians in the community of women of color, while Moraga, who teaches at U.C. Berkeley, focuses more on their role in the lesbian and gay world.

A striking aspect of Latino culture is the close connection between social politics and the arts—a connection most familiar to non-Latino Americans through the murals of Diego Rivera. A remarkable mural in Los Angeles, the "Great Wall of L.A.," is the work of over a hundred artists working under the direction of Latina lesbian Judy Baca. The half-mile-long mural, painted on the wall of a flood-control channel in the San Fernando Valley, depicts the social, cultural, and political history of Southern California, including the origins of gay and lesbian activism.

Luis Alfaro, a performance artist who runs VIVA, a Los Angeles-based lesbian and gay Latino arts agency, told us of the tradition of guerrilla theater as a means to educate and politicize Chicanos. During the 1960s and 1970s one such group, El Teatro Campesino (in which gays and lesbians were involved), took political theater to the fields to help organize Chicano agricultural workers. Today Alfaro and another performance artist, Monica Palacios, direct a similar project, whose aim is to raise awareness of HIV prevention and intervention issues among Latinos. The actors might show up outside a gay Latino bar on a Friday night and entertain the men waiting for admission with five-minute skits containing health care messages. Such skits, Alfaro told us, are more effective than written materials because young gay Latinos tend to live with their parents and would be reluctant to bring gay-relevant materials into their homes.

As examples of the diversity of gay male Latino writing, we can mention Reinaldo Arenas, who documented a life dedicated to an impassioned struggle for political and sexual freedom, and Michael Nava, author of a series of popular mystery stories whose main character, Henry Rios, is a gay Latino lawyer.[11]

African-Americans

Gay and lesbian African-Americans experience a double discrimination—as gay and black—that is at least as intense as the comparable discrimination against Latinos. In his essay "Brother to Brother: Words from the Heart," Joseph Beam[12] wrote of the sense of "home" that the black community offers to a black American, but went on: "I cannot go home as who I am and that hurts me deeply." Black gay history and culture is unknown to most blacks.

As with Latinos, there is a pervasive sense among black gay men that white gay men see them only as potential sex partners. In a piece titled "Does Your Mama Know About Me?"[13] the poet and essayist Essex Hemphill has written about the objectification of black bodies by gay white men, both in social interactions and artistic representations, such as in the photography of Robert Mapplethorpe:

> Mapplethorpe's "Man in a Polyester Suit," for example, presents a Black man without a head, wearing a business suit, his trousers unzipped, and his fat, long penis dangling down, a penis that is not erect.... What is insulting and endangering to Black men is Mapplethorpe's *conscious* determination that the faces, the heads, and by extension, the minds and experiences of his Black subjects are not as important as close-up shots of their cocks.

Hemphill concedes that the AIDS crisis has helped to bring the gay community together, but asserts that it "still operates from a one-eyed, one gender, one color perception of *community* that is most likely to recognize blond before Black, but seldom the two together." Several studies have analyzed how racism within the gay and lesbian community hinders the full identity development of gay and lesbian African-Americans.[14]

Another complaint that blacks (both gay and heterosexual) sometimes make about white gay people is that they too glibly compare the struggle for gay rights with the black civil rights movement. In this view, neither the oppression that gays and lesbians have undergone, nor the efforts they have made to liberate themselves, are comparable to the black experience. It has also been argued that equating gay people with a racially defined group such as blacks weakens the legal concept of protected classes and thus endangers the hard-won gains of the civil rights movement. According to Stephanie Smith, the Lesbians of Color Program Coordinator at the National Center for Lesbian Rights, the religious right has tried, with some success, to turn African-Americans against lesbians and gays by the use of this kind of argument.[15]

Several prominent black leaders, including Jesse Jackson, Coretta Scott King, and former NAACP Director Ben Chavis, have supported the gay rights movement, for example by speaking at gay rights marches. Minister Louis Farrakhan, on the other hand, has consistently denigrated black homosexuality, calling it the product of prison life and deficient role models.[16]

In spite of their poor image within their own community, black lesbians and gay men have made extraordinary contributions to African-American culture and politics. James Baldwin wrote a central document of the civil rights movement, *The Fire Next Time*, as well as one of the earliest novels to have a gay male theme, *Giovanni's Room*. Audre Lorde (who died in 1992) was one of America's most admired poets. Bayard Rustin was an aide to Martin Luther King, Jr., and an organizer of the 1963 March on Washington. Phill Wilson and A. Cornelius Baker are AIDS activists who direct public policy at AIDS Project Los Angeles and the National Association of People With AIDS, respectively (Wilson also founded the Black Gay and Lesbian Leadership Forum). H. Alexander Robinson is Senior Legislative Representative for the ACLU's Lesbian and Gay Civil Rights Project, and a veteran of innumerable African-American, gay and lesbian, and AIDS organizations. Barbara Smith is a writer who edited *Home Girls*, an important anthology of writings by black women, and is currently working on a history of lesbian and gay African-Americans. She also cofounded (with Audre Lorde) Kitchen Table: Women of Color Press, and currently its publisher. "Supermodel" RuPaul and dancer/choreographer Bill T. Jones have demonstrated that being openly gay is no bar to success in entertainment and the arts.

Asian-Americans

Asian-Americans tend to emphasize family history, family cohesion, and family achievement more than most Americans. The benefits and the drawbacks of this tradition for gay male Asian-American youth are illustrated by the following extracts from postings on the Gay Asian message board of America Online:

Subj: sex, disease and death
Date: 93-04-10 21:34:10 EDT
From: ToughTofu

The hardest thing about being gay/bi and Asian for me has been that the very fact of being out to my family breaks the three big traditional taboos ... never talk about sex, disease or death.... Of course, being gay is much more than sex, much more than HIV but some of my family members can't hear that. The wonderful thing about my family is that they continue to be there for me ... regardless. They accept my partner as another member of the family (like a brother-in-law), and they go out of their way to make sure I am at home among them. I guess I have learned to accept some of their idiosyncrasies like the implicit request not to talk about "those other folks" (meaning the gay community) while at the same time they have accepted me and mine....

Date: 93-04-12 01:32:16 EDT
From: Doodoo

Gosh, ToughTofu. I wish I can have it as easy as you did. Being Asian definitely plays a major role in my reluctance to come out: Being the first-born SON of my grandpa's first born SON, I can't help but always be the object of attention in the huge extended family. If others were to know of my gayness, my parents would undoubtedly die of shame overnite. And they thought I couldn't have done more to "lose their face" when I said I didn't want to follow in my grandpa, father, aunt and uncle's footsteps and become a doctor just yet....

Date: 93:04:12 03:48:43 EDT
From: Dotz

I guess I had it easier than most people because my uncle is gay.... However, I still am the first-born son of my grandfather's first-born son like you DooDoo. I remember my mom's comments when I first came out to her: "So does this mean that you won't have any kids?" I'm not sure if this is because of my Filipino background but every one has accepted my uncle and his partner for 10 years unconditionally.... My uncle said that everyone has known he is/was gay but they never talked about it. I think that applies to many of us. I'm trying to break that with my parents though....

This paradoxical impact of Asian family values on Asian-American gay men is also well illustrated in the 1993 feature film *The Wedding Banquet* (directed by Ang Lee), in which a gay man's marriage of convenience turns, under pressure from his Chinese parents, into too much of the real thing. By the end of the film, everyone knows the truth and accepts it, but on the condition that it not be publicly discussed.

We were invited to a recent meeting of the Los Angeles Asian Pacific Islander Sisters (LAAPIS), a social and educational group for Asian lesbians and bisexual women. Several women in the group said that the coming-out experience is especially difficult for first-generation Asian-Americans, whose parents may lack even the vocabulary in their mother tongues to describe gays and lesbians, and quite likely have never discussed the topic of homosexuality during their entire lives. They are prone to see their children's homosexuality as a specifically American influence and a sign that they are losing their child to an alien culture. Susan, a first-generation Chinese-American, told about her experience:

I came out to my family about six years ago. They were very worried. First of all, they completely didn't understand; they felt that I could change and they kept urging me to change. But what I found most significant for my parents in terms of their acceptance was their getting to know other Asian lesbian and bisexual women, and meeting my friends and seeing that these were real people out there. They'd always had this perception of "Who are these people you always hang out with?"—shadowy people that they didn't know, a bad influence or whatever—but as soon as they met other Asian women, who spoke the same language as we do at home (we speak Mandarin), it made a really big difference, and now they're meeting other parents, and it's just made a world of difference, because before they felt very isolated, they didn't want to tell anyone in their community—now they have other parents who they can talk to. They're not the types to go to PFLAG [Parents and Friends of Lesbians and Gays] and feel comfortable with a bunch of people who are non-Asian.

Another point, made by LAAPIS co-chair Shella Aguilar, is that Asians have been brought up in many different religious traditions. Many Filipinos are Catholics, for example, and many Koreans are fundamentalist Christians; these people may be opposed to same-sex relationships for that reason. Asians who are Buddhists, on the other hand, belong to a religious tradition that is relatively tolerant of homosexuality (see chapter 19).

Whatever the discomfort that many Asian-Americans may feel toward homosexuality, it does seem often to be overridden by a sense of loyalty to the Asian community. Lesbian and gay contingents take part in the Cherry Blossom and Chinese New Year parades in San Francisco, and are at least politely applauded by the crowd. Certainly there has not been the kind of opposition that has faced gay and lesbian Irish-Americans, for example, when they have attempted to participate in St. Patrick's Day parades in Boston and New York (see chapter 15).

An interesting example of a progay stance by an Asian-American organization was the 1994 decision by the Japanese American Citizens League (JACL) to support the constitutional right to same-sex marriage. Part of the reason for the JACL's interest in the topic is that there is a large Japanese-American population in Hawaii, where same-sex marriage has recently been the subject of intense legal and political debate (see chapter 15). In addition, several gay and lesbian Japanese-

Americans addressed the JACL convention and, in a thoroughly "un-Japanese" manner, talked about their own sexuality and the discrimination they had faced in their own community. Yet a third factor in the JACL's decision was a history of support by the gay community for "redress," that is, for national apology and compensation for the internment of Japanese-Americans during World War II. Openly gay congressman Barney Frank was a leader in guiding the enabling legislation through Congress, and the National Gay and Lesbian Task Force also supported redress. Evidently this support did not go unrecognized by the Japanese-American community.

The Deaf

Deaf people have a long history of stigmatization and exclusion. Only comparatively recently has American Sign Language (ASL) been recognized as a language in its own right, capable of sustaining a deaf culture equivalent in every way to the culture of hearing people. Differences of opinion still exist about the relative importance that should be placed on sign language and spoken language in the education of deaf children.

Deaf people have had to fight for the control of their own lives. Many deaf people, especially those deaf since birth, resent the paternalism of hearing people who regard deafness as a handicap to be alleviated or prevented, or who presume to speak on behalf of the deaf. Just as gays and lesbians have fought for the acceptance of homosexuality and against efforts to "cure" it, so some deaf people have resisted the introduction of invasive preventive measures such as the implantation of cochlear devices in infancy.

The integration of deaf people into mainstream society is very incomplete. Indeed, just as many gay people desire acceptance but still want to live in gay ghettos, so many deaf people, while working to improve the visibility of the deaf, still see the society of other deaf people as their "family of choice." In an article titled "Double Pleasure" deaf gay activist Gregg Brooks listed the advantages of gay relationships between deaf people over deaf-hearing relationships.[17] They included better communication, a shared culture, nonpaternalism, better acceptance by others, and greater durability.

We spoke with one gay male couple, Adam Novsam and Eric Scheir, who seem to exemplify Brooks's point of view. Scheir has easily comprehensible speech, while Novsam used ASL to talk with us. Novsam, while a student at Gallaudet College (the nation's leading college for the deaf, located in Washington, D.C.), was involved in the student demonstrations that led to the appointment of Gallaudet's first deaf president. Together for two years, Scheir and Novsam spoke of previous relationships with hearing gay men that had ended in part because of problems of communication and culture. "John, my ex-lover, felt comfortable with me," Scheir told us, "but he did not feel comfortable being around many deaf people. When I was with him, I always went with his hearing friends, and I'm lost—it's a lot of complications—with all the hearing people talking at the same time. I only understand clearly with one-to-one. Sometimes with John, he knows I'm angry, but he forgets that I'm here, he has the habit of talking.... But when I met Adam, it really took off, because we are both from an identical background—we both are gay, we both are deaf, and we both are Jewish. I'm a marriage-oriented person, I'd rather stay with a person for life." Novsam had a similar story with his ex-lover. "I'll give you an example. One night we went to a bar where all the people were, and there was a lot of music, and I didn't want to go, because of the music. He said 'Try it, why not? You'll enjoy yourself,' so I say OK ... so we're sitting with all these hearing people, and I'm the deaf person, and it's really boring for me to be there, it's like death, and I told him, I'm not happy being involved with that, I'm sorry, but he wanted to hear the music.... It just caused problems in the relationship." Adam and Eric plan to be married by a gay rabbi, with both their families in attendance.

In spite of some deaf gay people's preference for relationships with other deaf people, most of the actual partnerships of deaf gays and lesbians are with hearing people. Hank Stack, a deaf gay activist who is the treasurer of the Rainbow Alliance of the Deaf, has made a particular study of the relationships established by deaf gays and lesbians. He told us that the numbers are against deaf-deaf relationships: there simply are too few deaf gay people in most cities to make matches likely. Furthermore, the close-knit deaf communities tend to make everyone seem like members of one's biological family, and hence not like potential sex partners. He said that there is very little sex among gay deaf people who live in the same city; if deaf-deaf sexual relationships of any kind happen, it is generally through travel. Stack also pointed out there are practical advantages to deaf-hearing relationships, especially in helping the deaf partner communicate with the hearing world.

One deaf-hearing couple in their early twenties, Jeffrey Majors and Terry Tauger, had only been together for two weeks when we spoke with them. Majors moved to Los Angeles from Houston, where he told us, the deaf gay community is small and very conservative. Tauger is a professional ASL interpreter and has had long contacts with the deaf community. They met at the Six Gallery coffeehouse in West Hollywood (see chapter 7), an important center of deaf gay social life in the Los Angeles area. (The bars, with their dim lighting, are often avoided by deaf people.) Majors, who works as a housekeeper for an older gay man, is also organizing the first deaf gay cruise, a Caribbean trip with RSVP, a gay travel agency. Both Majors and Tauger acknowledged that deaf-gay relationships are "hard work," and neither of them had especially planned to engage in one. But what they have going for them, besides the obvious chemistry between them, are excellent bilingual skills on both their parts.

Many large cities have gay and lesbian deaf organizations, with names that usually include the word "Rainbow." The groups are loosely allied into a national Rainbow Alliance of the Deaf, which puts on a biannual conference. One city, San Francisco, has a Deaf Gay and Lesbian Center, which provides support for deaf gay people through advocacy, education, and counseling.

Lesbian and Gay Youth

"Coming out, for those of you who have been living under a rock, means that you are going to admit openly that you are gay." Thus Oprah Winfrey introduced a program on gay and lesbian teens in October 1994. With these words Oprah highlighted the two major differences between gay teenagers and their elders: first, that teenagers are dealing with the coming-out process, which their elders may have already completed; and second, that they are doing so in a society that is far more aware of, interested in, and well-disposed toward gays and lesbians than was true for an earlier generation. As a result, gay and lesbian teenagers have the opportunity not just to come out, but to join a self-aware youth movement within the larger gay community.

That is not to say that the current crop of lesbian and gay teenagers necessarily have an easy time coming to terms with their homosexuality, or making a clean breast of it to the world. On the contrary, some degree of pain and suffering is probably universal, because even the teenager who welcomes homosexuality must still grieve the loss of heterosexuality and the privileged life expected to go with it. And for some, rejection and isolation may still be the dominant experience of their teenage years. The diversity of teenagers' experience is well captured in a recent anthology of their own writings, *Two Teenagers in Twenty* (see Further Reading).

Coming out is a very different experience for gay and lesbian teenagers who are markedly gender nonconformist than for those who are more conventional in gender role. Feminine boys and masculine girls are effectively outed as gay or lesbian by their own gender nonconformity, regardless of what they choose to say or not say about themselves, and regardless of whether they are in fact homosexual. This is because children collectively believe in strict gender boundaries and the punishment of those who cross them. A nineteen-year-old lesbian on Oprah's show recalled a childhood history of tomboyism, and how it played out in her midteens: "Every day I was called a different name—'butch,' 'dyke,' 'lesbian,' 'what's it like to want to be a man?' I dreaded going to school. I thought maybe it was my fault I was gay and I deserved this abuse.... [In] weightlifting class, I was the strongest female, and when we had to do certain sports, when they'd break it up, you know, men on one side and women on the other side, they'd say, you know, 'Where are *you* supposed to go?'" The experience of such taunting and involuntary outing must be extremely painful, and when combined with other negative factors such as parental rejection or a predisposition to depression it may lead to attempted or completed suicide.[18] But teenagers who live through this experience often develop an inner toughness that serves them well in later life. This same nineteen-year-old, for example, went on to describe how, helped by the school psychologist, she rapidly came to terms with her lesbian identity. "I'm on *Oprah*, coming out," she said. "I think I've come a long way."

The situation for gender-nonconformist boys is similar. The British writer Quentin Crisp, for example, who was extremely effeminate from early childhood and took continual abuse for it, has had a long, robust life as the quintessential survivor, described in his autobiography *The Naked Civil Servant*. And, as mentioned earlier, it was drag queens, not more conventional gay men, who initiated the Stonewall Rebellion.

More conventionally gendered boys and girls have the choice to remain wholly closeted or to come out voluntarily. Such teenagers may go into an "overachiever" mode in which scholastic or athletic performance is used to distract attention from their problematic sexuality. They may carefully manage their coming out over a period of many years, weighing the exact pros and cons of each cautious step. The pseudonymous "John Reid" described exactly such a life path in his 1973 book *The Best Little Boy in the World*.[19]

Today, special-purpose organizations not only provide counseling, discussion groups, and social opportunities for newly emerging gay and lesbian youth, but also act as breeding grounds for a new generation of activists. One teenager from Lowell, Massachusetts, Troix Bettencourt, joined the Boston Alliance of Gay and Lesbian Youth, became its president, survived being kicked out of his home by his parents, persuaded his mother to accompany him in the Boston Gay Pride Parade, addressed the 1993 March on Washington, and was given the Human Rights Campaign Fund's Power of One Award, all before his nineteenth birthday. He tells his story in *Two Teenagers in Twenty*.

Anthropologist Gilbert Herdt and his colleagues at the University of Chicago have made a special study of a program for fourteen- to twenty-one-year-old gays and lesbians in Chicago, the Youth Group of the Chicago Horizons Community Services.[20] Founded in 1978, the Youth Group meets every Saturday at noon at Horizons' headquarters. After the introduction of new members, announcements of events, etc., the participants break up into smaller focus groups of about ten members each, to discuss topics chosen by the group members themselves. One of the focus groups contains the new members, and concentrates on coming-out issues. There is also a Wednesday evening "drop-in" session whose purpose is purely social. The Youth Group is far more racially mixed and racially harmonious than the city from which the members come. It is also has a rough balance of males and females, and its members tend to show much more physical and emotional intimacy across the sex lines than is commonly seen between lesbian and gay male adults. (In the Youth Group, as in this age group generally, both sexes refer to themselves as "gay.") The main purpose of the Youth Group is to help its members develop a sense of communal identity and communal pride. This is evident at Chicago's annual Gay Pride Parade, where the Youth Group by tradition forms the lead contingent. The Youth Group also provides panel or audience members for media events such as the *Oprah* show mentioned earlier. Although there have been no objective, controlled studies to assess the effects of the Chicago Youth Group or similar programs on the development of gay and lesbian youth, it seems likely that the provision of a communal space, outside of the endangering environment of their daily lives, permits its members to develop a sense of self-worth and group identity that would be much harder to acquire otherwise.

A few cities have gay and lesbian programs within the public school system. An example is Project 10 in Los Angeles, headed by Virginia Uribe, an openly lesbian teacher at Fairfax High School. Project 10 runs group sessions as well as individual counseling for gay, lesbian, and bisexual students, and it also attempts to educate the general student population about gay issues. The enormity of the task was evident to us when we visited this tough inner-city school. Not one of the gay or lesbian students we spoke to was out to his or her classmates; they all spoke of the likelihood of harassment or physical violence if their sexual orientation were known, and the glass windows in the doors of Uribe's classroom were carefully papered over. Yet the importance of the program to its students was evident in some of the plaques on the classroom walls. One of them, given by a group of Project 10 alumni/ae who had moved on to college at Cal State Northridge, was inscribed "To Dr. Virginia Uribe: For Inciting Queerness"—a joking reference to the commonly heard complaint that Project 10 actively recruits teenagers to homosexuality. Uribe herself is emphatic that Project 10 recruits no one: all it does, she says, is help students who are already gay, lesbian, or bisexual come to terms with their sexuality.

Massachusetts is probably the state with the most progressive attitudes toward gays and lesbians in the public school system. There is a Governor's Commission on Gay and Lesbian Youth (Troix Bettencourt is a member), and in 1994 Governor William Weld signed a state law—the first of its kind in the nation—that outlawed discrimination on the basis of sexual orientation in schools. High school students themselves can take much of the credit for this achievement: they organized a persistent, large-scale lobbying effort and staged candlelight vigils outside the statehouse. A poll conducted by the commission in

1993 showed that the majority of public school students in the state favor the idea of gay and lesbian support groups in the schools, and thirty-two public schools in Massachusetts now have such groups. Over 150 schools in the state have sent students to programs that teach methods to reduce homophobia in the school environment. There is also a teachers' organization, the Gay, Lesbian, and Straight Teachers Network, founded by Kevin Jennings, a gay history teacher in Cambridge, which works to liberalize attitudes toward the education of gay and lesbian youth. All these developments are remarkable for a state in which public expressions of antigay bias are still commonplace: in 1994, for example, the organizers of the Boston St. Patrick's Day Parade canceled the entire event rather than be forced to allow a gay contingent to participate (see chapter 15). Another state, Minnesota, is also notable for its many school-based youth groups, especially in the Minneapolis-St. Paul area.

Two cities, New York and Los Angeles, have special programs for gay and lesbian dropouts from the public school system. The New York program, named the Harvey Milk School, is run by the Hetrick-Martin Institute, a nonprofit group concerned with gay and lesbian youth, while the Los Angeles EAGLES Project is run by public school teacher Jerry Batty with the blessing (but without the financial support) of the L.A. Unified School District. Many of the students in both programs are markedly gender nonconformist, and as a consequence have horror stories to relate about their experiences in the regular school system. For these traumatized young people, just coming to class each morning is a minor triumph; obtaining a high school diploma may require extraordinary efforts on the part of the teachers and the students themselves.

Gay and lesbian youth have many other sources of support that were not available to their elders. Youth hot lines, like the one run by OutYouth in Austin, Texas, channel teenagers to youth groups and other resources. Youth newsletters like *insideOUT* (from San Francisco), as well as a kaleidoscopic array of "queer 'zines," inform gay youth about political and cultural trends. Youth-oriented television talk shows, like the one hosted by actress Ricki Lake, present gay and lesbian youth in a very matter-of-fact way, as people whose relationship problems are similar to those of their straight peers. And there are now gay and lesbian role models for virtually every career path, even if their numbers in some professions are still very small.

There are as yet no national groups organized by and for gay youth. The National Gay and Lesbian Task Force does put on youth-focused sessions at its annual Creating Change conferences. As a result of pressure from young activists at the 1993 conference, the Task Force decided to allot four seats on its board for young people. One of these went to *insideOUT* editor Rick Aguirre.

Old Gays and Lesbians

Until recently, old lesbians and gay men have been all but invisible, even within the gay community. Their invisibility arose from two causes. First, they grew up during a period when gays and lesbians had to make themselves invisible if they were to survive at all, and many of them learned only too well how to achieve this. Second, they have been the victims of a rejection that operates in the gay community just as it does among heterosexuals, a rejection of the no-longer-attractive and soon-to-be-dead by a society that prizes youth and beauty above all else. Of course, the gay community has always had its honored elders. But for every Harry Hay or Del Martin or Phyllis Lyon there have been thousands of old people whose gay or lesbian identity was known to few and celebrated by none.

If today there is a modest trend toward increased visibility and acceptance of the elderly within the gay and lesbian community, it is due primarily to the activism of older lesbians who responded to a central tenet of feminist thought—the concept that women should form their own identities rather that relying on identities assigned to them by others. Among the pioneers in applying this concept to the elderly was Barbara

Macdonald, whose 1983 book *Look Me in the Eye*[21] was an inspiration to more recent organizers of old lesbians.

In the late 1980s old lesbians on the West Coast began organizing annual conferences. Some of the participants at the 1989 conference, including Shevy Healey, formed a group known as Old Lesbian Organizing Committee (OLOC). This organization, which is open to lesbians age sixty and up, is dedicated to combating ageism within the lesbian and gay community. An example of OLOC's attitude is its use of "old" in its name, rather than "senior," "older," etc. "By naming ourselves 'old,'" said Healey, "we give up the attempt to pass. And as we thus break our silence, we empower ourselves and each other."[22]

OLOC opposes well-meaning attempts by younger lesbians and gay men to provide for old people by methods that perpetuate their exclusion from the main body of the community. It opposes, for example, the creation of housing specifically for old gays and lesbians. "Often young lesbians will tell me of their interest in establishing an Old Dykes Home," wrote Healey, "partly, I am sure, out of fear of what awaits them in their own old age in this homophobic world, and partly because of the belief that this would form a bond between us. It does the opposite. I think that they are a bit taken aback when I say that I'm not the least bit interested in a Home for Old Dykes, but I am very interested in intergenerational, intercultural housing for all dykes. My dream is not of a segregated old age."[23]

An important co-gender organization is SAGE (Senior Action in a Gay Environment). Based in New York City, SAGE is the only nationwide social services agency serving the gay and lesbian elderly. Its executive director, Arlene Kochman, told us that SAGE wants to emphasize the positive aspects of aging and to provide role models for younger lesbians and gay men. The specific services provided by SAGE in New York include services to the homebound or those in hospitals or nursing homes, health counseling, legal counseling on matters of special concern to older gays and lesbians (such as housing rights, durable powers of attorney, and wills), and co-gender and single-sex discussion groups. It has a branch organization in California and also operates as a nationwide advocacy organization.

Following Raymond M. Berger's pioneering study, *Gay and Gray: The Older Homosexual Man*,[24] a number of recent books and articles have focused on aging in the lesbian and gay community. Of particular interest is *Lambda Gray*, an anthology by Jeanne Adleman and others (see Further Reading).

Further Reading

Adleman, Jean et al. *Lambda Gray: A Practical, Emotional, and Spiritual Guide for Gays and Lesbians Who Are Growing Older*. North Hollywood, CA: Newcastle Publishing, 1993.

Gay American Indians. *Living the Spirit: A Gay American Indian Anthology*. New York: St. Martin's Press, 1988.

Hemphill, Essex, ed. *Brother to Brother: New Writings by Black Gay Men*. Boston: Alyson Publications, 1991.

Herdt, Gilbert, and Andrew Boxer. *Children of Horizons: How Gay and Lesbian Teens Are Leading a New Way Out of the Closet*. Boston: Beacon Press, 1993.

Heron, Ann, ed. *Two Teenagers in Twenty*. Boston: Alyson Publications, 1994. (An anthology of writings by lesbian and gay teens).

Luczak, Raymond, ed. *Eyes of Desire: A Deaf-Gay and Lesbian Reader*. Boston: Alyson Publications, 1993.

Moraga, Cherrie, and Gloria Anzaldúa. *This Bridge Called My Back: Writings by Radical Women of Color*. New York: Kitchen Table Press, 1983.

OLOC Handbook Committee. *Confronting Ageism: Consciousness Raising for Lesbians 60 and Over*. Houston: OLOC, 1992.

10
Sexual Diversity

The four groups we discuss in this chapter—bisexuals, leatherfolk, boy-loving men, and transsexuals—have in common that they are defined by their sexuality, and by the fact that this sexuality puts them in an uneasy relationship to the lesbian and gay community as a whole. In other respects they are very different, and we do not intend to suggest any social, biological, or political equivalence among them by dealing with them in the same chapter. With that disclaimer ...

Bisexuals

In chapter 5 we mentioned evidence that the reported incidence of bisexuality—the fraction of people who state that they experience significant sexual attraction to people of both sexes—has declined over the past few decades.

As a possible explanation for this change, we would suggest that the numbers of true bisexuals—people with a lifelong sexual attraction to both sexes—are fairly small, and have not changed over the years. In addition, however, there may be a pool of people who claim to experience bisexual attraction for more circumstantial reasons. This pool might include, for example, homosexual people who are forced by social pressures into opposite-sex relationships, or who have not yet fully accepted their sexual orientation. Supporting the existence of this latter group are data from a survey by *The Advocate* of its male readers, which reported that fully 40 percent of men who now consider themselves gay state that they did present themselves as bisexual earlier in their lives, usually between the ages of 18 and 25.[1] In other words, claiming a bisexual identity is a stage of the coming-out process for large numbers of gay men.

It seems reasonable to believe that liberalizing attitudes toward homosexuality are speeding and easing the coming-out process, and hence reducing the numbers of "circumstantial" bisexuals. We emphasize, however, that we are not trying to deny the existence of true bisexuality, nor are we predicting that bisexuals will disappear. On the contrary, we believe that true bisexuals will become more visible and accepted, and will have an easier time establishing a sense of community, when bisexuality is no longer used as a euphemism, refuge, or halfway house by people who are actually homosexual.

Just as homosexual men and women have to give up heterosexuality, or the expectation of heterosexuality, to develop their own identity as lesbians or gay men, so bisexuals also have to give up a prior sense of who they are. This prior sense may be either as heterosexual or homosexual. As Ann Fox, a bisexual psychotherapist, has pointed out, there are several barriers to making the transition to a self-affirming bisexual identity.[2] For a person coming from heterosexuality, an important barrier is homophobia, which may be strongly internalized just as it may be with lesbians and gay men. For a person coming from homosexuality, it is "biphobia," the discrimination against bisexual people that comes from both the heterosexual and homosexual camps. Biphobia may be expressed in such notions as that bisexuality is necessarily "fence-sitting," or that establishing sexual relationships with bisexual persons is futile because they will sooner or later need to express the other side of their sexual identity. In fact, there is no evidence that bisexuals are any more or less constant in their affections than lesbian, gay, or straight people, but when relationships with bisexuals do end there is a tendency to blame the breakup on some kind of biological imperative rather than the shortcomings of that particular relationship. Yet another expression of biphobia is the blame sometimes laid on bisexual women for supposedly bringing HIV into the lesbian community.

Another barrier to a bisexual identity has been the lack of a well-developed bisexual community. The community of lesbians and gay men is the safe space into which homosexual people come out. Bisexuals, however, must distance themselves from both the gay and straight communities without a strong sense of the social group which they are going to join. For this reason, bisexual activists have concentrated on creating such a community.

Efforts to develop a bisexual community reach back at least to the mid-1970s, when Maggi Rubenstein and Harriet Levy cofounded a Bisexual Center in San Francisco, and a Bisexual Forum was founded in New York. Although both organizations ceased operating in the early years of the AIDS epidemic, other local organizations, such the Boston Bisexual Women's Network, sprang up to replace them. Politically active groups also emerged. BiPOL, a group founded in San Francisco in 1983, was very active in demanding the inclusion of "bisexuals" in AIDS-prevention literature, and also ensured bisexual visibility by, for example, having the most outrageous floats in gay pride parades. On the East Coast, Lucy Friedland founded BICEP (Bisexual Community Engaging in Politics) as a media watchdog and lobbying organization in 1988. A national group, the Bisexual Network (BiNet) arose out of the bisexual contingent to the 1987 March on Washington, and the first National Bisexual Conference took place in San Francisco in 1990 under the sponsorship of BiPOL. An important anthology of writings by bisexuals, *Bi Any Other Name*, appeared in 1991 (see Further Reading).

In spite of these developments, it can hardly be said that there is yet a flourishing bisexual community with its own heritage, culture, or political agenda. Indeed, as discussed by Rebecca Shuster,[3] a possible strategy for bisexual activists, rather than aiming for a fully developed bisexual community, may be to concentrate on empowering bisexuals to claim simultaneous membership in both the lesbian/gay and the heterosexual communities. In a sense such a path may better express the nature of bisexuality, which is a *combination* of homosexuality and heterosexuality and not, as the Kinsey scale unfortunately suggests, something halfway between the two. It also might generate a group of people uniquely qualified to mediate between the lesbian and gay community and the larger heterosexual society. It will be interesting to see what direction bisexuals take as a group, as their identity as individuals becomes more widely recognized.

Leatherfolk

The word "leather," as currently used by gays and lesbians, has a broad range of meanings, from an interest in leather clothing and motorcycles through S/M,[4] fisting, dominance and submission, electro-torture and suffocation all the way to branding, piercing, and cutting as sexual or sexuo-theatrical acts. Leather has been the subject of numerous books that range from introductory manuals to psychological or socio-political studies.[5]

The connecting theme of the leather community is masculinity, in a certain sense of the word. But not only men are into this scene. In the more adventurous spirit of lesbian sexuality mentioned earlier, "leather" is an important component, especially for butch lesbians who identify as "dykes." One well-known lesbian who is into this scene is "Skeeter," a thirty-one-year-old "hard-core top and master" who was elected 1992 San Francisco Dyke Daddy. Skeeter emphasizes that masculinity and femininity are not tied to being a man or a woman. "I feel like a woman and I feel comfortable in my body and I don't feel the need to change gender," she told *Frontiers*,[6] "but one of the reasons that I don't feel I need to change genders is because I can take on a lot of attributes that one traditionally sees as male. So I don't feel like I am being denied anything. As a woman I get to be physically and emotionally strong; I get to be one of the boys. I also get to be really soft."

The first gay motorcycle club, the Satyrs, was founded in Los Angeles in the early 1950s; it included two members of the original Mattachine Society (see chapter 3). It was followed by similar clubs all round the country. Gay leather bars and clubs began to flourish in the mid-1960s and had their heyday in the late 1970s. In some cities they were aggregated in a particular area distinct from the more conventional gay centers; in San Francisco, for example, they were located in the area south of Market Street. Certain establishments, such as New York's Mine Shaft and San Francisco's Catacombs, which opened in the mid-1970s and closed in the mid-1980s, have achieved legendary status as temples of pre-AIDS sexuality.[7]

Organizations representing the gay and lesbian leather community have included the Chicago Hellfire Club, founded in 1971, and San Francisco's Samois, a lesbian S/M group that published a groundbreaking manifesto, *Coming to Power*, in 1981. Two groups founded in New York in 1980, the Gay Male S/M Activists (GMSMA) and the Lesbian Sex Mafia (LSM), have promoted understanding of S/M issues, training in techniques, and so on. The result has been an increasing acceptance of leatherfolk by the broader gay and lesbian community. Leather groups are now prominent participants in gay rights marches and cultural events. Magazines such as *Drummer* and *Leather Journal* cater to the leather community, and artists and photographers such as Tom of Finland and Robert Mapplethorpe have disseminated images of the leather culture to a not always receptive public.

What is the inner reality of leather and S/M? To some of its exponents, it represents catharsis, an almost literal "burning through" to mental health. According to journalist Mark Thompson, "S/M play is about healing the wounds that keep us from fully living; its intensity cauterizes our hurt and mends our shame.... Long-held feelings of inferiority or low self-esteem, grief and loss, familial rejection and abandonment, come to surface during S/M ritual. These extreme sensual acts undo memories of the past and thus provide passage between the unconscious underworld and the aboveworld of realization and present light."[8]

From leather as therapy it but a short step to leather as spirituality. Joseph W. Beam, for example, has written: "To extend into spirituality, a man may go head first as the yogis do, body first as fakirs do, heart first as monks do, or he may attempt the perilous task of going sexuality first as in certain tantric paths. Strangely, the submission required for bondage is not tantric in nature. It belongs to yet another class of spiritual paths which, because they act to bring all energy centers into alignment and move them 'up' together, are called 'noble' or 'balanced' ways. The spirit in the bondage dungeon is moving within all human energy centers at once."[9] We return to this topic in chapter 19.

The therapeutic and spiritual elements of leather are easier to perceive in the role of the person who is submissive or receives pain than in that of the person who is dominant or inflicts pain. Indeed, many people have seen the leather community's worship of the aggressively ultramasculine as a sign of devotion to fascism. Tom of Finland actually received his sexual initiation at the hands of the occupying Nazi soldiers, and his early art often featured swastikas and other Nazi imagery.[10] Such imagery is still found in the decor of some leather bars, and it is echoed in the military-style caps and other paraphernalia that form the leather uniform. Although it is obvious that these images are part of a fantasy, not an actual intention to go out and kill Jews or anyone else, the desirability of playing out such fantasies is open to debate.

Boy-Loving Men

If the leather community has had an uneasy relationship with the larger gay community, men who love boys are barely acknowledged as having anything to do with "regular" gay men. Indeed, there will be some who will be offended that we even mention such people in this book. During the publicity surrounding the lawsuit brought against singer Michael Jackson by a twelve-year-old boy and his parents in 1993,[11] many prominent representatives of the gay and lesbian community, such as Los Angeles Gay and Lesbian Community Services Center Director Lorri Jean, roundly denied that sexual attraction by an adult man to a twelve-year-old boy constituted homosexuality. Men who seek sex with children, it is widely claimed, are heterosexual regardless of the sex of the child.

Such a viewpoint might have some validity when discussing sex with very young children, but it is difficult to defend with respect to boys around the age of puberty or later. Sexual relationships between adult men and early- to mid-teenage boys were the very basis of cultures, such as that of classical Greece, that are universally recognized as homosexual (see chapter 2). Furthermore, men who are attracted to boys of pubertal or post-pubertal age are not generally attracted to girls, and if they have relations with adults it is with men, not women. To pick an example from among the safely dead, the philosopher Henry David Thoreau fell intensely in love with an eleven-year-old boy, Edmund Sewall, but also showed evidence of attraction to young adult men.[12]

The North American Man-Boy Love Association (NAMBLA) was founded in Boston in 1978, but is now based in New York. Its members are a mixture of "ephebophiles" (who are attracted to pubertal or post-pubertal boys), true pedophiles (who are attracted to pre-pubertal boys), and people who support NAMBLA's goals without being attracted to boys themselves. NAMBLA's central goal is the abolition of age-of-consent laws. According to NAMBLA, at least some children are capable of giving informed consent to sex, and of engaging in mutually satisfying sexual relationships with adult men. NAMBLA can claim some support for this viewpoint in psychological studies of boys who have engaged in such relationships.[13] NAMBLA does not advocate breaking the law or the legalization of non-consensual sex.

Although some prominent gay leaders such as Harry Hay have supported NAMBLA's right to participate in gay marches, the link between NAMBLA and the mainstream gay movement has always been tenuous. This became especially obvious in a dispute that broke out in late 1993 over NAMBLA's membership in the International Lesbian and Gay Association (ILGA), an umbrella organization of gay groups that had been appointed a consultative member of the United Nations' Economic and Social Council. After NAMBLA's membership became known, Senator Jesse Helms persuaded the U.S. Senate to withhold its annual payment to the United Nations until all its connections with "pedophile groups" were removed. In an improbable alliance, Helms was supported by Barney Frank, one of Congress's few openly gay representatives. "The question of age-of-consent doesn't seem to me to be a gay issue," he said, "and to buy into it is to buy into what I think is a very inaccurate and damaging argument—that gay people are more prone to have sex with children than other people."[14] Bowing to the pressure, ILGA members voted overwhelmingly to oust NAMBLA at their 1994 convention. But in spite of this action, ILGA itself was expelled from the U.N. Council in September 1994. This happened at the instigation of the U.S. delegation, which claimed that one ILGA member organization (the German Verein für sexuelle Gleichberechtigung) still advocated the repeal of age-of-consent laws. Thus ILGA failed to hold on either to its U.N. consultative status or to its principle of inclusivity.

Transsexuals

A transsexual is someone who is anatomically a woman, but has the subjective sense of being a man, or vice versa. As used by sexologists,[15] the word transsexual refers to two somewhat different groups of individuals. A "core group" of transsexuals has the following characteristics: a childhood history of marked gender nonconformity, gender nonconformity in adulthood as measured by sex-atypical scores in a number of standardized tests of "masculinity-femininity," a sexual attraction to persons of his/her own sex, aversion to the use of his penis/her vagina in sexual activity, a wish to live and be treated as a person of the other sex, and a wish to change his/her body as far as possible into that of the other sex. Another group of individuals also are very gender nonconformist and seek sex-reassignment surgery, but do not fit all the criteria listed above: for example they may be attracted to persons of the other sex, or they may enjoy using their penis/vagina in sex.

The "core group" of transsexuals fit the definition of "gay" or "lesbian" that we laid out in chapter 1, because they are sexually attracted to people of the same anatomical sex as themselves. (If they undergo sex-reassignment surgery they become heterosexual by this definition.) In fact, many "core-group" transsexuals do feel an affinity with lesbians and gay men, and show this by participating in gay pride parades, holding meetings at gay and lesbian community centers, and so on. Nevertheless, there is obviously a big psychological difference between feeling oneself to be a woman who is attracted to women (in other words a conventional lesbian) and feeling oneself to be a man who is attracted to women but who has the body of a woman (a core-group transsexual woman), or vice versa for men. Thus, many core-group transsexuals emphasize an identity separate from that of lesbians or gay men. Many of these transsexuals, while participating in "gay and lesbian" events and organizations, have demanded, often successfully, that these events or organizations be renamed to specifically include the words "transsexual" or "transgendered." Transsexuals who are attracted to the other sex (who are in the minority of all transsexuals who come to "gender-dysphoria" or sex-reassignment clinics) have even more reason to distance themselves conceptually from gays and lesbians, at least until they have sex-reassignment surgery.

Public awareness of transsexuality really began with the case of George (later Christine) Jorgensen, an American who underwent sex-reassignment surgery in Denmark in 1951. Since then, approximately 30,000 men and women have undergone this surgery worldwide, and there have been numerous books describing these people's experiences.[16] Transsexuality and sex-reassignment surgery are almost synonymous in many people's minds.

Surgery is indeed a sought-after goal for many transsexuals. Yet there are many reasons for emphasizing that surgery is not the centerpiece of transsexuality. First, transsexuality has existed in many, perhaps all cultures, long before the first sex-change operation. (Of course, emasculation of men was always an option, and it is still practiced by the *hijras* of India [see chapter 2].) Transsexual men and women have evidently found other ways to give expression to their identity than through surgery—through nonsurgical alterations in bodily appearance, cross-dressing, taking on the behaviors and social roles of the other sex, and passing as the other sex. Second, sex-reassignment surgery does not always lead to the desired psychological result, namely internal harmony. While many sex-changes have fulfilled the transsexual's expectations, others have been followed by disappointment, depression, even suicide. For that reason some centers have been performing fewer operations than in the past.

Even more significantly, there has been an increasing acceptance of gender variance that may make it less necessary for some transsexuals to change sex. Connie Norman, a Los Angeles-area activist and radio personality who had male-to-female reassignment surgery many years ago, told us that today she would not feel the need for it. "Nowadays it's OK to be nelly," she said. On the face of it, transsexuality is an entirely intrapsychic problem, an internal dissonance (it is still listed as a mental disorder in the APA's Diagnostic and Statistical Manual). Yet Norman's comment points up that social responses also play a significant role. This line of thinking has been explored by Kate Bornstein in her book *Gender Outlaw*:

> People think they have to hate their genitals in order to be transsexual. Well, some transsexuals do hate their genitals, and they act to change them. But I think that transsexuals do not "naturally" hate their birth-given genitals—I've not seen any evidence of that. We don't hate any part of our bodies that we weren't taught to hate. We're taught to hate parts of our bodies that aren't "natural"—like a penis on a woman, or a vagina on a man....[17] (p. 119)

Partly in response to these changing attitudes, there has been an increasing use of the term "transgender" in recent years. Although usage is by no means uniform, there is a tendency to use "transsexual" for people who are focused on sex-reassignment surgery and "transgendered" for people who claim the identity and role of the other sex but do not seek surgery.

To Bornstein, one answer to the "problem" of transsexuality is to get rid of society's entire concept of gender:

> Doing away with gender is key to doing away with the patriarchy, as well as ending the many injustices perpetrated in the name of gender inequity.... The struggle for women's rights (and to a lesser extent men's rights) is a vital stopgap measure until we can do away with the system whose very nature maintains the imbalance and prohibits any harmony." (p. 115)

It may be ambitious to think of doing away with gender, for several lines of research suggest that gender has at least in part a biological basis.[18] Yet there certainly does seem to be an increasing willingness to accept that gender is not a completely dichotomous trait—all masculine or all feminine—and is not inevitably tied to bodily sex. The comments of leatherwoman Skeeter, cited above, fit very much in the same vein. It is likely that the rise in the status of women over the past thirty years is a major factor behind the greater acceptance of gender variance: when women are more on a level with men, changing gender is less of a violation of caste.

Although transsexuals are considerably less numerous than conventional lesbians and gay men, they have organized to a remarkable extent. There are at least 100 groups and organizations nationwide that represent or cater primarily to transsexuals, and many more internationally.[19] The International Foundation for Gender Education, based in Waltham, Massachusetts, publishes a magazine, *Tapestry*, and sponsors an annual "Coming Together" convention. A radical group, Transexual[20] Menace, threatened to disrupt the 1994 Stonewall 25 march in New York in a dispute over the march's title. A more practical dispute concerned the criteria for the sex classification of transsexual athletes at the Gay Games prior to the march. Eventually the matter was resolved by allowing all athletes to choose their own category.

Further Reading

Bornstein, Kate. *Gender Outlaw: On Men, Women, and the Rest of Us.* New York: Routledge, 1994.

Feinberg, Leslie. *Stone Butch Blues.* Ithaca: Firebrand Books, 1994.

Hutchins, Loraine, and Lani Kaahumana. *Bi Any Other Name: Bisexual People Speak Out.* Boston: Alyson Publications, 1991.

Thompson, Mark, ed. *Leatherfolk: Radical Sex, People, Politics, and Practice.* Boston: Alyson Publications, 1991.

11
Special Interests

Gays and lesbians form all kinds of special-interest groups, some of which link people without regard to sexual orientation, while others are specifically gay-oriented. Of the latter group, we arbitrarily choose five to illustrate the diversity of interest-driven lesbian and gay society: the community of the New York vogueing balls, the lesbian and gay computer community, the lesbian softball leagues, gay and lesbian academics, and gay and lesbian publishers.

The Vogueing Balls

The drag balls of the Harlem Renaissance of the 1920s were mentioned in chapter 3. A tenuous thread of continuity links these events to the New York vogueing contests or "balls" that sprang up in the 1980s, contests that were the subject of Jenny Livingston's remarkable documentary film *Paris Is Burning*. Vogueing, which includes the dance of the same name, means the stylized parody of fashion shows. The contestants, mostly black or Latino gay men or male-to-female transsexuals, compete for trophies in the conventional runway categories like eveningwear and sportswear, but also in more unusual categories like military personnel, business executives, soap-opera stars, gang members, and so on.

What is so striking about the people who run and take part in the balls is the sense of community they have established. Mostly poor, often rejected by their families, and with little or no prospect of integration into the larger society, these men have constructed a parallel universe that is the focus of their lives. Starting as gay street-children, they enter one of the "houses" around which the contests are organized—the house of Xtravaganza, the house of Ninja, the house of Saint Laurent, and so on—and they take the name of the house as their new surname. Each house is run by a "mother," an older man who has established a reputation as a "legendary" contestant and who guides and trains the "future legends" who are under his protection. House members have a fierce allegiance to their house, comparable to that of gang members to their gang.

The clothes and accessories worn by the contestants are homemade, stolen, or received as presents from boyfriends or (if they are hustlers) from their clients. In many of the categories, the emphasis is on "realness" rather than on excess. Thus the atmosphere at the balls is not so much one of "camp" as of appreciation of detail and discerning connoisseurship.

What do the members of this community get out of their unusual life? A sense of belonging, certainly, of family and acceptance. And a place to act out an unrealizable dream: of wealth and power, of masculinity for some, or of femininity for others. To a viewer of *Paris Is Burning*, there is an infinite sadness in the vulnerability of many of the young people in the film. One of them, a waiflike transsexual who told of her desire to get her operation, marry into the gentry, and leave the world of the balls behind her, was brutally murdered during the making of the film. One can focus, as Essex Hemphill has in an insightful essay,[1] on the social injustice that makes this life of illusion necessary. But one can also recognize and admire an original, vibrant art form, whose practitioners do not merely lament their disconnection from the world they imitate, but also celebrate it.

Techno-Queers

People who live and breathe computers tend to be younger, better educated, and better-off that the average citizen. All these factors conspire to make the computer community remarkably gay-friendly. There is perhaps yet another reason: working with computers, and communicating though them, may instill a respect for intellect and clear thinking over nonintellectual aspects of personality such as sexuality.

The computer industry is years ahead of other industries in terms of its treatment of lesbian and gay employees. Many of the larger companies have domestic-partner policies that extend health and other benefits to same-sex partners. One large software company, Quark, Inc., was founded by a gay man, Tim Gill, who uses his personal fortune to the benefit of the gay and lesbian community (he was the largest contributor to the campaign that opposed the antigay Amendment 2 in Colorado).[2]

A San Francisco-based organization, Digital Queers, was founded in 1993 to help ensure that gay and lesbian organizations take advantage of the new technologies. Partly funded by the Gill Foundation, Digital Queers has helped overhaul the computer systems of organizations as large as the National Gay and Lesbian Task Force in Washington and as small as our own Institute of Gay and Lesbian Education in West Hollywood. It is particularly concerned with developing the on-line presence of gay organizations and gay people, in the belief that this is a cost-effective and efficient means to counter the big-dollar propaganda of the Christian right.

There have been gay and lesbian resources on the Internet for some years. An example is Sappho, a mailing list started in 1987 by Jean Marie Diaz. It now has about 600 subscribers and has spun off a number of splinter lists. It is open to all women, but is intended for the discussion of topics relevant to lesbian and bisexual women. Another important electronic facility on the Internet is the Queer Resources Directory, which is managed by a half dozen volunteers led by David Casti. The QRD has become the gay community's major clearinghouse for electronic information, particularly of a political nature. It receives more than 100,000 requests for information each month, and in response ships over 5 gigabytes of data—the equivalent of more that 2.6 million single-spaced printed pages or a small forest of trees. According to Casti, a strength of the QRD is its independence: it charges nothing for its services and receives no financial support from any other organization. It can therefore focus on providing an open line of communication among gay people without worrying about censorship, political correctness, and so on.

The Internet still presents problems of access for many people. Partly as a result, there has been a phenomenal growth of the private on-line services. AOL's Gay and Lesbian Forum, for example, includes announcements from community organizations such as the National Gay and Lesbian Task Force, downloadable files such as the judgments in important gay rights law cases and HIV research reports, current gay and lesbian news, a variety of special-interest message boards (from which the messages cited earlier were taken), a chat room for on-line gay discussions, and Heart-to-Heart, a section for personal ads. This latter service is much favored by gays and lesbians who do a lot of traveling and wish to meet congenial people in different parts of the country.

Besides these open or semi-open forums, there are also private electronic mailing lists that serve particular interest groups within the community. Dorsie Hathaway, a registered nurse who lives in Vancouver, Washington, manages nine such lists that are for groups such as politically active lesbians, disabled lesbians, lesbian parents, and so on. She told us that the lists provide not just a forum for special-interest discussions but a safe space where lesbians can be assured of acceptance and understanding, a space where putdowns and hostility ("flaming" in the jargon of the 'Net) are taboo. Hathaway also said that many lesbians, including herself, had found partners through electronic communication. "Men are so visual," she said, "when they finally meet face to face they often say 'No way!' But for me at least how a woman looks is secondary. Just by e-mail I know whether we're going to hit it off."

Lesbian Softball

Softball is the stereotypical lesbian pastime, and there are plenty of lesbians who fulfill the stereotype. Katy Wallace, a thirty-three-year-old law-school graduate who has played extensively on lesbian teams in the Seattle area, gave us her take on the attraction of the sport. "Many lesbians are naturally athletic," she said, "but in high school there's a mindset that you're not supposed to excel at something so physical—it's too masculine. Somehow we learned that there was something wrong with the gym teacher, she leered at the girls in the showers, you know—we didn't want to be like that. But when you're an adult and you join a lesbian team, it's really empowering, you get to relive the pleasure in sports, without any of the negatives. The environment is so supportive. It's just fun."

Wallace most recently played second base for the now-defunct team "R Place." Besides playing other local teams (both lesbian and nonlesbian), she traveled to regional and national events, such as the Gay World Series and the Gay Games. "It can really become your whole life," she said. "Maybe you practice twice a week, and play three times a week, and then on your day off, who's free to go out? The other team members, of course. Right now, that's all too much for me—I'm studying for the bar. For some people it's a way to date, to cruise, but mostly it's just a family, a pretty close-knit one. Seattle has lots of things for gays and lesbians to do, but in some places the softball team may be absolutely the only social outlet for lesbians."

Colleen Brady, a forty-two-year-old businesswoman who has been commissioner of the Emerald City Softball Association, explained the organization of lesbian and gay softball.

There's our local league—we'll have 12 lesbian teams in Seattle in '95, and about the same number of open teams—they're mostly gay men. Many of the teams are sponsored by businesses. Alex Veltri, who owns the Encore Bar and R Place and several other gay night spots, he's a big supporter of gay athletics here. There are teams of different levels of seriousness: competitive and recreational, though everyone is in it for the fun of it. For the regional tournaments, any team can go. For the Gay World Series, the winners in each level go, that's three men's teams and two women's teams. The World Series was held in Nashville in '94. About 35 cities in the U.S. and Canada send teams—about a hundred teams altogether. The event is run by the

North American Gay Amateur Athletic Association (NAGAAA). And then there's the Gay Games every four years.

Academia

In chapter 5 we cited a survey indicating that lesbians and gay men are twice as likely as heterosexuals to have received post-graduate education. It's therefore quite likely that lesbians and gay men are overrepresented on college faculties, but if so, their presence is much less obvious than it might be. The reasons for this are not hard to find. For one thing, the stigma of "corrupting the young," which causes such problems for gay and lesbian high school teachers, also operates, if not quite so forcefully, at the college level. In addition, the principle of academic freedom, which might seem to guarantee the freedom of gay expression at universities, is in practice hedged about with significant limitations. Most academics do not have tenure but would like to get it. Therefore their actions and words are often chosen with an eye to the likely reactions of senior faculty and administrators. By the time they do get tenure, they may be too set in their ways to come out of the academic closet. Other pressures to conform may come from funding sources, academic societies, publishers, and so on.

Yet recent years have seen a considerable increase in lesbian and gay visibility in academia, and especially in the numbers of lesbian and gay academics whose research and writings focus on gay issues. Some of these academics have banded together to start programs of gay and lesbian studies.

One of the pioneers among these programs has been the Center for Lesbian and Gay Studies (CLAGS) at the Graduate School of the City University of New York. CLAGS was founded by historian Martin Duberman in 1986. It organizes colloquia and conferences on such themes as "Gender Nonconformity and Homosexuality," "Great Dykes in American Literature," "The History of Lesbian and Gay African-Americans," and "Ethnographic Research on Male Prostitutes." It offers scholarships and fellowships in gay and lesbian studies, and it publishes a directory of gay and lesbian scholars around the country. CLAGS does not yet grant degrees, but it is working with other groups at the CUNY Graduate School to develop a Ph.D. program in multiculturalism, within which lesbian and gay studies could be an area of concentration.

The leader in college-level gay and lesbian education is San Francisco City College, a two-year community college that has offered courses on gay and lesbian topics since 1972. A gay and lesbian studies department was instituted in 1989; its current chair is art historian Jonathan David Katz.[3] Katz told us that about 2,000 students take classes in the department in an average year—a remarkable number even for a school as large as this one (it has over 90,000 students). The department currently offers twenty-one courses and is constantly expanding its curriculum: a new course on lesbians of color, for example, was added in 1995.

By way of giving some idea of the diverse approaches that lesbian and gay academics have taken to gay-related issues, we single out a few of these academics for mention. Lillian Faderman, a historian at California State University, Fresno, has illuminated the history of love between women in two notable volumes, *Surpassing the Love of Men* and *Odd Girls and Twilight Lovers*.[4] Faderman believes that sexual orientation is a product of life experiences—in *Odd Girls* she takes the time to cite no less than eleven scientific studies that repudiate a physiological basis for homosexuality. She is more interested in the modes of attraction between women, and how these modes have evolved through changing cultures, than in what women do or do not do in bed together. Faderman, unlike many gay and lesbian academics, succeeds in avoiding the buzzwords of queer theory and the polysyllabicity that so often usurps common sense[5]; her writing is direct and accessible, and she succeeds in bringing a rich diversity of historical women-loving women to life. Faderman and her partner, music professor Phyllis Irwin, were among the first lesbian couples to have a child through artificial insemination; their son Avrom was born in 1975.

Camille Paglia, who is on the faculty of the University of the Arts in Philadelphia, is a dazzling and combative critic whose book *Sexual Personae*[6] caused a minor sensation on its appearance in 1990. Whereas for Faderman sexuality is primarily a matter of relationships, for Paglia it is primarily a matter of identity. She recognizes, from civilization to civilization, the recurrence of certain sexual types, starting of course with men and women. To Paglia, intrinsic differences between men and women are at the origin of culture. Paglia infuriated feminists by asserting that "if civilization had been left in female hands, we would still be living in grass huts," but she also recognizes that men's "projective" nature brings disaster as well as triumph. Her "sexual personae" include the "femme fatale," the "nurturant male," the "woman-as-vampire," the "amazon," the "beautiful boy," and so on. An overarching theme in Paglia's work is the struggle between Dionysus and Apollo: between feeling, sensuality, and self-expression on the one hand, and divine beauty, order, and self-containment on the other. This conflict, says Paglia, is at the heart of gay works like Thomas Mann's *Death in Venice*, in which the beautiful, unreachable Tadzio is contrasted with the feverish Asiatic swamp of the Lido.

A lesbian academic of a very different flavor is Angela Pattatucci, an associate investigator in the Laboratory of Biochemistry at the National Cancer Institute in Bethesda, Maryland. Pattatucci has a Ph.D. in genetics from Indiana University in Bloomington. She was a co-author (with Dean Hamer and others) of the 1993 study that reported on the existence of a gene that influences sexual orientation in men (see chapter 4). Pattatucci is currently running a genetic, psychological, and health study of lesbians. Her aim is not to prove that lesbianism is genetic, but to identify genetic factors that influence many aspects of lesbians' lives, including their physical and mental health as well as their sexuality, and to understand how these factors interact with family environment, social forces, and so on. She is acutely aware that many gays and lesbians are alarmed by the prospect of genetic testing for homosexuality, with the attendant risks of selective abortion, employment testing, and so on. "Curing homosexuality genetically is not my goal," she told us.

"My purpose is not to see homosexuality as an abnormality, but as a normal variation of human behavior. Instead of focusing on what parents did wrong, I focus on what they do right. What has been instilled in children that gives them the strength to identify as gay or lesbian in a society that so stigmatizes them?" Pattatucci believes that it is important to stimulate public discussion of the ethical issues that surround all research on human genetics, and not just that aspect related to homosexuality.

Historian John Boswell of Yale University, who died in 1994, studied the development of Western attitudes toward homosexuality, particularly within the early Christian church. His 1980 book *Christianity, Social Tolerance and Homosexuality: Gay People in Western Europe from the Beginning of the Christian Era to the Fourteenth Century*[7] demonstrated that the history of homosexuality, even within the Christian tradition, is not one of unrelenting stigmatization and exclusion. On the contrary, Boswell traced a relatively gay-friendly tradition within the early Church that lasted until about the twelfth century. He suggested that the later Christian denunciation of homosexuality, for example by St. Thomas Aquinas, was not so much a product of received Christian tradition as it was a response to a general change in social attitudes, especially an increasing distrust of minorities that expressed itself in anti-semitism, homophobia, campaigns against witchcraft, and so on. As the book's subtitle indicates, Boswell believed that gays and lesbians existed throughout Western history, even if attitudes toward them changed considerably.

Frederick Whitam is a sociologist at Arizona State University, Tempe, who has studied homosexuality from a cross-cultural perspective. In *Male Homosexuality in Four Societies: Brazil, Guatemala, the Philippines and the United States* (co-authored with Robin Mathy)[8] and in other writings, Whitam has reported the existence of characteristic developmental patterns in the childhood histories of gay men and lesbians across widely different cultures. He distinguishes three kinds of homosexual people: those whose homosexuality is accompanied by marked gender nonconformity from childhood through adulthood, those who are moderately cross-gendered in childhood but become more conventionally gendered at adolescence (the majority of both lesbians and gay men fall in this group), and those who are conventionally gendered (except for their sexual orientation) throughout their lives. In strongly homophobic societies, Whitam believes, parents often detect and respond negatively to these early cross-gendered traits, contributing to their child's poor self-image long before he or she is aware of same-sex attraction. Whitam believes that the "social construction" of homosexuality is limited mainly to the ways in which society's responses to an individual's sexual orientation and gender identity mold his or her self-perception and self-esteem. Whitam's work has had a significant impact on local gay politics: the previously antigay editorial-page editor of the *Arizona Republic,* William Cheshire, switched dramatically to a progay stance after reading some of Whitam's papers, and this conversion probably played a role in the passage of a gay rights ordinance by the city of Phoenix in 1992.

Gay and lesbian studies, and multicultural studies in general, have done much to revivify academic thought in the United States over the last two decades. The "standard versions" of history, literary criticism, psychology, and so on have been uprooted and supplanted by a forest of new viewpoints. Scholarship has been reconnected with society. Lesbian and gay academics have had great success in rolling back the institutionalized homophobia that pervaded all these disciplines. Yet, as the distortions of the past are erased, new questions of objectivity arise. Where does "gay-positive" thought end and advocacy, even boosterism, begin? Will the gay community impose its own "standard versions," destined to become as fossilized as the old heterosexist dogmas? And will nongay scholars be allowed a voice in the debate?[9] As long as the battles over gay rights continue in the larger society, lesbian and gay studies will remain the focus of academic ferment and controversy.

Publishers

Until the recent upsurge of interest in gay- and lesbian-themed books, which has brought many mainstream publishers in the field, it fell largely to small gay- and lesbian-owned publishing houses to supply gays and lesbians with books that interested them. These houses still play a central role in creating a sense of shared experience in the gay and lesbian community.

The men and women who started these companies are people with a fervent belief in the redemptive power of the written word. Barbara Grier, for example, who founded Naiad Press with her partner Donna J. McBride in 1973, previously edited and wrote for *The Ladder*, the magazine of the Daughters of Bilitis, which for many lesbians was their sole lifeline to the lesbian community (see chapter 3). Grier told us that if Naiad did not exist, many lesbians would read nothing, something she would consider a tragedy. Naiad is located in Tallahassee, Florida. Although the first years of its existence were a struggle—no one was paid until 1982—the company now employs eight in-house staff and pays royalties to over 100 authors. Naiad has published over 300 books, of which about 200 are still in print, and it currently puts out about 24 new titles a year. Best known are its lesbian-themed romances and mystery novels (Katherine Forrest is probably the house's most well-known author). A good many of these books could fairly be described as "pulp fiction," with titles like *Passion's Legacy*, by Lori Page ("Sarah is swept into the arms of Augusta Pym in this delightful historical romance"), but it also publishes more substantial novels, by authors like Diane Salvatore and Jane Rule, as well as some nonfiction works and new editions of classic lesbiana like Gertrude Stein's *Lifting Belly*. Although Naiad's books are written primarily to entertain, the social issues that lesbians face are never far from the surface.

Sasha Alyson started Alyson Publications as a distribution company in the late 1970s, but began publishing his own books in 1980. Located in Boston, Alyson publishes a mix of fiction and nonfiction, and has so far put out about 200 titles. The company is notable for its dedication to minorities within the gay and lesbian community. For example, it recently published the first book about the gay deaf community, *Eyes of Desire* (see chapter 9), and it has put out many books for children and young people, including its ever-popular *Confessions of a Rock Lobster* by high school activist Aaron Fricke (see chapter 15). Two its children's books, *Heather Has Two Mommies* (by Lesléa Newman) and *Daddy's Roommate* (by Michael Willhoite), vie every year for the number-one slot on the list of books most frequently banned by school boards. A few of its adult books, such as Pat Califia's *Doing It for Daddy* (which deals with sadomasochism), have sparked controversy even within the lesbian and gay community.

Asked about the trend toward mainstream publishing of gay- and lesbian-themed books, Alyson's director, Alistair Williamson, conceded that Alyson cannot compete with the New York houses for "name" gay and lesbian authors. But he emphasized that the boom in gay books has helped everyone who publishes them. Because many of the chain bookstores now have a "Gay and Lesbian" section, for example, Alyson's books now have a place to sit and be noticed, when previously they got lost within inappropriate categories.

A number of small lesbian feminist presses have made important contributions to lesbian culture. The Kitchen Table: Women of Color Press, cofounded by Barbara Smith and Audre Lorde, is best known for the 1983 classic *This Bridge Called My Back* by Gloria Anzaldúa and Cherrie Moraga. Spinsters Ink in Duluth publishes four to six books per year, including a mix of fiction (such as Maureen Brady's novel *Give Me Your Good Ear*) and nonfiction (including Audre Lorde's *The Cancer Journals*, and *Why Can't Sharon Kowalski Come Home?* by Karen Thompson and Julie Andrzejewski). The press was founded in the late 1970s by Maureen Brady and Judith McDaniel, and it is currently owned by Joan Drury, a lesbian writer and activist whose other projects include the Harmony Women's Fund and the Norcroft Retreat for women writers. According to Spinsters' operations manager Nancy Walker, the company employs seven women, not all of whom are lesbian, and it depends to some extent on financial support from Drury. It also has its own softball team. Another important publishing company, Aunt Lute Press, based in San Francisco, was affiliated for a time with Spinsters Ink, but is now an independent nonprofit; it is best known for publishing poetry by women of color.

III Health

The majority of health issues that face lesbians and gay men are the same as those that face everyone regardless of their sexual orientation. But certain aspects of physical and mental health have special relevance to gays or lesbians, or need to be viewed in the particular context of gay or lesbian life. We deal with some of these—sexually transmitted diseases, breast cancer in lesbians, psychological problems, substance abuse, domestic violence, and gay-bashing—in chapter 12. Above all else, however, looms AIDS. Chapter 13 takes an objective look at AIDS as a medical condition; it provides the basic information about the disease with which everyone should be familiar. In chapter 14 we consider AIDS in its personal, communal, and political aspects. We describe ways in which AIDS, besides tearing the gay community apart, has also brought it together.

12
General Health Issues

In this chapter we survey a number of areas of physical and mental health that may be especially significant for lesbians or gay men. We then examine how gays and lesbians have responded to the general neglect of gay and lesbian health concerns by forming organizations that address these concerns and that attempt to influence national health care policy.

Breast Cancer

Women in general face about a 10–11 percent lifetime probability of contracting breast cancer. In the United States, about 180,000 women are diagnosed annually with the disease; in 1994, 46,000 women died of it. The number of new diagnoses has increased considerably in recent years, but most of this increase is due to the introduction of more sensitive diagnostic procedures. The death rate from breast cancer (after adjustment for changes in the age distribution of the population) has remained almost unchanged over the past sixty years, and women are about ten times more likely to die from heart disease than from breast cancer. In spite of these facts, there is a widespread misperception that breast cancer is the number-one health issue for women, and that it is increasing in epidemic fashion.

It has been suggested that the incidence of breast cancer may be higher among lesbians than among heterosexual women. There are no actual statistics comparing the incidence of the disease in the two groups. Among lesbians themselves, the belief in a higher incidence comes in part from direct experience of the disease in themselves or among their acquaintances. Lesbians have also been sensitized to the disease by written accounts, most notably by Audre Lorde's *Cancer Journals*, which documented her many-year struggle with breast cancer.[1]

Consideration of the risk factors for breast cancer lends some support to the idea that lesbians may suffer disproportionately from the disease. The known risk factors whose incidence might conceivably be elevated among lesbians are: nonmaternity, late age at first pregnancy, above-average height and weight, high-fat diet, and high consumption of alcohol. Of these, the most attention has been focused on nonmaternity. Actually, the incidence of nonmaternity does not appear to be much higher among lesbians than heterosexual women (see chapter 5), although the figures may change when one considers subgroups of lesbians, such as those who were aware of a lesbian orientation from an early age. In any case, nonmaternity by itself is a relatively weak risk factor, raising the incidence of the disease by less than twofold. Obesity and alcohol abuse may be more common among lesbians than among straight women, although the data are sparse (see below).

It is possible that the risk factors conspire together to produce a breast cancer rate than is severalfold higher among lesbians than among heterosexuals. In addition, it is possible that lesbians perform fewer breast self-examinations, receive less frequent mammographic examinations, and rely more frequently on unorthodox treatments than heterosexual women.[2] If so, one might expect breast cancer to be more advanced at diagnosis and to be more frequently fatal. Alternatively, there may in fact be no great difference in incidence or death rates in the two groups.

Ideally, one would resolve the issue by means of large-scale prospective studies. Unfortunately, past breast cancer surveys have not inquired about the participants' sexual orientation. This is of course part of a general neglect of lesbian issues in medicine and medical politics. One recent study of breast cancer from a feminist perspective, Sharon Batt's *Patient No More*,[3] steers clear of lesbians except to quote Audre Lorde. Even a prominent, out-of-the-closet lesbian doctor, Susan Love, barely mentions lesbians in her otherwise excellent book on breast cancer.[4]

Breast cancer has of course been a major focus of feminist activism. This activism has been very successful in drawing public attention to the disease and in increasing the levels of research funding devoted to it. Comparing breast cancer with prostate cancer, for example (a disease that causes about the same number of deaths per year in men), breast cancer receives about threefold greater media coverage and fourfold higher research spending.[5] This spending has paid off, for example, with the recent discovery of genes that predispose to breast cancer; this discovery will permit women who carry such genes to be offered earlier and more frequent breast examinations, and may also lead to improved treatments. Activism has also encouraged women to participate more directly in treatment decisions, for example in choosing between "lumpectomy" and mastectomy as the treatment for early stage cancer. Whether or not this participation results in better medical treatment, it clearly is of psychological benefit to some women with the disease. Probably lesbians are among those who benefit most from such participation, because they are likely to resent a paternalistic style of doctoring.

Sexually Transmitted Diseases

Sexually transmitted diseases, or STD's, include syphilis, gonorrhea, nongonococcal urethritis, vaginitis (due to a variety of organisms), herpes, venereal warts, chlamydial infections, and yeast infections. Viral hepatitis can also be transmitted sexually. (For a discussion of AIDS, which is also commonly transmitted through sex, see chapters 13 and 14.)

Most STD's are characterized by lesions at the site of infection. This site is not necessarily on the genitalia, however; gonorrhea, for example, can develop in the throat as a consequence of oral sex. Some STD's can spread to become systemic diseases: before the introduction of antibiotics, syphilis sometimes progressed to a fatal neurological disorder. Untreated gonorrhea in women can involve the internal reproductive tract and cause sterility. Viral hepatitis does not show symptoms at the point of infection (usually oral ingestion of the organism in the case of sexual transmission).

Some STD's, such as syphilis, respond readily to antibiotics. The treatment of gonorrhea has been complicated by the emergence of drug-resistant strains of the causative organism, but it is still curable in the great majority of cases. Herpes cannot be eradicated although the local symptoms can be alleviated by drug treatment. Hepatitis is generally a self-limiting infection, although progressive liver disease and liver cancer occur in some patients.

The risk of acquiring STD's depends on the number and identity of one's sexual partners, as well as the use or nonuse of safe-sex practices. Gay men tend to have more sex partners than lesbians, and thus to be at greater risk for STD's. The incidence of STD's in the gay male population declined in the early years of the AIDS epidemic, as gay men reduced the numbers of their sex partners and adopted the use of condoms. More recently, however, STD's have been making a comeback, especially in the younger age groups, presumably as a result of a return to unsafe sex and to greater promiscuity. It should be noted that the use of condoms is not as effective in preventing non-AIDS STD's as it is in preventing HIV transmission, because lesions can occur at sites not covered by the condom.

According to Jesus Ornelas, who is Senior Epidemiologist at the Los Angeles Gay and Lesbian Community Services Center, lesbians particularly need to look beyond their "protected" status and consider their actual sex practices. Many women who identify as lesbian nevertheless have sex with men, or with women who themselves have sex with men. Furthermore, there are lesbians who, contrary to stereotype, have large numbers of sex partners. Because it is difficult in practice to be sure of one's partners' sex history or health status, Ornelas emphasizes that all sexually active lesbians should be concerned about the possibility of acquiring STD's, and should seek prompt medical advice if symptoms develop. "If you're engaged in sex," Ornelas says, "you're at risk for something."

Obesity

There is a widespread belief that lesbians are more prone to obesity than other groups in the population. Although there are no statistically valid studies comparing the incidence of obesity in lesbians and heterosexual women, there is good reason to think that obesity is a major health concern for lesbians. In the National Lesbian Health Care Survey,[6] for example, which was based on questionnaires completed by nearly two thousand lesbians in 1984, being overweight was the most commonly cited health problem—one-third of the respondents said they were overweight, and two-thirds said they overate sometimes or frequently. In addition, many of the respondents cited other problems that can be caused or exacerbated by obesity, such as back pain or heart disease.

Attitudes toward obesity (usually defined as a body weight at least 25 percent above the actuarially ideal weight, caused by increased body fat) vary greatly. Some lesbians question whether lesbians are in fact any more likely to be overweight than heterosexual women. Others acknowledge a high rate of obesity among lesbians, but treat it as a positive phenomenon—a sign of liberation from the tyranny of the male gaze, or a return to the pre-patriarchal ideal of the fecund mother-goddess. In this vein, two bisexual women, Laurie Edison and Debbie Notkin, are collaborating on a book of photographic portraits of very fat women, to be titled *Women En Large.* In an interview with *Lesbian News,* Edison said: "Hopefully, this book will appeal to the women [who] are taught that being fat is the demon and taught to live in fear of that. We would like to help women let go of that fear."[7] A San Francisco group, Fat Lip Readers Theater, puts on performances and readings whose message is "Change the World—Not Your Body!" They have also made a video on the same theme, entitled "Nothing to Lose."

Still others consider that obesity is indeed a health problem for many lesbians and attribute it to the anxiety, poor self-image, and stress of belonging to a stigmatized group. However, there is little evidence that fat lesbians are more conflicted about their lesbian identity, or have been exposed to more stress (aside from stress caused by the obesity itself) than lesbians who are close to their ideal weights. Generally ignored is yet a fourth possibility, that the biological factors predisposing to homosexuality in women might also predispose to obesity, at least in a subset of lesbians.[8]

Alcohol and Drug Abuse

Numerous studies have reported that substance abuse is more prevalent among lesbians and gay men than among heterosexuals. According to a large-scale survey conducted in the late 1980s,[9] patterns of alcohol consumption among gays and lesbians differ in three major respects from those found among heterosexuals. First, drinking is as prevalent among lesbians as it is among gay men, whereas in the general population men drink more than women. Second, drinking does not decline with age in the homosexual population as it does among heterosexuals. Third, the increased rate of drinking among gays and lesbians is primarily caused by increased numbers of moderate drinkers; heavy drinking (contrary to the conclusions of some previous studies) is about equally common in the homosexual and heterosexual populations. The same study concluded that marijuana and cocaine use is elevated among gay men and lesbians.

Numerous factors have been proposed to contribute to the elevated use of alcohol and drugs by gays and lesbians.[10] Bars are their traditional meeting places, and bars still offer them the only congenial social environment in some communities. The stresses of discrimination, isolation, and being closeted, or equally those of coming out, all may predispose to substance abuse. Social factors that tend to reduce drinking after the teenage years, such as marriage and parenthood, are not operative for some gays and lesbians. In some groups, especially among young black men, drinking may be perceived as a validation of masculinity that gay individuals can ill afford to flout. Alcohol or drugs may be used by individuals who are conflicted about their sexual orientation to overcome inhibitions against participation in gay or lesbian sex. They may also be used to enhance or facilitate sexual acts, or to erase the memory of them. Drugs also are commonly used to ward off fatigue during all-night sessions at gay dance clubs.

The gay community as a whole has not squarely faced the problems posed by alcohol and drug abuse. These problems of course include the general medical and psychological consequences of substance abuse. In addition, substance abuse is believed to contribute in a major way to unsafe sex practices and the consequent spread of HIV infection, deterioration of the immune system in those who are already HIV-positive, employment problems, the breakdown of relationships, gay and lesbian domestic violence, prostitution, and of course traffic accidents. One reason that these problems do not receive adequate acknowledgment and discussion is that the alcoholic beverage industry has effectively muzzled the gay press through the heavy infusion of advertising dollars. It also cultivates a positive image in the community through sponsorship of gay organizations and AIDS fundraising events.

Lesbians and gay men who are alcohol-dependent need treatment services tailored to their needs. Programs designed for heterosexual men and women not only are likely to ignore the special factors that contribute to drinking by lesbians and gays, they also may create a climate in which lesbians and gays feel unable to discuss their sexual orientation, and hence to feel emotionally excluded from the group or alienated from the therapist. These problems are magnified when HIV is also an issue.

Alcoholics Anonymous has several hundred groups for gays and lesbians around the country. There are also a hundred or so gay-focused services provided by social service agencies, outpatient clinics, and so on. There are a handful of inpatient facilities for chemically dependent lesbians and gays, of which

Pride Institute, whose main facility is near Minneapolis, is the best known.[11] Pride Institute's approach is to combine the classic twelve-step program developed by Alcoholics Anonymous with specifically gay-positive programs. It establishes an environment in which gay lifestyles are seen as positive alternatives to heterosexual lifestyles, and it attempts to instill appropriate ways of coping with discrimination and rejection that may come from the client's family of origin or society in general. After an intake phase, in which the patient's family background, sexuality, relationships, and chemical dependencies are assessed, the patient enters a month-long treatment program that includes individual and group therapy, relaxation training, instructional sessions, twelve-step recovery meetings, recreation, meditation or prayer, and a homophobia program. After-care includes groups and workshops at the institute, twelve-step groups outside the institute, and a requirement for volunteer work in the gay and lesbian community. The institute also runs a family program for the lovers, friends, and relatives of inpatients. The aim of this program is to educate the family about alcoholism, help them confront their feelings about the patient's homosexuality, introduce the twelve-step principles, and identify co-alcoholics and refer them for treatment. The Pride Institute's executive director, Joseph Neisen, told us that the institute has a relatively good track record: at fourteen months after discharge, 74 percent of clients remain continuously abstinent from alcohol, and 67 percent remain abstinent from all drugs.

Domestic Violence

Most people conceive of domestic violence as being perpetrated by men on women, and indeed this probably does account for the great majority of cases. However, women do sometimes beat their male partners, and violence also occurs within the context of lesbian and gay male relationships.

In the past, violence within same-sex relationships has been hidden, either because the community as a whole did not want to deal with such a negative aspect of homosexuality, or because the victims were prevented from making the violence known by shame, embarrassment, or a fear of revealing their homosexuality. More recently the community's interest in same-sex domestic violence has been spurred by a number of articles and books,[12] as well by news stories of actual cases.

All victims of partner abuse, whether heterosexual or homosexual, share certain reactions. Often they are afraid to come forward for fear of provoking more attacks. Because of low self-esteem, they often feel that they are to blame for the violence perpetrated against them. Many suffer from classic post-traumatic stress syndrome: they feel numb, they disassociate; they can become hypervigilant or depressed.

Although the type of abuse seen within gay and lesbian couples is usually similar to that found in heterosexual relationships, lesbian and gay male perpetrators may also use the threat of outing the victim as part of the abuse or as a means to perpetuate it. Both gay male and lesbian victims may fail to come forward on account of fear of losing their job, friends, or family. A lesbian might also find it harder to come out as a victim of abuse because of the myth that abuse does not occur between two women, that lesbian relationships are loving and never violent. Thus her reporting it somehow represents a betrayal of the lesbian community and the concept of a lesbian utopia.

Victims often receive no support from friends. It is hard for people outside the relationship to understand the abuse, sometimes even to recognize it. Victims who broach the subject may be told, "She's smaller than you are, you should be able to handle her," or "He's such a nice guy, I can't believe he'd do something like that." If friends are aware of the abuse, they often have difficulty understanding why the victims stay, or even why they got involved with their abuser in the first place. Informing others of the abusive relationship may cause the victim to become isolated rather than to receive help.

Those victims who finally do come forward enter a system that is not prepared for them. Domestic violence laws in some states exclude same-sex couples or offer a less serious penalty for same-sex abuse. There is little provision for battered lesbians in shelters, and almost none for battered gay men. Shelter staffs are not usually educated about lesbian and gay issues, and even if they are, it is possible that other residents may be homophobic and rejecting. Families of origin, which provide an alternative to shelters for victims of partner abuse, are problematic as a refuge for gays and lesbians, since victims often fear that their families will blame what has happened on the victim's homosexuality rather than on a particular homosexual perpetrator.

Thanks in part to increasing awareness of the issues, services directed at gay and lesbian victims of domestic violence are making an appearance in some cities, especially New York, San Francisco, Los Angeles, Seattle, and Minneapolis. These services include hot lines, legal advice, shelters with staff trained in gay and lesbian partner abuse issues, and so on. Unfortunately, most of the country still lacks such resources.

Gay-Bashing

When a lesbian or gay man is assaulted on account of her or his homosexuality, the incident may qualify as a hate crime under state or federal statutes, thus making the perpetrator liable to increased penalties (see chapter 15). Nevertheless, hate crimes often go unreported because victims are afraid of the consequences of coming forward.

Of the hate crimes that *are* reported, the great majority are against gay men.[13] In Los Angeles in 1994, for example, there were 265 reported hate crimes directed against gay men and 30 against lesbians.[14]

Victims of any violent crime experience certain common psychological symptoms, in addition to any physical injuries they may sustain. They feel more vulnerable. They can no longer maintain the denial most of us do that something like this "could never happen to me." They may also experience sleep disturbances, uncontrollable crying, agitation and restlessness, increased use of drugs, and deterioration in personal relationships. In the context of a gay-bashing, the victim may develop feelings of worthlessness or self-blame associated with his or her homosexuality; in other words, the incident may reawaken an internalized homophobia.[15] Gay-bashing incidents can be especially traumatic for people in the early stages of their coming-out processes, because they have not yet developed a sufficiently strong gay or lesbian identity that might offer them some protection from the psychological insult. Even verbal assaults can threaten the identity development of lesbians and gay men, reinforcing as they do the notion that they are a stigmatized group and that physical violence may not be far away.

Mental Health

Prior to 1973, homosexuality itself was officially listed as a mental disorder by the American Psychiatric Association (see chapter 3). Since that time, attitudes within the mental health professions have improved to the point that, with a few exceptions, homosexuality is regarded as a normal variation of human nature, just as capable of contributing to a healthy mental, social, and sexual life as is heterosexuality.

In spite of the marked improvement in attitudes, bias can still influence the treatment received by lesbians and gay men from mental health professionals. For example, therapists may wrongly attribute the cause of a client's problems to her or his homosexuality, and therefore inappropriately focus discussions on that issue. Gay identity development and gay relationships may be seen from a heterosexual perspective. Bias may also exist in the area of family relationships: a therapist may conclude, for example, that the child of a lesbian or gay man has problems because of his or her parent's homosexuality.[16]

Of course, being homosexual does bring with it potential mental health problems, just as being heterosexual does. These problems include internalized homophobia, a lack of integrated self- and sexual identity, family conflicts, relationship difficulties, sexual dysfunction, compulsive sexual activity, chemical abuse or dependency, AIDS anxiety, and the effects of aging in a youth-oriented culture.[17]

Among these problems, the failure to fully integrate one's identity is perhaps the central one. As a consequence of exposure to antigay forces during childhood and adolescence, gays and lesbians often develop an unnaturally objective view of their own sexual orientation, seeing it from the outside, as it were, rather than simply experiencing it or acting on it as heterosexual people do. They tend consciously or unconsciously to develop strategies for coping with perceived conflicts between their identity as homosexual and other aspects of identity, such as their membership in ethnic groups, heterosexually oriented families and work environments, and so on. These strategies, which typically change over the life course, may not permit the individual to perceive him- or herself as a unified, coherent human being.

One common strategy is assimilation. As noted by Carmen de Monteflores,[18] assimilation is a survival mechanism in which members of stigmatized groups, including gays and lesbians, learn the language of the dominant group. Although of great practical utility, assimilation is largely a matter of externals, and it may conceal a sense of self-betrayal or inner splitting.

Opposed to assimilation is confrontation, in which individuals face up to their difference from the majority and acknowledge it publicly. Coming out, the central technique of confrontation, has been the subject of innumerable studies.[19] It has several aspects, including anger at previous rejection of one's homosexual identity by oneself and others, transformation of a perceived psychic deficit into a strength, a recasting of the past, and public acknowledgment of one's new self-awareness and group identity. Coming out is an extended process, not a single event, and may involve retrograde as well as forward steps. Coming out can proceed to a stage of "superminority" status, in which the individual denounces the majority culture and wages a continual "more-oppressed-than-thou" battle against it. According to some writers, such as Carmen de Monteflores, this may signal an impasse in the development of a mature identity, which must include a recognition of sameness as well as difference.

Yet another coping strategy is ghettoization, which may involve actual residence in a gay-identified locality (see chapter 7), or the adoption of the slang, dress, and attitudes of the gay and/or lesbian subculture. A thoroughly positive strategy in terms of gay identity development, ghettoization nevertheless may be accompanied by a rejection of other aspects of identity and hence may offer a hindrance to full identity integration. As discussed in other chapters, members of ethnic or religious minorities, the deaf, teenagers, and old people may feel compelled to conceptually abandon these other memberships in order to fit in with the gay and lesbian community. Alternatively, an individual may commute (physically or emotionally) between the gay ghetto and other sites of allegiance.

No doubt the desirable endpoint of identity development is the harmonious integration of different aspects of identity, a state Vivienne Cass terms "identity synthesis."[20] Probably no one fully attains such a state, given the complex and contradictory loyalties to which everyone is subject. But there are several ways in which progress in this direction can be facilitated. One is the full acknowledgment of an individual's diverse identities: when a Latina lesbian, for example, can acknowledge the importance of her lesbian identity to the Latino community, of her Latino identity to the gay and lesbian community, and of her identity as a woman to all groups, she is on the road to an integrated identity.[21] Another is the formation of contacts with others who share to some extent the individual's own combination of identities, as for example when an old gay man joins an organization of the gay elderly. Finally, the gay community itself helps greatly in this process when it acknowledges and celebrates the diversity of its members, just as it hinders the process when it attempts to impose a single cultural standard.

Sexual Dysfunction

Among the sexual dysfunctions that gay men most commonly bring to the attention of therapists are lack of sexual desire, difficulty in achieving penile erection, difficulty in reaching orgasm, and premature ejaculation. Such dysfunctions can have any number of causes including neurological disorders, intoxication, stress, and so on. According to Kenneth George and Andrew Behrendt,[22] a common cause of the lack of sexual desire in gay men is internalized homophobia arising from traumatic experiences in early life, and it can be relieved by working through those experiences.

In the context of a stable relationship, a perceived absence of sexual desire on the part of one partner may reflect a mismatch between the two partners in terms of their progression through the normal stages of a relationship. David McWhirter and Andrew Mattison have pointed out that declining sexual activity is a common feature of gay male relationships that last more than about two years; if desire declines earlier for one man than the other, the stage discrepancy is perceived as a problem.[23] The problem may be alleviated though discussion of the issue, or it may resolve itself naturally as the other partner "catches up."

Among lesbian couples, a marked decline in sexual activity over time is very common. Two years after the beginning of their relationship, according to one study,[24] only 37 percent of lesbian couples are still making love at least once a week or more. In contrast, 73 percent of heterosexual couples are making love this frequently. All kinds of reasons have been proposed to account for the phenomenon; most commonly, though, psychologists have focused on the extreme merging of identities that may occur within a lesbian relationship, a merging which may destroy the sense of "other" fundamental to erotic desire.[25]

According to Marny Hall,[26] an important therapeutic response to the de-eroticization of lesbian relationships is to normalize it, that is to make clear to the couple that their experience is common. In many cases, in fact, Hall recommends prohibiting all sex for a period of time, thus relieving the pressure to perform and demonstrating the therapist's indifference to standards of frequency. This breathing space can be followed, if the couple desires, by boundary-setting exercises and physical therapy (such as stroking sessions), which may lead to an increase in sexual desire and sexual activity in the relationship.

Health Care and the Community

Numerous community organizations are devoted to the health care issues of gays and lesbians. Clinics, either freestanding or associated with gay and lesbian community centers, exist in most large cities. Eleven of the largest of these clinics, which engage in research and policy development as well as patient care, joined in 1992 to form the National Alliance of Lesbian and Gay Health Clinics (NALGHC), in order to help promote a national health care agenda for lesbians and gay men. In 1994 it merged with another organization, the National Lesbian and Gay Health Foundation (NLGHF), an educational foundation that has been representing gay and lesbian health educators and health care providers since 1980. The combined organization (the National Lesbian and Gay Health Association or NLGHA) has three major missions: to respond to the AIDS epidemic, to increase the availability of lesbian health services, and to participate in the advancement of national health care reform on behalf of gays and lesbians. The association's new executive director, Christopher Portelli, immediately became embroiled in a controversy over HIV home-testing kits (see chapter 14).

The National Gay and Lesbian Task Force (see chapter 16) has also devoted considerable resources to health care issues. In 1993 it assembled a group of leading gay and lesbian advocates to make health care recommendations to the Secretary of Health and Human Services, Donna Shalala.[27] The recommendations stressed the importance of focusing attention on lesbians (especially the inclusion of lesbians in research), people of color (especially in HIV-prevention programs), youth (suicide prevention, services for runaways and homeless youth), and the elderly (training of service providers in the needs of old lesbians and gay men). They also emphasized the need for expanded programs directed against substance abuse, sexually transmitted diseases, and antigay violence. In the same year the task force issued a separate report on lesbian health, focusing on the barriers to health care that face lesbians, and the health risks that lesbians face in the areas of cancer, HIV, and substance abuse.[28]

Because the task force and NLGHA wield so little political influence in Washington, these reports and recommendations probably serve more to focus the gay and lesbian community's own attention on its health care needs, rather than to bring about any significant governmental action in the listed areas. Lesbian health concerns in particular were largely ignored by the gay and lesbian community during the first decade of the AIDS epidemic, and are only now beginning to receive the attention they require. Numerous health care clinics and services aimed at lesbians have been founded, or their services greatly expanded, during the last five years; they include the Lesbian AIDS Project in New York, the Mautner Project for Lesbians with Cancer in Washington, D.C., the Lyon-Martin Clinic in San Francisco, and the Audre Lorde Clinic in Los Angeles. In addition, articles dealing with the medical care of lesbians are beginning to appear in the mainstream medical press (see Further Reading). Nevertheless, in the face of the continuing onslaught of AIDS on the gay male population, issues of lesbian health continue to take a back seat.

There are numerous organizations for lesbians and gay men within the health care professions, including doctors, nurses, pharmacists, psychologists, and psychiatrists. The Gay and Lesbian Medical Association (GLMA), founded in 1981 as the American Association of Physicians for Human Rights, has about 1,200 member physicians. Like many gay and lesbian professional organizations, its has in part a social function, but it also seeks to combat homophobia within the medical profession and to promote the best possible health care for lesbians and gay men.

Further Reading

Coleman, Eli, ed. *Integrated Identity for Gay Men and Lesbians: Psychotherapeutic Approaches for Emotional Well-Being*. New York: Harrington Park Press, 1988.

Garnets, Linda D., and Douglas C. Kimmel, eds. *Psychological Perspectives on Lesbian and Gay Male Experiences*. New York: Columbia University Press, 1993. (An anthology of reprinted articles on a variety of topics including mental and physical health, alcoholism, etc.).

White, J., and W. Levinson. "Primary Care of Lesbian Patients." *Journal of General Internal Medicine* 8 (1993): 41–47.

13
AIDS: The Disease

The acquired immunodeficiency syndrome, or AIDS, has occupied a central place in the life of the gay community since the early 1980s. By the end of 1994, 440,000 Americans, the majority of them gay or bisexual men, had been diagnosed with the disease, and 270,000 of these had died. We have described the early history of the epidemic (now a pandemic) in chapter 3. In the present chapter we take a close look at AIDS as a medical phenomenon.

The Virus and Its Life Cycle

AIDS is a disorder of the immune system, caused by infection with the human immunodeficiency virus, or HIV. Like all viruses, HIV cannot live as an independent organism. Rather, it requires a cellular host to provide the nutrients and cellular machinery needed for replication. In the case of HIV, the main host is a type of human white blood cell known as the CD4 lymphocyte (sometimes called the T4 or T-helper cell), but some other cell types, both within the immune system and elsewhere in the body, can also be infected.

HIV actually exists in two major variants, known as HIV1, the kind responsible for virtually all infections in the United States, and HIV2, a form that exists (along with HIV1) in certain parts of Africa. HIV2 is closely related to viruses that cause immunodeficiency syndromes in various species of African monkeys (so-called simian immunodeficiency viruses or SIV). It has been speculated that HIV evolved from SIV at some time in the past, and that HIV1 has evolved further from SIV than

HIV2. The likely location for such evolution, and for the first cases of AIDS, is central Africa, but the details of this history, and the manner in which the virus first spread from monkeys to humans, are uncertain. Whatever the exact history, it is likely that urbanization and modern transportation facilitated the rapid spread of an infection that had previously existed in isolated locations or in an indolent form.

The HIV particle has three parts: an outer envelope, a protein matrix, and a dense inner core. The envelope consists of a three-layered membrane, into which are embedded spikelike proteins, whose heads stick out like studs from the virus's surface. These studs have the precise chemical structure to lock onto certain molecules, known as CD4 receptors, that cover the outer membranes of the cells that HIV infects. The function of the matrix is not well understood. The core contains the virus's genetic material, which is in the form of ribonucleic acid (RNA). As a RNA virus, HIV differs from many other viruses, as well as from all cellular organisms like ourselves, that use DNA as their genetic material. HIV's complement of RNA is extraordinarily limited: the entire genetic sequence of the viruses takes up only 9,749 "bases"—the chemical letters in which the genetic code is written. Each of our own cells, in contrast, contain a genetic code counted in hundreds of millions of bases. Yet we are no match for HIV.

It is believed that the genome (or complete genetic material) of HIV contains the sequences of only about nine genes (humans possess about 100,000 genes). Each gene codes for the synthesis of one or two proteins. The most well known of these proteins is the enzyme *reverse transcriptase,* which is packaged into the virus's core along with the RNA. Once the virus has entered its target cell, reverse transcriptase catalyzes the copying ("transcription") of HIV's RNA into DNA. A second virally coded enzyme, *integrase,* then inserts the DNA copy into the chromosomal DNA of the host cell. In this state, HIV is known as a *provirus*. Once the insertion is accomplished, HIV is extraordinarily well concealed: only by reading through the chromosomal DNA and looking for viral code might it be possible to locate it.

This conversion—of viral RNA into host DNA—defines HIV as a *retrovirus*. "Retro" because the direction of transcription is the opposite of what takes place in most organisms, such as ourselves. In us the genetic material, DNA, is transcribed into RNA, which acts as a messenger, bringing the genetic instructions out of the nucleus into the cell cytoplasm, where protein synthesis takes place. A few other retroviruses, besides HIV and SIV, are known. One of them, HTLV1, causes a kind of cancer of the immune system in humans.

Just sitting in among the host cell's DNA, HIV is unlikely to do harm. Sooner or later, however, the HIV proviral genes are transcribed back into RNA, and the RNA is translated into protein. The machinery for this process is, for the most part, the normal machinery of protein synthesis that every cell possesses; it has simply been subverted for the virus's purposes. But the virus's genes also regulate the process; in particular they ensure that the viral DNA is read off much faster than would normally occur. Large numbers of copies of the viral proteins are synthesized. These include not only the reverse transcriptase and integrase, but several other proteins: the proteins that form the envelope and matrix of the virus, a protein coded by a gene called TAT, which in some way accelerates the viral life cycle, an enzyme called protease that cuts other viral proteins into more active forms, and a protein called vpr that in some way triggers the production of viral particles. From some of these proteins, and from RNA transcripts of the proviral DNA, large numbers of new viral particles are assembled, and these are either budded off from the cell's outer membrane into the surrounding fluid, or the cell itself is destroyed and the particles are released en masse. The viral particles, now floating free in the blood or other bodily fluids, are able to home in on new target cells, and thus to repeat the cycle.

The CD4 lymphocyte, the main target of HIV's attack, is one of a class of lymphocytes known as T (for thymus-derived) lymphocytes, that together orchestrate much of the immune response to invading pathogens as well as to tumors. CD4 cells seem to be especially involved in defense against viruses and fungi, as well as against tumors. It is probably this selective role of CD4 in normal health that is responsible for the peculiar spectrum of illnesses that characterize the early stages of HIV disease.

Besides CD4 cells, however, HIV can infect other cell types. One such cell is the macrophage, another white blood cell, which plays an important role in the destruction of bacteria. It can also infect cells in the brain and spinal cord—not the nerve cells themselves, but a class of non-neuronal cells named microglia. Microglia and macrophages are closely related; in fact, macrophages can enter the brain from the blood and become microglia, bringing HIV with them.

Only a tiny fraction of all the CD4 cells, even in the blood of a person with advanced disease, actually contain the HIV virus. It therefore seems likely that the reduction in the numbers of CD4 cells, which is central to the pathological process in AIDS, is not simply a consequence of the virus entering and killing cells one after another. Rather, there seems to be some disturbance of the processes that regulate the production and lifetime of CD4 cells. Understanding these processes in greater detail might lead to the development of methods to correct this disturbance.

The Mechanism of Transmission

In terms of their biological makeup, all human beings are believed to be about equally susceptible to infection by HIV.[1] Infection can occur before birth, in childhood, adulthood, or old age. It can occur in both sexes and all races, in rich and poor, and in straight, bisexual, lesbian, and gay people. What matters, in the great majority of cases, is the behaviors in which people engage, not the category of people to which they belong. Thus "being gay" is not in itself a risk factor, though unprotected sex between men does carry a serious risk of HIV transmission. Conversely, "being lesbian" is not in itself a protection from AIDS, even though sex between women carries a low risk of HIV transmission. More than a few lesbians have acquired HIV via sex with men or the use of injection drugs.

HIV infection is transmitted from person to person through sexual contact or through exposure to blood or blood products. No other means of transmission are known. Among the myriad kinds of sex acts people engage in, penile-vaginal and penile-anal intercourse are the two most clearly associated with HIV transmission. In Africa, penile-vaginal intercourse is probably by far the commonest mechanism of HIV transmission. HIV is present at high levels in the semen and pre-ejaculatory fluids of HIV-infected men, and in the vaginal fluids of HIV-infected women. In vaginal intercourse, HIV transmission may occur more easily from man to woman than from woman to man, although this has been disputed by some scientists. It is believed that transmission from woman to man is greatly facilitated by the presence of genital sores or ulcers on the penis. Such sores are more prevalent in Africa than in the United States, on account of the lesser availability of effective treatments for them in Africa. Transmission from woman to man probably does occur in the absence of sores, however. The site of infection in such cases may be the urethral mucosa.

In the United States, penile-anal intercourse has been the commonest mechanism of transmission. The rectal mucosa is probably more easily penetrated by HIV than that of the vagina, either because of its histological makeup or because it is more likely to suffer microscopic tears during intercourse.

In penile-anal intercourse, transmission occurs much more readily from the insertive to the receptive partner than vice versa. Nevertheless, epidemiological studies, such as the Multi-Center AIDS Cohort Study,[2] have reported small numbers of men who claim to have engaged in insertive but not receptive anal intercourse during the period in which they became infected. It seems likely that the presence of blood in the rectum or anus (e.g., from hemorrhoids), or sores on the penis, would increase the likelihood of transmission from receptive to insertive partner, but it should not be assumed that either of these conditions are required for transmission to occur.

Proper use of latex condoms in vaginal and anal intercourse is believed to greatly reduce the risk of HIV transmission. "Proper use" means use of a new undamaged latex (not lambskin) condom. Any lubricant used should be water-based, not oil- or grease-based. The condom should be put on before the first insertion of the penis into the vagina or anus. After ejaculation, the penis should be withdrawn from vagina or anus before the erection is lost, and the bottom of the condom should be held with the fingers to prevent its coming loose before withdrawal.

Latex condoms are theoretically completely impermeable to the HIV virus. However, variations in the manufacturing process may cause occasional condoms to have microscopic pores that could permit transmission of HIV. More significantly, the use even of impermeable condoms does not render intercourse completely risk-free, because 100 percent "proper use" is difficult to attain. In the same way that condoms, though impermeable to sperm, are not completely effective as a means of birth control, so they offer valuable but not total protection against HIV transmission. The same is probably true of the recently introduced female condoms, which are made of polyurethane. The main advantage of these condoms is that they give the woman more direct control over the adequacy of protection.

Penile-oral intercourse ("fellatio") probably carries a significantly lower risk of HIV transmission than penile-vaginal or penile-anal intercourse. This is because levels of HIV in the saliva of infected people are low, and because the mucosal lining of the mouth is not easily penetrated by the virus. There is some dispute about the epidemiological evidence in this regard: there are small numbers of men who claim to have engaged only in receptive penile-oral sex during the period when they became infected, but there is evidence that many of these men did in fact engage in receptive anal intercourse also.[3] Obviously there is some theoretical risk (for the receptive partner) in oral sex, especially given the possibility of mouth ulcers or other lesions that might facilitate the absorption of the virus. Presumably the risk is greater when fellatio is continued to ejaculation than when it is discontinued prior to ejaculation, although one cannot totally discount the risk in the latter case, as the virus has been isolated from pre-ejaculatory fluid.

Oral-anal contact ("rimming") is stated by many authorities to carry a high risk of HIV transmission. There seems to be little epidemiological or theoretical evidence to back this assertion. But such contact does carry a high risk for transmission of other serious diseases, such as viral hepatitis.

Oral contact with the female genitalia ("cunnilingus") and female genito-genital contact carry an uncertain risk, probably not high. There are, however, a small number of cases in which oral-vaginal contact seems to have been responsible for HIV transmission. Contact with the female genitalia during the menstrual period increases the potential for HIV transmission if the menstruating partner is infected. The use of latex sheets (dental dams) probably decreases this risk.

Mutual masturbation carries little risk of HIV transmission. There is however a theoretical (though undocumented) risk of transmission via masturbation if semen or vaginal secretions from an infected partner come in contact with an open wound in the skin of an uninfected partner. Kissing is generally thought to be risk-free, though some authorities have suggested that deep kissing carries a low risk of transmission. Although insertive sex toys, such as dildos, are not a documented source of HIV transmission, it would seem prudent to disinfect them after use.

It is impossible to acquire HIV infection by having sex with a noninfected person, whatever sex acts are performed.

Besides the kinds of sexual behavior a person takes part in, the number of sex partners is also a factor affecting the risk of becoming infected. This was particularly true at the beginning of the epidemic, when the fraction of the population that was infected was very low. At that time, one had to have sex with hundreds of people to have a significant chance of meeting someone who carried the virus. Currently, the incidence of HIV-positivity in some groups, for example gay men in metropolitan areas, is so high that having sex with only a handful of people is very likely to bring one in contact with the virus. Therefore, the choice today for HIV-negative gay men is either to be in a mutually monogamous relationship with another HIV-negative man or to practice safer sex (especially the use of a condom in anal intercourse) in all sexual encounters. HIV-positive men should use condoms in insertive anal or oral intercourse. Most authorities recommend that they use condoms in anal receptive intercourse too, because of the risk of acquiring an added HIV load, a more virulent HIV strain, or another sexually transmitted infection. Although there is a theoretical risk of HIV transmission in female-female sex, lesbians probably do not significantly increase their chances of HIV infection by engaging in sex with other women.[4]

It should be mentioned that "safer sex" refers to the transmission of HIV only. There are other serious diseases, such as gonorrhea, syphilis, and herpes, that can readily be transmitted by some "safer-sex" practices, such as unprotected fellatio without ejaculation.

The preceding paragraphs have attempted to outline what is known about the risks of various sexual practices. But it is important to emphasize that unprotected anal sex is far and away the most dangerous practice for gay men. Gary Rose, Associate Director for Legislative and Regulatory Affairs at the National Association of People with AIDS, made the following statement during testimony before Congress: "We have to concentrate our efforts on stopping the one activity that we know causes most cases of gay transmission (anal sex without condoms as either the active or passive partner) and stop wasting our breath—and our credibility—on activities (oral sex, especially) that have minuscule impact and that very few people pay attention to. This approach undermines *all* prevention efforts."[5]

Of course, gays or lesbians who use injection drugs are at the same risk of acquiring HIV infection as heterosexual drug users. No one should share needles, syringes, or water for injection. Syringes and needles should be exchanged for new or sterilized with bleach after use.

The Stages of HIV Disease

The semen of HIV-infected men contains HIV, not only as free particles, but also as provirus in CD4 lymphocytes and macrophages that are present in semen. Some scientists believe that it is these cellular carriers of HIV, rather than the free particles, that transmit the infection to the receptive partner. According to this theory, the infected cells migrate through microscopic breaks in the rectal or vaginal mucosa, enter the lymphatic system, and reach the lymph glands. Here the infection is passed on to the host's cells, and over a period of days or weeks the levels of infected cells and free virus in the blood gradually increase. Although the virus is present, it can only be detected during this period by an expensive procedure known as the polymerase chain reaction (PCR).

At some point after exposure (usually between six weeks and six months), the levels of virus become high enough to elicit an organized response from the immune system. The B (or bone-marrow-derived) lymphocytes begin to secrete antibodies directed against the virus. It is these antibodies whose presence is detected in the commonly used HIV blood test, not the virus itself. The terms "HIV-positive" and "HIV-negative" generally refer to the results of the antibody test. It appears that all people who are HIV-positive are carrying the virus. This is unlike the situation with many infections, in which the infecting organism may be completely eliminated from the body, leaving only antibodies as an indicator of their earlier presence. The appearance of HIV-specific antibodies is known as *seroconversion*. Because HIV is present before seroconversion, being HIV-negative does not guarantee that a person is free of infection. This is the reason why blood banks reject donations from members of high-risk groups such as gay men, even though they can and do test all donated blood with the antibody test.[6]

Seroconversion is generally accompanied by a flulike illness of a few days' or weeks' duration, characterized by fever, muscle aches, nausea, and sometimes a skin rash. As the antibodies secreted by the B lymphocytes interact with the virus and reduce its concentration in the blood, so the symptoms subside. But the antibodies are not capable of reaching the provirus hidden among the genes of the CD4 lymphocytes and macrophages. Therefore a standoff is reached, which may persist for years. During this period, an HIV-positive person is capable of infecting others, but he or she has no overt signs or symptoms of disease.

The length of this standoff period is highly variable. Some people become seriously ill within a year of first infection. There are others who have remained symptom-free since becoming infected in the early days of the epidemic—twelve years ago or more. It is possible that some of these individuals will never show symptoms. The median interval between initial infection and diagnosis with AIDS (by criteria listed below) is thought to be somewhere between seven and ten years: that is, if one takes a large group of people, about half of them will have developed AIDS by seven to ten years after infection.

Although HIV-positive individuals show no symptoms during the long latent period, there are indications of pathological processes going on in their immune systems. The most well studied of these is a gradual decline in the numbers of CD4 (or T4) cells in the blood. In healthy, uninfected people the blood contains about one thousand CD4 cells per microliter (cubic millimeter). During the symptom-free period the numbers of CD4 cells decline at an average rate of about 80-100 cells per microliter per year. This is of course just an average: the rate of decline varies greatly between individuals, for reasons that are unclear, and also shows changes within one individual that may be related to stress, illness, diet, or other unknown factors.

The level of CD4 cells is the most accurate available indicator of an HIV-positive individual's likelihood of becoming ill. At a level of 500 cells per microliter, there is some risk of symptoms. By the time CD4 cells decline to 200 per microliter, the risk of disease is substantial.

The first symptoms or illness that an HIV-positive person experiences are generally not AIDS, because the term AIDS is reserved for a specific set of serious conditions. Therefore there is a period of time when an HIV-positive person is not entirely healthy but does not have AIDS. This state, which in the past was referred to as ARC (AIDS-related complex), is now known as *HIV-symptomatic disease*. The health problems that are common features of HIV-symptomatic disease are not life threatening, but they can cause considerable discomfort and disability. They include: thrush—an infection of the oral mucosa with a fungus called *Candida*; generalized swelling of lymph nodes; herpes zoster or shingles (a painful rash caused by reactivation of a latent chicken-pox infection in the cutaneous nerves); weight loss; unexplained fever, unexplained diarrhea, and night sweats.

As the CD4 cell count drops below 200, serious diseases forming part of the definition of AIDS become common. For that reason, the CDC has defined a CD4 count below 200 (in an HIV-positive person) as itself a criterion for a diagnosis of AIDS, even in the absence of other conditions.

The illnesses defining AIDS (in an HIV-positive person) include infections, cancers, and other conditions. The most common infection, especially as the AIDS-initiating illness, is *Pneumocystis carinii* pneumonia (PCP). Fully 80 percent of people with AIDS will experience at least one bout with PCP. Other infections include cryptococcal meningitis, toxoplasmosis of the brain, tuberculosis, *Mycobacterium avium* complex (MAC—an AIDS-defining illness when it occurs at sites other than the lungs), cytomegalovirus (CMV) disease, which may affect the intestines, the eyes, or the brain, and progressive multifocal leukencephalopathy, a viral infection of the brain or spinal cord. Cancers include Kaposi's sarcoma (which generally presents as purplish lesions in the skin but can spread to internal organs), lymphoma, and cervical cancer. Other AIDS-defining conditions include HIV encephalopathy, recurrent pneumonia of any cause, and wasting syndrome. Just one AIDS-defining illness is sufficient for a diagnosis, and if one of them is present, a low CD4 count is not required for a diagnosis.

The AIDS virus itself seems to become more virulent in the course of the disease. Person with late-stage AIDS tend to harbor variants of HIV that are *syncytium-inducing*. This means that, when added to lymphocytes in a laboratory culture, they cause the cells to fuse together, forming giant cells with multiple nuclei. The functional significance of this trait is uncertain, but it does seem to be associated with the ability to cause more severe disease. It is possible that some individuals are infected initially with the more virulent strains, and hence progress to AIDS with unusual speed.

Untreated, AIDS is uniformly and rapidly fatal. Even with the best treatment currently available, it has not so far proved possible to arrest the progress of the disease indefinitely. In the early days of the epidemic, survival after a diagnosis of AIDS was short—typically less than a year. By the late 1980s, after the introduction of antiretroviral therapy and improved treatment for opportunistic infections, median survival after diagnosis had increased to about two or two-and-a-half years. Persons receiving an AIDS diagnosis today can expect, on average, to live longer than this, because of the treatments developed in the last five years. Of course, it is likely that therapeutic developments in the next few years will improve these persons' life expectancy even further. One should also stress that the length of survival differs greatly among individuals. The reasons for these differences are poorly understood; besides the quality of medical care, the person's own self-care and will to live no doubt play a role. But the common tendency to attribute long survival to a person's "fighting spirit," positive attitude, etc., may exaggerate the role of psychological factors in controlling the course of the disease. There have been all too many people with positive attitudes who have succumbed to their first bout with pneumonia.

Treatment

Antiretroviral therapy is aimed at preventing the replication and dissemination of HIV within the body. Research in this area has taken two different tacks. The first is rational or semirational drug design, based on knowledge of the molecular biology of HIV and its potential points of attack. The other is the shotgun approach: the screening of large numbers of compounds for potential efficacy against the virus, with the hope of stumbling on a therapeutic compound. The two approaches actually overlap considerably, because the "rational" approach can so far only give a general idea of the classes of compounds that might be efficacious.

The obvious targets for rational attack are the enzymes or proteins coded by HIV genes. Of these, reverse transcriptase is the only one so far to have yielded significantly to this approach. Reverse transcriptase uses four *nucleosides*—adenosine, thymidine, guanosine, and cytosine—as the building blocks from which to string together a chain of DNA. These nucleosides are freely available in the cytoplasm of the host cell. Research in many laboratories has focused on synthesizing artificial nucleosides that are similar enough to the natural ones to be used by the reverse transcriptase, but which once used jam up the works, either by preventing further elongation of the chain or by making the finished chain unreadable or unstable. The complication is that they must *not* significantly interfere with the body's own DNA- or RNA-synthesizing enzymes, or have other toxic effects.

The first drug of this type to reach clinical use was of course 2-azido-thymidine, or AZT, now officially known as zidovudine or Retrovir. AZT is a slightly altered analog of thymidine. The original clinical studies, conducted in the mid-1980s, showed that AZT prolonged the survival of people who had a CD4 count below 200 and a history of at least one AIDS-defining illness. At that time there was optimism that AZT would work even better at earlier stages of HIV infection. Unfortunately these hopes were not realized. Some studies have indicated that AZT helps postpone the onset of AIDS for people with a CD4 count of 500 or less, although it did not seem to increase long-term survival in this group. For this reason the National Institute of Allergy and Infectious Diseases has recommended that AZT therapy be initiated at this level. A multicenter European study published in 1994, however, found no evidence for a postponement of the onset of AIDS in HIV-positive symptom-free individuals. All in all, it appears that the benefits of treatment with AZT alone are fairly short-lived, and may be most useful in people who already have some symptoms of AIDS. But the issue is still unresolved, and individual physicians vary widely in their prescribing policy. AZT has been shown to be quite effective in preventing the transmission from a pregnant woman to her fetus.

The problems with AZT are twofold. First, it causes side effects, especially anemia, that limit the safe dose and the length of time for which it can be administered. Second, it appears that the virus develops resistance to the drug, as measured by a less effective inhibition of reverse transcriptase in laboratory tests. Resistance seems to develop over a period of months. For these reasons, other reverse transcriptase inhibitors have been developed. Those introduced into clinical practice are ddC (zalcitabine), ddI (didanosine), and D4T (stavudine). Others are still at the experimental stage, such as 3TC (lamivudine). Some of these inhibitors have a selectivity for the viral enzyme that is considerably better than that of AZT. But clinical trials have not yet documented any clear superiority of these drugs over AZT. They are less liable to cause anemia but have their own serious side effects, including peripheral neuropathy and pancreatitis. They are commonly used as follow-on drugs for patients who can no longer tolerate AZT, or in whom AZT may have ceased to be effective, and they are currently being assessed in various combination and alternating regimens.

Much less advanced are efforts to find drugs that block other HIV functions. For example, there have been efforts to block the binding of the virus to the surface of CD4 cells. This binding involves a precise lock-and-key fit between a molecule on the surface of the virus (coded by a viral gene) and a receptor on the CD4 cell. The research aim was to develop a "soluble CD4 receptor," that is, a genetically engineered receptor that would bind to the virus in the bloodstream and thus prevent its ever reaching the body's own CD4 receptors. The drug was synthesized but, disappointingly, it turned out not to be useful clinically. Inhibitors of other HIV gene products, especially TAT and protease, have also been developed, but their clinical usefulness is so far unknown. Current information suggests that HIV readily mutates into a form that is resistant to protease inhibitors. The vpr protein has also come under study as a potential site of attack because, in a laboratory setting at least, antibodies to vpr can block the production of new viral particles by infected cells.

Rational development of antiretroviral drugs has proved frustratingly slow and has been beset by disappointments. Yet in the course of past failures, an enormous amount has been learned about HIV's molecular secrets. However long it takes, this line of research will ultimately succeed, and an effective therapy for AIDS will be found. The shotgun approach, on the other hand, has not yielded a single drug with significant utility so far, and has done little or nothing to advance our understanding of the disease.

In the absence, so far, of completely effective antiretroviral therapy, attention has also been focused on developing effective treatment and prevention for the complications of AIDS. It is successes in this area, more than in the development of antiretroviral drugs, that has been responsible for the improved prognosis for HIV-positive people. For example, it has proved possible to reduce the incidence of pneumocystis pneumonia with preventive regimens of trimethoprim-sulfamethoxalone (Bactrim, Septra) or inhaled pentamidine. New drugs have been introduced, such as acyclovir for herpes simplex, ganciclovir for CMV, fluconazole for fungal infections, and rifabutin for MAC. Unfortunately, the organisms responsible for opportunistic infections can develop resistance to drugs, particularly when, as is often the case with people with AIDS, the drug treatments have to be continued for long periods.

AIDS Vaccines

The development of AIDS vaccines has proved even more arduous than the search for therapeutic drugs. Three possible approaches have been explored: a live, attenuated (weakened) virus, a killed virus, and a synthetic vaccine engineered to resemble one or more of the proteins of HIV. On grounds of safety, the synthetic vaccine would be the most desirable, since it would not contain any genetic material from the virus and hence could not cause AIDS. For this reason, most research has been focused on this approach.

Several candidate synthetic vaccines are being tested in the United States. The small-scale trials currently under way are aimed only at testing the safety of the vaccines and establishing whether the vaccines cause people to develop antibodies that are capable of inactivating HIV. In 1993 it was reported that vaccinated individuals did develop such antibodies, but unfortunately the antibodies were active only against the laboratory strains of HIV that were used to generate the vaccine, not against HIV newly isolated from people with the disease. In mid-1994 it was reported that several vaccinated individuals have become infected with HIV, in spite of having anti-HIV antibodies in their blood prior to exposure (they became infected though sexual contact or other means, not from the vaccine). Both these reports suggest that the natural variability in the exact protein structure of HIV will make it hard to design a vaccine that offers broad protection. However, painstaking molecular studies of the virus indicate that there may be some regions of the virus's chemical architecture that cannot vary significantly without the virus losing its infectivity. If effective vaccines can be developed against such invariant regions, the problem of strain specificity may be solved.

Because of the time required for testing of safety and efficacy, it is unlikely that a vaccine will be widely available before the end of the century, even if one of the candidate vaccines under test at present turns out to be effective. Furthermore, there are serious financial and ethical problems associated with vaccine development. If, as seems likely, the major testing of a promising vaccine is conducted in a developing country where the infection rate is very high, will the finished vaccine be made available to that country, or to any other developing country, at an affordable price?

With all this talk of the limited success of medical science in the treatment and prevention of AIDS, one point needs to be emphasized. By identifying the cause of AIDS and its mechanism of transmission, medical science has already provided us with the knowledge by which everyone—gay, lesbian, or straight—can protect him- or herself against infection. Wisely used, this knowledge could stop the plague in its tracks.

The Natural History of the Epidemic

Epidemics tend to follow mathematically predictable paths. In the first phase, when relatively few people are infected, new infections increase exponentially within the pool of people at risk, meaning that the number of new infections doubles at fixed intervals. Later, the pool approaches saturation, that is, there are fewer and fewer at-risk people remaining to be infected. In this phase the rate of new infections stabilizes and then declines. Eventually the epidemic will die out completely, or, if there is a sufficient rate of new additions to the at-risk pool, it will continue indefinitely in an indolent or sporadic form. New additions might be immigrants or (in the case of AIDS) young people reaching the age of sexual activity. This simple model may be complicated by geographical considerations or, as in the case of AIDS, by the existence of multiple at-risk pools. In addition, the natural history of the epidemic can be altered by medical treatment, education, or public health measures.

The early exponential phase of HIV infection has been well documented for one very high-risk group, sexually active gay men who attended venereal-disease clinics in San Francisco. During the late 1970s, many blood samples from such men were taken as part of a research study on hepatitis B. These samples were stored by the CDC, and were available for testing when the HIV antibody test was developed. The fraction of the samples that were HIV-positive was as follows: 4 percent for bloods drawn in 1978, 12 percent in 1979, and 25 percent in 1980. In other words, during this period, before the first case of AIDS had come to medical attention, every HIV-positive man in that high-risk group was infecting a new sex partner every twelve months or less. (This is on average, and with the simplifying assumption that the group was isolated from other groups.) By 1984, when there had been a total of no more than 500 diagnosed AIDS cases in the city, 66 percent of the bloods were positive. In other words, the pool of at-risk men was already becoming saturated with HIV, and the rate of new infections was beginning to level off, at a time when only a tiny fraction of the men in this pool had actually come down with AIDS. The story was probably not very different in New York and Los Angeles.

The leveling off of the new cases of diagnosed AIDS should lag behind the leveling off of the HIV infection rate by the length of the average latent period, which is seven to ten years. By 1993 the rate of new diagnoses among gay and bisexual men indeed seemed to be leveling off at around 25,000 cases per year nationwide.[7] It is probable that the rate of new diagnoses among gay men will gradually decline over the next decade, even without medical advances, unless there is a major return to high-risk sex practices. (The new diagnosis rate among gay men will not drop to zero, however, because there is a stable or even rising rate of infection among young gay men who are new entrants to the at-risk pool.[8]) But other groups, especially those who acquire HIV infection through injection drug use or through heterosexual sex, will be diagnosed with AIDS at increasing rates for several years at least. Thus, even though currently about half of all new AIDS diagnoses are of gay men, the disease will become less and less identified with homosexuality over the next decade. Most likely, it will become identified with poverty and drug use, and the ethnic minorities who disproportionately suffer from these problems.

The prospects for a major expansion of the disease in the mainstream heterosexual population are still unclear. This pool is separated from the gay male pool by a bottleneck, namely by the relatively small numbers of men who practice both receptive[9] anal sex with men and insertive sex with women. This bottleneck caused a delay in the spread of HIV from one pool to the other, a delay that may have given time for education to limit the uncontrolled expansion of the disease among heterosexuals. In fact, heterosexual women at this point acquire HIV infection more commonly from heterosexual male drug users, or from their own drug use, than from bisexual men. The relative difficulty with which HIV is transmitted from women to men, in the absence of penile ulcers, may also be a factor in slowing the spread. But the fact that AIDS is spreading uncontrollably among heterosexuals in many developing countries means that there is no fundamental biological reason why the same thing could not happen here.

Further Reading

Fauci, A. S. "The Human Immunodeficiency Virus." *Science* 239 (1988): 617–622.

Frumkin, L., and J. Leonard. *Questions and Answers on AIDS,* 2d ed. Los Angeles: PMIC, 1994.

14
AIDS: The Response

AIDS differs from many other diseases in that it is associated with a defined group within the population—gay men. This association adds on to the disease a social dimension that influences everyone who comes in contact with it, however indirectly. The gay man who is afflicted with the disease is afflicted as a gay man—his homosexuality is afflicted. He struggles and suffers along with other gay men, dies along with them, is mourned and remembered along with them. Those who care for the AIDS sick, who raise money for them, or who fight for an end to the disease, are identifying, whether they are gay or straight, male or female, with homosexuality and with the gay community. Those who distance themselves from the disease are distancing themselves from homosexuality and from the gay community. This is the dimension of AIDS that we shall explore in this chapter.

Of course, the association between AIDS and gay men is imperfect and probably temporary. Only a minority of gay men have AIDS or will ever have it. Some lesbians, many heterosexual men and women, and children too young to know their sexuality have acquired the disease. The numbers of heterosexual people with AIDS will increase, and the numbers of gay men with the disease will decrease, until one day gay men and AIDS will be no longer be thought of together. It is important for people to know that. But that is not what this chapter is about.

Many writers have drawn parallels between AIDS and other infectious diseases—plague, syphilis, smallpox, tuberculosis, and so on—that have devastated populations in one period of history or another.[1] The parallels are valid in many ways, especially with regard to the stigmatization and alienation of the victims. With all these diseases, as with AIDS, the victims were rendered incapable of infecting "us" by distancing them: either physically, though flight, quarantine, immurement, hospitalization, and so on, or conceptually. This second kind of distancing often involved the establishment of a moral remoteness: the victims—especially those of syphilis—fell sick because of their own sinful behavior, a sinfulness that "we" will avoid.

Yet in some ways AIDS is more similar to that other great killer of young men—war. Those who are killed or injured in war are thought of almost entirely in terms of their membership of a group, the armed forces. They are honored in just or successful wars; in unsuccessful or unjust wars they are shunned. Dead or injured soldiers are valued in proportion to the degree that war itself is valued. Similarly, people with AIDS are thought of as casualties of homosexuality. This evokes an inordinate scorn, even hatred, of the victims of AIDS among those who scorn homosexuality. But it also evokes an extraordinary caring and love for those same people among those who respect and value homosexuality.

In this chapter we take a look at these responses to AIDS, responses at the level of the individual, the family, and the group. Most especially we are interested in the response of the gay and lesbian community as a group, because it is this response, in large measure, that has brought the community to where it is today—to a place where gays and lesbians are still stigmatized, blamed, and disadvantaged in all too many ways, but also where they are respected, even honored for their struggle against the disease, a struggle in which they have gained a group identity that they did not have before.

AIDS and Blame

AIDS is a natural disaster, which means that it can be blamed on almost anyone. And there certainly has been no shortage of blame for this disease. It has been blamed on gay men, on account of their homosexuality, their promiscuity, or their lack of religion. It has been blamed on heterosexual scientists and politicians and straight people generally, on account of their stupidity, their shortsightedness, or their homophobia. It has been blamed on the CIA. It has been blamed on people with AIDS, on account of their bad attitude or their willingness to collaborate in their own extermination.

The blame that has been laid on gay men by conservatives and the religious right is too familiar to need documentation. Of course, this kind of blame is not totally without foundation. It is true that if gay men in the late 1970s and early 1980s had had fewer sex partners, HIV would have spread more slowly, perhaps giving research and education a chance to stem the epidemic. Even some gay commentators have pointed out that gay men in the late 1970s were well aware that their sexual practices were spreading sexually transmitted diseases at an extraordinary rate. In *And the Band Played On* (see Further Reading) Randy Shilts described how Gaetan Dugas, supposedly the "Patient Zero" who brought the virus to the United States, continued to have unprotected, anonymous sex after being explicitly warned that he was spreading a fatal disease. Shilts also documented the resistance that some gay men put up to the idea of closing the bathhouses in San Francisco and other cities. Even today there are all too many gay men who, by failing to take precautions whose importance they are well aware of, are infecting others or becoming infected themselves.

But by and large, blaming gay men for the epidemic is not warranted. As documented in the previous chapter, enormous numbers of gay men became infected before AIDS was recognized as a disease. Since that time, thanks largely to educational programs run by gay men and lesbians, the rate of new infections among gay men has dropped dramatically. Furthermore, there was (and still is) a remarkable lack of governmental effort to educate gay men about the risk factors for HIV transmission and about safer sex practices. The greatest part of the blame laid on gay men for AIDS is motivated simply by hatred of homosexuality, a hatred that has found a convenient camouflage in a concern for public health.

The blame laid on the medical research establishment has been intense. Michael Callen, who died in 1994 after a twelve-year battle with AIDS, wrote: "I sometimes feel that my goal is to stay alive long enough to witness the AIDS equivalent of the Nuremberg trials, when all the scientists who've squandered so much money and so many lives pursuing dead ends in AIDS treatment research will be held accountable."[2] Playwright, author, and activist Larry Kramer has spent years castigating the NIH for their inaction. In a typical diatribe, he wrote: "In other words, it's not because of scientific ignorance but because of bureaucratic bullshit that there's never been a cure for any major illness to come out of the NIH. It's not what we don't know about AIDS that's prevented the cure; it's that there's no way the present system can allow for knowledge to be pursued in any mature, adult fashion."[3] Individual scientists have also been blamed, especially Robert Gallo of the National Cancer Institute, who, it has been suggested, may have "discovered" HIV, not in the blood of people with AIDS, but in a specimen of the AIDS virus sent to him by Luc Montagnier of the Institut Pasteur in France.[4] Sometimes the medical profession and the pharmaceutical industry are lumped together for purposes of blame, as in a slew of books whose titles are sufficiently explicit to make further perusal unnecessary: *Good Intentions—How Big Business and the Medical Establishment Are Corrupting the Fight Against AIDS, Alzheimer's, Cancer and More,*[5] *The AIDS War—Propaganda, Profiteering and Genocide from the Medical-Industrial Complex,*[6] and *Queer Blood—The Secret AIDS Genocide Plot.*[7]

Probably the most valid part of the blame directed at the research establishment relates to the delay in initiating research programs on AIDS, especially in the first two years of the epidemic. One research institute that claims to be at the forefront of virological research, the Salk Institute in San Diego, did no work on AIDS in the early 1980s; in fact it was only after the institute's own president came down with the disease, near the end of the decade, that research there began in earnest. Many other research organizations were equally tardy. Part of this delay was certainly connected with the image of AIDS as a gay disease. But it is not easy for scientists to quickly change the direction of their research, tied as they are to multiyear, federally funded programs. Nor is it easy for institutions to build the expensive containment facilities that research on HIV requires. The period in which the research community most flagrantly ignored AIDS—1981 and 1982—was also the period in which a large part of the gay community ignored the disease too. After this period, the pace of scientific discovery was extraordinarily fast, and AIDS is now one of the hottest and best-funded topics in the entire field of medical research. Unfortunately, this does necessarily mean that AIDS will soon be conquered. The "war on cancer" initiated by President Nixon did not succeed, in spite of a tremendous national effort; the problem of cancer was simply too difficult to be solved in the 1970s. In the same way, it may require years of progress in understanding the underlying biology before we can hope to devise a cure for AIDS.

The criticisms by Callen and Kramer, cited above, are far off target. In fact they contradict each other: Callen wanted someone to tell the scientists what to do, while Kramer wants people to stop interfering with scientists' work. The truth is that there will always be dead-ends in science, because one cannot know whether they are dead-ends until one has reached them. A scientist who reaches a dead-end in the course of a rational line of investigation into AIDS deserves our thanks, not our abuse.

What about the politicians, from President Reagan on down, who did so little to alert the country to the epidemic? Reagan himself exhibited a total failure of leadership. He did not speak about AIDS at all until May 1987, six years into the epidemic, and even in that speech he managed to mention only the "innocent" victims of AIDS—those who acquired the disease through blood transfusion or by being married to an intravenous drug abuser.[8] Of course, there was no talk of condoms or other measures that might serve some practical purpose in limiting the epidemic. Instead, he spoke up for mandatory premarital testing, a futile proposal to halt the epidemic at the gates of the traditional family. The entire administration, with the eventual exception of Surgeon General Everett Koop, took its cue from Reagan and turned a blind eye to AIDS, or minimized its significance or the amount of money needed to successfully combat it.

Yet even Reagan, in a sense, can be excused. His response to AIDS was exactly in accord with the minimalist principle of government he campaigned for, and for which he was enthusiastically elected and reelected. He responded the way most Americans wanted him to respond; anything else would have been a violation of his mandate. And if the Americans who voted for Reagan were able to distance themselves from suffering gay men, are not gay men themselves partly to blame for that—those gay men, at least, who were gay before AIDS and who did little to open lines of communication with straight America?[9] Blaming Reagan is subscribing to a view of history as a sequence of deeds and misdeeds by great men, a view that takes away our power to change history's course.

A subtle form of AIDS blame is directed at people with AIDS themselves. This is the blame that ascribes an HIV-positive person's progression to AIDS, and his or her worsening condition thereafter, to a failure of will. Rob Anderson, a San Franciscan who has remained in perfect health in spite of being HIV-positive since 1979 or earlier, said "I think of these friends of mine who worried themselves into the grave.... I truly feel that everything is influenced by the mind."[10] This kind of blame is often couched as its opposite: praise for those whose positive attitude, rage, or strategy for living seem to have stemmed the disease's advance. In Michael Callen's book, for example, appears the statement that "Long-term survivors are those who refuse to believe that AIDS is an 'automatic death sentence.'"[11] But regardless of how it is framed, the message is the same: you are responsible for your own (ill-)health.

This kind of blame is the least justified of all, since there is little if any evidence that a person's attitude influences the rate of disease progression. But it also illustrates most clearly the whole point and rationale of AIDS blame, which is to gain some sense, however illusory, of mastery over the disease. AIDS blame is saying "AIDS cannot touch me because I am not a godless sodomite," "AIDS can be cured by bringing wicked scientists to account," or "Only those who want to die do so." This is the psychological purpose of blame. Whether blame is deserved or not is secondary.

Because blame has a purpose, we should judge it, not just by its truthfulness, but also by its result. What is the effect of AIDS blame? Does it generate undeserved guilt in those blamed? Does it cause them to change their behavior and, if so, what is the effect of that change of behavior? Does it make people with AIDS healthier or sicker? Does it help to stop the spread of the disease?

AIDS blame has probably generated very little undeserved guilt. In fact, it has probably generated very little guilt of any kind. Gay men are certainly not about to take biblical rantings seriously. AIDS researchers have thick skins. And people with AIDS know that they are not conspiring in their own demise.

But AIDS blame *has* caused changes in behavior. Not by engendering guilt among the blamed, but by influencing the attitudes of the uninvolved majority, in other words by public relations. No group has striven more consciously to use blame in this way than ACT UP.

ACT UP

The AIDS Coalition To Unleash Power was founded in New York in March 1987. Foremost among its founders was Larry Kramer, who had previously been dismissed from the Board of Gay Men's Health Crisis on account of his confrontational stance and his opposition to GHMC's becoming an AIDS service organization. "I helped found Gay Men's Health Crisis and watched them turn into an organization of sissies," he told the *New York Times*, "I founded ACT UP and have watched them change the world."[12]

ACT UP was dedicated to direct action: to venting gay men's rage against their "murderers." It was the first gay organization to take the spirit of Stonewall anything like literally. Its logo, a pink triangle and the words SILENCE = DEATH, against a black background, has become one of the gay community's most familiar icons.

ACT UP's first action was a sit-in on Wall Street, aimed at protesting the slow pace of federal approval of AIDS-related drugs. Seventeen demonstrators were arrested. By the end of 1987 branches of ACT UP had been founded in several other cities around the country. In October 1987 demonstrators in Virginia disrupted Christian fundamentalist Pat Robertson's announcement of his presidential candidacy. In January 1988, nineteen ACT UP members were arrested in Burlingame, California, during a demonstration at the corporate offices of AZT manufacturer Burroughs-Wellcome. Numerous further actions took place later that year, including the disruption of a speech by vice presidential candidate Dan Quayle in September. The action that gained most attention, however, was the "die-in" conducted at St. Patrick's Roman Catholic Cathedral in New York on December 10, 1989, as Cardinal John J. O'Connor was celebrating mass. While some demonstrators littered the aisles of the church with their bodies, others interrupted the cardinal's words with shouts of "murderer" and demands for a change in the Church's policies on homosexuality, contraception, and abortion. One demonstrator crushed a communion wafer, the body of Christ according to Catholic doctrine. Meanwhile, several thousand protesters demonstrated in the street outside. One hundred and eleven protesters were arrested. A documentary film about the action, *Stop the Church*, was made by Robert Hilferty for PBS, but the network refused to air it.

By 1990, ACT UP had about sixty-five chapters nationwide. But from this high point, ACT UP went into a gradual decline. During 1990 there was considerable infighting over the question of whether ACT UP should stay focused on AIDS issues or expand its agenda. Partly as a result of this debate, another group, Queer Nation, was formed that devoted itself to combating homophobia generally. In March 1991 ACT UP earned the attention of President Bush: he said that its activities constituted "an excess of free speech." In 1992 ACT UP demonstrators harassed presidential candidates and attempted to disrupt both party conventions. But slowly ACT UP's actions began to lose their shock value. Attendance at ACT UP meetings declined, and by 1994 the organization had largely abandoned its confrontational approach. However, a spinoff organization, the Treatment Action Group (TAG), has been very active in conducting detailed analyses of NIH's drug development policies. It has become considerably more cautious in its recommendations than was ACT UP. In 1994, for example, TAG discouraged the Federal Drug Administration from inviting the pharmaceutical company Hoffmann-LaRoche to submit a request for accelerated approval of an AIDS drug (the protease inhibitor saquinavir).[13] ACT UP has continued to push energetically for new AIDS legislation such as the AIDS Cure Project introduced into Congress in 1994.

ACT UP has definitely contributed to public awareness of AIDS issues, and it should take credit for some of the progress that took place on these issues in the early 1990s, especially for the expedited approval of AIDS-related drugs by the FDA. In addition, ACT UP has given the gay community a renewed sense of power and control in the face of the numbing pressure of the epidemic. But ACT UP's policies, especially in its early years, were based on the false assumption that AIDS cures were sitting in the drug development pipeline, waiting to be let out. They were not. And even the expedited approval of drugs has been a two-edged sword: it has meant that drugs like AZT have been prescribed widely, and at vast expense to people with AIDS, with very little knowledge about their long-term benefits or hazards. Furthermore, it is uncertain whether the AIDS Cure Project, if enacted, would indeed hasten a cure, or whether it might actually delay it by creating a new centralized AIDS bureaucracy in which all independent thought is suppressed. Despised though the NIH is by many AIDS activists, it does a least have an established mechanism for fostering diversity and freedom in biomedical research.

More fundamentally, ACT UP may have been limited by its philosophy of blame. The American public may not be not willing to believe that Reagan, Fauci, O'Connor, and the rest are "murderers," that Burroughs-Wellcome is plotting genocide, and so on. As historian John D'Emilio has written, "A politics of rage weakens and destroys its proponents and their cause more effectively than it weakens and destroys an oppressive system.... A movement that mobilizes a constituency on the basis of pain will end up feeling its way to despair, disillusionment, and, ultimately, failure."[14]

The Person with AIDS

These days, when a gay man is diagnosed with AIDS, the diagnosis rarely comes as a bolt from the blue. Probably he has known his HIV-positive status for years. Very likely he has already experienced thrush, swollen glands, night sweats, or other harbingers of the disease. Perhaps he has been taking AZT for a considerable time. And almost certainly, he is already intimately familiar with the disease on account of its ravages among his friends and acquaintances. The transition from "HIV-positive person" to "person with AIDS" may be a sheer technicality: a drop in the CD4 cell count below the threshold 200 level.

For these reasons, a gay man who is diagnosed with AIDS will often attempt to continue living the same kind of life he led previously, a life characterized by all the activities, interests, and desires that make his particular life unique. In fact, some people with AIDS live so unremarkably in the pattern of their previous lives that many of their acquaintances and work colleagues have no idea that they are ill.

Yet there are psychological, physical, and practical changes that, whether suddenly or gradually, tend to become evident in the lives of people with AIDS. Employed gay men who are diagnosed with AIDS often leave their jobs, either at once or within a few months thereafter. This can be because they are not well enough to perform their duties, because of the benefits that disabled unemployed people are entitled to, because of pressure from their employers, or because of a strong desire to do something else with their lives. The transition from work to unemployment is a serious challenge, for those with AIDS like those unemployed for any other reason. It may be a psychological benefit, in terms of reduced stress or new opportunities, but it may also bring isolation, financial anxiety, and feelings of uselessness or of being a burden. When these problems are compounded by recurrent illness, increasing disability, and a bleak prognosis, depression is a common outcome. Almost all people with AIDS enter a state of moderate or severe depression at some point, although they often emerge from this depression into a more robust or accepting state of mind.

"I got AIDS in 1993, when the CDC changed their definition," Leon told us. He is a thirty-five-year old gay man of mixed African and European heritage.

I was 152 [CD4 cells], but I wasn't showing any symptoms. In December I developed a cough that wouldn't go away, and one night my temp went up to 104 and my sister wrapped me up and took me to the doctor, and that's when I found out I had *Pneumocystis*—AIDS had begun to materialize. I came through the first bout pretty good. Then in late January I had a relapse, and they started i/v pentamidine, and I've never been the same since. It took so much out of me.

I live with my sister and her husband. I get a check from the government, and I give them a certain amount. I feel very loved, very welcomed. I think she loves me more than her husband. She told me "I can get another husband—I can't get another you."

I began to notice that clothes didn't fit anymore—I put them on and they slid off. I took all the mirrors out of my room. I remember going to the bathroom one night, and I looked in the mirror, and I saw—a skeleton. It scared the life out of me, I stayed up all night long, I sat on the edge of the bed and I looked out of the window and cradled myself until the sun came up.

My sister did a lot of research, and she and her husband went to the Shanti program, and she was so worried about what I was going to do about money and where I would get medicine, all sorts of things. The gentleman that she spoke with said: "Don't worry, we take care of our own," and they got stacks of information. I found out about AIDS Project Los Angeles and the Minority AIDS Project and the AIDS Healthcare Foundation. I was introduced to Guy, my Buddy, in December 1993. I hadn't met many people, I was pretty much by myself—I've always been a loner. I'm not a bar person and I don't like picking people up. He's younger than me, but sometimes when I sit and talk with him he's very, very wise, and he shows me a different perspective that maybe I haven't thought about before. And he listens to me and gives me ideas and brings me up when I feel bad. You know, sometimes I really really feel bad, a lot of times I'm afraid. At times I'll look at my wrists, and my arms, and I see that skeleton.

I never thought it would happen to me. I've always been so careful. Then you sit and think about who did this to me. But at this point it's not important anymore.

I get tired really easy. I've had problems with my nervous system, that's why I support myself when I stand up. I'm going to start on a drug against the MAC, it's very prevalent. The doctor says it's not as bad as the pentamidine. I don't think I could take another dose of pentamidine, I really don't. I would pray that the Lord would take me right then and there.

I've thought about suicide. I went to the bookstore and got several books on how to do it. I know what to do. But I believe if they have enough sedatives to take the pain away that I would want to hang on to every bit of life I can. I love life, it's wonderful. People are so miserable and I don't know why.

Although statistics are hard to come by, it appears that suicide is very common among people with AIDS, especially among gay men with the disease. There have been estimates that as many as 25 percent of AIDS deaths among gay men are suicides or assisted suicides, and that over half of the gay men currently living with AIDS have made plans for suicide.[15] There is no doubt that many of these suicides would be better prevented, given that they may occur during potentially treatable or self-limiting episodes of depression common among people with AIDS. Nevertheless, suicide in the context of end-stage or debilitating AIDS is generally seen not as a cowardly or immoral way out, but as a fully justified assertion of the individual's control over his or her own life.

Assertion of control is a central psychological theme of AIDS in the gay community. While the right to suicide is an example, there are many other, perhaps more positive ways in which people with AIDS reject the status of passive victims. For example, they may develop a strong interest in the details of their illness and its treatment, and demand to participate in the medical decision-making process in their cases, in a way that patients with terminal illnesses have traditionally not done. They may seek alternative therapies in addition to or instead of the standard treatments offered by their doctors. They may join service organizations such as Gay Men's Health Crisis, not just to receive services but to participate actively in running the organizations and setting policy. They may externalize their experience with AIDS though art, writing, or other means of expression.

Finally, and most notably, they may join the political and public relations struggle for better treatment, education, and prevention, through membership in ACT UP, People with AIDS Coalition, Being Alive, or the National Association of People with AIDS. NAPWA, for example, runs a speakers bureau of people with AIDS from different communities and age groups who can communicate effectively with their peers: they teach HIV prevention and attempt to break down the social ostracism that still too often marks the disease. NAPWA, the National Minority AIDS Council, and the AIDS Interfaith Network collaborate to put on an annual National Skills Building Conference, which brings together medical personnel, volunteers, service agencies, and people with AIDS to provide technical training for dealing with the disease.

Among the many people with AIDS who have provided effective AIDS education to young people, one stands out—Cuban-American Pedro Zamora, who found out that he was HIV-positive in 1989, when he was seventeen years old. Zamora spoke at schools and other organizations, testified before Congress, made a television commercial for the Centers for Disease Control, and, most famously, participated in MTV's youth-oriented series *The Real World—San Francisco.* Zamora died on November 11, 1994, the day after the show's final segment was aired.

Friends and Lovers

Many gay men have a well-developed friendship network within the gay community, including current and previous sexual partners as well as nonsexual friends and acquaintances. This friendship network constitutes a space within which gay men are assured of being accepted, valued, and understood.[16] Oftentimes, when a gay man develops AIDS, the bonds within the friendship network intensify and contract. Perhaps an ex-lover will move in again and become the primary caregiver. Perhaps a gay neighbor will become a more intimate friend. Besides the practical assistance that the friendship network can provide, it also serves to assure the person with AIDS that he still belongs to the community, that he has not suffered the ostracism that so commonly has gone along with epidemic diseases.

Less obviously, the friends of a person with AIDS also receive assurance—assurance that they are not helpless in the face of the epidemic. They may be initiated into the mysteries of the Groshon catheter, or learn how to turn pentamidine into a breathable mist. They may perform the simple ritual of turning, which prevents bedsores. They may cook or shop or drive, or provide spiritual counsel, humor, or a sympathetic ear. By all these acts they are empowered to resist what may seem overpowering and irresistible. They may learn for their own future use how to live with AIDS.

Service Organizations

Community-based AIDS service organizations began in 1981 with the founding of the Kaposi's Sarcoma Foundation in San Francisco and the Gay Men's Health Crisis in New York. By 1983 there were 45 such organizations in the United States, and by 1991 there were over 600.[17] By 1994 there were over 500 different resources for people with HIV in just one city, Los Angeles.[18] Some AIDS service organizations, like GMHC in New York and AIDS Project Los Angeles (APLA), have hundreds of employees, thousands of volunteers, and annual budgets of many millions of dollars. Others are tiny groups of volunteers focusing on a single function—providing a free laundry service, for example, or staffing a hot line in a suburban or rural area. Furthermore, many organizations that existed prior to the AIDS epidemic have become largely devoted to providing AIDS services. Examples include the Shanti Project, founded in San Francisco in the 1970s to provide counseling to the dying and the bereaved, and the Gay and Lesbian Community Services Centers of several cities.

The services provided by these organizations are remarkable both in their quantity and diversity. Taking APLA as an example, in 1993 this organization conducted nearly 800 group counseling sessions, provided Buddies to over 300 people with AIDS, provided 48,000 hours of home attendant care, gave away 123,000 bags of food, performed 8,400 dental procedures, ran two residential facilities, answered 93,000 hot line calls, provided transportation, legal services, benefits advice, and treatment education for hundreds of clients, and educated 26,000 people though speakers and health fairs. APLA's income—$19 million in 1993—comes largely from private donations and other nongovernmental sources. Its fundraising division is an industry in itself. It consumes a large fraction[19] of APLA's total budget, blanketing Los Angeles's gay community with a blizzard of direct mail and magazine advertising, and putting on fundraising events that have become staples of the community's social calendar. These include the AIDS Walk, the Dance-a-thon, and the Universal Studios Summer Backlot Party. Above all, the annual Commitment to Life Show gives an idea of APLA's powerful connections and fiscal clout: the 1994 event featured Barbra Streisand, Elizabeth Taylor, Bruce Springsteen, Tom Cruise, and Liza Minelli, and honored Hillary Rodham Clinton and Disney Studios Chairman Jeffrey Katzenberg. It raised nearly $5 million in one evening.

APLA is only one piece of the AIDS action in Los Angeles. The Los Angeles Gay and Lesbian Community Services Center has an $11 million budget, 80 percent of which comes from governmental sources. The center runs an HIV clinic that receives 5,000 patient visits per month. Eighty percent of all persons who test positive for HIV in Los Angeles County are tested at the center. The center has a Lesbian Health Clinic, as well as a youth shelter where many of the clients are HIV-positive. Its telephone information and referral service answers about a quarter of a million calls every year. It also runs a very large AIDS prevention program and operates the Computerized AIDS Information Network, a database of 40,000 articles on AIDS and HIV. Other large players in Los Angeles are the AIDS Healthcare Foundation, that operates several clinics and hospices; L.A. Shanti, which concentrates on counseling; the Minority AIDS Project, which mainly serves gay men in the African-American and Latino communities; and the AIDS Service Center in Pasadena, which serves the San Gabriel Valley.

Most other large cities in the United States have numerous community-based AIDS service organizations. Some of these organizations have gone beyond the provision of services to become actively engaged in AIDS politics. GMHC, for example, has formed a spinoff organization, GMHC Action, which does not enjoy the same tax-exempt status as the parent corporation but is permitted to participate in electoral politics. Some of the AIDS organizations have banded together for political purposes, forming lobbying groups like National Organizations Responding to AIDS (NORA) and the AIDS Action Council. These and other groups have attempted to influence AIDS-related decisions in Washington, such as the establishment of the Office of National AIDS Policy, and the hiring and firing of President Clinton's first AIDS policy coordinator, Kristine Gebbie. (Gebbie's successor, legislative specialist Patsy Fleming, was appointed in November 1994.)

Another recent controversial issue in which NAPWA and other AIDS organizations became involved was the question of licensing the sale of HIV test kits for home use. (The kits do not give an immediate readout but require mailing in the kit for analysis; the findings are then conveyed to the client by telephone.) NAPWA and NLGHA (see chapter 12) opposed the licensing, claiming that a positive result conveyed over the telephone would lead to an increase in suicides by HIV-positive people. Proponents of the test cited surveys indicating that many more people would get tested if the kit were available, and pointed out that the clinics that NLGHA represents have a major financial interest in clinic-based testing.

In view of the number and scale of the AIDS service organizations, and their history of rapid growth, it is hardly surprising that significant organizational problems have arisen. Accusations of serious financial mismanagement have been leveled against several major AIDS organizations, including Shanti Project San Francisco, Philadelphia Community Health Alternatives, the Cascade AIDS Project, and AIDS Arms of Dallas.[20] Such accusations have led to the cancellation of government contracts, steep declines in donations, or the resignation or dismissal of administrative officers or board members. It can also happen that the different organizations in one city begin to compete with each other, not just for financial contributions, but also for qualified administrators and board members, volunteers, and even clients.

Perhaps the most notable services provided by community-based organizations to people with AIDS are the Buddy programs. These programs aim to establish one-on-one pairings between people with AIDS and volunteers, in an effort to provide a dependable, personal source of support. The volunteers are expected to visit their clients regularly and to provide support when they are in crisis. The tone of the relationship may vary from professional to intimate, but usually a strong bond develops between volunteer and client. The volunteers are themselves supported by group sessions with other volunteers and professional staff. Philip Kayal has made a sociological study of volunteerism at one AIDS service organization in his book *Bearing Witness* (see Further Reading).

Guy, an African-American man in his twenties who lives in West Hollywood, told us of his experiences as a Buddy.

I joined AIDS Project Los Angeles and made a lot of friends, which basically made me come out to myself. I saw an interview on television with a woman who was in a Buddy program—her last Buddy had just passed away—and she was saying about all the people dying alone, and I thought to myself, I can't imagine anyone dying alone. And so next weekend I joined the Buddy Program. I figured, what else can I do, I can't study it medically, I can't contribute a whole bunch of money, so I gave my time. The training was for two-and-a-half weekends. We had Buddy panels, client panels, sessions on death and dying, sessions on the disease itself, which was two or three hours of medical terms that went above everyone's head. It was a challenging thing. There's a final interview, then they match you up with someone. My first person was matched with me because we're both black, because there's such a shortage of black Buddies. We're not allowed to say "I don't want someone who's black, I don't want someone who's Latino, I don't want a woman." That's the client's choice, because they need to feel comfortable with whoever they're matched up with. I ended up with a black man, about 45 years old, he was infected through intravenous drug use. His family wrote him off. He said on his profile that he doesn't like affectionate men. I *am* really affectionate—whether it's gay, straight or whatever, I just tend to be "touchy." We had nothing in common. He wasn't gay, we had totally different backgrounds. I was afraid I would come across kind off snotty to him, and I did. And so we divorced.

I was reassigned to another man who I stayed with all the way to the end. We got along wonderfully. He got it through anal sex. He was about 36. He was White. We spent four out of seven days a week together. We would just spend time together. He was a set designer for a club, every Friday we'd go set up the stage, then go to the bar. APLA doesn't like you to drink with your client, but we're talking two adults. We went to the beach—things like that. I left on a three-week trip to Europe, and when I came back I went over to his house and he wasn't there. The neighbor across the hall told me, "He's in the hospital, prepare yourself, he looks like he's been in a concentration camp." I went to the hospital, but he died that day.

The Buddy programs are experiencing change and stress as the epidemic progresses. Originally, nearly all Buddy volunteers were gay white men, as were the majority of the clients. As the first generation of volunteers moved on, burned out, or fell sick themselves, they were replaced by a more heterogeneous group, including large numbers of women, both lesbian and heterosexual, and a more diverse ethnic mix. The clients too, have changed—many are nongay or nonwhite or do not live where most volunteers live. Meeting the wishes of clients and volunteers in the matching process has become much harder, and substantial waiting lists have developed in some cities.

A similar problem besets AIDS service organizations in general. Gay Men's Health Crisis, which in spite of its name is committed to serve all people affected by HIV, now has a client base of which nearly a quarter are women or heterosexual men, many of them Latino or African-American. Not only are the needs of these clients different from those of gay white men, there may also be problems of communication and trust between the different groups. To some extent, these problems are being addressed by attracting members of these newer groups to volunteer, employee, and leadership positions in the AIDS organizations. But the tradition of volunteerism, and the financial means to practice it, are less developed in the Latino and African-American communities than they are in white communities. Furthermore, it is at least a possibility that fundraising in the gay community will become harder as the donated dollars are used increasingly for nongay clients.

There are those in the gay community who believe that the AIDS service organizations have a harmful effect overall, by lessening the apparent impact of the disease and hence removing the issue from the public conscience and the political arena. Larry Kramer has lambasted those who work for these organizations as fools, dupes, and worse: "Organizations like GMHC and APLA are indeed our enemies," he wrote in a 1994 *Advocate* article.[21] "They're our exterminators. GMHC is our Dachau, and APLA is our Auschwitz—the places we send all our 'Jews' so that they can be put to death quietly, so that no one can hear our agonizing screams in the dead of night." If there is any grain of truth to Kramer's hyperbole, it is this: the AIDS service industry does tend to "infantilize" people with AIDS, to present them as lovable, helpless children who deserve our attention and our dollars, more than as adults with rights or a voice of their own. APLA's logo, two motherly hands soothing a limp-wristed victim, seems to epitomize this attitude: it stands in extreme contrast to the clenched fists of ACT UP.

Yet the service organizations have a record of accomplishment unparalleled in the history of American philanthropy. They have not cured a single case of AIDS, but they have prevented thousands of cases, and they have made AIDS a less painful, less lonely experience for hundreds of thousands. They are helping to find a cure and they are actively engaged in the political process. They have done all this while many of those who were truly charged with the nation's welfare did nothing.

Gay Professionals

The AIDS crisis has motivated many gay and lesbian professionals to change the focus of their work, either to join the battle against AIDS directly, or to assist in the community's general development. Doctors and other health professionals have of course had the most obvious opportunity to get involved. In the early days of the epidemic, gay and lesbian health professionals did heroic work, for example on the AIDS ward at San Francisco General Hospital. In the atmosphere of general hysteria and aversion that surrounded AIDS in the early 1980s, they (along with many heterosexual colleagues) struggled to provide effective treatment, or when that was not possible to at least give humane care. Since that time the treatment of AIDS has become much more broadly based and routine. There are still many gays and lesbians doing extraordinary work in big city hospitals, but they are no longer the ones who are recognized and sought out by the community. These days, the focus is on the "AIDS practice," the private medical practice or group practice whose patients are almost entirely gay men with AIDS. The physicians who head these practices may be very caring and skilled in AIDS treatment, and their patients can certainly be confident of a gay-friendly reception. But not seldom, the promise of great wealth that these practices offer leads to undignified competition for patients, suboptimal care, and a neglect of the medical needs of impoverished or uninsured people. These problems are not unique to AIDS: they are endemic to the American medical system. But they stand out in particularly stark relief given that so many people are devoting their lives to combating AIDS with little prospect of significant personal gain.

Many gay and lesbian lawyers, law students, and paralegals have also become directly involved in the battle against AIDS. They have done this by assisting AIDS service organizations with their incorporation and their ongoing legal needs, by volunteering in legal clinics, by providing legal counsel in HIV-related court cases, and by helping draft legislation protecting the rights of people with AIDS.

Priests and other religious workers have become involved, not only in their role of providing spiritual counsel to those affected by the disease, but also in more practical ways. They have started and run service organizations. In Los Angeles, for example, the charismatic Bishop Carl Bean and his Unity Fellowship Church founded the Minority AIDS Project, while members of the gay-friendly All Saints Episcopal Church in Pasadena founded the AIDS Service Center in that city. Gay and gay-friendly churchpeople have also done much to counter the propaganda of the religious right, and thus to foster a nonjudgmental attitude toward people affected by HIV. It should be stressed that church involvement in AIDS relief is not necessarily tied to an approving attitude toward homosexuality. The Roman Catholic diocese in Los Angeles, for example, has founded the Serra Project, which runs three AIDS residential facilities and is nondiscriminatory in its admission policy.

There are really very few occupations that have not provided the opportunity for gays and lesbians to join the struggle against AIDS. Gay journalists, led by Randy Shilts of the *San Francisco Chronicle,* have brought the plague into the consciousness of an unwilling public. Gay writers like Paul Monette have documented the personal impact of the disease. Gay teachers have promoted AIDS awareness among schoolchildren. Gay printers, publishers, accountants, designers, hairstylists, computer professionals, entertainers, and many others have donated their services to AIDS causes. Gay morticians have embalmed the dead, sometimes when others were too fearful to do so.

Several industries where gay men are well represented have formed industry-specific fundraising or educational organizations. The oldest of these is DIFFA, the Design Industries Foundation for AIDS. Founded in 1984, DIFFA has twenty chapters nationwide and has raised over $19 million for AIDS service organizations though cause-related marketing and fashion shows. In 1993 and 1994 the "DIFFA Collection," a traveling show and auction of 800 celebrity-customized Levis denim jackets, toured seven cities. In the entertainment industry the most prominent AIDS organization is Broadway Cares/Equity Fights AIDS. This New York-based fundraising organization acts as an AIDS benevolent fund within the industry, and also makes grants to AIDS service organizations across the country. Its major fundraising event is the annual Easter Bonnet Competition, in which the casts of rival Broadway shows model zany headgear. The 1994 contest raised $1 million.

Lesbians and AIDS

Because so few lesbians have contracted HIV, compared with gay men,[22] one might have expected lesbians to distance themselves from the epidemic. In fact, however, lesbians have been involved in the fight against AIDS from the start. At the beginning of the epidemic, for example, when AIDS services were almost nonexistent, a group of lesbians in San Francisco took dying gay men into their homes. Since then, lesbians have taken a highly visible role in forming and running AIDS service organizations.

One lesbian who has been outspoken in her concern about lesbians and AIDS is Amber Hollibaugh, head of GMHC's Lesbian AIDS Project in New York. Hollibaugh estimates that there are 8,000 lesbians nationwide who are HIV-positive.[23] Although most researchers would attribute these women's infection to sex with men or injection drug use, Hollibaugh believes that woman-to-woman transmission is seriously underreported because, she claims, a history of just one sexual encounter with a man is sufficient for a case to be labeled "heterosexual transmission," even when the woman is known to have an HIV-positive female partner. "You sit there and realize that people are just committed to a certain ideology," Hollibaugh said. "It doesn't matter what the facts are." Whether or not Hollibaugh is right about woman-to-woman transmission of HIV, she is clearly correct when she emphasizes two other points. First, the notion that "lesbians" only have sex with women and "straight women" only have sex with men is a serious oversimplification of what people actually do, an oversimplification that can spell danger for all women regardless of their sexual orientation. Second, the present low incidence of HIV among lesbians should be regarded as a challenge to action, not a reason for complacency. As Hollibaugh put it, "it's one of the few communities that could still actively construct prevention."

Outed by AIDS

Because of AIDS, the average American now knows the identities of far more gays and lesbians than he or she did in 1980. This new familiarity with homosexuals has come about through three mechanisms: the involuntary revelation of the sexual orientation of people with AIDS by the disease itself, the deliberate exposure of prominent gays and lesbians by AIDS activists, and the voluntary emergence of gays and lesbians from the closet in response to the epidemic.

The first widely known public figure who was revealed to be gay when he contracted AIDS was the actor Rock Hudson, in 1985. Since then, the list has grown inexorably year by year. Some of these have been people whose homosexuality was already widely known within the gay community and perhaps suspected outside it: Liberace and Rudolf Nureyev are examples. Others, like attorney Roy Cohn and Republican congressman Stewart McKinney, had been deep in the closet. Collectively, the list of celebrities who have contracted or died of AIDS has forced the public to realize that gay people are common in public life. But more significant than the few famous people who have fallen sick or died are the thousands of ordinary people who have done so. Many of these people have been gay men who, before they fell ill, were "out" only to a limited circle of gay acquaintances. All too often, their illness was the reason that relatives, work associates, and others found out about their homosexuality. It seems likely that millions of Americans have come to "know" gay men because they were diagnosed with AIDS. Many gay men with AIDS have returned to their families of origin, perhaps to small towns far from the gay-friendly coastal cities, and have forced the citizens of these towns to acknowledge for the first time that a gay man is one of their own.

The deliberate exposure of gay public figures—"outing"—is not necessarily tied to AIDS; in fact, the practice dates back at least to 1902, when the German industrialist Alfred Krupp was outed by the gay-friendly socialist journal *Vorwärts* (he committed suicide as a result). But the AIDS crisis has been the trigger for an explicit policy of outing by activists such as Michelangelo Signorile, who, after participating in several ACT UP demonstrations, felt himself called to expose closeted gays in public life. In his periodical *OutWeek*, and through other means, Signorile exposed a number of gay men in high places, including Pentagon spokesman Pete Williams and (posthumously) publisher Malcolm Forbes.

There has been considerable debate about outing. Some people have criticized the practice on moral grounds, that is, as an unwarranted invasion of privacy. Against this argument it can be said that homosexuality, like heterosexuality, is an important aspect of a person's identity, not a sleazy set of bedroom encounters. In this view, the public is entitled to know the sexual orientation of public figures, who, in essence, trade privacy for power. Another argument made against outing is that it inflicts significant harm on those outed. Yet it is hard to find documented examples of such harm. We no longer live in the kind of society that drove Krupp to suicide. In fact some people who have been outed in recent years have more or less thanked their outers for helping them do something they were not able to do on their own.[24]

Perhaps a more significant question concerns the effectiveness of outing as a instrument of gay politics. In his book, *Queer in America*, Signorile argues that outing has radically changed the climate for gays and lesbians in this country. He claims, for example, that the outing of Pete Williams "did indeed make a big dent in the military's policy against gays."[25] But it does not seem, at this point, that the policy has suffered a "big dent" at all, and it is certainly questionable whether Pete Williams's outing played a role in any favorable changes that may have occurred. One problem with outing is that people who are dragged kicking and screaming out of the closet are not good advertisements for homosexuality. Another problem is that the sheer number of people who can be forcibly outed is pretty inconsequential, compared with those who are openly gay or become so through AIDS or through their own actions. It may be that involuntary outing is motivated as much by rage and even by a desire for self-promotion as it is by any evidence that it serves a significant purpose.

Quite a different story is the "self-outing" of gays and lesbians in response to the epidemic. Motivated by their personal experiences of suffering or loss, or by the perceived threat to the gay community as a whole, gays and lesbians have come out of the closet in enormous numbers. And because coming out is a lifelong process, rather than a single event, each individual has been propelled some distance along his or her own path toward self-realization. Some people have come to acknowledge their homosexuality to themselves for the first time, some have come out to family and friends, some have made public announcements, become activists, or have involved themselves in the community in a variety of ways. This change of attitude, multiplied a millionfold, has brought about a sea change in gay and lesbian life—a new morality, in effect, which has made pride and service into obligations rather than options.

AIDS and the Community

AIDS is a disease of a hundred losses. The gay man with AIDS must face the loss of youth and beauty, of strength and self-sufficiency, sometimes of reason itself, before he comes to the ultimate loss. And the loss is shared by the lover who must go on alone, often to face the same fate, by parents who must bury the son who was to have supported them in their old age, and by the shrinking circle of friends whose lives are diminished, loss by loss. Beyond this individual, personal loss is the loss experienced by the entire gay community, not just of so many of its leaders and stars, but the loss of its very substance, the depopulation of the gay community. And even beyond this loss is the loss to society as a whole—a loss that can be counted in dollars, as so many young men are cut off at the beginning of their productive years, or that can be felt as a deep pain, as so much of the heart and wit and grace and magic of America is extinguished.

Not countering these losses, but existing alongside of them, are gains that also need to be recorded. Faced with AIDS, the gay community has grown and matured. Before AIDS, the gay movement was about gay rights. We do not diminish what was achieved in that era; on the contrary, we have a deepened respect for those who did not require the spur of AIDS to get involved. But since AIDS, the gay movement has been about more than rights: it has been about the duty of gays and lesbians to their community, and their pride as a community in fulfilling that duty. AIDS has given gays and lesbians a sense of unity and purpose and urgency, as nothing else has done. The results are to be seen everywhere, not just in the sphere of AIDS. Since the beginning of the epidemic, gays and lesbians have made enormous strides in visibility, acceptance, and respect, strides that would have been modest steps otherwise.

Further Reading

Jonsen, A. R., and J. Stryker, eds. *The Social Impact of AIDS in the United States*. Washington, D.C.: National Academy Press, 1993.

Kayal, Philip M. *Bearing Witness: Gay Men's Health Crisis and the Politics of AIDS*. Boulder: Westview Press, 1993.

Shilts, Randy. *And the Band Played On: Politics, People, and the AIDS Epidemic*. New York: St. Martin's Press, 1987.

IV Rights

What is the legal status of gays and lesbians, and how is this status evolving under the influence of gay activism and changing public opinion? We divide these questions, somewhat arbitrarily, into their legal and political aspects. Chapter 15 asks how the U.S. Constitution, the body of federal, state, and local laws, and the activities and opinions of lawyers and jurists influence the lives of lesbians and gay men. Chapter 16 describes the political processes, traditional and nontraditional, that are being used both to further and to hinder the evolution of gay rights.

15

The Law

Over the past forty years, the law has changed considerably for lesbians and gay men. In the 1950s, it was something to be avoided at all costs. Not just because of the sodomy statutes, but because one's identity as a homosexual, if known, was enough to damn one in any legal matter, however remotely connected with sex. Today, thanks to decades of tireless activism, the law offers gays and lesbians some specific protections, and a gay or lesbian identity is no bar to successful legal action in many fields of life. There are large numbers of openly gay or lesbian lawyers, a few openly gay or lesbian judges, and a handful of gay or lesbian legislators and political appointees in Washington.

In spite of these advances, the law still lags painfully behind what lesbians and gay men consider their due, and even behind general public opinion in some matters. But there are many active avenues for change, so much so that this chapter will probably be out of date in some respects before it reaches the bookstores. For this reason (and also because we are not lawyers) we do not attempt to cover legal matters in a how-to fashion. Rather, we will attempt to depict some of the general legal principles that affect the rights of lesbians and gay men, and to point out the areas of the law where changes are taking place.

The Constitutional Basis for Gay and Lesbian Rights

Because so many of those who came to North America were refugees from religious, political, or economic persecution, and because the United States were born in revolution from an oppressive colonial power, the Declaration of Independence placed an extraordinary emphasis on individual rights. Men were "created equal" and had "inalienable rights," including the right to "life, liberty and the pursuit of happiness." The 1787 Constitution did not incorporate these radical sentiments into its articles, but subsequent amendments laid out certain kinds of individual rights that could not be infringed on by federal or state law. Of special significance to gay men and lesbians are the right of free speech and assembly (First Amendment) and the right to due process and equal protection of the law (Fourteenth Amendment).

On the face of it, these amendments unequivocally establish a person's right to claim a gay or lesbian identity, to advocate homosexuality and gay rights, and to march in a gay pride parade. But the devil is in the details. May a city, for example, demand that a gay group post a bond before putting on a parade, and may the amount of the bond be higher for the gay group than for other groups, perhaps with the justification that greater expenses for security will be required? Thus the grand principles of the Constitution peter out into a thousand vexing instances, where one judge's opinion is as good as another's.

The Constitution, in spite of its protection of individual rights, was not read as prohibiting slavery or giving women the right to vote, until specific amendments were enacted to these ends. Similarly, the Constitution has not traditionally been interpreted to offer protection or rights to gays and lesbians, because homosexuality is not mentioned in that document. But the Constitution is subject to interpretation by jurists—men and women whose attitudes are shaped by contemporary standards. Even without amendment, the Constitution evolves along with American society, but the rate of evolution is greatly influenced by the particular individuals who constitute the judiciary, especially the Supreme Court.

Right to Privacy

One concept that has condensed out of judicial interpretation of the Constitution is the "right to privacy." This right is nowhere explicitly mentioned in the Constitution,[1] but it has been held to be a fundamental right implicit in the due process clause of the Fourteenth Amendment. The right to privacy has been a central issue in the evaluation of laws dealing with sexual matters. Most famously, the 1973 Supreme Court decision in *Roe v. Wade*[2] ruled that laws banning abortion were unconstitutional because they interfered with a pregnant woman's right to privacy in choosing whether to procreate. The right to marry and the right to use contraceptives have similarly been declared parts of the right to privacy.

The right to privacy was also the central issue in *Bowers v. Hardwick*,[3] the 1986 Supreme Court case in which state sodomy statutes were held to be constitutional. Michael Hardwick, a resident of Georgia, was arrested for sodomy when a police officer, who had entered his home legally in connection with another matter, observed him engaged in sex with another man. It would be hard to think of a case more appropriate for a constitutional challenge, and in fact the federal Court of Appeals decided in favor of Hardwick. But the Supreme Court reversed the decision by a five-to-four vote. According to the majority opinion, homosexual activity did not fall within the areas previously defined as entitled to privacy, namely the areas of family, marriage, and procreation. Justice Blackmun's dissent is quoted in chapter 3. One of the justices who voted with the majority, Justice Powell, later stated that he "probably made a mistake in that one," but added that he considered the case "frivolous."[4]

Seeking gay rights by appealing to the right to privacy is somewhat paradoxical: in a sense it is attempting to legalize the closet. Arrests under sodomy statutes are in fact extremely rare, because by and large it is the public aspects of homosexuality and gay culture that arouse antipathy, not what people do in their bedrooms.[5]

Equal Protection and Suspect Classes

The equal protection clause of the Fourteenth Amendment is also relevant to the sodomy statutes, and to the rights of gay people in general. Equal protection means not just that the laws should apply equally to everyone, but that laws should not discriminate unfairly against certain groups. The laws banning interracial marriage, for example, were struck down because, even though these laws might be enforced uniformly on everyone, they were bound to have a disproportionately restrictive effect on people belonging to racial minorities. Of course, equal protection does not prevent the law from discriminating against *any* group in society. Thieves, for example, are subject to imprisonment while nonthieves generally are not. What then are the criteria that decide whether a certain group may be discriminated against?

In general, if a law discriminates or permits discrimination against a group, there must be a rational basis for that discrimination. It is easy enough to find a rational basis for imprisoning thieves, or for preventing teenagers from purchasing alcohol. But the courts have recognized that apparently rational justifications may be used to mask irrational bigotry. It has therefore become a constitutional doctrine that legal discrimination against certain groups must have more than a "rational basis"; it must serve a "compelling state interest," which means essentially that it must be necessary for public safety. Groups entitled to this heightened level of judicial scrutiny are called "suspect classes": judges should suspect that laws that discriminate against them are based on bigotry.

To qualify as a "suspect class," a group must have a history of persecution, and must have been unable to obtain protection from this persecution by the usual political channels. There is little question that lesbians and gay men qualify on these grounds. A third requirement, however, is that the characteristic that forms the basis for discrimination be "immutable"—something, like race, that marks the individual as belonging to the group independently of any behavior, choice, etc.

In the case of gays and lesbians, this immutability requirement has been a significant stumbling block. Is homosexuality, or sexual orientation in general, immutable? Most gays and lesbians today feel that their sexual orientation is not a choice but something they became aware of and accepted, something given. The scientific evidence, reviewed in chapter 4, supports this notion to a considerable degree. The extreme difficulty, if not total impossibility, of changing one's sexual orientation (whether by punishment or by psychological, biological, or religious means) also supports the idea of immutability. In their book *Created Equal: Why Gay Rights Matter to America*,[6] Michael Nava and Robert Dawidoff state baldly that "being gay is what legal scholars call an 'immutable characteristic,' like race or gender."

But homosexuality has *not* generally been accepted by the courts as an immutable characteristic in the legal sense. Rather, the prevailing legal notion is that homosexuality is simply a set of behaviors that anyone might show, not an intrinsic characteristic. A good example of this was the decision in a recent case by a California Court of Appeal.[7] The plaintiff, Tim Curran, had been excluded from becoming a Scoutmaster on account of his being openly gay. In the decision, which went in favor of the Boy Scouts, Justice Fred Woods wrote: "An avowed homosexual scoutmaster would cause the boys to be ... more likely to engage in homosexual conduct.... Homosexuality is identifiable only by conduct or affirmation [saying that one is gay]; in other words, expressive activity: 'Homosexuality is behavioral and hence is fundamentally different from traits such as race.' It was Curran's conduct and advocacy, and not his status, that caused his exclusion."[8] In general, judges have not drawn a distinction between homosexual acts (e.g., sodomy) and a homosexual orientation. For this reason, the Supreme Court decision in *Bowers v. Hardwick* has been interpreted as ruling out the designation of gays and lesbians as a suspect class.

Freedom of Expression

Thanks to the First Amendment, government may not limit freedom of speech, assembly, or association (freedom of association is not explicitly mentioned in the First Amendment, but has been interpreted as arising from the other two freedoms). The Constitution does not prohibit *private* organizations from limiting these freedoms. Thus, in principle, gays and lesbians have better legal protection at public schools or in public employment than at their private counterparts. In practice, of course, many private colleges and corporations do take pains to protect these freedoms.

Freedom of speech (which covers the spoken and written word as well as certain behaviors that are essentially symbolic, such as flag burning) has certain limitations. One may not incite someone to commit a crime. Obscenity, libel, and slander are not protected, nor are "fighting words." Religious and political speech has the strongest protection, advertising the weakest. And while an interior designer, say, has the right to say "I'm color-blind," a public employer also has the right to fire him on the basis of the information imparted, if he can show a rational basis (not hard in this example).

One gay man who has tested the limits of free speech is Aaron Fricke. In 1979, as a high school senior in Rhode Island, Fricke requested permission to take another boy to the prom. After the school's refusal, Fricke sued and won in Federal District Court.[9] The court ruled that his proposed action was "symbolic speech." The case, and Fricke's book,[10] did wonders for gay and lesbian high school students. Nowadays it is generally acknowledged that gay and lesbian student groups at public institutions (whether high schools or colleges) have the same right to organize, speak out, use classroom space, and receive support as other student groups, at least insofar as their associations include advocacy as one of their functions.

A gay or lesbian teacher's freedom of speech varies with location. It is greatest away from the school: a gay public school teacher cannot be fired for advocating gay rights on television, for example, even if all of his or her students are watching, and even if the school has a legal policy of not employing gay or lesbian teachers. (If the teacher acknowledges being homosexual on television, however, the school board may fire him or her if it has such a policy, according to some court decisions). The teacher's freedom of speech diminishes on school property and is minimal in the classroom, where the school board has the right to control what is taught.

Organizing a gay rights march or forming a gay association is of course protected under the First Amendment. But there is no automatic right to form a gay contingent in someone else's march or parade, nor for gays or lesbians to join private associations of people who do not wish to admit them. This issue has come up in connection with the St. Patrick's Day parades in Boston and New York. In Boston the Massachusetts state courts ordered the parade organizers to admit gay contingents in 1992, 1993, and 1994. In retaliation, the organizers canceled the parade in 1994. In New York, on the other hand, the courts have consistently allowed the parade organizers to exclude gay groups. The differing judgments result from differing interpretations of the exact nature and purpose of the parade: especially whether it is essentially a political event, devoted to promoting the views of a particular group, or whether it is more like a public festival. In 1995 the United States Supreme Court ruled that the organizers of the Massachusetts parade also had the right to exclude gay groups.

Federal Law

Civil Rights Legislation

Federal legislation now greatly limits the power of employers to discriminate on the basis of race, sex, disability, and other grounds. Although each piece of civil rights legislation may be limited in scope, collectively such laws have a snowball effect: by bringing more African-Americans into Congress, for example, they make it more likely that the concerns of African-Americans will be addressed in future legislation.

As yet, there is no broad federal statute outlawing discrimination on the basis of sexual orientation. (The 1990 Americans with Disabilities Act, however, does offer protection to gay men who face discrimination on account of their HIV status.) A broad civil rights bill prohibiting sexual orientation discrimination in employment, housing, and services has been before Congress for many years, but it has never come close to passage. A more modest bill, restricted to the area of employment, was introduced in 1994.

Federal Employment

As an employer, the federal government has had a long history of discrimination against gays and lesbians. During the 1950s and 1960s many gays and lesbians were fired from the civil service, and the hiring of an openly homosexual individual would have been inconceivable. But a 1969 decision by the U.S. Court of Appeals for the District of Columbia (*Norton v. Macy*[11]) ruled that the mere fact that a civil service employee was homosexual or engaged in homosexual conduct was not sufficient grounds for dismissal. The Court wrote that "the notion that it could be an appropriate function of the federal bureaucracy to enforce the majority's conventional codes of conduct in the private lives of its employees is at war with elementary concepts of liberty, privacy, and diversity."[12] In 1973 the Civil Service Commission codified this ruling, stating that gay or lesbian employees may only be fired if their homosexual conduct compromises their fitness for their job. Whether the *Norton* decision protects federal employees' right to be open about their sexual orientation at work is uncertain. In a more recent case (*Singer v. U.S. Civil Service Commission*[13]) a federal court upheld the government's right to dismiss an openly gay employee. The decision was vacated by the Supreme Court, and the plaintiff eventually won reinstatement at an administrative hearing. It still appears, however, that an employee's openness about his or her orientation may be taken into consideration in dismissal hearings. For example, a 1982 case concerning a dismissed customs officer was decided in favor of the officer because his homosexuality "did not manifest itself in any way that resulted in notoriety or public censure which would reflect unfavorably on

Customs."[14] In other words, if a federal employee's open homosexuality did result in public censure, he or she might be liable to dismissal. The present legal situation, although a great improvement over what existed twenty years ago, is murky: a typical example of the situation generated by evolving case law in the absence of clear directives from civil rights legislation.

The Military

The U.S. armed forces operate more-or-less outside the law, or, to put it more tactfully, they have traditionally been accorded great latitude by Congress and the courts. As a result, the military has become one of the last bastions of unimpeded, unapologetic homophobia. Homosexuality, with or without evidence of homosexual conduct, has been both a bar to enlistment and grounds for discharge, often with less-than-honorable status. Nearly 7,000 military personnel were discharged for homosexuality in the period 1985–1989. The navy discharges its personnel for homosexuality at a higher rate than the other services, and women are at greater risk of discharge than men.[15]

This policy became the center of gay and lesbian attention in 1992, when Bill Clinton, during his campaign for the presidency, promised to overthrow it. After his election, however, he did not take immediate action, but instead referred the matter to the Secretary of Defense for study. This was the cue for Senate Armed Services Committee Chairman Sam Nunn to initiate a series of hearings designed to heighten public awareness of the supposed threat posed by gays and lesbians in the military. At one point, Nunn had himself photographed in the crowded sleeping quarters of a submarine, where crewmen apparently live in terror of homosexual advances. Nunn's strategy succeeded. Even though gay groups mounted campaigns of their own (notable among these was the Campaign for Military Service, spearheaded by legal activist Tom Stoddard), public opinion, as expressed by letters and phone calls to Congress, was overwhelmingly in support of Nunn's position. In July 1993 President Clinton announced a new policy, dubbed "don't ask, don't tell, don't pursue," which was incorporated into new regulations issued by the Pentagon in December 1993.

The new policy continues the ban on homosexual conduct in the military. Furthermore, part of the definition of homosexual conduct, according to the new regulations, is openly declaring oneself to be homosexual. Anyone who does so will be discharged unless they can prove that they have no propensity to engage in homosexual acts (a difficult thing for a homosexual person to prove, one might think). The new policy does end the practice of asking new recruits about their sexual orientation, and it also states that sex acts in private between consenting adults will normally not be investigated. But basically, gays and lesbians are allowed to serve only so long as they remain deep in the closet, which was exactly the situation before the new policy was enacted.

Consideration of the actual numbers of discharges illustrates how little the new policy has done for gay and lesbian service members. Although the total number of discharges for homosexuality fell from 949 in 1991 to 597 in 1994, this decline mirrors the shrinkage in the total size of the armed forces during the same period. The fraction of the total service personnel discharged for homosexuality has remained constant at 0.04 percent per year.[16]

There have been many legal challenges to the Pentagon's policies. In the 1970s two discharged servicemen, Leonard Matlovich and Vernon "Copy" Berg, brought suit against the Pentagon. The U.S. Court of Appeals instructed the Pentagon to find other grounds than homosexuality per se to discharge the two men. The cases were eventually settled out of court. Another case, brought by Army Sgt. Perry Watkins, was notable for the revelation that the army had allowed him to reenlist on three occasions with the knowledge that he was gay. In ruling in Watkins' favor, the Ninth Circuit Court actually found that gays and lesbians constitute a suspect class,[17] but this finding was not confirmed on appeal to the full court.

Two recent cases involved self-disclosure of homosexuality. In 1987 Joseph Steffan, then a cadet at the U.S. Naval Academy, was forced to resign after telling his commandant that he was gay. In November 1993 a panel of the federal appeals court for the District of Columbia ordered the navy to commission him as an officer, but a year later the full court ruled in favor of the navy.[18] The court argued that for a serviceperson to admit to being homosexual is for practical purposes the same as admitting to engaging in homosexual conduct. The case was not appealed to the Supreme Court. The other case involved Naval Petty Officer Keith Meinhold, who was discharged after coming out on national television in 1992. He reenlisted in December 1993 after a series of court victories, which included a court order by U.S. District Judge Terry Hatter Jr. that prohibited all discrimination against gays in the military.[19] In August 1994 the U.S. Court of Appeals in San Francisco upheld Meinhold's reinstatement, but threw out Judge Hatter's broad ban on antigay discrimination.

Considering that women are at greater risk than men for being discharged for homosexuality, it is ironic that most attention has been paid to men. Several important cases have been brought by women, including Dusty Pruitt, Miriam Ben-Shalom, and Zoe Dunning. Perhaps the best-known case is that of Army Col. Margarethe Cammermeyer, who was discharged from the Washington National Guard in 1992 after she volunteered the fact that she is lesbian. Cammermeyer, who was awarded a Bronze Star for her service in Vietnam, was under consideration for appointment as chief nurse of the National Guard at the time of her disclosure. She is the highest-ranking officer ever to challenge the Pentagon's sexual orientation policy. Her lawsuit was argued on an equal-protection basis. She won her case at the district court level in June 1994.[20] Judge Thomas Zilly wrote: "Mere negative attitudes, or fear, are constitutionally impermissible bases for discriminatory governmental policies.... The rationales offered by the government to justify its exclusion of homosexual service members are grounded solely in prejudice." An appeal is likely.

In late 1993 the ACLU and Lambda Legal Defense and Education Fund filed suit against the Defense Department on behalf of six gay service members who had not been the subject of investigation or discharge. The suit (*Able v. U.S.A.*) claimed that the new regulations infringed on their rights to free speech and equal protection. Because the suit itself exposed the six as gay, they also sought a court order prohibiting the Defense Department from discharging them during the litigation. In April 1994 U.S. District Judge Eugene Nickerson of New York issued such an order. A year later he decided the case in favor of the plaintiffs. His ruling emphasized the difference between status and actions. "This court concludes" he wrote, "that under the First Amendment a mere statement of homosexual orientation is not sufficient proof of intent to commit acts as to justify the initiation of discharge proceedings."

Thus there are a number of current cases that seem likely to lead to a Supreme Court ruling on the constitutionality of the military's policy toward gays and lesbians. A just resolution of this issue could do much to strengthen the legal position of gays and lesbians in all fields of employment.

Immigration and Naturalization

In the past, gays and lesbians could be denied permission to enter the United States under a clause of the Immigration and Nationality Act that excluded persons "afflicted with psychopathic personality or sexual deviation." In recent years, little effort has been put into enforcing the policy of exclusion, and in 1993 the Clinton administration officially ended it. A case in 1994 showed how far attitudes have changed: for the first time, an applicant was granted entry into the United States on the grounds that his homosexuality exposed him to danger in his native country. With respect to naturalization, sexual orientation has become a nonissue, thanks to a Fourth Circuit Court ruling in 1981.

Unfortunately, HIV status has replaced sexual orientation as an immigration issue for many gay men. Current policy denies entry, even on a visitor basis, to any HIV-positive individual.

During the Reagan-Bush years this policy was so strictly enforced that it led, for example, to the relocation of the International AIDS Conference to a foreign site. More recently there has been some liberalization—an exemption was granted for athletes attending the Gay Games in New York in 1994, for example. It is to be hoped that the policy will be recognized as unjust, not only in terms of the individuals affected by it, but also because the federal government has done so little to prevent the *export* of HIV, for example by American citizens participating in "sex tours" of Southeast Asia.

Budgetary Legislation

Even with the demise of revenue sharing, the federal government pours huge amounts of money into the states. This allows a substantial measure of federal control over matters that by their nature fall within the domain of state government, such as education. In 1994, for example, a bill passed the House that would have cut off federal education funds to any school district that offered programs supportive of gay and lesbian students. The effect of the bill was neutralized by an amendment that affirmed the right of schools to set their own curricula.

Equally, the federal government can use its budgetary powers to limit discrimination. It has used this power extensively to the benefit of women and minorities. A first example of the use of such powers to help gays and lesbians occurred in 1994: the California earthquake relief bill included a clause prohibiting discrimination on the basis of sexual orientation in the disbursement of emergency aid in the Los Angeles area. It is to be hoped that such language becomes standard in the nondiscrimination clauses of federal legislation.

State and Local Law

Gay Rights Legislation

Unlike the federal law, which barely makes mention of homosexuality, many states and localities have laws, executive orders, or ordinances that explicitly refer to gays and lesbians.

Some of these laws prohibit discrimination on the basis of sexual orientation in such areas as employment and housing. Laws of this type exist in the states of California, Hawaii, Massachusetts, Rhode Island, and Wisconsin, while Illinois, Michigan, Minnesota, New Jersey, New Mexico, New York, Pennsylvania, Ohio, and Washington have executive orders or civil service rules barring discrimination by government agencies. Most of the largest cities in the United States have some kind of gay rights ordinance or executive order in place; the major exceptions are Cincinnati, Dallas, Houston, St. Louis, and Miami. Four cities (San Francisco, Minneapolis, Seattle, and Santa Cruz) have enacted ordinances prohibiting discrimination on the basis of gender identity: these laws protect transsexuals and cross-dressers.

It is much less common for medium or small-sized cities to have antidiscrimination ordinances; those that do tend to be liberal or gay-friendly enclaves like Berkeley, Laguna Beach, Aspen, and Chapel Hill. Unfortunately, city and other local nondiscrimination ordinances are rarely enforced with any vigor, and they are easily overturned by local initiative or by countervailing state laws.

Examples of the conflict between states and localities in the area of gay rights are the battles that have raged in Colorado and Oregon. In Colorado, the cities of Denver, Boulder, and Aspen have for several years had nondiscrimination ordinances in place that include sexual orientation. In 1992 a group called Colorado for Family Values promoted a constitutional amendment ("Amendment 2") that would have repealed those ordinances and prohibited any future statewide or city ordinances of the same type. Amendment 2 passed by 53 to 47 percent at the November 1992 election. Opponents of the amendment challenged its constitutionality,[21] and a State District Judge, Jeffrey Bayless of Denver, granted an injunction suspending the enactment of the amendment before it was due to become law. A long trial in the fall of 1993 was a forum for the expression of every conceivable attitude toward homosexuality. Lawyers for the state of Colorado spoke of the "militant gay aggression" that was threatening the state's integrity. It was argued that discrimination against gays and lesbians was protected by the right to freedom of religion, since homosexuality is condemned in the Bible. On the other side, lawyers opposing the amendment argued that it was unconstitutional because it violated the fundamental right of a group to participate in the political process, as well as because it denied equal protection to a stigmatized "suspect class." In support of the suspect classification, witnesses such as molecular biologist Dean Hamer argued for a genetic influence on sexual orientation. In the end Judge Bayless did not buy the suspect class argument, but he did rule Amendment 2 unconstitutional as a violation of gays' and lesbians' fundamental right to political participation. The case was appealed, but in October 1994 the State Supreme Court sided with Judge Bayless by a six-to-one majority. Amendment 2, according to the high court, "alters the political process so that a targeted class is prohibited from obtaining legislative, executive and judicial protection or redress from discrimination, absent the consent of the majority of the electorate." The case has been accepted for review by the U.S. Supreme Court.

In Oregon the conflict has been even more complicated. The cities of Eugene and Portland have antidiscrimination ordinances in place. But in 1992 and 1993 an antigay group named Oregon Citizens' Alliance began persuading small towns to enact laws that prohibit antidiscrimination ordinances. Several towns enacted such laws, but a state law enacted in 1993 barred the enactment of the local antigay laws (the converse of the situation in Colorado). The Citizens' Alliance has in turn challenged the constitutionality of the state law. A statewide antigay initiative ("Measure 9") was defeated in 1992; a slightly watered-down version ("Measure 13") was reintroduced in 1994; it lost again, although the margin was closer. The intense conflict over homosexuality in Oregon reflects the changing demographics of the state, as large numbers of relatively young people migrate from California and elsewhere, bringing with them a liberal ethic that is at odds with the conservative traditions of the Northwest.

Of the several statewide antigay initiatives promoted around the country in 1994, only two actually made in onto the ballot (in Oregon and Idaho), and neither passed. (The only antigay initiative that did pass in 1994 was one in Alachua County, Florida, which repealed a local gay rights ordinance.) Nevertheless, it is clear that gay rights will remain a major political battleground. Part of the reason for this is that abortion rights, an issue even more divisive than gay rights, were taken out of the sphere of state law by the Supreme Court's ruling in *Roe v. Wade*. To some extent, gays and lesbians represent a substitute target: the public discussion of abortion and gay rights are both colored by moral attitudes toward nonprocreative sex.

The Sodomy Statutes

Although the U.S. Supreme Court has so far declined to rule sodomy statutes unconstitutional, such statutes have still been under attack at the state level. Such attack can be justified by peculiarities of the constitutions of individual states, or by peculiarities of the individual statutes. Pennsylvania's statute, for example, was ruled unconstitutional in 1980 on equal protection grounds: it outlawed oral or anal intercourse between unmarried, but not between married persons. Kentucky's statute, which outlawed oral or anal intercourse between same-sex but not opposite-sex partners, met a similar fate in 1992. The Nevada statute, which was similar to Kentucky's, was repealed by the state legislature in 1993. The Texas statute, also similar to Kentucky's, was ruled unconstitutional by a lower court in 1990, but a protracted legal battle led to the statute's reinstatement by the State Supreme Court in 1994. The sodomy statute in Massachusetts is more evenhanded: it condemns anyone guilty of anal intercourse to twenty years' imprisonment. Nevertheless it has been in legal limbo since 1974, when a parallel statute, barring "unnatural acts," was ruled not to apply to sexual behavior between adults in private. The states in which sodomy statutes are still fully operational are Alabama, Arizona, Arkansas, Florida, Georgia, Idaho, Kansas, Louisiana, Maryland, Minnesota, Mississippi, Missouri, Montana, North Carolina, Oklahoma, Rhode Island, South Carolina, Tennessee, Texas, Utah, and Virginia.

The sodomy statutes are rarely enforced—for every act of sodomy that leads to an arrest, millions must go unpunished. In fact, some cities in states with sodomy laws, such as Austin, Texas, and Phoenix, Arizona, have been able to enact antidiscrimination ordinances, thus giving protection to a class of people with a strong predisposition to break the law. (The Austin ordinance was overturned electorally in 1994.) But the sodomy statutes, dead letters though they mostly are, serve as a justification for the oppression of gays and lesbians in other fields, and as a general deterrent to gay rights legislation.

Other Sexual Offenses

The sexual offenses that really do affect gay men (though very rarely lesbians) are those variously termed public indecency, lewd and lascivious conduct, disorderly conduct, indecent exposure, importuning, soliciting, etc. Generally these offenses have to take place in public, although the word "public" is sometimes interpreted very broadly, to include for example a private sex club or a car parked in the darkest woods.

In the 1950s and 1960s, these laws were the mainstay of the legal oppression of gay men. Police busts of bars, clubs, and other gay meeting places led to mass arrests, often of men who were doing nothing more offensive than standing around talking. Oftentimes the charges were thrown out, but by then the harm had been done: the newspapers had published the names of the men concerned, and as a consequence they risked loss of job, marriage, and social position.

Nowadays, arrests of gay men on sex-related charges tend to be in parks, open spaces, or public toilets. It appears that the ready availability of gay bars, porno cinemas, and (in many cities) bathhouses and sex clubs has not diminished gay men's enthusiasm for outdoor encounters. Typically, a locality becomes established as a gay cruising-ground and sees increasingly heavy activity until nongay users of the space complain to the police. This leads to a police sweep that may be announced (in gay-friendly cities) or unannounced (elsewhere). A few arrests serve the purpose of moving the activity to some other location, at least for a while. Sometimes the police action is motivated by concern about crime perpetrated *against* gay men in cruising spots: Central Park in New York, Griffith Park in Los Angeles, and Balboa Park in San Diego, for example, have been the scene of numerous murders, assaults, and robberies of gay men.

Even in well-known cruising areas, it is often hard for police officers to observe actual sex in progress. Therefore it is common for undercover officers to pose as gay men and to make arrests when they are propositioned or when a man actually attempts a sex act with them. Entrapment is not a defense if the prosecution can show a predisposition to commit a crime. Nevertheless, juries tend to dislike the idea of a police officer spending his days in toilets waiting for someone to fondle him. It is relatively easy to obtain acquittal in such cases, particularly if the defendant and the police officer walked or drove to a more-or-less private location before sex was attempted.

Police busts of sex clubs still do take place, especially of clubs which encourage group sex. But convictions for lewd conduct or public indecency in such settings usually require that there was someone to be offended by the acts that took place. Sex clubs generally attempt to make this difficult to prove by asking every applicant whether he is gay and whether he is offended by seeing homosexual acts. Lesbian sex clubs, a relatively new phenomenon, have to take the same precautions.

Simply saying "Let's have sex" to an undercover officer is grounds for conviction for importuning or solicitation, at least in states that still have sodomy statutes. In other states such a statement may have First Amendment protection. Even loitering in a gay cruising area is an offense in many states, if there is intent to commit or solicit an indecent act.

Prostitution, whether male or female, is a crime almost everywhere. Both male and female prostitutes on the streets are subject to arrest for solicitation if they get into the car of an undercover officer and discuss terms. But in other ways male and female prostitution are quite different. Female prostitutes are often employed by pimps, or are part of businesses such as massage parlors, which are frequently made the target of undercover investigation. Male prostitutes, on the other hand, tend to be independent agents. If they operate off the streets, for example by advertising as "models" or "masseurs" in gay publications, they run little risk of arrest. A recent issue of *Frontiers*, a gay newsmagazine based in West Hollywood (see chapter 7), contained 544 such advertisements. It seems likely that male prostitution is a major industry in West Hollywood, yet aside from the arrest of a few streetwalkers, it is an industry that gets into little trouble with the law.

Hate Crimes

Hate or bias crimes are crimes against persons motivated by their membership in a group defined by such characteristics as race, national origin, religion, sex, disability, or sexual orientation. Violent crimes directed against gays and lesbians (gay-bashing) appear to have increased significantly in recent years. In Boston, Chicago, Minneapolis-St. Paul, New York, and San Francisco, reported antigay incidents increased by 127 percent between 1988 and 1993.[22] In Los Angeles County, antigay incidents increased by one-third between 1993 and 1994, surpassing reported hate crimes against any other group.[23] San Francisco experiences about the same number of incidents as Los Angeles, while New York sees about twice as many—632 antigay incidents were reported there in 1994.[24]

The law has traditionally looked leniently on crimes against gays and lesbians. Specious defenses such as "homosexual panic" were accepted in mitigation. (Homosexual panic is the supposedly involuntary violent reaction of a "latent homosexual" to meeting an openly gay person.) The trial of Harvey Milk's murderer Dan White in 1979 was highlighted by the infamous "Twinkie defense"—his supposed addiction to junk food—which helped to gain White an extraordinarily light sentence (see chapter 3).

More recently many states have attempted to clamp down on hate crimes by mandating increased penalties when a victim was targeted because of his or her membership in a group. Such hate crime laws, explicitly or implicitly including sexual orientation as a protected characteristic, now exist in twenty-two states and Washington, D.C. (New York is among the states that do not yet have such a law.) Many of the laws also mandate the collection of hate-crime statistics.

In 1993 the U.S. Supreme Court ruled (in *Wisconsin v. Mitchell*[25]) that such increased penalties for hate crimes are constitutional. Subsequently, Congress passed the Federal Hate Crimes Sentencing Enhancing Act, which allows increased sentences for federal crimes that are bias-motivated. Sexual orientation is explicitly mentioned as one of the bias categories in the act.

Whether the new laws are utilized depends greatly on the education of the legal community and the public in general. The California Department of Justice, for example, failed to collect hate-crime statistics in 1993 as mandated, citing budgetary constraints.

Employment

The basic legal principle regarding the hiring and firing of workers is that of "employment-at-will," that is, the notion that an employer has the right to select and dismiss employees for any reason or none. Obviously, this principle is injurious to lesbians and gay men, who commonly face discrimination in hiring and on the job. Over the years, however, the employment-at-will principle has been hemmed about with restrictions.

In public employment, there must generally be a rational basis for discriminating against any group. The situation for federal employees has been discussed above. For state or city employees, much depends on whether they live in a state or city that bars discrimination on the basis of sexual orientation in public employment. Even if they do not, however, they have certain protections. For example, public employees such as teachers may not be fired for exercising their constitutional rights, so long as this does not compromise their ability to perform their jobs. This has generally been interpreted to mean that a teacher may be openly gay or lesbian outside of school, march in gay rights parades, etc. (First Amendment protection), even if by this means his or her sexual orientation comes to the notice of students or parents. A teacher who reveals his or her sexual orientation or advocates gay rights legislation inside the classroom, on the other hand, may be dismissed by the school board. Education is of course one of the most sensitive areas for pro- and antigay advocates, since a large fraction of the population believes that teenagers can be "recruited" to homosexuality by gay teachers. Those educators who are openly gay or lesbian, and especially those who attempt to provide counseling for gay or lesbian students, face greater hostility than virtually any other gay group in this country. Luckily, progressive school boards, especially those that have at least one openly gay or lesbian board member, are beginning to lend support to their gay and lesbian teachers.

In private employment, the employment-at-will principle allows almost unfettered discrimination against gays and lesbians, except in states or cities that have laws specifically barring discrimination on the basis of sexual orientation, or in companies that have their own nondiscrimination policies that mention sexual orientation. Of course, these are the companies where problems are least likely to arise in the first place.

Gays and lesbians face discrimination in the workplace in ways that go beyond matters of hiring, firing, and promotion. For example, many companies offer medical insurance benefits to spouses of married employees, but not to domestic partners (whether of the same or the other sex). This discriminates against gay and lesbian employees because they are not able to marry their partners. Such policies are perfectly legal. It has even been ruled permissible for companies to remove a specific medical condition (AIDS) from medical coverage, even when this action was aimed at a single gay employee. Retirement benefits may be similarly restricted. Also, companies may ban indications of homosexuality (e.g., photographs of same-sex partners) while permitting equivalent heterosexual expression, at least in localities that do not have antidiscrimination statutes. All in all, the workplace can be a legal nightmare for gays and lesbians. In some ways it is a nightmare that is getting worse, as many gays and lesbians who were previously closeted at work begin to open up about their sexuality to their colleagues.

Housing and Services

As with employment, the areas of housing and services are governed by the at-will principle. In the absence of statutory provisions to the contrary, a landlord may refuse to rent to a gay person, a restaurant owner may refuse service to a gay person, and a club may refuse to allow a gay person to join. No rational basis for such discrimination need exist. However, several states and many large cities have enacted antidiscrimination laws or ordinances that cover housing and services. Furthermore, if the landlord or service provider is a government entity, a rational basis for discrimination is required under the equal protection clause of the Fourteenth Amendment. The Federal Housing Amendments Act prohibits housing discrimination on the basis of AIDS or HIV status.

A particularly fuzzy area of law deals with large organizations and their right to choose their membership in a discriminatory fashion. The Boy Scouts of America, for example, operates within this legal twilight. Founded by Lord Baden-Powell, who is widely believed to have been gay,[26] the Boy Scouts, or their American offshoot, have become stridently homophobic, banning gays as either Scouts or Scoutmasters. Claiming that their rejection of homosexuality is an essential component of the morality they wish to inculcate, the Scouts have argued that they are protected by the right of association, that is, the right of like-minded people to band together and exclude people who disagree with them. On the other hand it has been argued that the Boy Scouts of America is a business, subject to nondiscrimination laws that cover sexual orientation, such as California's Unruh Act.[27] The Curran case, which was decided in favor of the Scouts, was mentioned earlier in this chapter. In a more recent case (*Merino v. Boy Scouts of America*, 1994) the San Diego Superior Court ruled that the Boy Scouts *are* subject to the Unruh Act, and decided the case in favor of the plaintiff. During the case, the defense argued that homosexuality is merely a behavior that anyone might show, not an attribute capable of defining a group within society. One of us (Simon LeVay) testified as an expert witness against this argument, presenting the scientific evidence that gays and lesbians are indeed a definable class of people.

Marriage and Domestic Partnership

The usual legal definition of marriage is "the legal union of one man and one woman." This definition obviously excludes gay or lesbian couples from marriage. Marriage confers some significant legal benefits: these include the right to inherit property without a will, the right to workers' compensation after the death of a spouse, the right to assume leases and income tax and estate tax advantages, the right to sue for wrongful death of a spouse, the right to jointly adopt a child, hospital visitation rights, and the right to have sexual intercourse when one partner is below the legal age of consent. Thus gay and lesbian couples experience significant legal discrimination on account of their inability to marry, quite aside from the loss of any social or psychological benefits that marriage may bring. In spite of this, there has been considerable debate about the value of seeking the right to same-sex marriage. Some activists have expressed the view that marriage is an essentially heterosexual institution and that gays and lesbians should develop new, more liberated forms of relationship.[28]

There have been numerous unsuccessful attempts by same-sex couples to legally obtain marriage licenses. (Illegal same-sex marriage licenses have been common in some periods and places, for example in Harlem during the 1920s—see chapter

3.) In some states, the laws relating to marriage do not actually spell out that the couple must be of opposite sex, but the courts have always interpreted them to have that intention.

The most remarkable development in marriage law was a 1993 decision by the Hawaii Supreme Court. Three homosexual couples[29] had filed a complaint in 1991 against Hawaii's Department of Health, requesting a court declaration that the department applied the state's marriage law in an unconstitutional fashion, in that it refused to issue licenses to couples on the sole basis that the couple was of the same sex. In their decision in this case (*Baehr v. Lewin*) the State Supreme Court ruled that denying a marriage license to a same-sex couple violated the equal protection clause of the state constitution; in other words, the state must show a compelling governmental interest (such as a threat to public safety) to justify it. "Equal protection" in this context did not mean equal protection for gay and straight people, as one might have imagined. Such a decision would have been open to reversal by the U.S. Supreme Court, since *Bowers v. Hardwick* has been interpreted to deny suspect classification to homosexuals. Rather, it meant equal protection for men and women. The Court stated that denying a same-sex couple's right to marry discriminated against one of the partners on account of his or her sex—if he or she had been of the other sex, the marriage would have been legal.

The *Baehr* decision did not instantly legalize same-sex marriage in Hawaii. Rather, it left it up to the state legislature to come up with a "compelling interest" to prohibit it. Rising enthusiastically to the challenge, the legislature passed a bill in April 1994 that declared this interest to be the need to "foster and protect the propagation of the human race." The argument seems fairly specious, since the ability to produce children has never been a prerequisite for opposite-sex marriage. But with further judicial review and appeals, it could be years before the case is finally resolved.

"Domestic partnership" is a legal concept that has been developed as an alternative to marriage. It acknowledges that many couples, both same-sex and opposite-sex, live intimately together without being married, and that such couples should be accorded some rights. The advantages of domestic partnership over marriage, as a legal goal for the gay community, are twofold. First, avoiding the use of the word marriage may eliminate some of the conservative and religion-based opposition that same-sex marriage evokes. (In Hawaii, for example, the opposition to same-sex marriage has been led by the Catholic and Mormon churches.) Second, it is a new and flexible concept that can be tailor-made to particular ends, unlike marriage, whose legal apparatus is thoroughly fossilized.

The idea that gay or lesbian couples are entitled to legal protection similar to that which married couples enjoy, received a major boost from a New York case in 1989.[30] Miguel Braschi had lived with his lover in a New York rent-controlled apartment for many years; the lease was in his lover's name. After his lover died, Braschi attempted to continue the lease, something that only spouses or family members are entitled to do. The New York Court of Appeals ruled in Braschi's favor. It wrote:

> In the context of eviction, a more realistic, and certainly equally valid, view of a family includes two adult lifetime partners whose relationship is long-term and characterized by an emotional and financial commitment and interdependence. This view comports both with our society's traditional concept of "family" and with the expectations of individuals who live in such nuclear units.[31]

The judgment in *Braschi* means that committed same-sex couples may be accorded some of the rights of marriage, even when they are not in a legally documented domestic partnership.

Legislation defining the conditions, benefits, and obligations of domestic partnership has been enacted by a number of cities. Seattle's ordinance, for example, requires that domestic partners be unmarried (to anyone), not be close blood relatives, be over eighteen, live together, have a close personal relationship, and have agreed to be jointly responsible for each other's welfare and basic living expenses.

The legal benefits and obligations of domestic partnership, in most localities, are fairly slim, and generally extend only to those partnerships in which one member is a city employee. In the latter case they may grant leave to an employee if his or her partner is sick or has died. They may extend medical insurance benefits to the employee's partner or they may specify a monetary payment in lieu of such benefits. Sometimes they give rent-control benefits comparable to those established by *Braschi*. While such advantages are certainly worth having, they do not really advance the legal status of same-sex couples; they merely bring city halls up to the standards of those private employers that have such policies.

There is currently considerable interest in domestic-partnership legislation at the state level. Such legislation was introduced in California in 1994. The bill (AB 2810) established criteria for domestic partnerships and conferred rights in the various areas including inheritance and hospital visits. It was passed by the legislature but vetoed by Governor Pete Wilson. Comparable legislation may be introduced in Hawaii as an alternative to same-sex marriage, which the state legislature is trying to prevent. In the area of domestic partnership legislation, gays and lesbians find themselves in league with a much more powerful minority—old people, who quite commonly live as opposite or same-sex couples that need legal recognition and protection.

Children

Lesbians and gay men may have children from marriages or heterosexual relationships, or they may wish to adopt children or to become biological parents through sperm donation or other means. In any of these circumstances they can face formidable legal problems—problems that ultimately derive from society's notion of homosexuality as an infectious disease that spreads all too easily from adults to children.

If a married couple with children divorce, and one of the parents is lesbian or gay, that parent may be denied custody of the children, or even the right to spend time with them. The same thing may happen to an unmarried parent. Such tragic events were much more common in the past; their incidence has been reduced by changing social attitudes and by expert testimony on behalf of gay or lesbian parents.[32] But they still happen. In 1993 a lesbian woman living in Virginia, Sharon Bottoms, was denied custody of her two-year-old son on account of her sexual orientation and because she admitted to engaging in oral sex.[33] Oral sex is a crime under Virginia's sodomy statute, and the Bottoms case is an illustration of the pernicious influence of these "dead letter" statutes even today. The decision was reversed by the appeals court, but reinstated by the Virginia Supreme Court in 1995.

A homosexual parent's chances of obtaining custody of his or her child vary greatly from state to state. They are worst in the South, and best in states like Massachusetts, New York, and California, where courts have ruled that a parent's homosexuality must be proven harmful to the child for it to be considered as a factor in assigning custody.

There is a similar range of legal attitudes toward adoption by gays or lesbians, whether as individuals or couples. In New Hampshire and Florida, such adoptions are prohibited by state law. In some states, judges may take a dim view of the ability of gays and lesbians to provide an appropriate rearing environment. But in many states single-parent adoptions by lesbians or gay men are quite common, whether or not the adopting parent is in a homosexual relationship at the time.

If a gay or lesbian couple expand their family by means of a single-parent adoption, the nonadopting partner has no legal rights or obligations with respect to the child. The same is true when a gay or lesbian couple raise a child that is the biological son or daughter of one of them: the other has no legal tie to the child. This can lead to all kinds of problems, both in the details of day-to-day living as well as in case of death or separation. To some extent these problems can be reduced by powers of attorney, wills, etc. A more satisfactory solution, however, is two-parent or second-parent adoption. Two-parent adoptions are of course routine for opposite-sex couples, but there has been resistance to the concept for gay or lesbian couples on the grounds that the child will be exposed, not just to homosexuality, but to confused gender roles.

In spite of this resistance, two-parent and second parent same-sex adoptions are being approved by some jurisdictions. In September 1993 the Massachusetts Supreme Court allowed two surgeons, Susan Love and Helen Cooksey, to jointly adopt Tammy, a five-year-old child whom they had jointly raised from birth. Tammy is Love's biological child, conceived with sperm from Cooksey's cousin. The court ruled that Massachusetts law does not prohibit adoption by a same-sex couple. In California, there have been adoptions of biologically unrelated children by gay male or lesbian couples; although California law does not permit unmarried couples to adopt, the courts have approved a legal stratagem by which one member of the couple adopts as a single parent, then the second member adopts, with the first member becoming a "co-parent." Similar adoptions have been approved by courts in Oregon, Alaska, Washington, New York, New Jersey, and Washington, D.C.

Legal Organizations

In the early days of the gay rights movement, gay lawyers were deep in the closet, and legal support for gay men who got into trouble with the law came primarily from heterosexual lawyers. One of these, Herb Selwyn, handled the incorporation of the Mattachine Society in 1954, and defended numerous gay men charged with lewd conduct or other offenses. He even appeared on television several times during the 1950s to discuss homosexuality.[34]

Today the situation is very different. The gay community's flagship legal organization, Lambda Legal Defense and Education Fund, hires the country's top gay and lesbian attorneys to fight for the rights of lesbians and gay men in the courts. Founded in 1972 by William Thom, the Fund's first case was on its own behalf: it had to bring suit against the state of New York to obtain nonprofit status. Since then, the Fund has been involved in innumerable high-profile cases, either as counsel for gays and lesbians or by filing *amicus* briefs. These cases have included *Bowers v. Hardwick, Baehr v. Lewin*, the Colorado Amendment 2 case, *Steffan v. Cheney, Cammermeyer v. Aspin*, and a large number of child custody and HIV-related cases. The Fund is currently run by Executive Director Kevin Cathcart and has six full-time staff attorneys. It has an annual budget of $2 million, and maintains offices in New York, Chicago, and Los Angeles.

In defending the gay community against real or perceived infringements of their rights, the Fund sometimes has to weigh costs and benefits in highly controversial matters. In 1984, for example, the Fund brought suit to delay the introduction of the desperately needed HIV antibody test, citing its concern about mandatory testing. Luckily (in the view of many), the Fund lost this particular case. Even more controversial medico-legal issues may lie ahead. Current research on the biological basis of sexual orientation, for example, may eventually lead to the development of tests for genes that predispose to homosexuality (see chapter 4). What legal restrictions, if any, should be placed on the development or availability of such tests, or on actions that might be based on their results? Like many "gay rights" issues, these matters go beyond the purely legal arena to involve ethical questions that our community, and society at large, need to discuss.

The American Civil Liberties Union (ACLU) has handled gay rights cases since 1964. The early cases included challenges to bar raids and to the firing of gay or lesbian teachers. The ACLU has a national lesbian and gay rights project that employs five attorneys. Its recent cases have included the gays-in-the-military test case, *Able v. U.S.A.* (see above).

Another group, the National Gay and Lesbian Law Association, was formed in 1988 to put on biannual meetings of gay and lesbian lawyers and activists, known as the "Lavender Law Conferences."

Conclusions

Gays and lesbians still face significant legal obstacles in many fields of life: in the bedroom, in the family, in employment, and in services. But the law is beginning to recognize them as a distinct group of citizens. Just as the psychological identification of homosexual people was a vital step toward their full mental health, so their legal identification is a vital step toward their legal health. Until 1990 the phrase "sexual orientation" did not appear in the entire body of federal law. Now it appears in three different acts of Congress, all in contexts favorable to the protection of gay and lesbian rights.

The law is in transition. Extraordinary differences and paradoxes exist in the legal treatment of gays and lesbians, even within the laws of a single state. Piecemeal legislation by states and localities, often focused on narrow aspects of our rights, and often subject to erratic enforcement or legal interpretation, has generated confusion and unequal protection. Comprehensive, federally mandated protection against all forms of discrimination on the basis of sexual orientation is long overdue. But changing the law is politics, the subject of the next chapter.

Further Reading

Blasius, Mark. *Gay and Lesbian Politics: Sexuality and the Emergence of a New Ethic*. Philadelphia: Temple University Press, 1994. (Discusses legal and political issues from a Foucauldian perspective.)

Curry, Hayden, Denis Clifford, and Robin Leonard. *A Legal Guide for Lesbian and Gay Couples*, 7th ed. Berkeley: Nolo Press, 1993.

Harvard Law Review. *Sexual Orientation and the Law*. Cambridge, MA: Harvard University Press, 1990.

Hunter, Nan D., Sherryl E. Michaelson, and Thomas B. Stoddard. *The Rights of Lesbians and Gay Men: The Basic ACLU Guide to a Gay Person's Rights*. Carbondale: Southern Illinois University Press, 1992.

Rubenstein, William B. *Lesbians, Gay Men, and the Law*. New York: The New Press, 1993. (Court documents from important gay rights cases, along with background articles covering the same issues from a variety of nonlegal perspectives.)

Wolinsky, Marc, and Kenneth Sherrill, eds. *Gays and the Military: Joseph Steffan versus the United States of America.* Princeton: Princeton University Press, 1993. (Court papers from the Steffan case that offer a useful review of some general issues in gay rights, such as equal protection and suspect classification, from both a pro- and antigay perspective.)

16
Politics

In seeking political involvement and political advancement, gays and lesbians face significant theoretical and practical difficulties. Foremost among these, of course, is the fact that they are only a small minority, probably no more than 5 percent of the U.S. population (see chapter 5). They do not constitute a substantial voting bloc, except in a few areas of concentration such as San Francisco. Second, gays and lesbians face considerable political opposition, both from the homophobia of the radical right as well as from the ignorance and mistrust of much of mainstream America. Lastly, gay people, though sharing the same sexual orientation, are highly diverse in other ways: in sex, ethnicity, socioeconomic status, religion, education, occupation, and interests. While this diversity is a long-term benefit, providing the ferment that can keep a movement energized, in the short term it is a hindrance, preventing gays and lesbians from agreeing about what their political goals should be, or how to accomplish them. In fact, they do not agree on who is gay or lesbian, on whether gays and lesbians should include other groups, such as pedophiles, under their political umbrella, or even on whether homosexuality is an appropriate category on which to base a quest for political power.

On the positive side, gays and lesbians have one political advantage: many of them are highly motivated to work for their community. This motivation comes from energy released during their individual coming-out processes, from knowledge of their community's history of oppression, from the AIDS crisis, and from the belief that gays and lesbians have something special to contribute to this country's political and social life. Furthermore, as much as mainstream America has a tradition of prejudice against minorities, it also has a tradition of overcoming this prejudice. There are many groups who once were more despised than homosexuals are, and who wielded less influence than they do, who now enjoy political power, legal protection, and social acceptance. There is every reason to believe that the gay community can make society realize that they too deserve acceptance and fair treatment.

The National Organizations

The Human Rights Campaign Fund

The two largest organizations that represent the lesbian and gay community politically are the Human Rights Campaign Fund and the National Gay and Lesbian Task Force, both based in Washington, D.C. The Campaign Fund was founded in 1980. Although a relative newcomer to the gay rights scene, it has grown rapidly: its 1994 budget was about $8.5 million. The money comes from large individual donors, from the annual fundraising dinners it holds in several cities, and from direct-mail solicitation. It claims about 80,000 members, most of them individuals who have paid the Campaign Fund to deliver gay rights messages to congresspeople on their behalf. In January 1995 Executive Director Tim McFeeley was replaced by Elizabeth Birch, a thirty-eight-year-old attorney and former executive for Apple Computer.

The Campaign Fund's main aim is to influence federal legislation and federal administrative policy to the benefit of gays and lesbians. Of its forty or so employees, twelve are full-time registered lobbyists on Capitol Hill. It has assisted in the writing of several pieces of gay rights legislation, including the employment nondiscrimination bill introduced in 1994 by the House's two openly gay Democratic representatives, Gerry Studds and Barney Frank of Massachusetts. This bill, restricted to the field of employment, was much more modest in its aims than the omnibus gay rights bills that have languished in Congress for years, but so far it has not fared any better. The Campaign Fund also promotes the "National Coming-Out Day," an annual event in October when previously closeted gays and lesbians make a clean breast of their sexual orientation, and those already out of the closet are urged to increase their involvement in the community's affairs.

The Campaign Fund is a low-key organization that has successfully tapped into the relatively conservative, assimilationist element in the gay and lesbian community. It prides itself on doing important spadework for gay rights, mostly out of the media spotlight. One might be surprised that the organization that promotes Coming-Out Day itself uses a "closeted" name ("Human Rights" for "Gay and Lesbian"). But according to the Campaign Fund's communications director Gregory King, that's all part of the strategy. He told us that many affluent gays and lesbians would be too embarrassed to contribute to an explicitly gay organization.

To some observers, the Campaign Fund is so low key as to be of questionable usefulness. Torie Osborn, who was briefly executive director of the Campaign Fund's rival organization, the National Gay and Lesbian Task Force, has written that "HRCF still suffers a widespread reputation for staff underachievement and monochromatic mediocrity. The refrain reverberates widely here in Washington, D.C., and elsewhere: Just what do they do with all that money?"[1] To others, the Campaign Fund's deliberate style is the community's best hope for steady progress in the political arena.

The National Gay and Lesbian Task Force

The National Gay and Lesbian Task Force was founded in 1973. It has about 32,000 members, a full-time staff of twenty-three people, and a budget of $3.4 million (1994). The current executive director is Melinda Parras, who took over from Peri Jude Radecic in early 1995. The Task Force has experienced considerable organization turmoil and staff turnover recently.

The Task Force does some lobbying in Washington, although unlike the Campaign Fund it does not employ full-time lobbyists. Its main energy is directed outward toward the gay and lesbian community nationwide. It attempts to help gays and lesbians become involved in the community and in gay politics. For example, it puts on the annual Creating Change conference, a large gathering of gay, lesbian, and bisexual activists. The Task Force helps to educate the community through numerous carefully researched bulletins on subjects such as hate-crime statistics, congressional voting records, civil rights legislation, and lesbian and gay health care issues. It has a campus project aimed at encouraging the formation of gay and lesbian organizations at the college level. It also has made a particular study of right-wing political groups and how they may best be combated.

The National Center for Lesbian Rights

An organization that has resisted the trend toward co-gender activism is the National Center for Lesbian Rights, based in San Francisco. The Center, whose executive director is Liz Hendrickson, has filed *amicus* briefs in important lesbian-rights cases, for example the recent Sharon Bottoms custody case in Virginia (see chapter 15), and it seeks to influence public policy to the benefit of lesbians in the areas of health care, family law, and employment. It has a Lesbians of Color Project that organizes workshops and other events around the country.

The Gay and Lesbian Victory Fund

A new organization that has been making waves in gay politics is the Gay and Lesbian Victory Fund. The Fund was founded in 1991 by William Waybourn, who is now executive director (he has announced his intention to resign in 1995). The Fund is modeled after Emily's List, an organization that seeks to help women achieve political office. It gives financial support to openly gay or lesbian candidates who meet the following criteria: they must support the enactment of federal civil rights protection for gays and lesbians, they must have aggressive positions on lesbian and gay health care issues, they must be prochoice on abortion, and they must show evidence of running a substantial, professionally organized campaign. "We look to see if money will make a difference," Waybourn told us. The Fund does not give money to poorly run campaigns, nor to the campaigns of perennial shoo-ins like U.S. Representative Barney Frank of Massachusetts (though it does endorse Frank). Waybourn claims that the candidates supported by the Victory Fund do far better than nonsupported candidates, partly because of the Fund's support and partly because they are more viable candidates to start with.

As of 1994, the Victory Fund had about 4,000 members. Each member, on joining, pays $100 to the Fund. In addition, he or she undertakes to give at least $100 to each of two candidates out of the list of candidates the Fund supports in a given year. These checks are sent to the Fund, which forwards them to the candidates. The reason for operating in this fashion has to do with the laws that limit political contributions by political action committees (PAC's) like the Victory Fund. Because the checks are written directly by the members, the applicable limits are only those for individual contributions ($1,000 per person for a federal candidate), not those for PAC's ($5,000 total for a federal candidate). In addition to financial backing, the Victory Fund provides training to potential candidates, which is accomplished through a set of Training Institutes as well as through its comprehensive guide, *Out for Office* (see Further Reading).

In 1994 the Victory Fund supported twenty-six candidates. These included Tom Duane (candidate for the U.S. House of Representatives from New York City), Tony Miller (candidate for California secretary of state), Karen Burstein (candidate for New York Attorney-General), and several candidates for positions as state representatives, judges, and city councilmembers. The Fund gave a total of about $600,000 to these candidates, fourteen of whom were elected.

The Victory Fund's philosophy is founded on the notion that gays and lesbians themselves are the best representatives for our community in government. Yet the gay and lesbian electorate does not always seem to agree. In 1994, for example, Victory Fund-supported candidate John Duran was beaten in a primary for California state representative by several heterosexual but gay-friendly candidates; no more than about 10 percent of the gays and lesbians in the district (which includes West Hollywood) voted for Duran. The question of whether gays and lesbians should support their own in preference to gay-friendly heterosexual candidates (who may stand a greater chance of being elected) is one which the gay and lesbian community still has to come to grips with. The Victory Fund at least has made up its mind.

Minority Organizations

Two organizations that are focused on ethnic minorities within our community are the National Latino/a Lesbian and Gay Organization (LLEGO) and the Black Gay and Lesbian Leadership Forum (BGLLF). Gay and lesbian Latinos can take pride in the fact that Latinos—especially Puerto Ricans—took a prominent role in the Stonewall Rebellion. Since then, more than sixty Latino organizations serving gays and lesbians have formed, of which LLEGO, founded in 1987, is the national voice. Some of the issues that LLEGO is concerned with are racism, both outside and within the gay community, the rights of gay and lesbian immigrants and undocumented aliens, and health care and AIDS prevention within the Latino community. The Black Gay and Lesbian Leadership Forum, based in Los Angeles, was founded in 1988. It puts on an annual conference aimed at developing the organizational and leadership skills of gay and lesbian African-Americans. In addition, its AIDS Prevention Team provides education and counseling in an attempt to halt the rapid spread of the disease in the African-American community.

Washington

At present, there are only three completely out-of-the-closet members of Congress: Democratic representatives Barney Frank and Gerry Studds of Massachusetts, and Republican Steven Gunderson of Wisconsin. None of these was openly gay when first elected. Studds publicly acknowledged his homosexuality in 1983, after a congressional investigation revealed that he had had a sexual relationship with a male congressional page in 1973. He has been reelected five times since he came out. Frank came out in 1984 (in Boston) and again in 1987 (nationally), and has been reelected several times since then. He weathered a small scandal when his former boyfriend claimed to have been running a prostitution ring out of Frank's Washington apartment. Subsequently, the House Ethics Committee unanimously concluded that the charge was false. Gunderson's coming-out process was slow and painful, highlighted by an incident on the House floor when antigay congressman Robert Dornan of California said "He has a revolving door on his closet: he's in, he's out, he's in, he's out."[2] Gunderson finally made a clean breast of his homosexuality in 1995.

Studds and Frank have been long-time supporters of gay rights. Frank was the first sponsor of a gay rights bill in the Massachusetts state legislature in the 1970s. In Congress, the two men have repeatedly sponsored gay and lesbian civil rights legislation, most recently the 1994 employment nondiscrimination bill. Nevertheless, Frank lost a lot of credibility with the gay community in 1993 by supporting a compromise in the gays-in-the-military debate—a compromise that did not permit gay and lesbian service personnel to be open about their sexual orientation. Gunderson has also been supportive of gay rights legislation in recent years.

No doubt there are other gays or lesbians in Congress who are completely closeted. Such people are unlikely to take any positive stand for gay rights, and may even cloak their homosexuality with an antigay political stance. This was the case, for example, with Republican congressman Robert Bauman who, until he was arrested in 1980 for soliciting sex from a teenager in a gay bar, had made quite a career of antigay-rights propaganda.[3]

President Clinton carried through on his campaign promise to appoint gays and lesbians to positions within his administration. The Campaign Fund, the Task Force, and the Victory Fund worked together to provide Clinton with lists of suitable candidates. Those appointed have included Roberta Achtenberg, previously a member of the San Francisco board of supervisors, who was appointed as assistant secretary for fair housing (she resigned in 1995), Bruce Lehman (assistant secretary of commerce and commissioner of patents and trademarks), Richard Socarides (White House liaison to the Department of Labor), Bob Hattoy (White House liaison to the Department of the Interior), Nan Hunter (deputy general counsel to the Department of Health and Human Services), Andrew Barrer (senior advisor to the national AIDS policy coordinator), and several others. Clinton also nominated the country's first openly gay or lesbian federal court judge, Deborah Batts of New York, who was sworn in in June 1994.

Achtenberg and Lehman's positions were senior-level appointments requiring Senate confirmation. Achtenberg's confirmation was somewhat contentious, in part because of her history as a lesbian activist—as well as being a San Francisco supervisor, she had been executive director of the National Center for Lesbian Rights. Lehman was confirmed unanimously without any discussion of his sexual orientation. "I'm a Washington insider," he told us. "I've known all those senators for years; they weren't going to give me a hard time." Although Lehman's position is not especially relevant to gay rights issues, he said that he was introducing a nondiscrimination policy that included sexual orientation within the Patent Office (which employs 5,000 people) and was hopeful that the entire Commerce Department would follow suit. In addition, he takes seriously his responsibility as a role model, giving speeches at gay and lesbian events and mentioning his sexual orientation on other occasions. "The federal government is a pretty good place for gays and lesbians," he said. "There is no global protection, but it's beginning to happen on a department-by-department basis." He warned, however, that all bets were off if the Republicans regained the White House, and he took the opportunity of our interview to attack "rich, white gay men who think they naturally belong to the Republican Party."

Local Gay Politics

Local and state politics have been a more active scene for gays and lesbians than has Washington. Already in 1961 the San Francisco drag entertainer Jose Sarria ran for supervisor (see chapter 3). To our knowledge, the first openly gay or lesbian candidate to win a campaign was Elaine Noble, who was elected to the Massachusetts House of Representatives in 1974. Inspired by Noble's success, a sitting state senator in Minnesota, Allan Spear, announced that he was gay in the same year. The first openly gay man to be elected was Harvey Milk, who won a seat on the board of supervisors in San Francisco in 1977 (see chapter 3). More recently these sporadic successes have coalesced into a steady trickle: in 1992 and 1993, according to the Victory Fund's records, eight openly gay or lesbian candidates were elected to statewide office, and sixteen won local elections. However, there are still only a total of about seventy openly gay or lesbian elected officials in the United States—only about one in 7,000 of the men and women who currently hold elected office.

In some ways, a lesbian or gay man can be more effective in local politics than in Washington. For example, a lesbian or gay man elected to a school board can significantly improve the lives of gay and lesbian students in that school system. In Los Angeles Unified School District, openly gay school board member Jeff Horton has provided strong support for Project 10 (the district's gay and lesbian counseling program), the EAGLES Project (a special gay and lesbian high school), Gay and Lesbian Awareness Month, the Gay and Lesbian High School Prom, and other projects, all in the face of strident and persistent opposition from the Traditional Values Coalition and other antigay organizations in Southern California.

Of course, gays and lesbians are most likely to be elected in places where they are least needed—San Francisco, West Hollywood, and gay-friendly cities generally. But at last a few pioneers have demonstrated the potential for success in conservative areas lacking in organized gay life. Dale McCormick ran in 1990 as an openly lesbian candidate for the Maine

State Senate. She has described how she achieved this feat the old-fashioned way: by canvassing her rural district door-to-door on a bicycle named Tony.[4] McCormick was reelected in 1992 and has become an important spokesperson on gay and lesbian issues in a very conservative state.

Most large cities have partisan gay and lesbian political associations. The Democratic groups have a variety of names—Stonewall Club, Gay and Lesbian Democratic Club, Gertrude Stein Club, and so on. The Republican groups are called Log Cabin Clubs. The Log Cabin Clubs are organized into a national federation that has a Washington-based advocacy arm, the Log Cabin Republicans. Besides having a general social and networking function, the Democratic and Log Cabin Clubs endorse gay or gay-friendly candidates at primary elections. At general elections, it not seldom happens that the Democratic candidate is significantly more gay-friendly than the Republican. In such cases Log Cabin Clubs may issue "nonendorsements" of the Republican candidate, but they will not endorse across party lines. The political clubs also send delegates to state and national conventions, and thus play a role in setting their party's platform and in nominating candidates for state and national office.

Nonparty Politics

Gay politics extend far beyond the traditional political arena. This is partly because many gay activists have despaired of traditional politics as an instrument of change and have sought other forms of expression. In addition gays and lesbians, belonging as they do to a stigmatized and partially hidden minority, engage in a form of politics when they participate openly in any aspect of public life.

One group that flourished briefly at the margins of conventional politics was Queer Nation, founded in New York in 1990. Queer Nation grew out of ACT UP, but it differed from its parent organization in two respects: first, it attempted to address homophobia and gay invisibility generally, rather than focusing on AIDS issues, and second, many of its actions had the flavor of street theater rather than political protest. For example, Queer Nation members, dressed outrageously, went on "shopping trips" to suburban malls or took part in "kiss-ins" in heterosexual bars. Queer Nation, especially its West Coast chapters, was involved in outing celebrities in the entertainment industry such as Jodie Foster and David Geffen. Recently Queer Nation has faded into relative obscurity. It has, however, left one important mark on the gay landscape—the word "queer," which it celebrated in its name and in its slogan "We're here, we're queer, get used to it!" Familiar to older gay people as a standard derogatory expression for homosexuals, the word was adopted by Queer Nation as an in-your-face appropriation of the enemy's language. Since then, however, the word has accumulated an ever-broadening weight of meaning: first as a label for the younger, more rebellious element within the community, second as a co-gender alternative to "gay and lesbian," and lastly as a catch-all label for any antiestablishment or marginalized sector of society that might conceivably join a grand alliance against the existing power structure.

Another recently formed group is the Lesbian Avengers, founded in New York in 1992 by a group of women including writer Sarah Schulman. The group focuses on "issues of lesbian survival and visibility." The Avengers' first action was at Public School 87 in Middle Village, Queens, where they handed out lavender balloons labeled "Ask About Lesbian Lives" to the schoolchildren. During the boycott of Colorado over Amendment 2, they harassed the mayor of Denver when he came to New York to drum up trade and tourism. More recently they have organized "Dyke Marches" in parallel with co-gender gay and lesbian marches and parades. At the March on Washington in April 1993, the Dyke March took place on the evening before the main march and attracted 20,000 lesbians according to the organizers' count, making it "the largest lesbian event in the history of the world." (The *Washington Post* estimated the number of marchers at 6,000.)

More significant than anything the Lesbian Avengers may have achieved to this point is the possibility that they are symbolic of a new attitude in the lesbian community—a rising feeling that the interests of lesbians are not given proper consideration in co-gender organizations and events. In a recent piece, for example, Sarah Schulman wrote acidly: "The gay press, being totally misogynist, completely ignored us."[5] Remarks such as these are warning signals that gay men would do well to note, if another split in the community is to be avoided.

An organization that works hard to improve the gay community's public image is the Gay and Lesbian Alliance Against Defamation. GLAAD was founded in 1985 by a group of activists in New York, including Vito Russo and Larry Kramer; it now has chapters in eight cities. GLAAD looks out for and protests against antigay bias in the media. It has helped draw public attention to the negative portrayal of gays and lesbians in films such as *Basic Instinct* and *The Silence of the Lambs*, and it has persuaded several newspapers to improve their coverage of gay issues. It seems to us that GLAAD may sometimes be too eager to impose a gay "party line." In early 1995, for example, it put out a statement urging gays and lesbians to boycott talk shows whose hosts had not taken a GLAAD-run sensitivity training course. Certainly no single committee, however well meaning, can be the arbiter of correct attitudes concerning the diverse gay and lesbian community.

Another nationwide organization whose mission overlaps partially with GLAAD's is the Parents and Friends of Lesbians and Gays. PFLAG chapters provide support for the relatives and friends of gay people, who often have a difficult coming-out process of their own to go through. In addition, PFLAG members have been diligent in writing letters to newspapers in response to negative stories about homosexuality or gay people.

Because a central aim of gay politics is the removal of stigma and discrimination against gays and lesbians, which still pervades so many aspects of American life, the daily life of gays and lesbians is a continuous string of possibilities for political action. We mentioned Aaron Fricke's struggle to bring a male date to his school prom in chapter 15. Among the myriad more recent examples, we arbitrarily choose to mention two. The first is the case of Wanda and Brenda Henson, already mentioned in chapter 6, who attempted to start Camp Sister Spirit, a feminist education center and retreat, in tiny Ovett, Mississippi. Local opposition to their plans was expressed in such unsubtle ways as the placing of a bullet-ridden dog on their mailbox, as well as by threatening phone calls. Led by a Southern Baptist minister, an attorney, and a salesperson, the locals formed Mississippians for Family Values, dedicated to forcing the Hensons out of Jones County. In early 1994 U.S. Attorney General Janet Reno, under pressure from the NGLTF and other groups, sent federal mediators to meet with the Hensons and with residents of Ovett, but without significant result: the residents (or the vocal ones at least) are still adamant that the Hensons must leave, while the Hensons are just as determined to stay. Although the Hensons have received considerable moral and practical support from the lesbian and gay community nationally, their thanks are not unqualified. "I believe that the gay and lesbian community holds a big responsibility for what is happening to us right now," said Brenda Henson in a typically forthright interview with *insideOUT*.[6] "If all the teachers, lawyers, nurses, doctors and social workers came out, then this wouldn't be happening. Middle Americans judge gays and lesbians by the people they see marching and making noise. If they don't know any gays, then they can just make up whatever the fuck they want."

The other example, chosen for its very insignificance, concerns a gay couple in Pasadena, California. Raul Caudillo, a nineteen-year-old student at Pasadena City College, called radio station KOST-FM in April 1994, during its nightly "Love Songs" program, and requested a song to be dedicated to his boyfriend and fellow student Brian Dreesman. The station refused, citing a policy against same-sex dedications. The couple initiated a series of protests in which GLAAD and five gay and lesbian publications became involved. The matter culminated in September 1994 with a massive gay and lesbian call-in that tied up the station's phone lines for hours. KOST saw the light and changed its policy. "I've been studying Martin Luther King and Gandhi all my life," said Dreesman. "This is the first time I've had the chance to apply what I've learned."[7]

The Opposition

The most well organized opposition to the gay community's struggle for equal rights comes from the radical right, and in particular the religious right—the conservative and ultraconservative political organizations whose power base lies mainly within the evangelical churches. In the late 1970s and early 1980s, Jerry Falwell's Moral Majority was the main standard-bearer of the religious right. The Moral Majority never achieved significant political power because the Republican Party was focused on issues such as anticommunism and Reaganomics, not on moral or religious issues. When both communism and Reaganomics collapsed, however, the center of energy within the Republican Party shifted toward a moral conservatism. In this atmosphere a new organization, the Christian Coalition, began to change the political landscape. Founded by Pat Robertson, and run by Executive Director Ralph Reed, the coalition now claims over 600,000 dues-paying members and a budget of $20 million. Even this figure understates the coalition's size, because the national organization, based in Chesapeake, Virginia, has partially independent branch organizations in nineteen states. The coalition claims to have a total of 872 chapters.[8]

The Christian Coalition is opposed to gay rights, not only because of the traditional concept of homosexuality as a sin, but also because the gay and lesbian community is seen as the focus of an antireligion, antifamily, antitradition movement in modern American society. For that reason it is the organized, public aspects of the gay and lesbian community that the coalition tries to combat, as much or more than homosexuality itself. The Christian Coalition completely rejects the idea of homosexuality as an aspect of a person's identity. As an example of the political application of this stance, a 1994 initiative proposed by the Oregon Citizen's Alliance (which is supported by the Christian Coalition) included the following wording: "Children, students and employees shall not be advised, instructed or taught by any government agency, department or political unit ... that homosexuality is the legal or social equivalent of race, color, religion, gender, age or national origin." Instead, the Christian Coalition takes the view that homosexuality is an aberrant behavior pattern that can be "taught" (by sexual molestation, by example, or by persuasion) and that can also be "corrected" (by psychotherapy or by religious conversion).

The Christian Coalition's principal strategy is to obtain political power by taking over the Republican Party. According to Sidney Blumenthal,[9] by 1992 the coalition had gained dominance or significant leverage over the Republican Party in about twenty states. In Oregon, for example, the party is under the control of the coalition-supported Oregon Citizens' Alliance. In Virginia the coalition-supported candidate, Oliver North, easily won nomination for U.S. senator at the 1993 state convention, but lost the election in 1994. In Texas in 1993, the coalition engineered the election of Steven Hodge, who has publicly advocated the death penalty for homosexuality, to the chairmanship of the advisory committee of the Harris County Republican Party. By 1994, conservative Christians controlled thirty-two of California's fifty-two county Republican central committees.[10] Many of the Republicans newly elected to Congress in 1994 were supported by the Christian Coalition, and can be relied upon to oppose any gay rights legislation.

Besides the Christian Coalition a host of other organizations are opposed to gay rights. They include the Free Congress Foundation, founded in 1974 with financial support from the Coors family, and Lou Sheldon's Traditional Values Coalition, based in Anaheim, California, which has been involved in antigay politics in California and nationwide. James Dodson's Focus on the Family, based in Colorado Springs, has 1,200 employees and an annual budget of $94 million in 1993[11]; it supported Colorado for Family Values, the promoters of the 1992 antigay Amendment 2. The American Family Association, based in Tupelo, Mississippi, has a $5 million budget and runs a tireless campaign to eliminate positive references to homosexuality from the media. Lyndon Larouche, who sponsored AIDS quarantine initiatives in California in the 1980s, is currently in jail for mail fraud, but he still spearheads a movement that is violently hostile to gays, Jews, and other minorities.[12]

Sensing that Americans generally oppose the intrusion of religion into politics, the radical right tends to soft-pedal the religious basis for its antigay stance. Instead, antigay campaigns are based on the attempt to depict the gay "lifestyle" as destructive to the family, obsessed with sex, and offensive to common decency. This was the message of "The Gay Agenda," a videotape circulated during the gays-in-the-military controversy. The videotape also asserted that gays and lesbians could revert to "normal" heterosexual behavior. Another antigay argument, which has been pursued with considerable success by Lou Sheldon and Colorado for Family Values, is that gays and lesbians already *have* equal rights, and are now attempting to obtain "special privileges" under the law.

Political conservatism is not inevitably accompanied by homophobia. Former senator Barry Goldwater of Arizona, for example, who was for years a pillar of the Republican Party's right wing, has become an ardent supporter of gay rights, and is honorary chairman of Arizonans for Fairness, the group that successfully fought an antigay initiative drive in 1994. "There is no place in our life for these political hooligans," he said of the Traditional Values Coalition of Arizona, sponsors of the initiative. "Let's hope once and for all that we just don't do things that way in Arizona."[13] Goldwater may have been influenced in his attitude by the experience of having an openly gay grandson. There is also a new breed of fiscally conservative, socially liberal Republicans, such as Governor William Weld of Massachusetts, who support gay rights. It remains to be seen whether such people can save the party from the encroachments of the Christian Coalition and its allies.

The Gay Agenda

What is the real "gay agenda?" What do gays and lesbians want from the political process? The answer, of course, is that each person wants something different. But within this diversity, one can discern two major trends, one more conservative, one more radical.

The more conservative view has been enunciated by writers such as Bruce Bawer. Bawer shares the religious right's distaste for the gay community's celebration of sexuality. He also agrees to some extent with the religious right's denial of homosexuality as a aspect of identity. The following passage from his book *A Place at the Table* illustrates this viewpoint:

> Gays exist as a group, then, largely because there is anti-gay prejudice. If gay relationships were taken for granted by everyone and accorded the same legal and moral status as heterosexual marriages, and if gay children were educated to be as comfortable with their sexuality as straight children, and given courtship rituals comparable to those of straight children, much of what we think of as the "gay subculture" would disappear. Individual gays would still gravitate to each other because of sexual or romantic attraction, but there would be nothing to bind homosexuals together en masse in gay bars and restaurants, gay churches or synagogues, or Gay Studies programs. It is precisely because anti-gay prejudice does exist that some gays, in the interest of self-protection, cling to their sexual identity, and (in some cases) accordingly become preoccupied with sex.[14]

Bawer is not totally denying that there are different classes of humans—gay and straight—but he is saying that, in the absence of antigay prejudice, this classification would be trivial, as socially irrelevant as classification by handedness is in our society today. Therefore Bawer's political goal is simply the elimination of entrenched antigay bias: the opening of marriage to same-sex couples, for example, and perhaps the enactment of nondiscrimination legislation. Following the success of this program, gays and lesbians will assimilate into mainstream society and become more or less invisible as a group.

The more radical view is that gays and lesbians not only have a separate identity, but that this identity propels them, regardless of any future change in attitudes, toward socialism. The experience of being a gay or lesbian child, according to writers such as Tony Kushner, sets him or her apart from the group as a permanent and natural outsider. This experience is not going to change with any likely change in social attitudes. For this reason, gays and lesbians have a natural affinity with other marginalized groups, and have a natural interest in bonding with them in a struggle to create a new, nonhierarchical social structure. In a recent article (see Further Reading), Kushner agrees that an important goal for gays and lesbians is to live free of the fear of homophobia, but he adds:

> But what of all the other things gay men and lesbians have to fear? What of the things gay children have to fear, in common with all children? What of the planetary despoilment that kills us? Or the financial necessity that drives some of us into unsafe, insecure, stupid, demeaning and ill-paying jobs? Or the unemployment that impoverishes some of us? Or the racism some of us face? Or the rape some of us fear? What about AIDS? Is it enough to say, Not our problem? Of course gay and lesbian politics is a progressive politics: It depends on progress for the accomplishment of any of its goals. Is there any progressive politics that recognizes no connectedness, no border-crossings, no solidarity or possibility for mutual aid?

A point of view somewhere between Bawer's and Kushner's has been articulated by Michael Nava and Robert Dawidoff. In their book *Created Equal*, these authors base their argument for gay rights on fundamental freedoms such as the right to privacy, rather than on the assertion of a distinct gay or lesbian identity or on a natural affinity between gay people and other outsiders. In this they follow Bawer. But they do not believe that all gays and lesbians will eventually assimilate. They write: "There will always be lesbians and gay men who prefer a gay-oriented way of living, who live in urban gay communities and pursue the attractions and diversions those communities offer. Other gays and lesbians live lives undistinguished by sexual orientation except in their private lives."[15]

Nava and Dawidoff are right to make clear that there are differences among gays and lesbians that inevitably affect political attitudes. Gay and lesbians who wish to lead "undistinguished" lives, and there are many of them, may vote for nondiscrimination statutes, but they will never go to the barricades to overthrow the capitalist world order. They just want to be left alone. The more radical sector of our community, to whom the word "queer" signifies an ever-expanding coalition of the disaffected, will never disappear into the woodwork of American society, or not until society has been changed beyond all recognition.

Perhaps the most important point is one made at the beginning of this chapter, that gays and lesbians are a small minority. For their political demands to be heeded, they must reach out to others. Bawer and Nava and Dawidoff believe this should be done by appealing to the fundamental reason and decency of the majority of society. This means, by and large, that gays and lesbians should keep a low profile and present themselves as average citizens, no less or more deserving of legal protection than anyone else. More radical gays and lesbians believe that the gay community should join arms with ethnic minorities, the poor, and so on, to gain sufficient political clout to achieve its aims in the face of the resistance of Middle America. Both strategies may have something to offer. But the fact is, leading "undistinguished" lives is exactly the strategy that failed in the past. Without a moral stance that links their identity with the identities of others, gays and lesbians may assimilate into society, but their assimilation will be a constant invitation to renewed discrimination.

Further Reading

Bawer, Bruce. *A Place at the Table: The Gay Individual in American Society*. New York: Poseidon Press, 1993.

DeBold, Kathleen, ed. *Out for Office: Campaigning in the Gay Nineties*. Washington, D.C.: Gay and Lesbian Victory Fund, 1994.

Kushner, Tony. "A Socialism of the Skin." *The Nation* (July 4, 1994).

Schulman, Sarah. *My American History: Lesbian and Gay Life during the Reagan/Bush Years*. New York: Routledge, 1994.

Signorile, Michelangelo. *Queer in America: Sex, the Media, and the Closets of Power*. New York: Anchor Books, 1993.

V Culture

In the final section of the book we discuss art and religion, two central aspects of gay and lesbian culture. Art has probably been the least inhibited mode of lesbian and gay expression, one that has provided a sense of continuity to a people who have not been the automatic recipients of family or community traditions. We treat lesbian and gay male art separately (in chapters 17 and 18), partly because there are significant differences between their styles of artistic expression, and partly to give us the opportunity to approach the subject from two different perspectives, one focusing more on the process of art, the other more on the psychological motifs to which art gives form. Religion, the subject of chapter 19, represents perhaps the *most* inhibited mode of lesbian and gay expression, yet one for which, paradoxically, lesbians and gays seem to have a unique gift.

17
Lesbian Art

Lesbians and gay men learned to read and to see through the eyes of the dominant culture, a culture in which the lesbian is mostly invisible. Lesbian art is about shifting that view, creating a self-defined identity rather than one defined by others. Lesbian artists work from the margins, tugging at the center. They document and celebrate the diversity of a minority culture. They contest taboos, sometimes subtly, sometimes confrontationally. They form the point of a wedge to be driven into the pretensions of society.

In the introduction to her collection *Rude Girls and Dangerous Women,*[1] Jennifer Camper makes a statement on the subject of why she became a cartoonist: "I was looking for images of women that were familiar to me, women who had adventures and were tough and sexy. Women who had fun. Generally, what I saw in the arts and media were women who were victims and dykes who were confused, so I created the images I wanted myself." This motivation is heard over and over in each discipline covered in this chapter.

Is There a Lesbian Sensibility?

Lesbians have spent most of their lives learning, studying, and absorbing heterosexual culture, art, literature, popular media—images with which they have little identification, and to which they always must do a certain amount of transposing of gender to fully comprehend. Now there exists a vital and extensive world of lesbian art that we will explore in this chapter. For our purposes, we define lesbian art as art made by lesbians.

Obviously this issue of sensibility affects one's definition of lesbian art. Can a lesbian open about her lesbianism create anything *but* lesbian art? The answer varies. Dorothy Allison reports that she could not write out of a straight sensibility, though at the same time she maintains that discussions about what qualifies as lesbian art are really debates about fashion and politics. Photographer Catherine Opie believes not in a sensibility but in a "cultural aesthetic, based in the culture and experience. Being a lesbian is only part of it." Kaucyila Brooke, a visual artist, does not think a lesbian sensibility exists. She thinks lesbian artists are trying to carve out a place for themselves, make a category for themselves rather than be invisible. "Lesbian artists may make work around the same kind of topics out of a sense of belonging, but the more people produce works the more diverse it becomes." If there are dominant themes or a sensibility, says video artist Jane Cottis, it is because "lesbians work in a different way from others because they're approaching work from a different standpoint, from outside the dominant culture. Therefore critique of the dominant culture is often a part of the work." Any lesbian sensibility, she continues, comes from the audience; she gets the best response from a predominantly lesbian audience that understands the jokes in her videos.[2]

With any culture, it is not in general possible to separate art from the culture. Lesbian art of the late 1960s and early 1970s was virtually inseparable from lesbian culture of the time, which started out being about community—the community that lesbians sought and built for themselves based on their desire to be around other women in general and other lesbians in particular. Until going to a women's music festival, or buying a Meg Christian album, many lesbians had little sense of themselves as a group or community. But when they participated in this way—buying music, seeing theater, being in the audience when comedians Kate Clinton or Karen Williams performed—lesbians saw themselves. Finally they were in on the jokes, could identify with the songs, and saw themselves reflected in paintings, photographs, and sculpture. They recognized themselves, maybe for the first time, in books, films, poetry, music, and humor by, about, and for lesbians. Lesbian culture became a way to make lesbians visible in a world that refused to recognize them.

Lesbians today are too diverse to be defined as one community. There are the bad girls, the Lesbian Avengers, closeted lesbians, lipstick lesbians, fat lesbians, sporty lesbians. Some lesbians call themselves dykes, some queer. Some refuse to utter the word lesbian. Similarly, lesbian art ranges from the tame, positive, politically correct representations of lesbians in Naiad Press books to Hothead Paisan, Homicidal Lesbian Terrorist, the Uzi-toting main character of cartoonist Diane DiMassa's comic book quarterly.[3] Lesbian artists today do not cluster around the same cultural center of the early lesbian feminist movement, a utopian woman-only haven. They have scattered in all directions, causing controversy and creating discussion, just the way art should.

The Link to Feminism

Lesbian content can be seen over time in art, particularly in poetry and fiction, but the current incarnation of lesbian art and culture is strongly linked to feminism and the women's movement of the 1970s. For many women, feminism allowed them to be lesbians by giving them an analysis of society and of the world that had not been previously available to them. Prior to the women's movement, there were a few courageous women who were out as lesbians, but even they were usually out only in a local sense, to just a few people. Only a handful of lesbians or gay men were known as such outside their immediate society. Feminism was about women finding their voices; it gave them the courage to speak out as women, and finally to speak out as lesbians. Feminism sought to redefine society in women's terms and to create a women-identified culture. Women who were already living as lesbians when feminism burst onto the political and social scene in the late 1960s and 1970s often found that they had been living a feminist life all along.

In the 1970s when there was an explosion of women's art, lesbians and straight women worked together to develop and present women's art in all its forms—visual, multimedia, performance pieces, the written word. Inevitably, there were some splits between straight women and lesbians, where lesbians wanted more lesbian content in their work and some straight women most firmly did not want to be identified with lesbian content or to work with lesbians who insisted on being out. (There were also straight women who had no problems with lesbian content in their work or with working with lesbians.)

Lesbian audiences were and are often more interested in lesbian-focused cultural expression than in women-focused expression, and what might be described as lesbian art started to appear in the early 1970s. At first lesbian expression, whether through music, visual art, literature, or usable art (jewelry, crafts, clothing), was found in clearly lesbian venues such as music festivals or concerts advertised among lesbians, or at political demonstrations. Performances such as music, comedy, and some theater became popular and spread across the United States. Performances were popular because they were, said Liebe Grey, an early participant in women's and lesbian music and theater, "live bodies in a room sharing something," and for many lesbians it was the first time they saw more than ten (and up to one hundred) lesbians together, sharing their culture.[4]

We will separate lesbian art into five different realms: music, comedy, literature, film, and the visual arts. As we shall see, the line between these areas often blurs.

Music and Music Festivals

The concept of a Lesbian Nation, a state of mind rather than an actual place, "helped to change the meaning and the image of lesbianism by giving love between women greater visibility and by presenting visions of self-affirmation through lesbian-feminist music and literature. In its success in reaching large numbers of lesbians, women's music was perhaps the most effective of all the enterprises undertaken by the lesbian-feminist community in the 1970s."[5] Starting in the early to mid-1970s, large crowds of lesbians gathered at concerts and festivals, and recordings of some of the music performed there went back into their homes, with self-affirming lyrics about lesbian politics, lesbian love, and lesbian unity. These performances not only helped create a community but proselytized for the cause.

Two songs became unofficial lesbian anthems in the 1970s: "Leaping Lesbians" (by Sue Fink and Joelyn Grippo) and "Waterfall" (by Cris Williamson). "Leaping" is a humorous take on what "they" (the straight world) thought of lesbians, while "Waterfall," introduced on the album as "A song about the deep cyclical waters of life,"was written as an affirmation of the positive effects of change.

Sometimes it takes a rainy day
Just to let you know everything's gonna be all right.
I've been dreaming in the sun, won't you wake me up someone
I need a little peace of mind
Wake me from this dream that I have dreamed so many times
I need a little peace of mind, oh I need a little peace of mind.

When you open up your life to the living, all things come spilling in on you.
And you're flowing like a river, the Changer and the Changed.
You've got to spill some over, spill some over, spill some over over all.

Filling up and spilling over, it's an endless waterfall
Filling up and spilling over, over all.
Filling up and spilling over, it's an endless waterfall
Filling up and spilling over, over all.

Like the rain falling on the ground.
Like the rain falling all around.[6]

Women musicians and performers started their own recording companies in order to circumvent the sexism and resistance to women, never mind the homophobia, in the music industry. Musicians such as Meg Christian and Cris Williamson of Olivia Records, and Linda Tillery, Alix Dobkin, and Kay Gardener recorded their own and others' work, and distributed their recordings at concerts and festivals and through women's bookstores. There were tours of women musicians in the early 1970s, concerts in church basements and high school auditoriums before crowds of women anxious to hear music that described their lives.

Women's music festivals started about the same time as women's music, and existed partly to showcase the music and partly to give lesbians a place to gather. The earliest (and largest) festivals that still exist, such as the Michigan Womyn's Music Festival, the National Women's Music Festival in Indiana, and the West Coast Women's Music and Comedy Festival, featured music and comedy as well as workshops on political and social topics. Today these festivals have become institutions unique to lesbian life. There are twenty to thirty held around the United States and Canada every summer, with attendance ranging from a few hundred to ten thousand women. The music and the comedians' stories affirm same-sex relationships between women. Art becomes a reflection of life, not something that has to be translated before it can be appreciated.

Women's music has branched into the mainstream with two nationally known recording artists who came out as lesbians in 1993: k.d. lang and Melissa Etheridge. These women are stars, not just performers, and both have won Grammy Awards. Neither writes or sings explicitly lesbian lyrics. Etheridge says "I write from a genderless place. I don't think I will ever write or sing 'I love *her*.' I like that my music reaches not just gay but straight fans—men and women both."[7] Some other mainstream artists who have come out do deal with lesbian or gay issues, such as coming out and AIDS. For example, the Indigo Girls (Amy Ray and Emily Saliers), in their song "this train revised," refer to homosexuals killed in the concentration camps.[8] Yet, in the end, it is not the explicitly lesbian content, or the lack of it, that is important. What matters to lesbians is that there is a visible lesbian presence—strong voices, out in the world, not denying who they are.

Comedy

The spotlight of "lesbian chic" and the gay moment of the early 1990s focused mainstream attention on lesbian comics for the first time. Several of them appeared on national talk shows, and a great buzz was created about lesbian comedy going mainstream. These comics may have been new to the general viewing public, but they have been known to lesbians for years; lesbian comedy is as much a part of the culture as women's music. Lesbian comedians used to emcee the women's music festivals, introducing acts and providing commentary in between. According to Kate Clinton, a comedian who started performing in 1981, the comics gradually convinced the festival organizers that they had more to offer than amusing patter between singers. Soon lesbian comedians were booking their shows the way women's music performances were organized: two forty-five minute sets with an intermission in between, not the standard fare of comics who work up ten to fifteen minutes worth of jokes for a comedy club.

Lesbian comedians today work in many different styles, from the political humor of Kate Clinton to the in-your-face hyperactivity of Lea DeLaria to the Jewish borscht belt comedy of Sara Cytron. Suzanne Westenhoefer does not like to play only lesbian venues, while Lynda Montgomery "plays almost exclusively to lesbian and gay audiences because she feels they deserve her focused attention and that her own people's acceptance is the most powerful reward."[9]

Marga Gomez straddles the line between stand-up comedy and performance art. Her comedy is characterized by long pieces, not just one-liners, that are topical and address current affairs with a lesbian focus. Her performance pieces are autobiographical vignettes about growing up in a Puerto Rican performing family—her parents acted in Spanish theater in New York. This work can be poignant and not always funny.

Kate Clinton thinks of comedy as folk art. She relates it to the notion of the clown in native tribes, and views lesbian comedians as "comic Cassandras." "We're the ones who tell on the community ... and there's a lot to tell on."[10] While Clinton believes that comedy is comedy, she stresses the importance of a separate lesbian comedy. It should be identified as lesbian as much as possible, to stake out a territory until there is no longer a need to do so, until attitudes toward lesbians and gay men have changed.

At best, says Clinton, comedy is like poetry: imagistic, surprising, compact, and inspired at times. It is immediate. Plenty of jokes may be understood by straight audiences, but lesbians are going to understand them at the deepest level. Lesbian comics have fun with stereotypical lesbian images—softball and sports—and women's topics such as menstruation, but also deal with topics all comics use: sex, religion, relationships, family. But the spin on them becomes unique to lesbians (and gay men at times) because of common experiences such as coming out to family.

Canadian comic Elvira Kurt does a monologue about being the only child—and a lesbian at that—of Hungarian immigrants. On any given night the number of children of Hungarian immigrants in the audience may be quite small, so the laughter comes not from that specific shared experience but from the general understanding of anger and disappointment leveled at lesbians by their families. It is at just such times as these that lesbians recognize from their own lives moments of truth that are so individual as to be almost inexpressible, and yet here is someone expressing it. Everyone has a different association, yet everyone laughs at the same time.

Clinton says she and other lesbian comics have been affected by the work of gay male comedians. Lesbians were too serious to make fun of because they were too threatened by society at large. The men were so outrageous and had an attitude of having nothing to lose. This proved infectious to Clinton, who credits some of her edgier, borderline vicious routines to the influence gay male comics have had on her work.[11]

Referring to herself and other lesbian comedians, Clinton speaks of an "odd kind of political sense about our work." She calls it humor activism. She loves material that challenges the status quo, and believes she and other lesbian comics are working for social change. So does Karen Williams, one of the few African-American lesbian comics. "I think comics have really pushed the movement forward.... We've bridged the kind of gap between the totally invisible lesbians and the politicians. Comics acknowledge people's experience, in a way politicians never can."[12]

Humor paves the way for dialogue, and can be informative and enlightening as well as entertaining. Comics are artists in their stance as outsiders commenting on society. Lesbian comics are thrice distanced: as artists, as women, and as lesbians.

Lesbian humor is not limited to stand-up comedy. The comic book reappeared as a serious form of alternative expression in the 1980s and several lesbians are using comic strips to speak about issues of concern to lesbians.

Alison Bechdel's syndicated comic strip *Dykes To Watch Out For* runs in over forty-five publications, mostly in the United States and Canada, as well as in a gay paper in Scotland, with bootleg copies appearing in Japan, Italy, and Denmark. Bechdel calls her strip "part documentary, part soap opera—entertainment with this archival job on the side."[13] While she states that her real goal is to capture the present, she admits she tries to keep an accurate picture of lesbian culture as it evolves, including the little details an archivist safeguards, everything from the most recent political/intellectual theory to the latest fashion trend.

Traditionally, comic strips and books have been seen as a very lowbrow art form. Their appeal for Bechdel lies in a complex visual grammar that we take for granted but that has infinite possibilities and power to communicate. Like the stand-up lesbian comedians, Bechdel's work comes out of an integrated worldview that is part of being a lesbian. As she puts it, for lesbians, "politics is not separate from what you're having for breakfast."

Diane DiMassa is much more on the edge than Bechdel, though they share some of the same audience. She's angry and funny in a style that does not appeal to everyone. Her character, Hothead Paisan, homicidal lesbian terrorist, roams her nameless city with an Uzi, which she has no compunctions using against men—in this strip they are all homophobic, sexist, and racist. She will use a hand grenade if she has to. Along with the violence comes a healthy release of the rage that lesbians feel both as lesbians and as women in this society, as well as a heavy dose of humor.

DiMassa originally captured the more underground 'zine audience. Other lesbian cartoonists have staked out territory, much the way the stand-up comedians have. Andrea Natalie's "Stonewall Riots," syndicated in many gay and lesbian papers, are editorial in nature. Rhonda Dicksion's work covers the home life of lesbians. Fish and Terry Sap are two underground cartoonists who could be called, in the words of Bechdel, who admires their work, the "bad girls" of lesbian comics. Fish's work documents explicit S/M sex, and Sap draws "baby dykes."

The humor in any of these women's work is immediately evident, but with it come powerful messages of anger, hope, renewal, and community. As with oral comedy, written and illustrated comedy presents its audience with truth in an easily heard form, simple on the surface but capable of effecting change. Alison Bechdel told us that humor is just a side effect of what she does. She is "basically interested in narrative," and feels much more connected to lesbian writers than to lesbian comics. With good reason: the themes she deals with have been present in lesbian writing since it was first recognized.

Literature

Lesbians today can read about themselves in everything from escapist to literary fiction. Lesbian authors go on promotional book tours and give readings. All this is a far cry from times past when an author's homosexuality was a closely guarded secret, one that was pushed into the closet by relatives and survivors, sometimes even surviving partners.[14] Nor were biographers immune, choosing to avoid the topic of sexuality rather than discuss the lesbianism of their subject. For centuries, love between women was hinted about, written around, and only occasionally dealt with directly. More often than not readers had to read between the lines to find the lesbian content of a story or poem. Until early in this century the lesbian, though present, had been all but invisible in literature.

Today lesbians can look to literature for ways to live their lives, for affirmation of their existence, in any number of ways. In this section we examine written work over time in an effort to trace the course of the lesbian in literature, and see where current lesbian writing stands and what it offers about human as well as lesbian experience.

47 I have had not one word from her

Frankly I wish I were dead.
When she left, she wept

a great deal; she said to
me, "This parting must be
endured, Sappho. I go unwillingly."

I said, "Go, and be happy
but remember (you know
well) whom you leave shackled by love

"If you forget me, think
of our gifts to Aphrodite
and all the loveliness that we shared

"all the violet tiaras,
braided rosebuds, dill and
crocus twined around your young neck

"myrrh poured on your head
and on soft mats girls with
all that they most wished for beside them

"while no voices chanted
choruses without ours,
no woodlot bloomed in spring without song ..."

Sappho[15]

Sappho is the first lesbian writer. In fact, her poetry antedates heterosexual lyrical poetry.[16] The term lesbian comes from Sappho's home, the Greek island of Lesbos. Sappho, who lived around 600 B.C., was considered throughout antiquity to be the greatest of the lyric poets, and her poetry was so admired that she was called the "tenth muse" by Plato. Her work consists primarily of passionate love poems to women and about love of nature. She was extensively quoted, and it is primarily through these quotes that we know anything of her work. She wrote nine books of poetry (about two good-sized volumes in today's terms), but her work was deliberately destroyed during the early Middle Ages. Until very recently, many classicists tried to deny that Sappho's poetry portrayed erotic love between women.

There may have been women-identified or even lesbian writers earlier than Sappho in her or other cultures, but her work is the earliest we have. However, the Hebrew Bible certainly shows a strong woman-to-woman relationship in the story of Ruth and Naomi.

We can find a rich tradition of woman-to-woman erotic and love literature, starting in seventeenth-century England with the tradition of poetry and letters between women. The relationships between these women has been described as "romantic friendship."[17] This type of correspondence between women ranged from the poetry of Katherine Fowler Phillips and her circle in the seventeenth century to the letters of Eleanor Roosevelt in the twentieth century. With some classics, such as the work of Emily Dickinson, Willa Cather, and Virginia Woolf, the reader has to guess at the lesbian content or read between the lines. Some of Gertrude Stein's work is much more explicitly lesbian than the widely read *Autobiography of Alice B. Toklas* and *3 Lives*; none of Stein's lesbian work appeared during her lifetime.[18] The French writers of the 1920s and 1930s such as Renee Vivien and Natalie Barney are explicitly lesbian, but for many American lesbians the writers are more known than the work, having served as models for characters in the fiction of Djuna Barnes and Radclyffe Hall, among others.

Explicitly lesbian fiction first appeared in 1928 with Radclyffe Hall's classic *The Well of Loneliness*. Influenced by the theories of sexual inversion and gender variance put forth by Richard von Kraft-Ebbing and Havelock Ellis (whom she had write a preface for *The Well of Loneliness*), Hall believed she was a man trapped in a woman's body. Her main character, Stephen Gordon, is the prototypical gender-reversed lesbian whose lovers were very feminine women.

Calling her "love's mendicant," "invert," "one who stands between the sexes," Hall wrote about Stephen and "people like her" as being "afflicted." And yet at the end there is ultimate self-acceptance of that place, and a plea for acceptance: "'God,' she gasped, 'we believe; we have told You we believe.... We have not denied You, then rise up and defend us. Acknowledge us, oh God, before the whole world. Give us also the right to our existence.'"[19]

In America, that world was relatively accepting of lesbians for a short time in the 1930s, but the period after that and until the Stonewall Riots in 1969 was rather grim and cold. The only refuge many lesbians found was in books.

Lesbian pulp fiction of the 1950s and 1960s was sometimes written by men for men, but also by lesbians for lesbians. Ann Bannon's Beebo Brinker series, published from 1957 through 1962, depicted lesbian life in New York City, focusing on several characters followed in each book.[20] They painted a rather grim picture of lesbian life, though it was no doubt accurate. The women—Laura, Beebo, and Beth—spend a lot of time in the bars, get drunk, have drunken fights (especially in *Beebo Brinker*). Gay men are represented primarily by one character, Jack Mann, who never has a satisfying gay relationship and ends up marrying Laura, and they have a daughter. Bannon states in a note at the beginning of each of the reprinted books:

> Looking back from the mid-80s to the distant 1950s and 60s, let me share a thought with you. The books as they stand have 50s flaws. They are, in effect, the offspring of their special era, with its biases.

But they speak truly of that time and place as I knew it. I would not write them today quite as I wrote them then. But I did write them then, of course. And if Beebo is really *there* for some of you—and Laura and Beth and the others—it's because I stayed close to what felt real and right.

What felt real and right to many lesbians was to live openly as lesbians. In 1969, Isabel Miller's *Patience and Sarah* introduced readers to a lesbian couple who ended up together. Despite the fact that the novel was set in New England in 1816, twentieth-century lesbians could see what was possible for them in the present.[21]

Canadian author Jane Rule does not write about lesbian values or politics, though she wrote one of the most popular coming-out novels, *Desert of the Heart*,[22] which was made into the popular film *Desert Hearts* by director Donna Deitch. The lesbian characters in her books, as well as the gay male and heterosexual characters, form a community, but not the lesbian community that appears in later lesbian fiction.

The books of these and the few other authors venturing to write about lesbians were published at the time by mainstream presses. Soon another influence emerged: independent lesbian feminist presses.

In 1973, with *Rubyfruit Jungle*[23] Rita Mae Brown gave lesbians something they had been waiting for for years: a popular novel that had a lesbian hero who not only didn't have a problem with being a lesbian, she had to fashion her own sense of what that identity was. Brown's hero, Molly Bolt, goes to New York's Greenwich Village to find other lesbians, and she does. She also eventually returns home to reconcile with her adoptive mother, something she needs to do before she can make her way back to the city.

Rubyfruit Jungle was published by Daughters, Inc. Though it no longer exists, Daughters and other independent lesbian presses made a vision of lesbian life possible for many women. Dorothy Allison expresses her gratitude in an essay: "I would never have begun to write anything of worth without the example of those presses and magazines reassuring me that my life, and my family's life, was a fit subject for literature."[24]

Today's lesbian fiction deals less frequently with coming out and more with lesbian characters living their lives. Much of this work falls under the genres of mystery and romance, though the themes of lesbian fiction are certainly evident. A lesbian consciousness, where the personal is political, is still at work, and even escapist fiction has content. One of the most popular genres is the lesbian detective novel. Barbara Wilson, author of the Pam Nilson series, includes political and social topics and analysis in her work. Each volume of Katherine V. Forrest's Kate Delafield series has made the lesbian best-seller lists. *Amateur City*, published in 1984, introduced readers to Detective Kate Delafield of the Los Angeles Police Department. In that and the three other books in the series, Forrest not only presents readers with mysteries to solve but also moves her character through stages of her personal life, which in this case means a lesbian life lived more and more openly as Delafield comes out to her partner and begins to take her place in the Los Angeles lesbian community. Other issues are presented through the crimes themselves: homophobia and McCarthyism, a brutal gay-bashing, a mother's complete intolerance of her lesbian daughter.[25]

Some authors have expanded the insular view of lesbian life and issues. In 1994 novelist Sarah Schulman published a collection of political manifestos written during the Reagan/Bush years. Her 1990 novel *People in Trouble* chronicles the social activism, art, and ACT UP involvement of its main character. Schulman's work is not a lyrical extolling of the virtues of lesbian lives but gritty accounts of lesbian and gay life in the time of AIDS.[26]

Lesbians are also reclaiming their sexuality, not just in the romantic "filling up and spilling over" gentle metaphors of the 1970s but in work that is raunchy, defiant, and unashamed. Jane DeLynn's novel-in-stories *Don Juan in the Village*[27] features a nameless narrator, a writer, who picks up women in bars, has anonymous sex—including fisting—and goes out with a woman she finds so ugly she's attracted to her.

Lesbian sex has been included in lesbian fiction from the beginning—the popularity of Katherine V. Forrest's classic *Curious Wine*[28] attests to lesbians' desire to read about lesbian sex for affirmation, recognition, and arousal—and now most lesbian presses and some mainstream ones have published anthologies of lesbian erotic fiction, from "vanilla" to S/M with a full range of tastes in between.

The emergence of contemporary lesbian poetry follows a similar pattern to that of lesbian fiction. From Sappho through the time of romantic friendships, women wrote not necessarily explicitly lesbian poetry but poetry addressed to women, work ranging from the seemingly homoerotic "Goblin Market" by Christina Rossetti to Emily Dickinson's much more masked poetry of her frustrated love for various important women in her life.

The multifaceted nature of some lesbian poets almost defies categorization: Judy Grahn—historian, mythologist, playwright, poet, and publisher; Dorothy Allison writes novels, short stories, and essays; Adrienne Rich and the late Audre Lorde—each has produced essays that influenced both lesbian and feminist thought. The breakthrough volume for lesbian poetry that reflected early lesbian-feminist concerns with multiculturalism and issues of radical revision of society (race, class, gender roles, and age) was *Lesbian Poetry: An Anthology*.[29]

Influenced by feminism and then lesbian feminism, contemporary lesbian poetry is part of the multifaceted lesbian voice, expressed through the nature poems of Pulitzer Prize winner Mary Oliver and the work of other lesbian poets such as Olga Broumas, Minnie Bruce Pratt, Chrystos, and Pat Parker.

Whether writing influential essays such as "Compulsory Heterosexuality and Lesbian Existence"[30] or poetry, Adrienne Rich encourages and reminds lesbians that they are creating new paradigms and structure for themselves and their communities.

In one poem, "XIII" from "Twenty-One Love Poems," Rich talks of rules breaking "like a thermometer." She tells her lover that whatever they do together is "pure invention"; having been given maps that were outdated "by years," they are charting new territory. This concept of breaking new ground applies equally to lesbians in general. The poems of Dorothy Allison and Cheryl Clarke, among others, stand in sharp contrast to the more subtle sexuality of Adrienne Rich. They carry even further the idea that because lesbians are not governed by the constraints of conventional society, they can therefore configure their lives differently.[31]

The changes in the expression of lesbian sexuality and the maturation of the lesbian novel into something beyond the coming-out story (though those will always be with us) signify the expansion and perhaps disintegration of the old notion of Lesbian Nation. Some of the old spirit can be found today in literary journals like *Common Lives, Lesbian Lives,* and *Sinister Wisdom.* These perhaps paved the way for magazines like *Brat Attack* for leather dykes, *Fat Girl,* and any number of possibly transitory publications. Today's lesbian literature no longer expresses the utopian vision of one lesbian community, but rather reflects the potentially inclusive diversity of lesbians today. Its stories will continue to chart the course lesbians are taking into the future, a course, as Adrienne Rich tells us, that is governed by no rules, and with no maps to guide them.

Theater

As with lesbian music, lesbian theater as we know it today started with the women's movement of the 1970s. In the early 1970s several small theater groups tried to start women's theater in major cities, but with little success. Early on, many of the straight women involved did not want to do anything explicitly lesbian or even feminist, while lesbian audiences did not want to see theater that was not explicitly lesbian. Throughout the 1970s small theaters would occasionally pull together a show that could be considered women's theater; there was often some lesbian content in the plays produced, although they would not be considered lesbian plays. Many of the women experimenting with theater in the 1970s were not doing traditional plays and plots. There has been a Women's Theater Festival for several years, but unlike the women's music festivals, it is not primarily lesbian in focus. There are lesbian playwrights, actors, and plots at the festival, but there are also many straight women who participate. It is truly a women's (rather than "women's" as a euphemism for lesbian) festival.

Starting in the 1980s, Jane Chambers's plays, particularly *Last Summer at Bluefish Cove,* drew big crowds. *Bluefish Cove* has an explicitly lesbian plot, is accessible to audiences, and still enjoys popularity in productions staged today. Perhaps its continued success is due to the positive light in which it portrays a lesbian community, the interaction of a group of friends, including the coming out of one as they all face the death of the central character.

More recent work deals with more than coming out, though in San Francisco playwright Claire Chafee's *Why We Have a Body,* one of the main characters is having an affair with a married woman on the cusp of coming out. The play's themes of love and searching are consistent with lesbian themes. That it has no standard plot line seems particularly lesbian and female. Chafee's answer to criticisms about the play's rather loose plot line is: "This is the way life goes."[32]

Through the 1980s, performance art became more popular, and it is among performance artists like Holly Hughes and Marga Gomez that we find some of today's most vibrant lesbian theater. All of Hughes's work directly confronts and challenges mainstream society's concepts of women's roles and sexuality and AIDS through graphic, sometimes violent, sometimes humorous images conveyed through various types of narrative, both visual and oral.

Also criss-crossing the line between performance and theater are the Five Lesbian Brothers, a company that writes and performs original work, and also does spoofs on classic lesbian-themed films and plays such as *Mädchen in Uniform* and *The Children's Hour.*

Highways, a performance space in Santa Monica, California, and Wow Cafe, a cafe and performance space in New York, are both venues in which lesbian performers can get started and participate in workshops to improve their art. Sleeveless Theater is another such space (see chapter 6). Alice B. Theatre Company, established in the 1980s in Seattle, bills itself as a "gay and lesbian theater for all people" and is part of the thriving theater scene there.

Film

Over the years Hollywood has presented very few images of lesbians, and those it has offered reflected a mainstream view of lesbian life. Lesbians have been portrayed on the movie screen as pathological, suicide-prone, evil, sometimes literally blood-sucking. This tradition still persists, as for example in the icepick-wielding psychopath played by Sharon Stone in *Basic Instinct*. There is clearly a modest trend toward more positive portrayals, as for example in the lesbian character portrayed by Whoopi Goldberg in *Boys on the Side*, yet even here the price of being a lesbian character seems to be to give up any hope of a sex life.[33]

In the late 1970s and early 1980s independent lesbian filmmakers started producing and directing their own short and feature films about lesbians. When Donna Deitch was preparing to make *Desert Hearts* (1985), the adaptation of Jane Rule's 1964 novel *Desert of the Heart*, she says, "There hadn't been a film about a relationship between two women that hadn't ended in suicide like *The Children's Hour* or in a bisexual triangle. I wanted to make just a love story, like any other love story between a man and a woman, handled in a frank and real way."[34]

Go Fish (1994, directed by Rose Troche) can be seen as a transitional work between the slick production values of *Desert Hearts* and the grittier quality of underground independent movies. Like *Desert Hearts* and *Claire of the Moon* (1993, directed by Nicole Conn), *Go Fish* is a lesbian love story. Unlike the two earlier films, however, it is not a coming-out tale but a story about two lesbians who meet and fall in love. The characters dress in a very hip 1990s style, and the look and feel of the film are quite contemporary. It felt generationally different from its predecessors, dealing as it did with a self-contained community of dykes who discussed the politics of being a lesbian in a straight society (the invisibility of lesbians in the culture; whether a woman can call herself a lesbian if she sometimes sleeps with men). And though one of the characters has to move out of her home because her mother will not accept her homosexuality, *Go Fish* is not about coming out. The departure point is different from films made by older lesbians. Lesbians have come out; now what?

The diversity of the answers to that question is evident in a sampling of the topics of the current crop of lesbian films and video: dealing with one's family after coming out, the balance of power in relationships, lesbian marriages, gender-bending, and sex. As in lesbian literature, lesbian films and videos are beginning to move past coming-out stories to a point where a character's lesbianism is one fact about her and not necessarily the central point of the story. For example, *Fresh Kill,* Shu Lea Cheang's avant-garde feature, is a mystery about an environmental catastrophe, and the character who explores the mystery is a lesbian.

Jan Oxenberg, who wrote and directed the 1970s lesbian classics *Home Movie* and *A Comedy in Six Unnatural Acts,* is working on a number of projects, several of which have lesbian themes. Elaine Holliman's short film *Chicks in White Satin,* nominated for an Academy Award in 1993, told the story of two lesbians who invited their mothers to their wedding, and how the parents dealt with the event and the relationship; it is being made into a feature film, and Holliman was also hired to write a screenplay of Rita Mae Brown's classic *Rubyfruit Jungle.* She is but one of many lesbian filmmakers with work in production at the time of this writing. Their success in finding Hollywood distribution for their films may mean more varied and accurate representation of lesbians in film.

Video is a less expensive medium than film, and the advent of small cameras and portable equipment enabled independent artists to make videos on a shoestring budget. Lesbians have taken to this form for the freedom it allows them. Writer/director Jane Cottis teamed with artist Kaucyila Brooke to make "Dry Kisses Only." The seventy-eight-minute video is a send-up of academic readings of film texts. A hunt for the covert lesbian texts in classic Hollywood movies is thrown into different perspective by having the dry academic narration take place in a rose garden, in the bathroom, at a cocktail party, and in bed, among other unusual locations. If viewers simply listened to the soundtrack, they would hear valid discussions of social constructionism vs. essentialism, classic linear narrative, covert readings of films. But the discrepancy between the voice-over and the location highlights the video-makers' point of view, an irreverent lesbian stance.

What critics and theorists tend to forget about film and video is that, no matter what the layers of meaning and topics dealt with, most filmmakers are making movies they want to see—this is a consistent fact expressed in magazine interviews with directors Donna Deitch and Rose Troche, writer Lauran Hoffman, and in our conversation with writer/director Jan Oxenberg. These works are being made for entertainment. It just so happens that in entertaining their audiences, today's lesbian filmmakers are bringing an authentic lesbian vision to life, instead of what passes for lesbianism as seen through the eyes of heterosexuals.

Photography, Painting, Sculpture, Conceptual Art

Lesbian art of the 1970s was influenced by the political correctness of lesbian feminism. The 1977 "Lesbian Art and Artists" issues of *Heresies: A Feminist Publication on Art and Politics* was a catalyst to the major exhibits of lesbian art in the 1970s, two of which were held in New York and Los Angeles: in 1978 the 112 Greene Street Workshop presented "A Lesbian Show," and in 1980 in Los Angeles the Women's Building mounted "The Great American Lesbian Art Show" (GALAS). Artist/critic

Harmony Hammond describes much of the work of that time as simplistic and idealizing of lesbians. Though "fairly asexual and safe," these early exhibits still generated a public lesbian presence and discussion of that presence in the art world.[35] For the first time a wide range of artists were willing to be public about being lesbians, although some of them still kept lesbian content as a suggestion rather than an overt statement in their art. Lesbian themes of "anger, concealment, secrecy, guilt, coming out, celebrating the female body, and generally creating a visible lesbian presence" were represented visually by "landscape, fruit, and flower imagery."[36]

Typical of the time was the visual work done for lesbian-feminist journals and publishers. Photographers JEB (Joan E. Biren) and Tee Corinne illustrated the early years of lesbian feminism with their politically conscious images of women. Both document writers, artists, musicians, the music festivals, and lesbian events—just about every aspect of the lesbian community. Corinne manipulated some of her images in the darkroom, using solarization and superimposition to create abstract patterns of female body parts. Women's bodies were not objectified in lesbian art, and although they might be portrayed hugging or kissing, direct depiction of lesbian sex was mostly absent from lesbian art of the 1970s. This was quite a contrast from the purely sexual terms in which lesbians were shown on the covers of pulp fiction of the 1950s (mostly designed to appeal to male fantasies of lesbian eroticism). This swing back was due to the feminist stance against the representation of women as sexual objects in the media and to lesbians demanding to be considered in other than purely sexual terms.

In the 1980s new attitudes toward lesbian sexuality emerged. Lesbians began to explore S/M and leather, and to rethink the concepts of butch-femme and gender.[37] The lesbian sex radicals were more evident in literature than visual art, though some artists began exploring some of these issues in the late 1980s.[38] Many lesbians were (and still are) active in the movements against pornography and violence against women, and objected to these new attitudes. Some artists saw this militant antipornography stand as a dangerous threat to their creative expression.[39]

Much lesbian art in the 1990s explores power and authority and radical sex. This is both a reflection of a culture and a push at its margins. Over the years, as sex became more visible in the lesbian community and the debate over pornography and erotic art raged in feminist circles, lesbian artists dealt more directly, even confrontationally, with lesbian sexual content. Lesbian artists are reintroducing sexuality as one focus of being a lesbian.

Two of Catherine Opie's photographic self-portraits leave no room for the viewer's doubt as to who the photographer is or what she stands for. "Pervert" shows Opie seated facing the viewer. She wears pants but no shirt, a leather hood covers her entire head. Down each arm is a parade of temporary piercings, twenty-three eighteen-gauge needles basted into the skin of her arms. A fresh carving on her chest spells out "Pervert." There is a carving on the artist's back in the other portrait; this one of a house with chimney, a family close by. Opie has done a series of portraits of other leather dykes and of female-to-male transsexuals. While these may alarm or startle some, they are in fact classically beautiful portraits, documents of a community, as is all of her work. Her self-portraits locate her within the leather and S/M community, a deliberate statement on her part, a naming of who she is, a declaration: "This is what you're buying when you buy a piece of mine." The dream of domesticity—the house and the picket fence, two parents and a child, the classic American dream—etched not just in the mind of the artist but literally on her back. Her photographic images are immediate, accessible—startlingly beautiful and beautifully startling.

Opie told us she wondered about some of the buyers of her work. What did it mean that heterosexual married men were purchasing "Pervert"? This has been an issue for some lesbian artists, resulting in a hesitancy to depict lesbian sex because they have no control over their audience (a hesitancy that does not seem to exist in lesbian fiction, especially in romantic novels; but perhaps this is because the writer is less intimate with her audience, and more books are produced than editions of a work of visual art).

Just as there is no one Lesbian Community, there is no one Lesbian Art. Whether exploring the edge of the edge (S/M, leather, etc.) or the somewhat more comfortable center, lesbian art has been a search for the marginal, a search for identity and self-definition. This is where ideas and minds are changed, on the edges. The "bad girls" of conceptual art and photography and comics and fiction may be the most radical, but all lesbian artists are driving a wedge into the status quo. That's the whole search lesbian culture has explored from the earliest days of the 1970s, a search for identity and self-definition. All the work done on the edges is what got k. d. lang and Melissa Etheridge into the mainstream. Lesbian artists no longer promote an idealized, utopian culture, but work at the edges of their own sensibilities. Whether those sensibilities can be defined as lesbian or not is not the key question. Key is what do they have to say about themselves, about being a lesbian, about being a woman, about being a person in the world today. The more lesbian artists there are, the less uniform the work becomes, in whatever artistic discipline. Lesbian artists working today are creating their own identity, refusing to be defined from the outside.

Further Reading

Boffin, Tessa, and Jean Fraser, eds. *Stolen Glances: Lesbians Take Photographs.* London: Pandora Press, 1991.

Faderman, Lillian. *Surpassing the Love of Men: Romantic Friendship and Love between Women from the Renaissance to the Present.* New York: William Morrow, 1981.

Faderman, Lillian, ed. *Chloe Plus Olivia: An Anthology of Lesbian Literature from the Seventeenth Century to the Present.* New York: Viking, 1994.

Foster, Jeannette. *Sex Variant Women in Literature.* Tallahassee, FL: The Naiad Press, 1985.

Gever, Martha, John Greyson, Pratibha Parmar, eds. *Queer Looks: Perspectives on Lesbian and Gay Film and Video.* New York: Routledge, 1993.

Penelope, Julia, and Susan Wolfe, eds. *Lesbian Culture: An Anthology.* Freedom, CA: The Crossing Press, 1993.

Weiss, Andrea. *Vampires and Violets: Lesbians in Film.* New York: Penguin Books, 1993.

Zimmerman, Bonnie. *The Safe Sea of Women: Lesbian Fiction 1969-1989.* Boston: Beacon Press, 1990.

18
Gay Men and the Arts

Gay men are artistically inclined—that is the stereotype, at least. People may differ about why this is so: whether it is a natural endowment of creative genes, or the experience of oppression that channels gay men's energy through "artificial" outlets. But it is widely agreed that gay men are especially at home in the creative arts.

Not that every gay man is an artist by trade, of course. Gay men are soldiers, teachers, carpenters, homemakers, scientists, flight attendants. But even for the majority of gay men whose job description is not "artist," artistic feeling and artistic expression seem often to be second nature. In the Yankelovich survey (see chapter 5) gay men (as well as lesbians) were significantly more likely than heterosexuals to believe that creativity is not just the province of artists, but exists in everyone. This blurring of the boundary between life and art is a truly "gay" characteristic.

Within the artistic professions, the prevalence of gay men was for years a matter of speculation and conjecture. AIDS has changed that. With sad regularity the obituaries list designers, musicians, actors, writers, artists, and photographers who have succumbed to the disease, and the activism provoked by AIDS has motivated hundreds of other members of those professions to come out of the closet. Of all spheres of artistic expression, dance has been most devastated by the disease. If there was ever any question about the matter, it is now a certainty that dance in all its forms—ballet, modern dance, figure-skating, and the rest—is a field of expression in which gay men are preeminently successful. But the other arts are not far behind.

This affinity between gay men and the arts is a phenomenon that is not limited to the contemporary United States. It seems to have been generally true throughout Western history. And even when one looks beyond Western culture, the connection is still discernible. Gay men, especially those with relatively nonmasculine gender identity and gender role, have been performance artists in widely diverse cultures. One could mention the hijras of India, who perform ritual dances at marriages and births; the mahu of Polynesia, who were also often ritual dancers; the berdaches of native North America, who often sang or carried out ritual performances as shamans; and the kabuki actors of pre-Western Japan, who frequently were involved in sexual relationships with men (see chapter 2). Whether more conventionally masculine gay men gravitated to the arts in non-Western cultures is much less certain, because such men were not often recognized as a distinct subgroup within the male population.

Aspects of Gay Creativity

What is it that draws gay men to the arts? And is there anything special about gay art that distinguishes it from heterosexual art? Do gay men have a special way of perceiving the world, of expressing their feelings, or of relating to other people, that gives their art a characteristic quality? In attempting to answer these questions, we feel compelled to look beyond the contemporary gay cultural scene in the United States, for if certain modes of expression are truly part of the gay male experience, they should recur wherever and whenever gay men have existed.

One attribute of some gay men that clearly influences their mode of artistic expression is gender variance. Whether one prefers to say that some gay men are more feminine that straight men, or that they are more in touch with the female principle that resides within all of us, the fact is that feminine traits do often influence gay expression in characteristic ways.

Empathy, for example, and caring, nurturing qualities in general, are thought of as feminine—they are more typically shown by women that by men. These same qualities in some gay men allow creative expression to take place within the context of personal service. The culinary arts, hairdressing, fashion, interior design, and floristry all take place to a greater or lesser extent within this context. No doubt it is this same element of personal service that also "taints" these forms of expression, as if such service involves a shameful abandonment of the male principle of oblivious egotism.

The gay male community seems to go through cycles in which it alternately rejects and accepts gender variance. As mentioned in chapter 3, the 1970s were a period in which any kind of departure from masculinity was deeply suspect. More recently, there has been increasing respect for sexual variance, both in gay men's lives and in their art. The play *Angels in America*, for example, made the thoroughly unmasculine Prior into the central character, the person whose spiritual growth is the main dramatic line of the play. Until recently, Prior would have been a comic sideshow.

Although femininity and ambiguous sexual identity figure prominently in gay male art, they are not its key or central features. Rather, gay creativity is characterized by a tendency to perceive the world, and human nature, in layers, as if the screen we call the observable world is but one of many screens on which reality plays itself out. Perhaps an apt metaphor is the toy theater: the wooden cutout of the proscenium arch, which defines where one is pretending to "really" be (in a theater), the wings and moveable scenery that represent the inner worlds of dramatic action, and the cardboard figures that, thanks to a convenient system of rods or wires, carry out that action under the guidance of the watcher himself.

Gay writers have often presented themselves, or characters like themselves, as having this kind of vision, a mode of seeing somewhere between clairvoyance and voyeurism. In Thomas Mann's *Buddenbrooks*, for example, young Johann (Hanno), who dies in childhood, is portrayed as the archetypal prehomosexual, artistic boy. He spends hours alone with his toy theater, and in "real" life sees through people's social exteriors to what he perceives as their lonely, suffering hearts:

> But the little Johann saw more than he was supposed to see: his eyes—those timid, golden-brown, blue-shadowed eyes—observed too well. He saw not just the confident amiability with which his father treated everyone he met, he also saw, with his strange, penetrating glance, how terribly hard a performance it was for him. He saw how, after every visit, his father would lean back in the carriage, ever more silent and pale, his eyes closed, his eyelids reddened. With horror he saw, as they approached the next house, a mask slide over his father's features, and a suddenly renewed elasticity of movement seize his tired body.[1]

The narrator in Proust's *Remembrance of Things Past* has the same gift. Although the narrator is not explicitly portrayed as homosexual, he is clearly in many respects Proust's self-portrait, especially in his childhood. In one scene the young narrator has a privileged insight into the soul of the composer Vinteuil:

> On the day when my parents had gone to pay him a visit, I had accompanied them, but they had allowed me to remain outside, and as M. Vinteuil's house, Montjouvain, stood at the foot of a bushy hillock where I went to hide, I had found myself on the level with his drawing-room, upstairs, and only a few feet away from its window. When the servant came in to tell him that my parents had arrived, I had seen M. Vinteuil hurriedly place a sheet of music in a prominent position on the piano. But as soon as they entered the room he had snatched it away and put it in a corner. He was afraid, no doubt, of letting them suppose that he was glad to see them only because it gave him a chance of playing them some of his compositions. And every time that my mother, in the course of her visit, had returned to the subject he had hurriedly protested: "I can't think who put that on the piano; it's not the proper place for it at all," and had turned the conversation aside to other topics, precisely because they were of less interest to himself.[2]

The window through which the child sees is a framing device that serves much the same purpose as a proscenium arch, setting off the action seen through it as representing a separate level of reality, a level to which his parents, being inside the room, do not have access. In fact, Proust's narrator was, like Hanno Buddenbrook, passionately enamored of the theater. Later in the novel he becomes a true voyeur, using windows to spy on both gay male and lesbian encounters.

Sometimes the framing device is literally a frame. Francis Bacon's famous paintings of screaming popes, for example, are mounted in frames of unusual weight and opulence, frames that are echoed by the cubicle of white lines within which the pope sits. These frames say both "It's OK, this is just a painting," and "This is the *inside* of the pope." They further represent the pope as a prisoner, an actor being forced to recite lines written for him by Bacon—presumably a torrent of homophobic abuse.

More often, though, the same framing effect is achieved by stylistic devices. In the *Epic of Gilgamesh*[3] (ca. 1700 B.C.), the story proper is prefaced by an introduction in which the narrator invites the listener to view the city walls of Uruk and to read an engraved tablet, set in the wall by Gilgamesh himself, which carries the text of the ensuing epic. In Plato's *Symposium*, which is devoted largely to the topic of male homosexual love, the conversation is relayed to the reader through a chain of hearsay, and the climax of the work, Socrates' account of the nature of beauty, is represented as having been told to him by the priestess Diotima. The effect is of stepping though a sequence of doors into ever deeper levels of reality, from which we are jarringly returned by the entrance of the drunken Alcibiades. In Benjamin Britten's opera *Billy Budd*, based on Melville's homoerotic sea story, the old captain steps in front of the curtain to introduce the story as if from his recollection, or perhaps as a voyage into his own unconscious. Shakespeare is a master of such devices. The "play within the play" in *Hamlet*, the various levels of real and pretended madness in *King Lear*, the three witches who control the human drama in *Macbeth*, the cross-dressing in the comedies, and the alternation of Falstaffian buffoonery and earnest statesmanship in the histories—all these devices serve to suggest the multilayered nature of reality as seen through gay eyes.

In some gay art, a sense of multiple reality is conferred by reference to previous works of other artists. In Gus Van Sant's film *My Own Private Idaho,* modern-day hustlers lapse into speeches from Shakespeare's *Henry IV* plays. In Jonathan Tolins's play *The Twilight of the Golds,* which concerns an upscale Manhattan couple and their gay fetus, the characters and scenery of Wagner's *Ring* cycle intrude progressively into their lives. And Bacon's screaming popes, mentioned above, are a conscious homage to Velasquez, and perhaps thus to Picasso, who also reinterpreted Velasquez's paintings.

The layered quality of gay reality may be perceived in many ways. Sometimes, the immediate reality of everyday existence is seen only as a drab curtain that obscures a brilliant, even threatening inner world. Edmund White, for example, described life as a "dull brown geode that eats at itself with quartz teeth."[4] Or, conversely, there may be a self-conscious focus on surfaces—a resolute denial of inwardness that, by its very fervor, draws attention to what it denies. The profound superficiality of Oscar Wilde is a case in point. Obviously, this mode of expression goes over into parody and camp, of which more later.

Gay Silence

Because stigmatization, persecution, and censorship have historically placed such severe constraints on gay men, both in their lives and in their art, silence has been a characteristic mode of gay expression. In Tennessee Williams's play *Cat on a Hot Tin Roof,* for example, the central character, Brick, is essentially mute, rising to passion only in order to deny his homosexuality in the face of overwhelming evidence. Of course, Brick's silence is not Williams's silence. But Williams, like most gay creative artists of his period and earlier, was faced with the problem of expressing his identity in a hostile culture. The most common solution was the displacement of homosexual ideas into a heterosexual context. Thus, Williams's Blanche

DuBois, Proust's Albertine, Albee's George and Martha, and hundreds of characters like them have been construed, with varying degrees of confidence, as gay men in female or heterosexual male guise. The problem of expression has been even more acute for gay performing artists, who generally have had little choice in the sexual orientation of the characters they have played or in the sex of the person with whom they have danced.

Of course there are universals, like love and betrayal, that can play identical roles in gay and straight relationships. And self-expression is only one aspect of art: an artist who cannot step outside his own individual experience, who cannot see and represent the world through the eyes of someone radically different from himself, is a poor artist indeed. There have been innumerable authentic representations of heterosexuality by gay men, and even a few of homosexuality by straight men. To that extent, the gay artist's silence may not be material to his art, but only to his mental health, driving him to drink or suicide, perhaps, while leaving the world a string of unsullied masterpieces. But there are also many ways in which the experience of homosexuality is not parallel or equivalent to the experience of heterosexuality: in being a stigmatized, minority condition; in involving a process of self-recognition, acceptance, and assertion, or conversely of denial and rejection; in creating relationships of purely "elective affinity" and hence ones that are more intense and closer to nature and sometimes more short-lived; and in facing AIDS. Gay artists who do not deal explicitly with homosexuality must either be silent about these aspects of themselves or must represent them falsely.

Another way in which gay artists have dealt with the expression of homosexuality is to be silent about the sexual aspects of the relationships they are describing. In other words, homo*sexual* relationships have often been portrayed as homo*social*. This kind of silence is a mask that is extraordinarily difficult to penetrate. For one thing, there is considerable disagreement as to whether "brotherly love," "male bonding," and the like are intrinsically different from male homosexuality or not. In our view they are: we believe that close friendship between heterosexual men is a real but nonsexual phenomenon. We also acknowledge, however, that in cultures or periods where homosexuality is strongly stigmatized, gay men may express their attraction to other men in the form of nonsexual friendship. Thus, if sexuality is not explicitly mentioned in the depiction of a friendship between men, it can be hard to tell whether the artist transposed homosexuality into homosociality, portrayed repressed homosexuality, or portrayed genuine homosociality.

There can be internal clues as to the artist's intention, however. If, for example, a character who is engaged in an intimate male-male friendship is also represented as valuing that friendship above heterosexual love, it is reasonable to suspect that the friendship is intended to be understood as sexual. This is the case, for example, in *Gilgamesh*, where the hero rejects the advances of the love-goddess Ishtar in favor of his friendship with Enkidu, and is in fact punished for that rejection with Enkidu's death.[5] Or, there may be suggestive imagery, as in the opening scene of Joseph Conrad's[6] short novel *The Secret Sharer* (1910), in which a sea-captain, standing watch during the night, spots a naked young man in the phosphorescent water alongside the ship. In John Schlesinger's film *Midnight Cowboy*, a single gesture illuminates the homoerotic subtext: the embrace that the cowboy (Jon Voigt) gives the dead Ratso (Dustin Hoffman) at the close of the film.

Because gay silence has its roots in oppression, we are justified in hoping that the current liberalizing trend in American society, if it continues, will break the silence and open the doors to an unprecedented flowering of gay creativity.

Coming Out

Coming out is the opposite of gay silence. Much gay art, especially writing, has to do with the coming-out process. In this, of course, gay art shares a tradition with nongay art, expressed particularly in the *Bildungsroman*, the novel of personal growth or spiritual education. The novel in this genre best known to

American readers is J. D. Salinger's *Catcher in the Rye* (1951), in which, incidentally, homosexuality is presented as just another snare on the hero's path to self-awareness.

Early gay writers were very ambiguous about the coming-out process, as one might expect from the social climate in which they wrote. The theme might be cloaked in cryptic allegory, as in Hans Christian Andersen's *The Ugly Duckling*. If homosexuality was even vaguely hinted at, as in Oscar Wilde's *Picture of Dorian Gray*, then coming out was portrayed as a process of inexorable decline and degradation. Even a comparatively recent and explicitly gay work, Andrew Holleran's 1978 novel *Dancer from the Dance*, echoes *Dorian Gray* in many respects. The central character, Malone, is a workaholic, closeted New Yorker who falls in love with an Italian youth from New Jersey. After a briefly serene love affair, Malone throws himself into the New York gay scene, and the remainder of the book is the story of his downwardly spiraling addiction to sex and drugs and disco music. Malone comes out to himself and to the gay world, but only toys with the idea of telling his family, and he cuts himself off totally from his previous heterosexual acquaintances. His coming out is an exchange of one alienation for another, and the ultimate resolution is suicide.

Published only four years after *Dancer from the Dance*, Edmund White's *A Boy's Own Story* (1982) seems to belong to a different age. Like Hanno Buddenbrook, White's narrator as a child has a privileged, almost pathological insight into his father's psyche:

> Later, an hour later, he'd descend to his squire's breakfast, shaved and dressed in a white shirt, silk tie and double-breasted suit, his eyes young, sharp and intelligent in a head I'd seen earlier from an odd, wounded angle. He was now polite to the cook, deferential to my mother and lighthearted and cutting with my sister and me—he who'd been nothing but a felled deity exuding a cold sweat an hour before.

Like Hanno, he finds more reality in the toy theater than in real life:

The toe of a big brown shoe protruding from beneath the hem of the proscenium draperies kept in mind real dimensions only for a few more minutes; soon the reduced scale of the stage had engulfed me, as though I'd been precipitated through a beaker and sublimated into another substance altogether.... In this lighted cube my emotions coalesced because they were given a firm bounding line and because things devolved with the logic of art, not life.

But in drastic contrast to Hanno, White's narrator is not killed off in childhood, but is allowed to become a gay man. This process of becoming is full of pain and turmoil, of laughable efforts to love men while avoiding the label of "homosexual." But it is ultimately successful, because he is allowed to develop his own unmediated vision of the world and his place in it.

The coming-out genre was pretty much wrapped up by David Leavitt with his 1986 novel *The Lost Language of Cranes*.[7] In this novel a young man comes out to his parents, only to have his father come out to him. The story highlights the cultural differences between the generations that allow the younger man a far smoother road to a gay identity.

Lamentation

Loss is an inescapable part of the human condition. In this age of AIDS, gay men experience this loss not only as individuals but also as a community. However each man reacts to his loss, whether through tears, silence, depression, rage, humor, compassion, or activism—or most likely through some combination of all of these—he is taking part in a social ritual whose formulas have been prescribed since time immemorial.

For gay men, part of the ritual is artistic expression. Long before AIDS, there was a tradition of expression of grief at the loss of a lover, a tradition that often framed the grief in song or incantation. A beautiful example is the lamentation of Gilgamesh for his dead friend Enkidu[8]:

Enkidu, your mother, the gazelle,
and your father, the wild donkey, engendered you,
four wild asses raised you on their milk,

and the herds taught you all the grazing lands.
May the Roads of Enkidu to the cedar forest mourn you
and not fall silent night or day.
May the elders of the broad city of Uruk-Haven mourn you.
May the peoples who gave their blessing after us mourn you.
May the men of the mountains and hills mourn you.
...
May the brothers go into mourning over you like sisters;
The lamentation priests, may their hair be shorn off on your behalf.
Enkidu, your mother and your father are in the wastelands,
I mourn you ...

The repetitive, chantlike style of Gilgamesh's lament, although exquisitely personal, also has a liturgical quality, perhaps echoing the formulas of the "lamentation priests." Something of the same character exists in Walt Whitman's lamentation for President Lincoln, *When Lilacs Last in the Dooryard Bloom'd*. Of course, Whitman and Lincoln were not lovers. Nevertheless, the poem reads as a depiction of the most intimate bereavement:

As you droop'd from the sky low down as if to my side, (while the other stars all look'd on,)
As we wander'd together the solemn night, (for something I know not what kept me from sleep,)
As the night advanced, and I saw on the rim of the west how full you were of woe,
As I stood on the rising ground in the breeze in the cool transparent night,
As I watch'd where you pass'd and was lost in the netherward black of the night,
As my soul in its trouble dissatisfied sank, as where you sad orb,
Concluded, dropt in the night, and was gone ...

AIDS has engendered a culture of grief. A song that captures the quality of AIDS grief as well as any work of art (although it is not explicitly about AIDS) is "The Crying Game," in its performance by Boy George. The lyrics (by Geoff Stephens) are generic: rather than lamenting a single loss, the lines express the numbing of feeling caused by loss after loss. Read on the printed page, the lines have a flat quality, but the sung version is full of contrasts. Boy George alternates between a more feminine and a more masculine vocal tone, setting up an ambiguous sexuality that stamps the work as gay art.[9] There is also a contrast between the heavy, incantatory quality of the first part of each line, and the greater emotion at the end. The first line, for example ("I know all there is to know about the crying game"), ends with a sweeping descending sixth, and the end of the first stanza ("And then before you know where you are, you're saying goodbye") is marked by an unexpected modulation on the last syllable. Yet another contrast is between the pattering, dance-music backing and the melancholy songline. These contrasts give the song a quality of mystery, as if, however often one has heard it, one has not quite heard it through.

"The Crying Game" expresses "pure" grief: a totally self-absorbed sadness, unmixed with positive thoughts about the persons lost or with hope for the future. Much of the art related to AIDS, especially the works of people with AIDS themselves, goes beyond sadness to express acceptance, love, even joy. This could be said, for example, of the ballet *Empyrean Dances*, choreographed by Edward Stierle for the Joffrey Ballet. The premiere of *Empyrean Dances* is described by Diane Solway in her biography of Stierle:

> The curtain came up on a stage littered with architectural fragments, the facade of a half-finished or abandoned building visible on a backdrop. From the wings, dancers entered the desolate setting and became sculptural friezes themselves, posing on and then soaring from the ruins in a continuous cascade of lifts and leaps. "You are in this destroyed place," Eddie had instructed the dancers during rehearsals, "and you are rebuilding it with your spirit." He had wanted to share with them the discovery of his own spiritual strength, which he was convinced was helping to keep him alive. Hope and rebirth were the twin themes he sought to convey with this ballet; its closing image would feature the entire cast standing in an ascending pattern, gazing upward and offstage towards a celestial light.[10]

A recurring theme in AIDS art is that of bereavement as exclusion: the feeling of the survivor that, by not having AIDS, he has been shut out from the group of true homosexuals, or has betrayed his dead or dying lover. In Tony Kushner's play *Angels in America*, for example, a dying man's ex-lover deliberately engages in unprotected anal sex in order to join the ranks of the afflicted. The sex act is played out with the utmost realism, although with the two actors separated from each other by several feet. It reminds us that pornography is a staple of gay culture, but it turns pornography to a different use, namely to convey the strength of the man's desire to join the culture of death.

A film that expresses AIDS grief in an original way is entitled, simply, *Grief*. A low-budget comedy by Richard Glatzer (1993), the film follows the soap-opera-like goings-on in the offices of a TV production company. Among the attractive, gay young men in the office, Mark (Craig Chester) is facing the anniversary of the death of his lover. Grief, thoughts of suicide, and a sense of pointlessness mingle with clumsy attempts to get involved in new relationships and to develop his career. The "real" story is intercut with hilarious episodes from the tacky courtroom series, *"The Love Judge,"* which the company is engaged in making. These courtroom scenes, with their flickering light, cheap color, and ugly, histrionic litigants, are a typical gay framing device. By their extreme falsity they serve to drive the real story, which is itself tacky enough, into the foreground, making the characters warmer, more real and more sexy, and their problems more involving, than they would otherwise have been.

Of the works of art created out of AIDS grief, none has received so much attention as the AIDS Memorial Quilt. The quilt was the concept of Cleve Jones and the Names Project in San Francisco. Each three-by-six-foot panel of the quilt remembers a single individual who died of AIDS, and is the work of a surviving lover, family, or group of friends. The quilt presently has over 25,000 panels.

Although not every panel of the AIDS Quilt commemorates a gay man, or was made by gay men, the quilt's concept, design, and total effect is the quintessence of gay male art. For one thing, it is gender-variant: no heterosexual man would think to commemorate another through so unmasculine an art as quilting. In addition it depicts, in the relationship between the individual panel and the entire quilt, the relationship between the individual gay man and the community to which he belongs. Each panel is strikingly different—in color, pattern, wording, in the objects sewn onto the panel, in every muted, quirky, or flamboyant detail. In this, the quilt prizes individuality, even flaunts it, just as gay men prize or flaunt their own individuality. Yet each panel is sewn to its neighbors, and those neighbors to others, and so on. As one's gaze pulls back from the details of a single panel to take in the vast multicolored patchwork of the entire quilt, one cannot help thinking, not just of the vast numbers of those who have died of AIDS, but also of the strength of a community that connects so much diversity. Viewing the quilt is an achingly painful experience. But it also powerfully rejects homophobia and the stigma of AIDS, and it joyfully unites those who have died with each other, with the living, and with the unborn.

Two novels that deal, in very different ways, with the suffering and loss caused by AIDS are Paul Monette's *Afterlife*[11] and Dale Peck's *Martin and John*.[12] Monette's novel concerns Steven, Dell, and Sonny, the "widowers" of three men who died of AIDS at the same time in the same hospital. Meeting periodically during the ensuing months, the three men go through a divergent evolution. Dell becomes increasingly the victim of his own murderous rage, Sonny seeks oblivion in sexual indulgence, while Steven works his way painfully toward a new relationship, a relationship that is intensified by the shadow of the advancing plague. The novel is notable not for a distinct literary style but for its sympathetic account of the differing ways in which different people (or perhaps even one person) can respond to horror and loss.

Peck's *Martin and John* is a series of short stories and vignettes in which the narrator or narrators, all called John, recall episodes from their childhood or from their relationships with their lover or lovers, all called Martin. In one episode, John as a small child witnesses his mother's bloody miscarriage; in another, he watches Martin, emaciated by AIDS, die in his bathtub by rectal hemorrhage. There are also scenes of all-too-transient tenderness: Martin and John as teenagers, both facially scarred, meet on a farm in Kansas, before Martin mysteriously disappears; Martin as John's stepfather, who rescues his mother from drink and makes love to both of them, only to be driven away by her addiction to the memory of John's father. Told with a haunting spareness, the stories are brilliantly illuminated glimpses of disparate lives united by suffering and love, or perhaps one life chaotically recombined, as if viewed through splintered glass.

Rage

Rage—the conjunction of energy and blame—is hardly a predominant theme in gay male art, but in the context of the AIDS epidemic it has taken on a special significance. In Larry Kramer's 1985 play *The Normal Heart*, for example, the protagonist Ned (based on Kramer himself) lives in a state of rage. He even becomes furious with his beloved brother Ben, a heterosexual lawyer, because Ben is more interested in building himself an expensive house than in joining the fight against AIDS, and because Ben is not willing to admit that homosexuality is as normal and innate a state as heterosexuality:

BEN: My agreeing you were born just like I was born is not going to help save your dying friends.

NED: Funny—that's exactly what I think will help save my dying friends.

BEN: Ned—you can be gay and you can be proud no matter what I think. Everybody is oppressed by someone else in some form or another. Some of us learn how to fight back, with or without the help of others, despite their opinions, even those closest to us. And judging from this mess your friends are in, it's imperative that you stand up and fight to be prouder than ever.

NED: Can't you see that I'm trying to do that? Can't your perverse ego proclaiming its superiority see that I'm trying to be proud? You can only find room to call yourself normal.

BEN: You make me sound like I'm the enemy.

NED: I'm beginning to think that you and your straight world are our enemy. I am furious with you, and with myself and with every goddamned doctor who ever told me I'm sick and interfered with my loving a man. I'm trying to understand why nobody wants to hear we're dying, why nobody wants to help. Two million dollars—for a house! We can't even get twenty-nine cents from the city. You still think I'm sick, and I simply cannot allow that any longer. I will not speak to you again until you accept me as your equal. Your healthy equal. Your brother![13]

In a political sense, Ned's rage seems justified: he is right that straight people's refusal to concede an identity to gay men underlies their ability to ignore the AIDS crisis. But in a psychological sense, breaking off his friendship with his brother seems terribly wrong—a product, as Ben perceives, of Ned's inability to establish his own sense of self-worth. At the end of the play, after Ned has succeeded in carrying a gay relationship through to its tragic conclusion, the brothers embrace once more.

The words that close the scene quoted above—"Your healthy equal. Your brother!"—echo the famous closing line of Baudelaire's poem *Au Lecteur*: "Hypocrite lecteur,—mon semblable,—mon frère!" (Hypocritical reader,—my likeness,—my brother!). The reference, whether intended or coincidental, seems to affirm that Ned's speech, his anger and his plea for acceptance, is directed at each of the play's viewers or readers, not just at Ben.

Humor, Parody, and Camp

Humor is of course universal, but gay humor often has a particular quality known as "camp." To talk about camp, according to Susan Sontag, is to betray it, whereupon she wrote the classic account of the subject (see Further Reading). Camp is easier to recognize than to define, but it is generally marked by parody, excess, deliberate artificiality, and sexual suggestiveness or gender confusion. Camp is a point of view, not only on the part of the artist, but also of the reader or watcher. Take the Triumphal March from Verdi's *Aida.* Even without the elephants, every element of camp is there: the blaring circus music, the strutting extras (most of them no doubt gay) in their overdone costumes, the half-naked slaves craving for the lash. But unless the audience begins to titter, the spectacle is merely magnificent, not camp.

The element of parody in camp is another example of the "layered" quality of gay vision. Parody is simultaneously representing a point of view and criticizing it, often by exaggeration. For gay men, like any marginalized group, the obvious target of parody is the Establishment, especially in its emphasis on customs such as heterosexual marriage that ignore the needs of gay men. Oscar Wilde was of course the master of this kind of parody. His technique was to take conventional phrases or attitudes and stand them deftly on their head, as in this passage from *The Importance of Being Earnest* in which Lady Bracknell is vetting Jack's suitability for marriage to her daughter:

LADY BRACKNELL: ... Now to minor matters. Are your parents living?

JACK: I have lost both my parents.

LADY BRACKNELL: To lose one parent, Mr. Worthing, may be regarded as a misfortune; to lose both looks like carelessness. Who was your father? He was evidently a man of some wealth. Was he born in what the Radical papers call the purple of commerce, or did he rise from the ranks of the aristocracy?[14]

Wilde's mockery of marriage and social snobbery was very likely derived from his own sense of exclusion. Wilde was a snob himself: his famous attachment to Alfred Douglas was certainly influenced by the fact that Douglas was a minor aristocrat. In his novel *The Picture of Dorian Gray,* published in 1891 shortly before he met Douglas, Wilde reversed the relationship: Henry Wotton, the decadent cynic, was the lord, while Gray, the beautiful airhead, was the commoner. What is so remarkable in Wilde is that this bitter wellspring of creativity becomes so transmuted as to generate characters, like Lady Bracknell, who are positively lovable in their fanatical conservatism. Perhaps the ability to achieve such transformation is a gay trait. In Shakespeare's *Twelfth Night*, for example, Malvolio is a tireless spoiler of fun, but Shakespeare draws him in a human enough way as to make one feel sorry for his ultimate undoing. As an example of an equivalent character created by a nongay artist one could point to Beckmesser, the stickler for musical order in Wagner's opera *Die Meistersinger*. There is an ugliness in Beckmesser's character, and the music written for him to sing, which distorts the emotional balance of the opera, and which leaves raw and exposed the animosity Wagner felt toward the person he was parodying (the music critic Eduard Hanslick).

Because writers like Wilde did not deal explicitly with homosexuality, they could not directly parody homophobia. Shakespeare did manage it on one occasion, although the passage is hidden away in *Troilus and Cressida*, one of his lesser-known plays. The curmudgeonly Thersites berates Patroclus for his relationship with Achilles (act 5, scene 1):

THERSITES: Prithee be silent, boy; I profit not by thy talk; thou art thought to be Achilles' male varlet.

PATROCLUS: Male varlet, you rogue! What's that?

THERSITES: Why, his masculine whore. Now, the rotten diseases of the south, the guts-griping, ruptures, catarrhs, loads o' gravel i' th' back, lethargies, cold palsies, raw eyes, dirt-rotten livers, wheezing lungs, bladders full of impostume, sciaticas, limekilns i' th' palm, incurable bone-ache, and the rivelled fee-simple of the tetter, take and take again such preposterous discoveries!

PATROCLUS: Why, thou damnable box of envy, thou; what mean'st thou to curse thus?

THERSITES: Do I curse *thee*?

PATROCLUS: Why, no, you ruinous butt; you whoreson indistinguishable cur, no.

THERSITES: No? Why art thou then exasperate, thou idle immaterial skein of sleave-silk, thou green sarsenet flap for a sore eye, thou tassel of a prodigal's purse, thou? Ah, how the poor world is pestered with such waterflies, diminutives of nature!

PATROCLUS: Out, gall!...

The diseases that Thersites wishes on sodomites are sexually transmitted (the "disease of the south" is syphilis). The thought is similar to the religious right's notion of AIDS as God's punishment for homosexuals.

The heart of camp has to do with gender. Often it means taking masculinity, femininity, or androgyny to their absurd limits. The masculine, outdoorsy persona projected by Walt Whitman in his poetry and in his life strikes most modern readers as camp: in *Song of Myself*, for example, he describes himself as "turbulent, fleshy, sensual, eating, drinking and breeding," and in real life he claimed to have fathered bastards in numerous cities, though none of them ever showed up to claim their patrimony. The same kind of camp masculinity is evident in the world of leathermen, and in art that portrays them such as the drawings of Tom of Finland. An example of the same phenomenon in film is the character of Luke, a spaced-out, HIV-positive urban cowboy in Gregg Araki's film *The Living End*. Among other feats, Luke shoots three gay-bashers who come at him with baseball bats in a parking garage. The scene seems to be a parody of the climax of a classic Western. At any event, it evoked wild applause when the film played to gay audiences, an indication that the film was read as admiring as well as mocking Luke's masculine pose.

Camp femininity is the life and art of the drag queen. Again, there is an ambivalent mixture of mockery and admiration, even longing. In the past, drag queens have often been seen as degrading to the image of gay men, or to that of women, but recently they have made a comeback. In Stephan Elliott's 1994 film *The Adventures of Priscilla, Queen of the Desert*, three drag entertainers camp it up in the Australian outback. In the film's "message" scene, one of the three realizes, much to his surprise, that his young son accepts and admires his drag persona and his homosexuality. The film also points up the diversity among those who do drag: one of the three is a conventional gay man, one is gay but also has a wife and son, and the third is a postoperative male-to-female transsexual.

Even androgyny has its camp extreme. One could trace the evolution of the phenomenon in the portrayals, over the centuries, of the martyrdom of Saint Sebastian, beginning with paintings whose spirituality is only slightly undermined by the martyr's akimbo stance, and culminating in masterpieces of kitsch such as the rendering by the photographers Pierre et Gils, who represent Sebastian as a doe-eyed youth dreamily awaiting sex, death, or both..

Love

Gay love exists outside the forms and conventions of heterosexual life. Love between men and women was, and still often is, sanctified by the institution of marriage. In theory at least, marriage provided public recognition of the love between man and woman, transformed sex from a vice into a virtue, protected the couple from sexual invasion by third parties, connected the couple to their families of origin, offered a clear social and sexual role to each member of the couple, and provided a secure environment for the raising of children. During the long period in which marriage was loaded with so much psychological and economic responsibility, same-sex love always carried with it the experience of alienation and exclusion. But it also carried, for those who sought it, a sense of freedom and adventure that could be an inspiration to art.

Christopher Marlowe's play *Edward II* (ca. 1592) portrays the love between the fourteenth-century English king and his favorite, Piers Gaveston. The play is deeply pessimistic—it paints their love as helpless against the homophobia of the barons, who eventually murder both of them. Marlowe himself was killed in a "tavern brawl," conceivably also a victim of homophobia. The play (as well as the 1992 film based on the play, directed by Derek Jarman) emphasizes that it is Edward's rejection of heterosexuality, as much as his relationship with Gaveston, which caused his downfall.

Many artists have praised the freedom of gay love; a freedom conferred by its disconnection from established ways of behavior. This feeling is intense in the work of Walt Whitman, for example in the poem *I Hear It Was Charged Against Me*:

I hear it was charged against me that I sought to destroy institutions,
But really I am neither for nor against institutions,
(What indeed have I in common with them? or what with the destruction of them?)
Only I will establish in the Mannahatta and in every city of these States inland and seaboard,
And in the fields and woods, and above every keel little or large that dents the water,
Without edifices or rules or trustees or any argument,
The institution of the dear love of comrades.

The same feeling is evident in the works of gay artists as diverse as James Fenimore Cooper, Jean Genet, Allen Ginsberg, and Werner Fassbinder. Genet in particular presented an image of himself as the Outsider, whose cult has been central to twentieth-century art.

Gus Van Sant's film *My Own Private Idaho* (1992) also presents gay love in terms of freedom. The two hustlers, Scott and Mike, enjoy the freedom of the streets until Mike falls in love with Scott. Scott's response is to reject homosexuality, marry, and join the Establishment, while Mike is left to decay on the streets. Yet Mike is seen as the fortunate one, the one who remains free.

If gay love is intensified by its atmosphere of outsiderdom, what will happen to it if gays and lesbians cease to be outsiders? We are in fact beginning to see books and films in which a gay or lesbian character is part of the group, and in which his or her homosexuality is fairly incidental to the action. An example is Andrew Fleming's 1994 film *Threesome,* a comedy about three college roommates: a straight man, a gay man, and a straight woman. The gay man's coming out is a relatively painless affair, and the unrequited love triangle that establishes itself (woman→gay man→straight man→woman) has a threefold symmetry of frustration. It's the same thing, the film seems to be saying, to be rejected for your sex as to be rejected as an individual. For a while, this frustration is submerged by an intense friendship among the three, but eventually the straight couple begins a sexual relationship from which the gay man is excluded. The film ends up highlighting differences in the experience of homosexual and heterosexual love. For one thing, as a member of a small minority, the gay man must leave the straight majority, at least temporarily, in order to find requited love. Also, there are differences between gay and straight men that will affect the quality of their relationships in any circumstances. In the film this point is made in fairly stereotypical fashion, by making the gay man a sensitive intellectual and the straight man a mindless party animal. Beyond this, and perhaps more true to life, the gay man is the narrator, the one who frames the story by recollecting the events months or years after they happened, while the others merely act in it. The gay man is the observer, the artist, the born Outsider.

Body and Soul

Nowhere is the layered view of the world more obvious than in gay men's attitudes to the physical and spiritual sides of human nature. In the typical nongay conception, these two aspects of our nature are contradictory or mutually exclusive. One is either talking about the body or about the soul, but not both. In early Christian iconography, for example, the saints stood in rows, their bodies hidden from neck to ankle by identical robes, with little in their facial appearance to distinguish them as individuals or even as men or women. Each carried an identifying token—Saint Catherine had her wheel, Saint Agatha her pincers. Because these tokens were often the instruments of their martyrdom, they not only identified the saints as individuals, they also symbolized the negation of their bodies and hence their spirituality. In life, scourging, fasting, and celibacy served the same purpose.

Of course, fasting and celibacy are out of fashion even among heterosexuals today, and scourging survives, if at all, as a sexual turn-on. But even today we see, in the standard heterosexual view, a contradiction between the physical and the spiritual. Pornography, for example, is denigrated as intrinsically immoral, or, in a more liberal environment, as degrading to women. There is little connection, therefore, between heterosexual pornography and heterosexual "art."

Gay men, and specifically gay artists, have never felt this kind of contradiction. Rather, the body has been revered, both for its own pleasures, and as the screen on which our inner life is played out. The Greeks sculptors, who were either gay themselves or were influenced by a gay-friendly culture, attempted to represent spirituality by an ideal bodily beauty—both male and female. Gay artists of the Renaissance, especially Michelangelo, gave their male nudes a more individual sexual beauty, but also used it to express religious truths (Baudelaire described Michelangelo's art as "the no-man's land where Christs and Herculeses intermingle"). And gay pornography today is not separate from gay art, but an accepted part of it. There is little sense, in the gay community, that male pornography degrades gay men in general or the actors who perform it.

Spiritually inclined gay men have typically revered the entirety of the physical world, of which the body is part, as God's creation. In his poem *I Sing the Body Electric,* Walt Whitman lovingly details every part of the body, outside and in, and concludes:

O I say these are not the parts and poems of the body only, but of the soul,
O I say now these are the soul!

Gerard Manley Hopkins was a gay poet of a very different religious and sexual outlook from Whitman. He was a Roman Catholic priest and was probably celibate. But, like Whitman, he found the spiritual in a series of brilliant instances of the observed world, and he emphasized the physical aspects of spirituality. In his sonnet *The Caged Skylark,* for example, Hopkins begins with a traditional Christian representation of the body as a mere encumbrance to the soul:

As a dare-gale skylark scanted in a dull cage
Man's mounting spirit in his bone-house, mean house, dwells—...

But at the end of the poem he affirms that

... Man's spirit will be flesh-bound when found at best,
But uncumberèd: meadow-down is not distressed
For a rainbow footing it not he for his bónes rísen.

In other words, the soul in its finest state (at the Resurrection) will once again inhabit its human body, but will no longer be imprisoned by it.

Further Reading

Baker, Rob. *The Art of AIDS: From Stigma to Conscience.* New York: Continuum Publishing Co., 1994.

Bergman, David, ed. *Camp Grounds: Style and Homosexuality.* Amherst, MA: University of Massachusetts Press, 1993.

Dyer, Richard. *Now You See It: Studies on Lesbian and Gay Film.* London: Routledge, 1990.

Klusacek, Allan, and Ken Morrison. *A Leap in the Dark: AIDS, Art, and Contemporary Culture.* Montreal: Véhicule Press, 1992.

Sontag, Susan. "Notes on 'Camp'," in *Against Interpretation and Other Essays.* New York: Dell, 1966.

19
Religion and Spirituality

Religious life presents a deep paradox for lesbians and gay men. On the one hand, many organized religions have anathematized homosexual behavior, and have attempted to exclude gays and lesbians from participation in religious life. On the other hand, many gays and lesbians have a particular affinity with the spiritual, an affinity that seeks expression both in religious participation and in the forms of daily living.

In this chapter we explore this paradox in three ways. First, we survey the attitudes of several world religions toward homosexuality, in an attempt to discover the origins of antigay doctrine. Second, we describe the efforts made by lesbians and gay men to practice and serve within the traditional framework of organized religion. Finally, we explore the ways in which lesbians and gay men have sought to create new forms of spiritual community, forms that are more accepting of their sexuality and more expressive of their inner lives.

World Religions and Homosexuality

Islam

Founded by the seventh-century Arabian prophet Mohammed, Islam has some historical and doctrinal themes in common with Judeo-Christianity. Islam recognizes Abraham and Jesus as pre-Mohammedan prophets; indeed, Sunni Moslems (who predominate in Turkey, North Africa, and the Arab countries) share the Christian belief that, at the end of the world, Jesus will return in power. The main elements of Islamic teaching—

strict patriarchal monotheism, and the obligations to religious observance, charity, and pilgrimage—are all echoed in Christianity. Hebrew religious law, the *halakhah*, strongly influenced Islamic law, the *shari'a*.

Mohammed was a worldly man: he had several wives and was a successful general and governor. Perhaps for this reason Muslims (except for the monastic Sufis) did not develop an ascetic, renunciatory tradition to the same degree as did the early Christian church. Sexual desire and sexual pleasure were therefore not held to contradict spirituality. In spite of this relatively liberal attitude toward sex in general, Islam's holy book, the Koran, as well as the recorded teachings of Mohammed, explicitly denounce homosexual behavior and condemn the person who practices it to hell-fire. "God will cancel all his good deeds," said the Prophet in his "Farewell Sermon."[1]

In Islamic countries, there have traditionally been strict legal proscriptions against homosexuality, and public affirmation of a gay or lesbian identity has been impossible. On the other hand, these legal proscriptions have been directed mainly against the public expression of homosexuality, rather than against homosexual behavior. In fact, some Islamic countries, such as Iran, have had a long literary and artistic tradition of homosexual expression. Furthermore the segregation of the sexes, which is so marked a feature of traditional Islamic culture, serves to facilitate and conceal same-sex relationships. A lesbian who lives in Beirut told us that she and her lover can walk arm-in-arm and hold hands in public spaces without arousing any concern.

There are about 5 million Muslims in North America, of whom about 10 percent are observant. Most are recent immigrants, but there are also substantial numbers of converts, especially among African-Americans. The extreme antigay stance of the Nation of Islam leader Louis Farrakhan was mentioned in chapter 9. More typically, American Moslems have conservative but not stridently hostile views toward gays and lesbians.

Hinduism

Hinduism is a catchall designator for the innumerable Indian sects that acknowledge the Vedas as sacred books. Hindu mythology is rife with sexual ambiguity: the destroyer god Siva, for example, took on a hermaphroditic form on occasion, while Brahma gave rise to the goddess Satarupa through a process of binary fission, not unlike that imagined in Plato's *Symposium* (see chapter 2). This gender-defying tradition no doubt explains the tolerance still extended to the sects of gender-variant or transsexual men, the *jogappas* and *hijras*, who frequently engage in sex with conventional men (see chapter 2).

Classical Hindu teachings take either a positive attitude toward homosexual acts (as in the *Kamasutra*), or a moderately negative one. The broader Hindu culture, however, has taken a more strongly negative view. Typically, homosexuality has been viewed as an alien import, brought by invaders of the Indian subcontinent such as the Greeks or, ironically, the Islamic Moguls. "When Kabul was conquered by the Muslims," wrote an eleventh-century scholar, "and the Ispahbad of Kabul adopted Islam, he stipulated that he not be bound to eat cow's meat nor to commit sodomy (which proves that he abhorred the one as much as the other)."[2]

The sense of homosexuality as something alien is widespread, not only in modern India, but among Hindu immigrants to the United States. Gay or lesbian youth in first-generation immigrant families may be at a loss even for the words to describe themselves to their parents: the term *hijra* for example, with its associated images of mutilation, mendicancy, and prostitution, hardly offers a delicate entry into the topic.

Hindu religion and philosophy attracted numerous groups of American disciples during the 1960s and 1970s. The most enduring of these sects has been the Society of Krishna Consciousness, which still has temples and residential communities in many cities. Although KC's adherents are young, peaceable, vegetarian, and dedicated to a joyful deity, their attitude to sex is uncompromising: it should only take place within the context of procreation. Homosexual behavior is therefore not sanctioned.

Buddhism

Of all the major world religions, Buddhism is probably the most alien to contemporary Western ideas. Buddhism teaches a life-negating philosophy: to escape the cycle of reincarnation and suffering, individuals must attempt to extinguish desire, and thus to enter a state of blissful nonexistence (*nirvana*). Buddhism sees sex simply as an undesirable departure from celibacy, and thus makes little distinction between homosexuality and heterosexuality. The ascetic principles of Buddhism apply mainly to the monastic orders, however; the lay communities in which they are embedded are expected to engage actively in life, including sexual relations.

The neutrality of Buddhist teachings with respect to homosexuality permitted different Buddhist cultures to develop a variety of attitudes toward same-sex behavior. The most positive attitudes were found in Japan where, prior to Westernization, male homosexuality was widely practiced and praised, even within the confines of Buddhist monasteries (see chapter 2). In Tibet, on the other hand, monastic homosexuality was proscribed, although monks sometimes took advantage of loopholes in the regulations, such as the failure to prohibit intercrural penetration. Little information about lesbianism in Buddhist cultures is available, although Chinese literature does contain references to lesbian love, even in Buddhist convents.[3]

Buddhist institutions in the United States are also relatively tolerant of homosexuality and gay people. As mentioned in chapter 9, this religious tolerance may ease the position of lesbians and gay men in families that are Buddhist or that have immigrated from countries with strong Buddhist traditions.

Judaism

Judaism is a monotheistic religion with a received Law (the Torah), an ancient body of scripture partially shared with Christianity, a traditional set of laws derived from these (the *halakhah*), and a system of ethical obligations (*mitzvot*) that govern interpersonal relations. Thus observant Jews are guided by deep moral principles (such as *chesed ve'emet,* compassion and truth) as well as by detailed injunctions concerning the minutiae of daily living. While Orthodox Jews follow the Law as literally as possible, the adherents of Reform Judaism, which arose in the eighteenth century, have rejected some of the traditional restrictions and have simplified the rituals. Reform Judaism includes a Conservative branch that maintains some orthodox traditions. Of course, not all Jews (in the sense of being descendants of the tribes of Israel) are adherents of Judaism. The total Jewish population in North America numbers about 6 million.

In Jewish tradition, the main purpose of sex is procreation, and this is encouraged. Celibacy is not a desirable or admired state. Sexual acts between men are prohibited by biblical injunctions, and the halakhah extends this prohibition to women. Because there is no concept in traditional Jewish law of sexual orientation, but only of sexual acts, the law does not concern itself with the rights or needs of homosexual people.

American Jewish hostility to homosexuality began to weaken in the 1970s, when the more liberal branches of the Reform movement recognized the existence of gays and lesbians as people with distinct identities and civil rights. Gay and lesbian congregations began to appear, and in the 1980s rabbinical schools began accepting openly gay or lesbian students. In 1988 the State of Israel legalized homosexuality. In the early 1990s the Conservative movement also acknowledged the existence and needs of gay and lesbian congregants, but did not permit their admittance to rabbinical schools. Orthodox Jewry remains opposed to homosexuality and gay rights.

The many synagogues that now serve gay and lesbian Jews not only provide spiritual communion; they also are sources of gay-positive education as well as practical assistance to gays and lesbians. Prompted by the mitzvah of *bikur cholim* (visiting the sick), numerous synagogues and other Jewish organizations provide services to people with AIDS and other illnesses, and they attempt to overcome homophobia and AIDS stigma among Jews generally.

Gay and lesbian Jews view their homosexuality not just in the context of the Judaic religion, but also in the perspective of Jewish history. Jewish gay leaders are especially conscious of the Holocaust, the fact that gays as well as Jews were its victims, and the moral lessons to be drawn from it. The Holocaust featured prominently in the speeches of Harvey Milk (see chapter 3), as it has more recently in the writings of Larry Kramer (see chapters 14 and 18). American Jews are conscious not only of the history of anti-Semitism, but also of the remarkable extent to which they have overcome anti-Semitism through education, politics, and group-based social action. In that sense Jews present the gay and lesbian community not just with a warning from the past, but also with a vision for the future.

Christianity

Christianity is founded on the same biblical law and ethical principles as Judaism, but includes in addition the doctrine that God was made man in the person of Jesus. Essentially patriarchal, Christianity has nevertheless at times come close to deifying Mary, mother of Jesus, who at the very least is considered the principal saint. Christians, to varying degrees, believe in an afterlife with rewards or punishments for earthly deeds, as well as an ultimate day of judgment when souls will be rejoined with their bodies.

The great success and expansion of the Christian religion has led to innumerable schisms. Today, there is such a diversity of churches, ranging from the autocratic to the freethinking, that no general statements about Christian attitudes toward homosexuality can usefully be made. We therefore treat individually some of the major branches of Christianity, with emphasis on those well represented in the United States.

Roman Catholicism

Citing Romans 1:26 as authority (see chapter 4), the Catholic church unequivocally condemns all homosexual behavior. Although St. Paul did not acknowledge the existence of homosexual people, the modern church does so, and it divides them into two classes, "temporary" and "incurable" homosexuals. The latter are entitled to considerate pastoral care, but moral justification of their sexual behavior (on the grounds that it is in keeping with their innate homosexuality) is not permitted.[4]

The Catholic position on homosexuality is consistent with its traditional position that sex is intended only for procreation. Thus it can be traced back to the antisex stance of the early Christian church, as well as to Judaic law. As historian John Boswell has shown, however (see chapter 11), the church's condemnations of homosexuality only began in earnest around the twelfth century, when social attitudes toward many minority groups hardened. Thus the current antigay stance is as much the product of social intolerance as it is the perpetuation of a moral tradition established by St. Paul.

The Catholic church has shown some signs of softening its position in matters of sex. It has recently accepted the notion, put forward by Protestants centuries ago, that sex has a psychological function in cementing the spousal bond, although the couple must be "open to procreation." However tentative, this step could eventually lead to a recognition of a role for sex in other loving relationships. In concordance with such a prospect, Catholic leaders nowadays tend to be more positive in their statements about homosexual people than they were twenty years ago, even if homosexual acts are still considered "morally disordered."

These modest steps have of course done nothing to placate gay activists in the United States, who see the Catholic church as a major source of antigay sentiment and a cause of needless self-hatred among lesbian and gay youth. In the 1980s, when the gay community began to advocate the use of condoms as a protection against HIV, they were appalled by the opposition of the Catholic church to safe-sex education and to condom distribution in schools. Angry protests ensued, including the disruption of Catholic services (see chapter 14). The hostility continues more or less unabated today; in fact other issues have added fuel to the flames, such as the political engagement of the Catholic church in Hawaii in the debate over same-sex marriage (see chapter 15).

Caught in the middle of these conflicts are lesbian and gay Catholics themselves. Some have organized into groups such as Dignity, which attempts to support the development of an integrated Catholic-gay identity. Some simply ignore the church's teachings on the matter (just as many heterosexual Catholics ignore the church's strictures on masturbation, contraception, and abortion). Others, especially gay priests, sacrifice their homosexuality, or its public expression, in favor of their religious beliefs. One such man, the retired leader of a prestigious Catholic institution, spoke eloquently with us about the pain he had suffered, not on account of his own sexuality, but because of his inability to offer adequate support to the innumerable gays and lesbians who had been under his pastoral care.

Conservative Protestantism

While the Catholic position on homosexuality can be conceptualized as an external influence on American society, no such view is possible with respect to fundamentalist Protestantism, which is American to the core. Fundamentalists of course worship Jesus as the son of God and believe that he offers the only path to salvation. Nevertheless, in fundamentalist thought there often seems to lurk the suspicion that Jesus, in his human form, was a dangerous innovator, or at least a bleeding-heart liberal who failed to adequately condemn homosexuality and other vices. Fundamentalists are more comfortable with the Old Testament view of homosexuality as an "abomination before the Lord" than with St. Paul's more intellectualized "crime against nature," a conception that opens the door to nit-picking arguments about the nature of "nature," animal homosexuality, and so forth.

Fundamentalism is particularly associated with the Southern Baptist church, and the Southern Baptist Convention has unequivocally condemned homosexuality on several occasions.

Nevertheless, the Baptist denomination is "congregational," meaning that each church has considerable doctrinal autonomy, and attitudes among Southern Baptist churches toward gays and lesbians vary considerably. In fact, some Southern churches belonging to more "liberal" denominations such as Methodism are more hostile to gays and lesbians than are many Southern Baptist congregations. Again, this points up the fact that Christian views on homosexuality do not merely set social attitudes; they are themselves influenced *by* those attitudes, in this case by the moral conservatism of the American South.

Another important conservative branch of Protestantism is the Church of Jesus Christ of Latter-day Saints (Mormons), founded in 1831 by Joseph Smith. Like Jesus, Smith neglected to denounce homosexuality, and in its early years the church seemed but little concerned with the topic. In the mid-twentieth century, however, as Senator McCarthy and others brought the threat of homosexuality to the nation's attention, the Mormon authorities began to issue stern condemnations, based on the usual scriptural authorities. A policy of excommunication was instituted for unrepentant homosexuals, and at Brigham Young University agents were designated to spy on the off-campus activities of the students. Those students whose activities suggested homosexuality were expelled or treated with various forms of aversion "therapy." These treatments are no longer used.

A group of gay Mormons, called Affirmation, was founded in Los Angeles in 1977; it now has eighteen chapters nationwide, including one in Utah. Numerous articles, as well as a 1991 book, *Peculiar People*,[5] have presented a sympathetic account of the trials and tribulations of gay Mormons. In response to the generally improving social attitudes toward gays and lesbians, the Mormon church has slightly softened its stand on the issue. Excommunication is no longer favored, a distinction is drawn between homosexual identity and homosexual acts, and more than one gay person is now permitted to attend the same group-therapy session. But every Brigham

Young student still has to vow not to engage in sex outside of marriage—and same-sex marriage is not coming to Utah any time soon.

Mainstream Protestantism

The mainstream Protestant denominations in America, such as Presbyterians, Lutherans, Methodists, and Episcopalians, are mostly offshoots of churches founded in various European countries, and their American adherents are to some extent the descendants of emigrants from those countries. But, with doctrinal differences between them being fairly minor, American Protestants increasingly attend whatever church is convenient or congenial to them.

The importance of private judgment in matters of faith is a central feature of Protestant belief. This obviously works to the advantage of gays and lesbians, and in fact most mainstream Protestant denominations support gay rights legislation, the repeal of sodomy statutes, and so on. Many congregations specifically reach out to gays and lesbians: these are sometimes termed "Reconciling" or "More Light" congregations. Most of the denominations have active gay or progay organizations, such as Integrity (Episcopalian), Lutherans Concerned, and Kinship (Seventh Day Adventist). These organizations work to support gay and lesbian members of their denominations, as well as to influence their churches toward more gay-positive policies.

The sticky issues for many of these denominations concern the ordination of openly gay and lesbian ministers and the question of same-sex marriage. The Presbyterians, for example, have been debating whether to ordain gays and lesbians for years. Divided themselves, and fearful of splitting their church, Presbyterian leaders have shuffled the issue from study group to study group. Other denominations have done likewise. Meanwhile, quite a few already-ordained Protestant ministers have come out of the closet. One of the earliest was Malcolm Boyd, a Episcopalian priest who came out in the 1970s. He has written movingly of life in the clerical closet:

> Many gay priests were beloved within their parishes for their sensitivity, androgyny, gaiety of spirit, wisdom, wit and sophistication.... Yet at the least suggestion of homosexuality, they could be simply and peremptorily dismissed. Within a matter of hours, many were sent on their way into ignominious exile. For numerous older men it was too late to start a new career; their "security" was smashed by rumor and angry retaliation, leaving a gay priest without resources, mercy or love.[6]

Few mainstream Protestant churches will marry or bless the unions of same-sex couples, but they have by and large taken a neutral stance on the question of the legalization of civil same-sex marriage. This may be because the issue has not yet become a matter of great public interest, outside of Hawaii. In addition, however, doubts about the morality of such marriage may be balanced by a respect for gay and lesbian civil rights.

The most freethinking of the Protestant denominations, such as the Unitarian-Universalists and the Society of Friends (Quakers), have long supported the gay and lesbian community. One particular Unitarian-Universalist church's involvement with the community is described in chapter 6.

Gay and Lesbian Denominations

In reaction to the less than welcoming attitude of many established churches, there have been efforts to organize denominations specifically for lesbians and gay men. Of these, the Universal Fellowship of Metropolitan Community Church (MCC) is by far the largest.

MCC is one of the world's largest gay and lesbian organizations. Founded 1968 by the Rev. Troy Perry, an ordained Pentecostal minister, MCC now has almost 300 churches in sixteen countries. It counts 42,000 members, and can boast an annual income of $10 million. It is still rapidly growing.

MCC's churches are united more by their gay-friendliness than by any special doctrinal theme. Its ministers come from diverse backgrounds: they establish diverse styles of liturgy and may emphasize different religious ideas. Nevertheless Perry, who still heads the church, emphasizes three major principles. First, all believers shall be saved—salvation is unconditional and cannot be taken away by any church. Second, the church is family to all who need it. Third, the church struggles for both the religious and the secular rights of gays and lesbians.

MCC takes its role as family seriously. Besides welcoming worshippers unconditionally, it has a very active AIDS ministry in many cities, and in places it has lesbian health ministries and prison ministries too. In terms of rights, it strives to persuade other denominations to treat gays and lesbians equally with their heterosexual members, and has also immersed itself in general gay political issues such as the gays in the military debate. MCC has been repeatedly refused membership in the National Council of Churches (NCC), but it has not taken this rejection lying down: it has organized protests outside the NCC headquarters, and it has berated the NCC for its homophobic stance. According to the NCC, the rejection has more to do with doctrine—especially the question of whether MCC has one—than with its gay and lesbian membership. But the member churches of NCC who have opposed MCC's admission are those that have traditionally been homophobic: orthodox denominations and those that have predominantly black congregations.[7]

Another gay and lesbian denomination is the Unity Fellowship Church, founded by Bishop Carl Bean. It has churches in Los Angeles, Washington, D.C., and Detroit, and it caters primarily to the African-American gay and lesbian community. It is nondenominational and has many non-Christian members. It is also strongly involved in AIDS outreach through its sister organization, the Minority AIDS Project (see chapter 14).

An Overview

In our view, religious doctrines are constructed by humans, not handed down by deities. To the extent that this is true, doctrines that oppose homosexuality or homosexual expression arise from the particular views of the founders, as well as from general social attitudes at the time of founding and through subsequent history. In that sense, religious homophobia is little different from homophobia in general, in whatever terms it may be cloaked. Fear of the Other and patriarchal sexism are the key ingredients. This is why Buddhism, which is relatively nonpatriarchal, is also relatively nonhomophobic. It is striking that, over the long term, religious views on homosexuality evolve along with changing social views, even though these views may remain couched in the language of the founders. This bodes well for religiously minded lesbians and gay men in America today; it seems likely that the churches, albeit with varying degrees of foot-dragging, will follow the larger society and become more accepting of their gay and lesbian members.

In chapter 18 we suggested that gay men (and it is true for lesbians too) make less clear a distinction between the body and the spirit than do heterosexuals. We will take up this theme again below. But the separation between body and spirit is an important concept in many organized religions, especially Christianity. For one thing, it is what allows Christians to reconcile belief in an afterlife with the obvious fact that the body disintegrates after death. Body-spirit dualism is what makes mummification unnecessary. Gays and lesbians represent a threat to the separation between body and spirit, as well as to that between male and female.[8] These threats affect several religions, including the more authoritarian denominations of Christianity. It remains to be seen how these denominations will respond.

Spirituality

For many gay men and lesbians, even the best efforts of homosexual religious groups are not enough to convince them to participate in anything that smacks of traditional organized religion. Rather than struggle within the religion in which they were raised, or join a newly established gay and lesbian congregation, some just leave their faith. For some, Christianity is all too compatible with many forms of oppression; others find Judaism no longer relevant to their lives. Lesbian feminists in particular may find both too patriarchal. Yet many gays and lesbians feel the need for something greater than themselves, something outside themselves, whether as an organizing principle in their daily lives or a container for soul-searching.

We have already seen one group of lesbians who have incorporated formal and informal rituals into their daily lives (chapter 8). As gay men and lesbians develop their community of friends and family (both of choice and of origin) they invent their own rituals, whether or not they choose to label them as such: coming together over a traditional holiday, commemorating a birthday or special occasion. These unconscious gatherings speak to the need to celebrate their lives in a meaningful way. Coming together in community can be the first step of a spiritual search.

Some people believe that it is in this area of spirituality that the unique nature of gay men and of lesbians comes to light. In past cultures, lesbians and gay men have been healers and artists and musicians and magicians, scientists, scholars, priests and priestesses. Judy Grahn, Randy Conner, and Walter Williams are among those who have documented the links between spirituality and homosexuality in past cultures over the course of centuries.[9] Many lesbians and gay men are seeking out those links and connecting to them today.

Two-Spirit People

As discussed in chapter 2, other cultures not only accepted gender-variant men and women but respected and encouraged them to become useful, contributing members of their tribe. Nonpatriarchal cultures did not attach the same stigma to gender variance as does our society.

The Judeo-Christian tradition, in which an all-powerful God created all things, does not accord equality, according to the beliefs of some gays and lesbians, but instead establishes a hierarchy of spiritual worth. The spirituality of Native American tribes was animism, which emphasized not one creator, God, but a multiplicity of spirits in the physical universe. Spirit commands respect. Thus in Native cultures if a woman has the spirit of a man, or a man that of a woman, she or he is viewed as being blessed with two spirits, not as something less but something more. Western culture has no concept like this. Nor does basic respect for the feminine exist in Western culture. Unlike our society, Native cultures have a tradition of encouraging two-spirit people, which in turn enables them to make their best contribution to the tribe. Two-spirit people are seen as sacred, spiritually gifted people who can assist others in their spiritual needs.

No wonder then that gay men and lesbians are drawn to these cultures and traditions, and have incorporated their beliefs into their own spiritual practices.

Feminism, Witchcraft, and Goddess Worship

Many lesbians and some gay men currently practice various forms of Goddess worship and Witchcraft. Certain aspects of these religions are similar to those of Native American culture.

Goddess religions provide a complete paradigm shift from patriarchal religion; their adherents view them as a return to an original, matriarchal paradigm: god is not a male outside the individual, rather the Goddess is immanent, in everything. Each Witch has the Goddess within herself, there is no separation of the religious and the secular.

This idea of everything being connected is central to Witchcraft. All human needs and desires are "sacred evidences of the life-force."[10] Witches have a responsibility to respect all life forms, and to be involved in the world community. Politics and spirituality are interconnected.

Rituals in Witchcraft are used to transcend the present and achieve an altered state of reality because it is only in such a state that one can truly understand the secrets of the religion. Witches celebrate life passages, seasonal rituals, lunar stages—full, dark, new—and each has its purpose. For example, the dark moon rituals are about saying no, setting limits, giving permission to get angry, and making space to honor emotions seen as negative. All their rituals celebrate the cyclical aspect of life, death, and rebirth, keeping practitioners in touch with that connection to everything.

Of particular relevance to many lesbians is the Dianic tradition, in which some covens can be joined by women only, although some of the rituals may be attended by men. The Dianic tradition is a celebration of women's mysteries, the blood mysteries of birth, menstruation, menopause, and death. The Goddess appears in three forms: the maiden, the mother, and the crone. Women celebrate passage into a new stage of their life through an appropriate ritual, such as a Queening Ritual for the celebration of Middle Age and Responsibility, or a Croning Ritual for a woman who has reached the age of 56, the Sage Age. Each stage has its inherent wisdom and value, and is part of a complete cycle. The concept of the maiden, or virgin, has a somewhat different meaning in the Dianic tradition than it does in common parlance. A virgin is a woman who is her own woman, independent, wild, uncontrolled at times; a much more powerful image than that of a sexual virgin. Thus are women's bodies validated in all stages of life.

Radical Faeries

Men, gay men especially, suffer in patriarchal society. In Witchcraft, they no longer have to suppress their feminine side. Nor do they have to suppress anything among the Radical Faeries, a national movement of gay men exploring what it means to be a gay man today.

The Radical Faeries is an anarchic group, though Mark Thompson, an early participant, told us that it has been in existence long enough to start getting codified.[11] Still, he maintains that at the basic level the Faerie groups help gay men break the straightjacket of heterosexual conformity. Freed from gender norms and restrictions, they are able to get in touch with their feminine side, and with a spiritual side different from whatever they were brought up in.

Harry Hay, one of the founders of the Faerie movement (and of the gay movement itself—see chapter 3), believes in the essential difference of gay men; they constitute a third gender (lesbians are possibly a fourth). This belief in the "neitherness" of gay men—they are not like heterosexual men nor like heterosexual women—and his search to discover their purpose in society provided the spiritual basis for his political activism. This quality of neitherness makes gay men mediators between the seen and the unseen. In this quality, Hay believes, lies gay men's gift to the heterosexual world.

Activities at a Faerie gathering might involve heart circles—the men sit in big circles and speak from the heart; any number of rituals involving chanting, drumming, or singing or evoking spirits; men wandering off to make love; sometimes there are group explorations. As they partake in these experiences, the men are urged to let go of the competition they face in their daily lives, release the striving they assume in the heterosexual world.

Faeries are the embodiment of the trickster, the jester. Many playfully cross-dress during gatherings, but do not give up male attributes such as beards.

In Faerie gatherings gay men have the opportunity to confront and release their internalized homophobia. Simply changing outwardly—the politics of coming out and being gay—is not enough: one must deal with the spiritual aspects of self, of soul, before being able to make any lasting changes. This means a continual coming out, each time reaching a deeper level of personal awareness and, simultaneously, a greater interconnectedness to the world. As for Witches and lesbian feminists, for Radical Faeries the personal is political.

Conclusion

Assimilation of lesbians and gay men into heterosexual society is seen by some as a loss of spirit, a disconnection to that which truly gives one's life meaning. Coming out as a lesbian or gay person is not a one-time experience but a continual process. It is a death and birth experience, a letting go of one identity and the assumption of another. As the lesbian and gay movement grows, so does the need of its people for answers to existential questions. These questions can be raised by AIDS, the political state, homophobia, the loss of a love. Whether it is fear of dying or just a sense that political activism can take them only so far, gay men and lesbians are looking for ways to explore their lives in a faith relevant to their lives.

The twenty-five years since Stonewall have matured gays and lesbians. At one point they might have been content with the common spirit felt in a gay or lesbian bar, or at a pride parade. But that's just boosterism, says Mark Thompson: "What we need is soul."[12] In that remark he echoes the comments of a traditional Hawaiian *mahu,* when asked by Walter Williams about the differences between *mahu* and gay identity. "Gays have liberated themselves only sexually," he said, "but they have not yet learned their place in a spiritual sense."[13]

Further Reading

Budapest, Zsuzsanna. *The Holy Book of Women's Mysteries: Feminist Witchcraft, Goddess Rituals, Spellcasting, and Other Womanly Arts.* Oakland, CA: Wingbow Press, 1989.

Conner, Randy P. *Blossom of Bone: Reclaiming the Connections between Homoeroticism and the Sacred.* San Francisco: HarperSanFrancisco, 1993.

Grahn, Judy. *Another Mother Tongue: Gay Words, Gay Worlds.* Boston: Beacon Press, 1984.

Starhawk. *The Spiral Dance: A Rebirth of the Ancient Religion of the Great Goddess* (10th anniversary edition). San Francisco: HarperSanFrancisco, 1989.

Swidler, Arlene, ed. *Homosexuality and World Religions.* Valley Forge, PA: Trinity Press International, 1993.

Thompson, Mark, ed. *Gay Spirit: Myth and Meaning.* New York: St. Martin's Press, 1987.

Thompson, Mark. *Gay Soul: Finding the Heart of Gay Spirit and Nature.* San Francisco: HarperSanFrancisco, 1994.

Epilogue

In this book we have explored some of the ways that, as lesbians and gay men, we interact with each other and the world around us. But we are left with the question: Are we truly a community? Are we "family"—the word we so casually use to refer to people like ourselves? And if so, are we family by blood, by choice, or by mere expediency?

Of course, there are hierarchies of communities, starting with the entire human race, and ending with the household. Everyone belongs to various groups at different levels of the hierarchy, but each individual experiences a sense of community within a more restricted set of these groups. Few people feel much sense of community with the entire human race. That may be unfortunate, but it's unlikely to change, at least until such time as we make contact with alien civilizations. What gives a group a sense of community is not so much the similarities among its members, but the differences between its members and those outside the group, especially when those differences are sensed as an external threat.

Gays and lesbians have certainly been exposed to an external threat, homophobia, and this has worked in the past as an effective glue binding all homosexual people together. It has made them into a secret society complete with its own hidden meeting places, its passwords, and its underground literature.

But the threat of homophobia is steadily diminishing. Even in 1994, a bad year politically for gays and lesbians, only one of the many antigay initiatives—a county ordinance in Florida—got onto the ballot and passed, and several fresh lesbian and gay faces succeeded in winning elected office. The trend toward acceptance and visibility of gays and lesbians is not a momentary easing of restrictions: it is a long-term trend whose origins are partly understood and whose continuance is reasonably assured.

There are two major factors responsible for the decline of homophobia. First, the women's liberation movement has succeeded in greatly reducing the perception that men and women belong to superior and inferior castes (see chapter 3). Because homosexuality is viewed (rightly, in our estimation) as a kind of gender nonconformity, it has traditionally been stigmatized as a violation of these castes. Such violations have been losing significance as the difference in rank between men and women diminishes. On this account both lesbians and gay men owe an enormous debt to feminists and their achievements.

The other factor is the effort by gays and lesbians themselves (many of them feminists too) to better their own position. If it is possible for many of us to be openly gay now, it is because generations of lesbians and gay men demanded their rights in the most adverse of circumstances—a tradition started by Karl Heinrich Ulrichs (the centennial of whose death we mark in 1995), and greatly accelerated in the last decade by men and women who have been personally touched by the AIDS epidemic. Of course the process continues, as lesbians and gay men in recalcitrant corners of America—the military, the rural South, and the schoolhouse especially—continue to risk their careers, their social status, and even their lives for the good of the community. But no one seeing the parade of unapologetic homosexuals on talk shows, in books, newspapers and films, in the workplace, and in social and political groups could reasonably deny that the floodgates of gay liberation have opened wide.

Yet as homophobia recedes, what if anything will take its place as the unifying force in our community? The victim mentality will not serve, in the long run, as a cohesive force for our community, and already it is taking on a strained, artificial quality, as if it is beginning to be used in a petulant quest for attention and for the crushing of dissent.

What are the true bonds that hold our community together? The strongest and most fundamental, of course, is sexual desire. This is what has always compelled lesbians and gay men to seek out the company of others like them. It is at the heart of everything, from the sex clubs of the gay ghettos to the demurest lesbian couple hidden away in the suburbs. Because gay men and lesbians are sexually drawn to people of the same sex as themselves, sexuality can act like a polymerizing agent to form dense, extended networks. For gay men particularly, many of their friends and associates are likely to be their past, present, or future sex partners, or *their* partners, and so on. For heterosexual people, such networks do not form so readily.

The trouble with sexual desire is that it arises from a part of our mind that is singularly uninterested in co-gender issues, multiculturalism, political correctness, confronting ageism or anything of that kind. Sexual desire takes one outside one's own self like nothing else does, but it is also incomparably selfish. And falling in love means excluding the world (except for one person) from one's sphere of concern. Thus sexual desire divides as well as binds our community. Most fundamentally, sexual desire forms a chasm between lesbians and gay men.

A much broader aspect of gay and lesbian identity that does impose some unity on our community is gender nonconformity. Of course, same-sex desire itself is gender-nonconformist, but being gay or lesbian goes further. As discussed in several places in this book (see chapters 2, 4, and 9), people who experience same-sex desire as adults tend to exhibit a range of gender-nonconformist traits as children, even if limited to a mild sissiness in boys or a moderate tendency to adventurousness and leadership in girls. Even though the relationship often becomes less noticeable after puberty, it can still be measured by cognitive psychologists, affecting traits like spatial and verbal ability, and probably many more. Some gays and lesbians, of course, are openly at war with the norms for their sex throughout their lives. Gender nonconformity in one degree or another, we believe, influences career choice, social and cultural interests, and sexual roles.

The attitudes of lesbians and gays concerning gender are not entirely healthy. First comes the belief, subscribed to by many lesbian and gay therapists, that gender identity and gender role are solely the products of socialization. Not only is there little scientific evidence to support this belief; it is also damaging, in that it makes gays and lesbians who are gender nonconformist, as well as transsexual men and women, search futilely in their childhood memories for what made them so, and it also leads them to separate off their gender nonconformity conceptually from their homosexuality, which many gay and lesbian therapists *do* consider innate. In fact, whatever their causes, homosexuality and gender nonconformity are intimately related.

Second, many gays and lesbians, especially in the past, have disliked and, as best they could, concealed their own gender nonconformity. Of course this is understandable, given childhood teasing and adult sexism. In the 1970s the gay male community as a whole rejected effeminacy in favor of an exaggerated masculinity (see chapter 3).

Gender nonconformity is much more accepted today. But still gays and lesbians refuse to simply *be* gender-nonconformist. Instead, they have to *act* gender nonconformist, to have an intellectualized reason for it. Either they are intent on overthrowing the patriarchy, and have chosen the abolition of gender as the means to that end, or they are cultural trendsetters for whom "genderfuck" is the *mode du jour*. Either way, their act gives them some room for self-expression but ultimately denies an important truth, that gender nonconformity is special to homosexual people. Heterosexuals, by and large, have conventional genders—they set the standards by which gender is defined. Gays and lesbians have mixed-up, patchwork, iridescent genders, not truly changeable but seeming to change with every shift in the light.

Although sexual desire and gender nonconformity are unifying factors in our community, there are also deep divisions, most obviously between lesbians and gay men. Lesbians feel part of the community of women much more than gay men feel part of the community of men. Many lesbian activists consider themselves feminists and have been or still are active in feminist politics and culture. Yet the blurred boundaries of "women's music" and "lesbian music," or of "feminist politics" and "lesbian politics," are not matched by any equivalent blurring of the male lines. The so-called men's movement is minuscule in scope and uncertain in direction.

Lesbians are rightly concerned about being ignored or treated as second-class citizens within the gay and lesbian community. The public debate about "gays" in the military, which focused on gay men even though the major issue was that of lesbians, was a perfect example (see chapter 15). AIDS is another issue where lesbians have every right to be sensitive. AIDS is primarily a disease of gay men; we disagree with efforts to make it seem otherwise, even as we recognize the importance of AIDS education among lesbians (see chapter 14). But if the AIDS epidemic aroused little interest, in its early years, on account of its association with gay men, how much less interest would it have elicited if lesbians had been the prime victims? Would America even have heard of the disease? Are there other epidemics—breast cancer is the one most spoken of—that do indeed ravage the lesbian population while the world looks away (see chapter 12)? It is incumbent on gay men especially, who have been the recipients of extraordinary assistance from lesbians in the context of AIDS, to make sure that lesbian health issues are given proper attention and respect.

Another area where gay men need to show more vocal support for lesbians is that of parenting, child custody, adoption, and so on. Both gay men and lesbians may have children or want to have children, but numerically the issue is a bigger one for lesbians (see chapter 5), whether we are talking about children from a heterosexual marriage or relationship or children born or adopted within the context of a same-sex partnership. Lesbians and gay men must be united and unceasing in their efforts to eliminate all remaining antigay discrimination in the area of parenting.

Yet another area of potential strain between gays and lesbians concerns sex. In her book *Cherry Grove*[1] Esther Newton described how two lesbians walking in the Meat Rack came upon a naked gay man with an erection, a sight that meant one thing to them—rape. "I guess they think all of [the Rack] is theirs," they commented angrily, "there *is* no public path." The episode illustrates how sex, which seemingly should create no problems between gays and lesbians, actually does so. Gay men are more promiscuous, more sexually adventurous, and more interested in thrusting their sexuality into public view than are lesbians. Of course, we are no longer living in the 1970s: gay men have moderated their excesses to some extent, and some lesbians are embarking on a sexual revolution of their own. But still, there is an enormous gap between lesbians and gay men in their degree of focus on the genitals and what can be done with them, and this gap leads to obvious tensions. A "public path" has still to be established.

If lesbians are sometimes torn between allegiance to women and to the lesbian and gay community, other groups experience similar, perhaps even stronger tensions. An African-American gay man, for example, has to develop a sense of two identities, as black and as gay, and then he has if possible to recombine them into yet a third identity, that of a black gay man. Members of many marginalized groups, including ethnic minorities, the deaf, the disabled, the old, and sexual minorities such as bisexuals, feel some resentment to the "mainstream" gay and lesbian community for failing to help them in this developmental process. The resentment is expressed in a variety of negative beliefs: that white gay men seek out nonwhites only for erotic purposes, not for real social intercourse; that lesbians and gays want to pack their aging sisters and brothers out of sight in gay old folks' homes; that homosexuals "don't believe in" bisexuality, and so on.

The lesbian and gay community is probably less racist, less ageist, less biphobic, and less inclined to ignore the handicapped than is heterosexual America. But that is not enough. Gays and lesbians who belong to ethnic or age-defined minorities are far more exposed, more marginalized, than the straight members of these same groups. Even if their complaints sometimes ring false, they need and deserve far more support in their search for self-acceptance and social acceptance. It is gays and lesbians who are most able to give them that support, by explicitly recognizing their existence, by acknowledging their social, political, and cultural achievements, and by ensuring that their voices are heard in gay and lesbian organizations.

Another division in the lesbian and gay community is a political one, between its conservative and progressive wings. The conservatives minimize the differences between homosexual and heterosexual people and seek simply the elimination of the last vestiges of antigay discrimination; the progressives consider gays and lesbians to be natural outsiders who should ally themselves with other marginalized groups in an effort to remake American society from the bottom up (see chapter 16).

Progressives are far more visible and influential than conservatives at present, but its likely that conservative voices will be heard more clearly as time goes by. Even a simple measure of political stance—party affiliation and voting record—supports this expectation. Gays and lesbians are Democrats, Republicans, and Independents in about the same ratio as the general population, but many gay and lesbian Republicans stayed away from the polls in 1992 (see chapters 5 and 16). In 1994, on the other hand, many of them did vote, and for their own party.[2] This did not happen merely because of disillusionment with the Clinton administration's policies toward gay rights. The 1994 election, with its heavy emphasis on conservative ideals, was an opportunity for many conservative lesbians and gay men to finally vote their principles, even at some risk to the community's short-term interests. It is likely that the gay political movement will become more factional as its goals come closer to reality.

One could go on listing these divisions within the community: between S/M practitioners and those who abhor S/M, between suburban assimilationists and ghetto-dwelling separatists, between pagans and Christians, between balletomanes and rodeo buffs, and (most divisive of all) between rich and poor. The gay community is about as diverse and conflict-ridden as the larger society.

What holds our community together, more than sexual desire or gender nonconformity, is a sense of being different. Too often this sense of difference is confused with the effects of homophobia. Stigmatization can make a difference into a disease, certainly, and that has happened all too often with homosexuality. But removing stigmatization does not remove the difference, it only removes the pathology.

Many gays and lesbians recall having felt different at a very early age. Not oppressed or victimized—that came later if at all—but simply different, in a way that they typically find hard to verbalize. Different from their sisters or brothers, different from their parents' expectations, different perhaps from their own wishes for themselves. More self-aware, more inner-directed, lesbians and gay men develop apart from the regular world, not just in matters of sex but in every sphere of life. They look at the world from the outside, not with the bitterness of loners, but with the irony and sympathy of commentators, artists, helpers, and mediators.

Gay people form a community, not because they have been marginalized, but because they *are* marginal. They occupy the borders of society and fill its interstices, like veins of bright ore in blank rock. They live in places like West Hollywood, a shard of land unclaimed by other cities. They speak a language that sounds like English but is really an occult creole, constructed of borrowings; its phrases are pitched for the gay ear. Gay life is a tone of voice, a look, a style as much as a sexuality. In the main, these things pass straight people by; unless they are to be wasted on thin air, gay people need each other.

The product of this community, the culture of lesbians and gay men, is densely interwoven. A Jewish/African-American couple forms a revolutionary dance ensemble. Two lesbians in Mississippi harangue the entire community. A camp musical stars the AIDS virus. Dentists, American Indians, and Catholics march together to demand equal rights. Latino actors bring safe-sex theater to the streets. Lawyers from New York and San Francisco plead for a mother in Virginia. Ten thousand "gaydars" go off when a closeted official appears on television. Sadomasochism and spirituality are taken as metaphors for each other. A quilt unites us all. Taking our community apart for inspection, as we have tried to do in this book, means tearing irretrievably at its vital fabric.

If we have a vision for our community that goes beyond protecting our own rights and interests, if we believe that our private traditions can be the basis for a new, more humane world, then our task is challenging indeed. We must first create that world in little; we must make our own community into a robust model for how the larger world could be. That means overcoming the barriers of mistrust that still too often separate lesbian from gay man, white from black, and old from young. It means respecting the diversity and sense of difference that defines our community, and using them for a common purpose. And it means creating, not an army of lovers, but a company of free spirits, in whose ardor and art and seriousness and foolish antics the world can be slowly and magically entwined.

Notes

Chapter 1

1. For a discussion of some of these issues, see "Sex or Gender," a special section in *Psychological Science* 4 (1993): 120–126, with commentaries by Douglas Gentile, Rhoda Unger, Mary Crawford, and Kay Deaux. We agree with Deaux's comment (p. 125): "For terminology to depend on theoretical stance when demographic categories are at issue only exacerbates confusion and proliferates terms."

2. New York: Carol Publishing Group, 1989.

3. Adrienne Rich, *Blood, Bread, and Poetry: Selected Prose, 1979–1985* (New York: W. W. Norton, 1986), p. 51.

Chapter 2

1. For a colorful history of amazons, see chapter 7 of Judy Grahn's *Another Mother Tongue: Gay Words, Gay Worlds* (Boston: Beacon Press, 1984).

2. Pedro de Magalhães de Gandavo, cited in Walter L. Williams, *The Spirit and the Flesh: Sexual Diversity in American Indian Culture* (Boston: Beacon Press, 1986), p. 233.

3. Our description of berdaches and amazons in Native American cultures is based primarily on *The Spirit and the Flesh.*

4. Paula Gunn Allen, "Lesbians in American Indian Cultures," in Martin Duberman, Martha Vicinus, and George Chauncey, Jr., eds., *Hidden from History: Reclaiming the Gay and Lesbian Past* (New York: Meridian Books, 1989), pp. 106–117.

5. Some reports assert that parents did cause their daughters to become amazons. For example, it has been claimed that among the Kaska Indians of the Subarctic, parents who had insufficient sons would arbitrarily assign their youngest daughter to malelike status: "When the youngest daughter was about five years old, and it was obvious that the mother was not going to produce a son, the parents performed a transformation ceremony. They tied the dried ovaries of a bear to a belt which she always wore. That was believed to prevent menstruation, to protect her from pregnancy, and to give her luck on the hunt" (*The Spirit and the Flesh*, p. 235). If this account is correct, it would appear that innate gender variance played little part in the development of the Kaska amazons. In his preface to the second (1992) edition of his book, however, Williams makes a broader claim for the innate gender variance of amazon/berdache individuals in Native American cultures. He suggests that written sources that posit a parental role may be unreliable.

6. Cited in *The Spirit and the Flesh*, p. 137.

7. Francisco Palóu, 1787, cited in Jonathan N. Katz, *Gay American History: Lesbians and Gay Men in the U.S.A.* (New York: Meridian Books, 1992), p. 292.

8. The "biological" argument for the explanation of homosexuality and gender variance does not require, as is sometimes assumed, that these traits occur with the same frequency in all parts of the world and in all periods of history. For one thing, genes do not occur with the same frequency in different races—that is why races exist. For another, not all "biological" diversity results from differences in genes. See Simon LeVay, *The Sexual Brain* (Cambridge, MA: MIT Press, 1993).

9. For accounts of the mahus, and further references, see *The Spirit and the Flesh*, pp. 255–258; Serena Nanda, *Neither Man Nor Woman: The Hijras of India* (Belmont, CA: Wadsworth, 1990), pp. 134–137.

10. Cleland S. Ford and Frank A. Beach, *Patterns of Sexual Behavior* (New York: Harper and Brothers, 1951), p. 131.

11. *Neither Man Nor Woman*, pp. 129–131.

12. Interview with Robert Levy, cited in *The Spirit and the Flesh*, p. 256.

13. *Neither Man Nor Woman*, p. 75.

14. John Boswell, *Christianity, Social Tolerance, and Homosexuality: Gay People in Western Europe from the Beginning of the Christian Era to the Fourteenth Century* (Chicago: University of Chicago Press, 1980), p. 74.

15. *Gay American History*, pp. 232–238.

16. K. J. Dover, *Greek Homosexuality* (Cambridge, MA: Harvard University Press, 1978), p. 58.

17. *Greek Homosexuality*, p. 52.

18. Plato, *Symposium*, trans. B. Jowett (New York: Walter J. Black, 1942), p. 180. Translation slightly modified for clarity.

19. *Greek Homosexuality*, p. 177.

20. Paul G. Schalow, "Male Love in Early Modern Japan: A Literary Depiction of the 'Youth,'" in *Hidden from History*, pp. 118–128.

21. C. Strehlow, cited in *Patterns of Sexual Behavior*, p. 132.

22. *Patterns of Sexual Behavior*, p. 132.

23. An age-disparate male homosexual relationship in a British public school is depicted in Lindsay Anderson's 1968 film *If*. . . . The classic film depiction of an age-disparate lesbian relationship is the German film *Mädchen in Uniform* (Leontine Sagan, 1932), which is set in a Prussian-style girl's academy. For a history of the "crush" in British girl's boarding schools, see Martha Vicinus, "Distance and Desire: English Boarding School Friendships, 1870-1920," in *Hidden from History*, pp. 212–229.

24. Lillian Faderman, *Odd Girls and Twilight Lovers: A History of Lesbian Life in Twentieth-Century America* (New York: Columbia University Press, 1991), p. 1.

25. Martin Duberman, "'Writhing Bedfellows' in Antebellum South Carolina: Historical Interpretation and the Politics of Evidence," in *Hidden from History*, pp. 153–168.

26. Cited in Harry Oosterhuis, "Homosexual Emancipation in Germany—Two Traditions," in Harry Oosterhuis and Hubert Kennedy, eds., *Homosexuality and Male Bonding in Pre-Nazi Germany* (New York: Harrington Park Press, 1991), pp. 1–27.

27. R. L. Meisel and I. L. Ward, "Fetal Female Rats Are Masculinized by Male Littermates Located Caudally in the Uterus," *Science* 213 (1981): 239–242. A similar phenomenon occurs in cattle, producing so-called freemartins: behaviorally sterile females who were twins with males. It is not believed to occur in human male-female twins, because the blood supplies of human dizygotic twins are more or less independent.

28. A. Perkins and J. A. Fitzgerald, "Luteinizing Hormone, Testosterone, and Behavioral Response of Male-Oriented Rams to Estrous Ewes and Rams," *Journal of Animal Science* 70 (1992): 1787–1794.

29. G. L. Hunt, Jr. and M. W. Hunt, "Female-Female Pairing in Western Gulls (*Larus occidentalis*) in Southern California," *Science* 196 (1977): 1466–1467.

30. J. C. Hall, "Courtship among Males Due to a Male-Sterile Mutation in *Drosophila melanogaster*," *Behavior Genetics* 8 (1977): 291–312.

31. *Christianity, Social Tolerance, and Homosexuality*, p. 80.

32. See, for example, C. M. McCormick and S. F. Witelson, "A Cognitive Profile of Homosexual Men Compared to Heterosexual Men and Women," *Psychoneuroendocrinology* 16 (1991): 459–473.

Chapter 3

1. "Miss E.M.," *ONE Magazine*, April, 1953, cited in Jonathan N. Katz, *Gay American History: Lesbians and Gay Men in the U.S.A.* (New York: Meridian Books, 1992), pp. 102–103.

2. Lillian Faderman, *Odd Girls and Twilight Lovers: A History of Lesbian Life in Twentieth-Century America* (New York: Columbia University Press, 1991), p. 140.

3. Martin Duberman, *Cures: A Gay Man's Odyssey* (New York: Dutton, 1991).

4. Jonathan N. Katz, *Gay American History: Lesbians and Gay Men in the U.S.A.* (New York: Meridian Books, 1992), pp. 129–207.

5. Don D. Harryman, "With All Thy Getting, Get Understanding," in Ron Schow, Wayne Schow, and Marybeth Raynes, eds., *Peculiar*

People: Mormons and Same-Sex Orientation (Salt Lake City: Signature Books, 1991), pp. 23–35.

6. Esther Newton, *Cherry Grove, Fire Island: Sixty Years in America's First Gay and Lesbian Town* (Boston: Beacon Press, 1993). See also chapter 6.

7. See for example Judith C. Brown, *Immodest Acts: The Life of a Lesbian Nun in Renaissance Italy* (Oxford: Oxford University Press, 1986); Lillian Faderman, *Surpassing the Love of Men: Romantic Friendship and Love between Women from the Renaissance to the Present* (New York: Quill, 1981); Kent Gerard and Gert Hekma, eds., *The Pursuit of Sodomy: Male Homosexuality in Renaissance and Enlightenment Europe* (New York: Haworth Press, 1988).

8. Randolph Trumbach, "The Birth of the Queen: Sodomy and the Emergence of Gender Equality in Modern Culture, 1660–1750," in Martin Duberman, *Hidden from History: Reclaiming the Gay and Lesbian Past* (New York: Meridian Books, 1989), pp. 129–140.

9. George Chauncey, Jr., "Christian Brotherhood or Sexual Perversion? Homosexual Identities and the Construction of Sexual Boundaries in the World War I Era," *Journal of Social History* 19 (1985): 189–212.

10. Eric Garber, "A Spectacle in Color: The Lesbian and Gay Subculture of Jazz Age Harlem," in *Hidden from History*, pp. 318–331; *Odd Girls and Twilight Lovers*, pp. 67–79; George Chauncey, Jr., *Gay New York: Gender, Urban Culture and the Making of the Gay Male World 1890–1940* (New York: Basic Books, 1994).

11. *Gay American History*, p. 377. For Goldman's own involvement in an erotic same-sex relationship, see *Odd Girls and Twilight Lovers*, pp. 33–34.

12. Currently available from Anchor Books.

13. Philadelphia: W. B. Saunders.

14. In a critique of the second volume (on women), Mead wrote that the book's sale should be restricted, because young people's "desire to conform was protected by a lack of knowledge of the extent of nonconformity" (cited in Wardell B. Pomeroy, *Dr. Kinsey and the Institute for Sex Research* [New York: Harper and Row, 1972], p. 362).

15. Alfred C. Kinsey, Wardell B. Pomeroy, Clyde E. Martin, and Paul H. Gebhard, *Sexual Behavior in the Human Female* (Philadelphia: Saunders, 1953).

16. Stuart Timmons, *The Trouble with Harry Hay: Founder of the Modern Gay Movement* (Boston: Alyson Publications, 1990), pp. 136–137.

17. In an interview for the documentary *Before Stonewall*, Hay said, "We didn't know at that point, none of us knew, that there had ever been a gay organization of any sort anywhere in the world before; we had absolutely no knowledge of that at all." But Hay's biography (*The Trouble with Harry Hay*, p. 141) states that Hay already knew about the Chicago Society for Human Rights in 1930, and that Rudi Gernreich knew about Hirschfeld's movement and discussed it with Hay in 1950 before the society was founded. Furthermore, Hirschfeld himself gave a highly publicized lecture tour of the United States in 1930–31, including a number of lectures in San Francisco (Charlotte Wolff, *Magnus Hirschfeld: Portrait of a Pioneer in Sexology* [London: Quartet Books, 1986], p. 286). It seems improbable that Hay, then a student at Stanford University, could have been unaware of Hirschfeld's activities.

18. Dorr Legg et al., *Homophile Studies in Theory and Practice* (San Francisco: ONE Institute Press, 1994).

19. The quirky names of the DOB and the Mattachine reflect the personalities of the people who were motivated to start such organizations. Bilitis was a fictitious Greek lesbian invented by the nineteenth-century writer Pierre Louys. The Mattachines were a company of masked dancers in fifteenth-century France.

20. *Making History*, p. 132.

21. *Odd Girls and Twilight Lovers*, p. 144.

22. Evelyn Hooker,"The Adjustment of the Male Overt Homosexual," *Journal of Projective Techniques* 21 (1957): 18–31.

23. *Making History*, p. 16.

24. *Making History*, pp. 93–103.

25. Judy Grahn, *Another Mother Tongue: Gay Words, Gay Worlds* (Boston: Beacon Press, 1984).

26. A clip from the news conference is shown in *Before Stonewall.*

27. See John D'Emilio, "Gay Politics and Community in San Francisco since World War II," in *Hidden from History,* pp. 465–473.

28. January 21, 1966, excerpted in *Making History,* pp. 89–90.

29. Irving Bieber et al., *Homosexuality: A Psychoanalytic Study of Male Homosexuals* (New York: Basic Books, 1962).

30. *Odd Girls and Twilight Lovers,* p. 211.

31. In one study carried out in San Francisco in 1969, only 1 percent of gay men said they were attracted to "feminine" qualities in a man (Alan P. Bell and Martin S. Weinberg, *Homosexualities: A Study of Diversity among Men and Women* [New York: Simon and Shuster, 1978], p. 312).

32. Ibid., p. 308.

33. Ibid., p. 256.

34. It is estimated that about 5,000 men were sent to forced-labor camps for homosexuality. (The majority of them died there, but they were not gassed.) There are only one or two documented cases of women being sent to the camps for homosexuality. Milk's figure of 300,000 could only be justified by including some arbitrary fraction of the total number of people who died in the camps. See Richard Plant, *The Pink Triangle: The Nazi War against Homosexuals* (Henry Holt and Co., 1986), p. 154, quoting research of Rüdiger Lautmann; Günter Grau, *Hidden Holocaust? Gay and Lesbian Persecution in Germany 1933–45* (London: Cassell, 1995), pp. 6, 15.

35. The full text of Milk's speech is reprinted in Randy Shilts, *The Mayor of Castro Street: The Life and Times of Harvey Milk* (New York: St. Martin's Press, 1982), pp. 364–371.

36. Ibid., p. 334.

37. Jill Johnston, *Lesbian Nation: The Feminist Solution* (New York: Simon and Shuster, 1973).

38. Cited in Randy Shilts, *And the Band Played On: Politics, People, and the AIDS Epidemic* (New York: St. Martin's Press, 1987), p. 238.

Chapter 4

1. Hubert Kennedy, *Ulrichs: The Life and Works of Karl Heinrich Ulrichs, Pioneer of the Modern Gay Movement* (Boston: Alyson Publications, 1988).

2. Magnus Hirschfeld, *Die Homosexualität des Mannes und des Weibes* (Berlin: Louis Marcus, 1914). See also Charlotte Wolff, *Magnus Hirschfeld: A Portrait of a Pioneer in Sexology* (London: Quartet Books, 1986). For a critical analysis of Hirschfeld's ideas from a social constructionist perspective, see Manfred Herzer, *Magnus Hirschfeld: Leben und Werk eines jüdischen, schwulen und sozialistischen Sexologen* (Frankfurt: Campus Verlag, 1992).

3. Sigmund Freud, *Three Essays on the Theory of Sexuality*, trans. James Strachey (New York: Basic Books, 1975).

4. Sigmund Freud, "The Psychogenesis of a Case of Homosexuality in a Woman" (1920), in *The Standard Edition of the Complete Psychological Works of Sigmund Freud*, ed. James Strachey, vol. 18 (London: Hogarth Press, 1955), pp. 147–172.

5. For a contemporary gay psychoanalyst's views on the development of homosexuality, see Richard A. Isay, *Being Homosexual* (New York: Farrar, Straus, Giroux, 1989).

6. In a 1994 survey by *The Advocate* of its gay male readership, 90 percent asserted that they were "born with their orientation." (Janet Lever, "The 1994 Advocate Survey of Sexuality and Relationships: The Men," *The Advocate* [August 23, 1994], pp. 17–24.)

7. Kathleen Bourne, *Lesbian Identity Formation*, Dissertation in Counseling Psychology, University of Southern California (1992).

8. Richard C. Pillard and James D. Weinrich, "Evidence of Familial Nature of Male Homosexuality," *Archives of General Psychiatry* 43 (1986): 808–812.

9. J. M. Bailey and D. S. Benishay, "Familial Aggregation of Female Sexual Orientation," *American Journal of Psychiatry* 150 (1993): 272–277.

10. J. M. Bailey and R. C. Pillard, "A Genetic Study of Male Sexual Orientation," *Archives of General Psychiatry* 48 (1991): 1089–1096.

11. J. M. Bailey, R. C. Pillard, M. C. Neale, and Y. Agyei, "Heritable Factors Influence Sexual Orientation in Women," *Archives of General Psychiatry* 50 (1993): 217–223.

12. F. L. Whitam, M. Diamond, and J. Martin, "Homosexual Orientation in Twins: A Report on 61 Pairs and 3 Triplet Sets," *Archives of Sexual Behavior* 22 (1993): 187–206.

13. D. H. Hamer, S. Hu, V. L. Magnuson, N. Hu, and A. M. L. Pattatucci, "A Linkage Between DNA Markers on the X-Chromosome and Male Sexual Orientation," *Science* 261 (1993): 321–327.

14. R. A. Gorski, R. E. Harlan, C. D. Jacobson. J. E. Shryne, and A. M. Southam, "Evidence for a Morphological Sex Difference within the Medial Preoptic Area of the Rat Brain," *Journal of Comparative Neurology* 193 (1980): 529–539.

15. L. S. Allen, M. Hines, J. E. Shryne, and R. A. Gorski, "Two Sexually Dimorphic Cell Groups in the Human Brain," *Journal of Neuroscience* 9 (1989): 497–506.

16. S. LeVay, "A Difference in Hypothalamic Structure between Heterosexual and Homosexual Men," *Science* 253 (1991): 1034–1037.

17. Most of the gay men studied by LeVay died of complications of AIDS, and their sexual orientation was known because they had been asked about risk factors for acquiring HIV infection. The grounds for believing that the small INAH3 seen in these men was linked to their sexual orientation and was not a disease effect are presented in LeVay, *The Sexual Brain* (Cambridge, MA: MIT Press, 1993), p. 121. Most pertinently, LeVay had a comparison group of heterosexual men who also died of complications of AIDS; in these men INAH3 was large. For women who come to autopsy, there is rarely if ever any indication of their sexual orientation in their hospital records.

18. L. S. Allen and R. A. Gorski, "Sexual Orientation and the Size of the Anterior Commissure in the Human Brain," *Proceedings of the National Academy of Sciences of the U.S.A.* 89 (1992): 7199–7202.

19. A. Scamvougeras, S. F. Witelson, M. Bronskill, P. Stanchev, S. Black, G. Cheung, M. Steiner, and B. Buck, "Sexual Orientation and Anatomy of the Corpus Callosum," *Society for Neuroscience Abstracts* (1994), p. 1425.

20. A. Perkins, J. A. Fitzgerald, and G. E. Moss, "A Comparison of LH Secretion and Brain Estradiol Receptors in Heterosexual and Homosexual Rams and Female Sheep," *Hormones and Behavior* (in press, 1995).

21. See for example C. L. Williams, "Organizational Effects of Early Gonadal Secretions on Sexual Differentiation in Spatial Memory," *Behavioral Neuroscience* 104 (1990): 84–97.

22. D. Lunn and D. Kimura, "Spatial Abilities in Preschool-Aged Children," University of Western Ontario, *Department of Psychology Research Bulletins* 681 (1989).

23. J. Hall and D. Kimura, "Performance by Homosexual Males and Females on Sexually-Dimorphic Motor Tasks," University of Western Ontario, *Department of Psychology Research Bulletins* 718 (1993).

24. Doreen Kimura, "Sex Differences in the Brain," *Scientific American* (September 1992), pp. 119–125. The sex differences in verbal skills are less consistent than those in spatial skills, and have not been replicated in all studies.

25. C. M. McCormick and S. F. Witelson, "A Cognitive Profile of Homosexual Men Compared to Heterosexual Men and Women," *Psychoneuroendocrinology* 16 (1991): 459–473.

26. C. M. McCormick, S. F. Witelson, and E. Kingstone, "Left-handedness in Homosexual Men and Women: Neuroendocrine Implications," *Psychoneuroendocrinology* 15 (1990): 69–76.

27. J. A. Y. Hall and D. Kimura, "Dermatoglyphic Asymmetry and Sexual Orientation in Men," *Behavioral Neuroscience* 108 (1994): 1203–1206.

28. E.g., A. P. Bell, M. S. Weinberg, and S. K. Hammersmith, *Sexual Preference: Its Development in Men and Women* (Bloomington: Indiana University Press, 1981); M.T. Saghir and E. Robins, *Male and Female Homosexuality: A Comprehensive Investigation* (Baltimore: Williams and Wilkins, 1973); N. L. Thompson, Jr., D. M. Schwartz, B. R. McCandless, and D. Edwards, "Parent-Child Relationships and Sexual Identity in Male and Female Homosexuals and Heterosexuals," *Journal of Consultative and Clinical Psychology* 41 (1973): 120–127; E. A. Grellert, M. D. Newcomb, and P. M. Bentler, "Childhood Play Activities of Male and Female Homosexuals and

Heterosexuals," *Archives of Sexual Behavior* 11 (1982): 451–478; R. Blanchard and K. Freund, "Measuring Masculine Gender Identity in Females," *Journal of Consultative and Clinical Psychology* 51 (1983): 205–214; J. Harry, *Gay Children Grown Up: Gender Culture and Gender Deviance* (New York: Praeger, 1982).

29. F. L. Whitam, "The Prehomosexual Male Child in Three Societies: The United States, Guatemala, Brazil," *Archives of Sexual Behavior* 9 (1980): 87–99; F. L. Whitam and R. M. Mathy, "Childhood Cross-Gender Behavior of Homosexual Females in Brazil, Peru, the Philippines, and the United States," *Archives of Sexual Behavior* (1991): 151–170.

30. J. M. Bailey, J. S. Miller, and L. Willerman, "Maternally Rated Childhood Gender Nonconformity in Homosexuals and Heterosexuals," *Archives of Sexual Behavior* 22 (1993): 461–469. In the case of lesbians, mothers who knew their daughters were lesbian were significantly more likely to recall them as having been gender nonconformist in childhood than mothers who were unaware of their daughters' homosexuality. This could either be because knowledge of their daughters' homosexuality distorted their memories of their daughters' childhood personality, or because mothers of more gender-nonconformist lesbians are more likely to become aware of their daughters' sexual orientation.

31. The other study is by B. Zuger, "Early Effeminate Behavior in Boys: Outcome and Significance for Homosexuality," *Journal of Nervous and Mental Disease* 172 (1984): 90–97.

32. S. A. Berenbaum and M. Hines, "Early Androgens Are Related to Childhood Sex-Typed Toy Preference," *Psychological Science* 3 (1992): 203–206.

33. E.g., R. W. Goy, "Differentiation of Male Social Traits in Female Rhesus Macaques by Prenatal Treatment with Androgens: Variation in Type of Androgen, Duration, and Timing of Treatment," *Fetal Endocrinology* , M. J. Novy and J. A. Resko, eds. (New York: Plenum Press, 1974), pp. 23–247.

34. See for example Richard R. Troiden, "The Formation of Homosexual Identities," in Gilbert Herdt, ed., *Gay and Lesbian Youth* (New York: Harrington Park Press, 1989), pp. 43–73. Troiden writes: "People construct their sexual feelings to the extent that they actively

interpret, define and make sense of their erotic yearnings into systems of sexual meanings articulated by the wider culture." For critiques of the biological approach from a variety of perspectives, see Anne Fausto-Sterling, *Myths of Gender: Biological Theories about Men and Women* (New York: Basic Books, 1992); Janet E. Halley, "Sexual Orientation and the Politics of Biology: A Critique of the Argument from Immutability," *Stanford Law Review* 46 (1994): 503–568; William Byne, "The Biological Evidence Challenged," *Scientific American* (May 1994), pp. 50–55.

Chapter 5

1. *10%* is the name of a national gay and lesbian magazine, as well as that of the newsletter of the gay and lesbian students' group at UCLA. *Two Teenagers in Twenty* is the name of an anthology by gay and lesbian teens, and *One Teacher in Ten* is a book about lesbian and gay teachers. *Project 10* is the name of a counseling service for gay and lesbian high-school students in the Los Angeles Unified School District.

2. J. A. Davis and T. W. Smith, *General Social Surveys. 1972–1990: Cumulative Code Book* (Chicago: National Opinion Research Center, 1990); T. W. Smith, "Adult Sexual Behavior in 1989: Number of Partners, Frequency of Intercourse, and Risk of AIDS," *Family Planning Perspectives* 23 (1991): 102–107.

3. Robert T. Michael, John H. Gagnon, Edward O. Laumann, and Gina Kolata, *Sex in America: A Definitive Survey* (Boston: Little, Brown and Company, 1994).

4. J. O. G. Billy, K. Tanfer, W. R. Grady, and D. H. Klepinger, "The Sexual Behavior of Men in the United States," *Family Planning Perspectives* 25 (1993): 52–60. For a critique of this study, see H. Taylor, "Number of Gay Men More Than 4 Times Higher Than the 1 Percent Reported in a Recent Survey," *The Harris Poll* 20 (1993): 1–4.

5. Unpublished results of A. Pattatucci and D. Hamer, cited in D. H. Hamer, S. Hu, V. L. Magnuson, N. Hu, and A. Pattatucci, "A Linkage between DNA Markers on the X-Chromosome and Male Sexual Orientation," *Science* 261 (1993): 321–337.

6. Bettina Boxall, "Statistics on Gays Called Unreliable," *Los Angeles Times* (May 1, 1994), p. A3, and personal communication. It should be

borne in mind that the 1992 election was of particular significance to gays and lesbians, which may have increased their representation among voters.

7. *A Yankelovich MONITOR Perspective on Gays/Lesbians* (Norwalk, CT: Yankelovich Partners, 1994). In this chapter, where we mention differences between gays and nongays reported in the Yankelovich study, these differences were significant at the 95 percent confidence level, except where indicated to the contrary.

8. K. Wellings, K. Field, A. M. Johnson, and J. Wadsworth, *Sexual Behaviour in Britain—The National Survey of Sexual Attitudes and Lifestyles* (London: Penguin, 1994), p. 183.

9. P. Aldhous, "French Venture Where U.S. Fears to Tread," *Science* 257 (1992): 25.

10. G. van Zessen and T. Sandfort, *Seksualiteit in Nederland* (Amsterdam: Swets and Zeitlinger, 1991).

11. F. Whitam and R. M. Mathy, *Male Homosexuality in Four Societies: Brazil, Guatemala, the Philippines, and the United States* (New York: Praeger, 1986).

12. Charlotte Wolff, *Magnus Hirschfeld: A Portrait of a Pioneer in Sexology* (London: Quartet Books, 1986), pp. 58–59.

13. A totally unreliable but footnote-worthy piece of demography survives from fourteenth-century France. A gay man, Arnaud de Verniolles, testified to the Holy Roman Inquisition in Pamiers that three thousand people in that town were "infected with sodomy" (E. L. Ladurie, *Montaillou—The Promised Land of Error*, trans. B. Bray [New York: Vintage Books, 1979], p. 147; John Boswell, *Christianity, Social Tolerance, and Homosexuality* [Chicago: University of Chicago Press, 1980], p. 206, footnote). If Arnaud's assertion is correct, the high incidence of homosexuality is probably to be accounted for by the presence of a seminary in the town: most of the reported instances involved seminary students.

14. Dean Hamer and Peter Copeland, *The Science of Desire* (New York: Simon and Schuster, 1994).

15. One cannot fully discount the possibility that differences such as these might simply reflect differences in people's willingness to admit

to being gay or lesbian. Because the Yankelovich survey reported a higher incidence of homosexuality than most other surveys, however, it seems less likely that underreporting distorted their results. In addition, interviewees were not required to state their sexual orientation directly to the pollsters.

16. Janet Lever, "Sexual Revelations: The 1994 Advocate Survey of Sexuality and Relationships: The Men," *The Advocate* (August 23, 1994), pp. 17–24.

17. The sex of the subscribers was based on first names—ambiguous names were eliminated. We thank John Knoebel, Vice President for Circulation, for providing us with the printouts.

18. The studies have been summarized and reviewed in J. D. Weinrich, "Nonreproduction, Homosexuality, Transsexualism, and Intelligence: I. A Systematic Literature Search," *Journal of Homosexuality* 3 (1978): 275–289.

19. M. Willmott and H. Brierley, "Cognitive Characteristics and Homosexuality," *Archives of Sexual Behavior* 13 (1984): 311–319; C. M. McCormick and S. F. Witelson, "A Cognitive Profile of Homosexual Men Compared to Heterosexual Men and Women," *Psychoneuroendocrinology* 16 (1991): 459–473.

20. "Statistics on Gays Called Unreliable."

21. M. V. Lee Badgett, "The Wage Effects of Sexual Orientation Discrimination," *Industrial and Labor Relations Review*, 48, no. 4 (1995, in press).

22. The Yankelovich data indicate that the "average" gay man lives in a household with 2.03 other individuals whose average incomes are much less than his own, while the "average" lesbian lives with 1.78 people whose average incomes are close to her own, and significantly higher than those of gay men's household members. This result is somewhat puzzling, since the obvious candidates for low-income household members—children—were twice as common in the households of lesbians as in those of gay men. Most likely, part of the answer lies with opposite-sex spouses: the wives of married gay men are likely to earn less than the husbands of married lesbians. Gays and lesbians living together may also contribute to the observed data.

23. The survey question did not specify "biological mother," so some fraction of the affirmative answers may refer to adoptions or to informal assumptions of maternal status.

Chapter 6

1. The expression "Boston marriage" is now sometimes used to refer to two lesbians who live together but are not sexual partners.

2. In a 1992 opinion piece Dunn wrote: "The press have effectively made the label stick not through reporting news, but through repetition of innuendo. Lack of facts, statistics or data of any kind have not precluded their recycling old misrepresentations with new quotes. Why should we eschew a 'lesbian school' label even as we affirm our support of the lesbian members of our community? Because it is misleading—we are not predominantly lesbian by any measure—and because we are recruiting students from high school environments where any suggestion of homosexuality can be stigmatic enough to discourage a student from applying for admission" (Mary Maples Dunn, "The 'L-Word Label,'" *NewsSmith*, Spring 1992, p. 12.)

3. In West Hollywood, for example, the ratio of lesbians to gay men increased from 1:9 to 1:7 between 1988 and 1993, according to surveys conducted by the city.

4. Among the pioneers of lesbian-directed porno movies are Nan Kinney and Debi Sundahl of San Francisco, whose company Blush Entertainment puts out titles like *Suburban Dykes*, with its "hot and nasty garage fuck scene."

5. Two recommended books are Susie Bright's *Susie Sexpert's Lesbian Sex World* (Pittsburgh: Cleis Press, 1990), and Pat Califia's *Sapphistry: The Book of Lesbian Sexuality*, 3d ed., revised (Tallahassee, FL: The Naiad Press, 1993).

6. Loulan cites the following personal ad: "Brat Needs Discipline. Jewish, 33-yr-old bottom, new to S/M, rediscovering the lil' kid in me who wants to play (when the mistress is away . . .). This recovering 'p.c. fascist' gets off on bondage, whipping and feathers; food and rubber cat fetishist. Need a top w/sensitivity that can make me mind my p's and q's. No abuse, drugs, alcohol, tobacco, 12-steppers highly preferable; Jewish wimmin most welcome."

7. Cited in Steve Weinstein, "Hot Winter Cruising and Other Gay Odysseys," *Metrosource* (Autumn/Winter 1994), pp. 26–35.

Chapter 7

1. A domestic partnership bill was passed in 1994 but vetoed by Governor Pete Wilson.

Chapter 9

1. In Raymond Luczak, ed., *Eyes of Desire: A Deaf-Gay and Lesbian Reader* (Boston: Alyson Publications, 1993), p. 38. (Reprinted by permission of the author.)

2. Lillian Faderman, *Odd Girls and Twilight Lovers: A History of Lesbian Life in Twentieth-Century America* (New York: Columbia University Press, 1991), p. 287.

3. Walter L. Williams, *The Spirit and the Flesh: Sexual Diversity in American Indian Culture* (Boston: Beacon Press, 1992), pp. 201–229; Paula Gunn Allen, *The Sacred Hoop: Recovering the Feminine in American Indian Traditions* (Boston: Beacon Press, 1986).

4. Will Roscoe, "Living the Tradition: Gay American Indians," in Mark Thompson, ed., *Gay Spirit: Myth and Meaning* (New York: St. Martin's Press, 1987), pp. 69–77.

5. "Hispanic" and "Latino" have approximately the same meaning but different connotations, rather like "homosexual" and "gay": "Hispanic" is an objective term favored by demographers, while "Latino" is more popular as a self-identification.

6. Carla Trujillo "Chicana Lesbians: Fear and Loathing in the Chicano Community," in Carla Trujillo, ed., *The Girls Our Mothers Warned Us About*, pp. 186–194.

7. Unpublished survey by Lourdes Arguelles, cited in *The Girls Our Mothers Warned Us About*, p. 186.

8. L. R. Jaffe, M. Seehaus, C. Wagner, and B. J. Leadbetter, "Anal Intercourse and the Knowledge of Acquired Immunodeficiency Syndrome among Minority-Group Female Adolescents," *Journal of Pediatrics* 112 (1988): 1055–1057; B. Voeller, "AIDS and Heterosexual Anal Intercourse," *Archives of Sexual Behavior* 20 (1991): 233–276.

9. Reinaldo Arenas, *Before Night Falls: A Memoir*, trans. D. M. Koch (New York: Viking Penguin, 1993), p. 113.

10. See Eric Marcus, *Making History: The Struggle for Gay and Lesbian Equal Rights, 1945–1990* (New York: Harper Perennial, 1992), pp. 187–196.

11. E.g., *The Little Death* (Boston: Alyson Publications, 1986). Nava is also co-author, with Robert Dawidoff, of *Created Equal: Why Gay Rights Matter to America* (New York: St. Martin's Press, 1994), which is discussed in chapter 16.

12. Joseph Beam, "Brother to Brother: Words from the Heart," in Joseph Beam, ed., *In the Life: A Black Gay Anthology* (Boston: Alyson Publications, 1986), pp. 230–242.

13. In Essex Hemphill, *Ceremonies: Prose and Poetry* (New York: Plume, 1992), pp. 37–42.

14. J. DeMarco, "Gay Racism," in M. J. Smith, ed., *Black Men/White Men: A Gay Anthology* (San Francisco: Gay Sunshine Press, 1983); L. Icard, "Black Gay Men and Conflicting Social Identities: Sexual Orientation versus Racial Identity," *Journal of Social Work and Human Sexuality* 4 (1986): 83–93; D. K. Loiacano, "Gay Identity Issues among Black Americans: Racism, Homophobia, and the Need for Validation," in Linda D. Garnets and Douglas C. Kimmel, eds., *Psychological Perspectives on Lesbian and Gay Male Experiences* (New York: Columbia University Press, 1993), pp. 364–375.

15. Stephanie Smith, "NCLR's LOC Project Promotes Leadership Roles for People of Color in the Lesbian and Gay Civil Rights Movement," *NCLR Newsletter* (Spring 1994), p. 6.

16. An example of Farrakhan's antigay rhetoric is the following: "Those of you—who are homosexual—you weren't born [that] way brother—You never had a strong male image.... [These] are conditions that are forced on black men. You're filling up the jails and they're turning you into freaks in the jails." Cited by Ron Simmons in "Some Thoughts on the Challenges Facing Black Gay Intellectuals," in Essex Hemphill, *Brother to Brother: New Writings by Black Gay Men* (Boston: Alyson Publications, 1991), pp. 229–252.

17. Gregg Brooks, "Double Pleasure," in *Eyes of Desire*, pp. 147–148.

18. An often-cited but highly questionable statistic is that one-third of all teen suicides are by gay or lesbian youth. This derives from an estimate, based on a study of teenagers who entered shelters and counseling facilities, that the suicide rate among gay and lesbian youth may be two to three times the rate among heterosexual youth (Paul Gibson, "Gay Male and Lesbian Youth Suicide," in U.S. Department of Health and Human Services, *Report of the Secretary's Task Force on Youth Suicide* [Washington, D.C., 1989], vol. 3, pp. 110–142). The applicability of this figure to the general gay and lesbian teen population is very uncertain. In any event, multiplying this figure by an even more questionable number, the famous "10 percent" incidence rate of homosexuality (see chapter 5), and generously rounding up the result, one arrives at the "statistic" that one-third of all teen suicides are gay—one of the least plausible and most damaging of all myths about gay and lesbian people. "We have to stop using those statistics because they make us look foolish," said Teresa DeCrescenzo, executive director of Gay and Lesbian Adolescent Social Services in Los Angeles, "like we don't have legitimate enough claims without using pumped-up statistics." (Karen Ocamb, "Risky Business," *Frontiers* [May 20, 1994], pp. 64–68.) For articles on gay teen suicide from a variety of perspectives, see Gary Remafedi, ed., *Death by Denial: Studies of Suicide in Gay and Lesbian Teenagers* (Boston: Alyson Publications, 1994).

19. New York: G. P. Putnam's Sons.

20. Camille J. Gerstel, Andrew J. Feraios, and Gilbert Herdt, "Widening Circles: An Ethnographic Profile of a Youth Group," in Gilbert Herdt, ed., *Gay and Lesbian Youth* (New York: Harrington Park Press, 1989), pp. 75–92; Gilbert Herdt and Andrew Boxer, *Children of Horizons : How Gay and Lesbian Teens Are Leading a New Way Out of the Closet* (Boston: Beacon Press, 1993).

21. Barbara Macdonald with Cynthia Rich, *Look Me in the Eye: Old Women, Aging, and Ageism* (Minneapolis: Spinsters Ink, 1983).

22. Shevy Healey, "Why OLOC Has an Age Cut-Off of 60? Why We Call Ourselves 'Old?'" OLOC Handbook Committee, *Confronting Ageism Consciousness Raising for Lesbians 60 and Over* (Houston: OLOC, 1992), p. 101.

23. Shevy Healey, "Beyond Barriers," in *Confronting Ageism*, p. 152.

24. Urbana-Champaign: University of Illinois Press, 1982; reprinted by Alyson Publications, 1984.

Chapter 10

1. *The Advocate*, August 23, 1994.

2. Ann Fox, "Development of a Bisexual Identity," in Loraine Hutchins and Lani Kaahumana, *Bi Any Other Name: Bisexual People Speak Out* (Boston: Alyson Publications, 1991).

3. Rebecca Shuster, "Beyond Defense: Considering Next Steps for Bisexual Liberation," in *Bi Any Other Name* , pp. 266–274.

4. S/M stands for sadomasochism, although some practitioners are reinterpreting it as "sensuality and mutuality" or "sex magic." In any event, it refers to the infliction and reception of pain as sexual acts.

5. E.g., Joseph W. Beam, *Leathersex: A Guide for the Curious Outsider and the Serious Player* (Los Angeles: Daedalus Publishing Company, 1994); Pat Califia, *Sensuous Magic: A Guide for Adventurous Couples* (New York: Masquerade Books, 1993); Guy Baldwin, *Ties That Bind: The SM/Leather/Fetish Erotic Style: Issues, Commentaries, and Advice* (Los Angeles: Daedalus Publishing Company, 1993); Mark Thompson, ed., *Leatherfolk : Radical Sex, People, Politics, and Practice* (Boston: Alyson Publications, 1991).

6. Wickie Stamps, "Dyke Daddy Dearest," *Frontiers* (September 23, 1994), p. 71.

7. Gayle Rubin, "The Catacombs: A Temple of the Butthole," in *Leatherfolk*, pp. 119–141.

8. *Leatherfolk*, p. xvii.

9. Joseph W. Beam, "The Spiritual Dimensions of Bondage," in *Leatherfolk*, pp. 257–266.

10. Arnie Kantrowitz, "Swastika Toys," in *Leatherfolk*, pp. 193–209.

11. Jackson has consistently denied all the charges. The civil case was settled out of court and criminal proceedings were dropped after the boy refused to testify.

12. Jonathan Ned Katz, *Gay American History: Lesbians and Gay Men in the U.S.A.* (New York: Meridian Books, 1992), pp. 481–494.

13. Reviewed in Richard Green, *Sexual Science and the Law* (Cambridge, MA: Harvard University Press, 1992), pp. 154–155.

14. Brent Hartinger, "Separating the Men from the Boys," *10 Percent* (Sept./Oct. 1994), p. 45.

15. N. Bubrich and N. McConaghy, "Two Clinically Discrete Syndromes of Transsexualism," *British Journal of Psychiatry* 133 (1978): 73–76; American Psychiatric Association, *Diagnostic and Statistical Manual of Mental Disorders* (3rd. ed.) (Washington, D.C.: A.P.A., 1980); R. Blanchard, "Typology of Male-to-Female Transsexualism," *Archives of Sexual Behavior* 14 (1985): 247–261; F. Leavitt and J. C. Berger, "Clinical Patterns among Male Transsexual Candidates with Erotic Interest in Males," *Archives of Sexual Behavior* 19 (1990): 491–505.

16. For example, Jan Morris, *Conundrum: An Extraordinary Narrative of Transsexualism* (New York: Henry Holt and Company, 1974); Carmen, *My Life, as told to Paul Martin* (Auckland, New Zealand: Benton Ross, 1988).

17. Kate Bornstein, *Gender Outlaw: On Men, Women, and the Rest of Us* (New York: Routledge, 1994), p. 119.

18. See Simon LeVay, *The Sexual Brain* (Cambridge, MA: MIT Press, 1993), pp. 131–135.

19. They are listed in *Tapestry* 69 (Fall 1994).

20. In choosing to spell its name with one "s," Transexual Menace has etymological principles on its side: the prefix "trans-" shortens to "tran-" before a subsequent "s" (compare "transudation").

Chapter 11

1. Essex Hemphill, "To Be Real," in *Ceremonies: Prose and Poetry* (New York: Plume Books, 1992), pp. 11–121.

2. For an interview with Tim Gill, see *Victory!* (May 1994), pp. 18–21.

3. He should not be confused with the historian Jonathan Ned Katz, some of whose work is referenced in chapters 2 and 3.

4. Lillian Faderman, *Surpassing the Love of Men: Romantic Friendship and Love between Women from the Renaissance to the Present* (New York: Quill, 1981); *Odd Girls and Twilight Lovers: A History of Lesbian Life in*

Twentieth-Century America (New York: Columbia University Press, 1991).

5. We found an example of the latter by opening at random a volume of *GLQ—A Journal of Lesbian and Gay Studies*. We stabbed the page and read "Mohr assimilates contemporary work to perennial philosophical controversies regarding metaphysical realism and essentialism. . . ." (Morris B. Kaplan, "The Last Liberal," *GLQ* 1 [1994]: 199–208.)

6. Camille Paglia, *Sexual Personae: Art and Decadence from Nefertiti to Emily Dickinson* (New Haven: Yale University Press, 1990). Paglia's most recent work is *Vamps and Tramps: New Essays* (New York: Vintage Books, 1994).

7. Chicago: University of Chicago Press. Boswell's most recent book is *Same-Sex Unions in Pre-Modern Europe* (New York: Villard Books, 1994).

8. New York: Praeger, 1986.

9. As examples of heterosexual scholars who are currently making important contributions to gay and lesbian studies, we can mention Amy Richlin, a classicist at the University of Southern California who has explored the gay and lesbian life of ancient Rome; Michael Bailey, a psychologist at Northwestern University who is interested in the mental traits associated with sexual orientation (his twin studies are mentioned in chapter 4); and Eve Sedgwick, a Professor of English at Duke University, who has analyzed social aspects of sexual orientation in books such as *The Epistemology of the Closet*.

Chapter 12

1. Audre Lorde, *The Cancer Journals* (Argyle, NY: Spinsters Ink, 1980).

2. Personal communication from Suzanne Haynes, chief of the health education section at the National Cancer Institute. Both Audre Lorde and Flame (the lesbian with breast cancer interviewed in chapter 8) rejected medical advice in favor of nontraditional treatments at some point in their illness.

3. Sharon Batt, *Patient No More: The Politics of Breast Cancer* (Charlottetown, Prince Edward Island: Gynergy Books, 1994).

4. Susan M. Love with Karen Lindsey, *Dr. Susan Love's Breast Book* (Reading, MA: Addison-Wesley Publishing Co., 1990). In a presentation at the June Mazer Lesbian Collection, Los Angeles, in November 1994, Love generally downplayed the notion that lesbians are at markedly higher risk for breast cancer than heterosexual women. For Love's involvement in lesbian parenting issues, see chapter 15.

5. David Shaw, "Does Rise in Breast Cancer Constitute Epidemic?" *Los Angeles Times* (September 13, 1994), p. A16.

6. Judith Bradford and Caitlin Ryan, *The National Lesbian Health Care Survey* (Washington, D.C.: National Gay and Lesbian Health Foundation, 1987).

7. Cheryl Smith, "Women of Size," *Lesbian News* (January 1993), p. 40.

8. The brain region that, from animal experiments, is known to play a central role in the generation of female-typical sex behavior is the ventromedial nucleus of the hypothalamus (For a brief review, see Simon LeVay, *The Sexual Brain* [Cambridge, MA: MIT Press, 1993], pp. 77–79). This same nucleus (though probably not precisely the same nerve cells) is also responsible for the control of feeding behavior. Destruction of the ventromedial nucleus in humans as well as in experimental animals commonly leads to obesity, although the exact location of most sensitive region is disputed; see A. W. Hetherington and S. W. Ranson, "Hypothalamic Lesions and Adiposity in Rats," *Anatomical Record* 78 (1940): 149–172; R. M. Gold, "Hypothalamic Obesity: The Myth of the Ventromedial Nucleus," *Science* 182 (1973): 485–490. Obesity in humans is under partial genetic control: the recently discovered weight-regulatory gene "Ob," which is probably responsible for some human obesity, is believed to code for a satiety factor that is secreted by adipose tissue and exerts a regulatory control of the activity of neurons in the ventromedial nucleus. Thus one could postulate that the association between homosexuality and obesity in some women arises from hormonal or neuronal interactions between weight-regulatory and sex-regulatory circuits at the hypothalamic level. We mention these admittedly speculative ideas to counter the belief that any association between obesity and lesbian orientation must of necessity have a psychosocial origin.

9. D. J. McKirnan and P. L. Peterson, "Alcohol and Drug Use among Homosexual Men and Women: Epidemiology and Population Characteristics," *Addictive Behaviors* 14 (1989): 545–553; D. J. McKirnan and P. L. Peterson, "Psycho–social and Cultural Factors in Alcohol and Drug Abuse: An Analysis of a Homosexual Community," *Addictive Behaviors* 14 (1989): 555–563.

10. P. M. Nardi, "Alcohol and Homosexuality: A Theoretical Perspective," *Journal of Homosexuality* 7 (1982): 9–25; L. Icard and D. M. Traunstein, "Black, Gay, Alcoholic Men: Their Character and Treatment," *Social Casework: The Journal of Contemporary Social Work* (May 1987), pp. 267–272; D. J. McKirnan and P. L. Peterson, "Stress, Expectancies, and Vulnerability to Substance Abuse: A Test of a Model among Homosexual Men," *Journal of Abnormal Psychology* 97 (1988): 461–466; D. Mosbacher, "Lesbian Alcohol and Substance Abuse," *Psychiatric Annals* 47 (1988): 49–50; E. F. Ratner, "Treatment Issues for Chemically Dependent Lesbians and Gay Men," in Linda D. Garnets and Douglas C. Kimmel, eds., *Psychological Perspectives on Lesbian and Gay Male Experiences* (New York: Columbia University Press, 1993), pp. 567–578.

11. E. Ratner, "A Model for the Treatment of Lesbian and Gay Alcohol Abusers," *Alcoholism Treatment Quarterly* 5 (1988): 25–46.

12. S. L. Morrow and D. M. Hawxhurst, "Lesbian Partner Abuse: Implication for Therapists," *Journal of Counseling and Development* 68 (1989): 58–62; N. Hammond, "Lesbian Victims of Relationship Abuse," *Women and Therapy* 8 (1989): 89–105; D. Island and P. Letellier, *Men Who Beat the Men Who Love Them* (New York: Harrington Park Press, 1991); C. Renzetti, *Violent Betrayal: Partner Abuse in Lesbian Relationships* (Newbury Park, CA: Sage Publications, 1992).

13. National Gay and Lesbian Task Force Policy Institute, *Anti-Gay/Lesbian Violence, Victimization, and Defamation in 1993: Local Trends, Victimization Studies, Incident Descriptions, Official and Community Responses* (Washington, D.C.: NGLTFPI, 1994).

14. Los Angeles County Commission on Human Relations, 15th anual report, reported in *Los Angeles Times* (March 30, 1995).

15. L. Garnets, G. M. Herek, and B. Levy. "Violence and Victimization of Lesbians and Gay Men: Mental Health Consequences," in *Psychological Perspectives*, pp. 579–597.

16. American Psychological Association Committee on Lesbian and Gay Concerns, *Final Report of the Task Force on Bias in Psychotherapy with Lesbians and Gay Men* (Washington, D.C.: American Psychological Association, 1990).

17. E. Coleman, *Integrated Identity for Gay Men and Lesbians* (New York: Harrington Park Press, 1988).

18. C. de Monteflores, "Notes on the Management of Difference," in *Psychological Perspectives*, pp. 218–247.

19. Several key articles are included or reprinted in Eli Coleman, ed., *Integrated Identity for Gay Men and Lesbians: Psychotherapeutic Approaches for Emotional Well-Being* (New York: Harrington Park Press, 1988) and *Psychological Perspectives* .

20. V. C. Cass, "Homosexual Identity Formation: A Theoretical Model," *Journal of Homosexuality* 4 (1979): 219–235.

21. O. M. Espín, "Issues of Identity in the Psychology of Latina Lesbians," in *Psychological Perspectives*, pp. 348–363.

22. K. D. George and A. E. Behrendt, "Therapy for Male Couples Experiencing Relationship Problems and Sexual Problems," in *Integrated Identity*, pp. 77–88.

23. D. P. McWhirter and A. M. Mattison, *The Male Couple* (Englewood Cliffs, N.J.: Prentice-Hall, 1984).

24. P. Blumstein and P. Schwartz, *American Couples* (New York: William Morrow, 1983).

25. P. Kaufman, E. Harrison, and M. Hyde, "Distancing for Intimacy in Lesbian Relationships," *American Journal of Psychiatry* 141 (1984): 530–533.

26. M. Hall, "Sex Therapy with Lesbian Couples: A Four-Stage Approach," in *Integrated Identity*, pp. 137–156.

27. National Gay and Lesbian Task Force Policy Institute, *Gay and Lesbian Health Recommendations* (Washington, D.C.: NGLTFPI, 1993).

28. National Gay and Lesbian Task Force Policy Institute, *Lesbian Health Issues and Recommendations* (Washington, D.C.: NGLTFPI, 1993).

Chapter 13

1. There do appear to be some individuals who, judged by their behavior, are likely to have been repeatedly exposed to HIV, but have not become permanently infected and remain HIV-negative with the usual antibody tests. These include some female prostitutes who have had repeated unprotected sex with men in regions of Africa where HIV infection is very common. Furthermore, laboratory tests on the lymphocytes of some of these individuals indicate that they were previously exposed to HIV. Thus it is possible that some individuals are capable of completely eliminating HIV at a very early stage of infection. There has been speculation that this elimination occurs, not through the production of soluble antibodies, but by the other major weapon of the immune system, cell-mediated immunity. This consists of specialized lymphocytes that carry antibody-like molecules on their outer membranes. Studies are currently under way to determine whether there are biological differences between these individuals and those who do become permanently infected. Alternatively, there may be differences in the details of the first exposure event, for example in the amount of virus entering the body, which determine whether permanent infection results or the virus is eliminated. Recently it has been reported that some HIV-infected infants are capable of completely eliminating the infection, although such elimination may be a very rare event.

2. R. Detels, et al., *Journal of the Acquired Immune Deficiency Syndrome* 2 (1989): 77.

3. L. Frumkin and J. Leonard, *Questions and Answers on AIDS*, 2d ed. (Los Angeles: PMIC, 1994).

4. One Italian study followed eighteen sero-opposite lesbian couples who engaged in practices including unprotected orogenital and oro-anal sex, anal manipulation, sex during menses, and reciprocal use of sex toys. The sero-negative partners all remained sero-negative six months after completion of the study. The authors interpret the results to support the view that the risk of sexual transmission of HIV between women is nonexistent, but they acknowledge that a larger

sample size would be required to confirm the results. (R. Raitiri, R. Fora, and A. Sinicco, "No HIV-1 Transmission through Lesbian Sex," *Lancet* 334 [1994]: 270.) For a dissenting view, see comments of Amber Hollibaugh in chapter 14.

5. U.S. House of Representatives Committee on Energy and Commerce, Subcommittee on Health and the Environment, July 12, 1994. Full transcript available from NAPWA.

6. The risk of HIV transmission from a single blood transfusion in the United States is currently somewhere between 1 in 50,000 and 1 in 200,000.

7. The issue is complicated by the broadened diagnostic criteria introduced in 1993. This brought about 25,000 gay male cases forward into the 1993 reporting year that otherwise would have been reported in subsequent years.

8. According to a 1992 study funded by the National Institute of Allergy and Infectious Disease, nearly 3 percent of gay and bisexual men aged 18–29 living in San Francisco become infected every year (*NIAID AIDS Agenda* [Summer 1993], p. 5). If this figure is correct and the situation continues unchanged, nearly a third of these men will be infected or dead before they reach their thirtieth birthday.

9. As discussed earlier, unprotected anal sex can sometimes lead to infection of the insertive partner. But the epidemiological studies cited earlier indicate that this route of transmission is infrequent enough to discount in a broad discussion of the spread of the disease.

Chapter 14

1. For discussions of AIDS in the context of other epidemic diseases, see Arien Mack, ed., *In the Time of Plague: The History and Social Consequences of Lethal Epidemic Disease* (New York: New York University Press, 1991).

2. Michael Callen, *Surviving AIDS* (New York: HarperCollins, 1991), p. 237. Callen's book is far more positive and upbeat than this single angry sentence might suggest.

3. *The Advocate* (May 17, 1994), p. 80.

4. Randy Shilts, *And the Band Played On: Politics, People, and the AIDS Epidemic* (New York: St. Martin's Press, 1987), pp. 528–530. For

Gallo's side to the story, see his book *Virus Hunting—AIDS, Cancer, and the Human Retrovirus: A Story of Scientific Discovery* (New York: Basic Books, 1991).

5. Bruce Nussbaum (New York: Penguin Books, 1991).

6. John Lauritsen (New York: Asklepios, 1993).

7. Cantwell, Alan, Jr. (Los Angeles: Aries Rising Press, 1993).

8. *And the Band Played On*, pp. 594–596.

9. Among whom Simon LeVay includes himself.

10. Sheryl Stolberg, "Still Alive: Defying an Epidemic," *Los Angeles Times* (September 8, 1993), p. A14.

11. *Surviving AIDS*, p.45. He cites unpublished research by Drs. Temoshok and Solomon.

12. *New York Times* (August 7, 1990), p. A11.

13. David Thomas, "TAG, ACT UP in Hot Fax War," *POZ* (October/November, 1994), pp. 18–19.

14. John D'Emilio, *Making Trouble: Essays on Gay History, Politics, and the University* (New York: Routledge, 1992), pp. 220–223.

15. See Leslie Knowlton, "A Time for Dying?," *Los Angeles Times* (July 19, 1994), p. E1.

16. Peter M. Nardi, "That's What Friends Are For—Friends as Family in the Gay and Lesbian Community," in K. Plummer, ed., *Modern Homosexualities: Fragments of Lesbian and Gay Experience* (London: Routledge, 1992), pp. 108–120.

17. A. R. Jonsen and J. Stryker, eds., *The Social Impact of AIDS in the United States* (Washington, D.C.: National Academy Press, 1993).

18. *HIV L.A.: A Directory of Resources for People with HIV* (AIDS Project Los Angeles, Summer 1994).

19. According to APLA's 1993 Annual Report, fund-raising formed 13 percent of APLA's expenditures. According to IRS documents examined by the *Los Angeles Times*, it formed 31 percent of expenditures. The 13 percent figure, according to APLA's Chief Financial Officer William Misenheimer, was arrived at by excluding

the direct expenses of putting on fund-raising events. He told us that APLA is attempting to move toward less costly fund-raising strategies.

20. Ingrid Ricks, "Pain Management," *The Advocate* (May 31, 1994), pp. 41–43.

21. Larry Kramer, "After Seeing Schindler's List," *The Advocate* (April 19, 1994), p. 80.

22. In a national survey of people with HIV infection or AIDS conducted by the National Association of People With AIDS, 1,247 respondents identified as gay men and 12 as lesbians. Of these 12 women, one claimed to have been infected through sex with women. These figures may not be fully representative. (*HIV in America* [NAPWA: Washington, D.C., 1992], p. 11.)

23. Casey Davidson, "Hey, Listen! GMHC's Amber Hollibaugh Tells Lesbians the Truth," *POZ* (August–September, 1994), p. 28.

24. For example, a British Member of Parliament, Michael Brown, responded to his outing by a tabloid newspaper by saying "Thanks to the *News of the World*, I can be a little freer tonight" (*Frontiers* [December 2, 1994], p. 41).

25. Michelangelo Signorile, *Queer in America: Sex, the Media, and the Closets of Power* (New York: Anchor Books, 1994), p. 161.

Chapter 15

1. Some state constitutions do explicitly confer a right to privacy. California, for example, adopted this provision by general vote in the early 1980s, but its relevance to gay and lesbian rights has yet to be tested.

2. 410 U.S. 959 (1973).

3. 478 U.S. 1039 (1986)

4. *Washington Post* (October 26, 1990), p. A3.

5. See discussion in Mark Blasius, *Gay and Lesbian Politics : Sexuality and the Emergence of a New Ethic* (Philadelphia: Temple University Press, 1994), pp. 132–137.

6. New York: St. Martin's Press, 1994, p. 18.

7. *Curran v. Boy Scouts of America*, 23 Cal. 4th. 1307 (1994). An appeal to the California Supreme Court is pending.

8. Quoted in *Frontiers* (April 22, 1994).

9. *Fricke v. Lynch*, 491 F. Supp. 381 (D.R.I. 1980).

10. *Confessions of a Rock Lobster* (Boston: Alyson Publications, 1981).

11. 417 F. 2nd 1161 (1969).

12. Quoted in Nan D. Hunter, Sherryl E. Michaelson, and Thomas B. Stoddard,*The Rights of Lesbians and Gay Men: The Basic ACLU Guide to a Gay Person's Rights* (Carbondale, IL: Southern Illinois University Press, 1992), p. 20.

13. 530 F. 2nd 247 (1976) (vacated and remanded 429 U.S. 1034).

14. *U.S. Customs v. National Treasury Union*, cited in Harvard Law Review, *Sexual Orientation and the Law* (Cambridge, MA: Harvard University Press, 1990), p. 49.

15. Statistics cited in*The Rights of Lesbians and Gay Men*, p. 41.

16. U.S. Department of Defense data, cited in Art Pine, "Few Benefit From New Military Policy on Gays," *Los Angeles Times* (February 6, 1995), p. A1.

17. *Watkins v. United States Army* 875 F. 2nd 699 (1989). The suspect classification was based on the opinion that immutability is not a requirement.

18. *Steffan v. Cheney* 920 F. 2nd 74 (1990).

19. *Meinhold v. U.S. Dept. of Defense* 34 F. 3rd 1469 (1994).

20. *Cammermeyer v. Aspin* 850 F. Supp. 910 (1994).

21. *Romer v. Evans* 94-1039.

22. National Gay and Lesbian Task Force Policy Institute, *Anti-Gay/Lesbian Violence, Victimization, and Defamation in 1993* (Washington, D.C.: NGTLFPI, 1994).

23. Los Angeles County Commission on Human Relations, 15th annual report, reported in *Los Angeles Times* (March 30, 1995).

24. The New York figure reflects incidents reported to gay and lesbian agencies.

25. 113 U.S.S.C. 2194 (1993).

26. Martin Greif, *The Gay Book of Days* (New York: Carol Publishing Group, 1989), p. 47.

27. The Unruh Act states that "All persons within the jurisdiction of this state are free and equal, and no matter what their sex, race, color, religion, ancestry, national origin, or disability are entitled to the full and equal accommodations, advantages, facilities, privileges, or services in all business establishments of every kind whatsoever." Although the Act does not mention sexual orientation explicitly, the California Supreme Court ruled in *Harris v. Capital Growth Investors XIV*, 52 Cal. 3rd 1142 (1991), that it applied to prevent arbitrary discrimination against gays and lesbians.

28. For contrasting points of view, see Thomas Stoddard, "Why Gay People Should Seek the Right to Marry," and Paula Ettelbrick, "Since When Is Marriage a Path to Liberation?" in William B. Rubenstein, *Lesbians, Gay Men, and the Law* (New York: The New Press, 1993), pp. 398–401 and 401–405, respectively.

29. The plaintiffs were two lesbian couples, Ninia Baehr and Genora Dancel, and Tammy Rodrigues and Antoinette Pregil, and one gay male couple, Pat Lagon and Joseph Melilio.

30. *Braschi v. Stahl Associates Co.* 74 N.Y. 2nd 201 (1989).

31. Quoted in *Sexual Orientation and the Law*, pp. 162–163.

32. See for example Richard Green, *Sexual Science and the Law* (Cambridge, MA: Harvard University Press, 1992), pp. 18–49.

33. *Bottoms v. Bottoms* 444 S.E. 2nd 276 (1994).

34. For Selwyn's account of his activities, see Eric Marcus, *Making History: The Struggle for Gay and Lesbian Equal Rights, 1945–1990* (New York: HarperCollins, 1992), pp. 54–58.

Chapter 16

1. Torie Osborn, "Star Search," *The Advocate* (July 12, 1994), p. 80.

2. March 24, 1994, during a debate on a bill to cut off funding to schools that "encourage homosexuality" (see chapter 15). Dornan's remarks were stricken from the congressional record, but not before they had been broadcast live on C-SPAN. See also *Frontiers* (April 22, 1994), p. 15.

3. Michelangelo Signorile, *Queer in America: Sex, the Media, and the Closets of Power* (New York: Anchor Books, 1993), p. 191. The charges were dropped but Bauman lost his bid for reelection. See also Eric Marcus, *Making History: The Struggle for Gay and Lesbian Equal Rights, 1945–1990* (New York: HarperCollins, 1992), pp. 356–367.

4. Dale McCormick, "Running in a Rural District," in Kathleen DeBold, ed., *Out for Office: Campaigning in the Gay Nineties* (Washington, D.C.: Gay and Lesbian Victory Fund, 1994), pp. 223–225.

5. Sarah Schulman, *My American History: Lesbian and Gay Life during the Reagan/Bush Years* (New York: Routledge, 1994), p. 284.

6. Mindy Ridgway, "Manufacturing Hate," *insideOUT* (Summer 1994), p. 12.

7. Joseph Hanania, "KOST-FM Officially Lifts Ban on Same-Sex Music Call-ins," *Los Angeles Times* (September 14, 1994), p. F2.

8. Sidney Blumenthal "Christian Soldiers," *New Yorker* (July 18, 1994), pp. 31–37.

9. "Christian Soldiers."

10. Jack Nelson, "GOP Moderates Warn of Religious Right Takeover," *Los Angeles Times* (July 28, 1994), p. A1.

11. Louis Sahagun, "Rise of Religious Groups Divides Conservative Town," *Los Angeles Times* (July 6, 1994), p. A1.

12. Jean Hardisty, "Constructing Homophobia—Colorado's Right-Wing Attack on Homosexuals," *The Public Eye*, Newsletter of Political Research Associates, Cambridge, MA (March 1993), pp. 1–10.

13. *Frontiers* (July 29, 1994), p. 17.

14. Bruce Bawer, *A Place at the Table: The Gay Individual in American Society* (New York: Poseidon Press, 1993).

15. Michael Nava and Robert Dawidoff, *Created Equal: Why Gay Rights Matter to America* (New York: St. Martin's Press, 1994), p. 137.

Chapter 17

1. Bala Cynwyd, PA: Laugh Lines Press, 1994.

2. Interviews with the artists: Dorothy Allison (by phone) November 25, 1994; Catherine Opie, November 26, 1994; Kaucyila Brooke, November 28, 1994; Jane Cottis, November 28, 1994.

3. Two years' worth of the quarterly have been anthologized in one volume: Diane DiMassa, *Hothead Paisan, Homicidal Lesbian Terrorist* (Pittsburgh and San Francisco: Cleis Press, 1993).

4. Interview, September 22, 1994.

5. Lillian Faderman, *Odd Girls and Twilight Lovers: A History of Lesbian Life in Twentieth-Century America* (New York: Columbia University Press, 1991), p. 220. Faderman devotes a chapter to Lesbian Nation, pp. 215–245.

6. "Waterfall" on Cris Williamson's album *The Changer and the Changed*, coproduced by Margie Adam, Meg Christian, and E. Marcy Dicterow. Words and music by Cris Williamson. © 1975 Bird Ankles Music. Used by permission.

7. Judy Wieder, "Melissa: Rock's Great Dyke Hope," *The Advocate* (July 1994), pp. 45–56.

8. 1994 emi virgin songs, inc. and gohap music (bmi), on the compact disc *Swamp Ophelia*, Epic Records Group, 1994.

9. Katie Cotter, "Lynda Montgomery," *Lesbian News* 20 (October 1994), p. 44.

10. Interview with Kate Clinton, November 16, 1994.

11. Gay comic Frank Maya does a routine about Anne Frank, certainly an edgy piece; the audience finds itself laughing when Maya makes pointed references to the family's hiding in the attic, saying if it had been his family he'd have worn heavy shoes and tromped around saying "We're up here." That kind of edge has crept into some of Clinton's work when she uses cultural icons such as Rose Kennedy and does not treat them with the almost sacrosanct respect they usually receive.

12. Victoria Brownworth, "Karen Williams," *Lesbian News* 20 (October 1994), p. 45.

13. Interview with Alison Bechdel, November 2, 1994.

14. Emily Dickinson was in love with several women during her lifetime, among them Sue Gilbert and Kate Anthon. Dickinson's family and literary executor went so far as to alter the chronology of some of her work so that it would better fit the theory of a male suitor who served as her muse and eventually spurned her.

15. Mary Barnard, *Sappho: A New Translation* (Berkeley: University of California Press, 1958).

16. Lillian Faderman, ed., *Chloe Plus Olivia: An Anthology of Lesbian Literature from the Seventeenth Century to the Present* (New York: Viking, 1994), pp. ix–x.

17. Lillian Faderman *Surpassing the Love of Men: Romantic Friendship and Love between Women from the Renaissance to the Present* (New York: William Morrow, 1982).

18. *Lifting Belly* is an erotic lesbian poem Stein wrote between 1915 and 1917. It was not published until 1953, and it was rediscovered by scholar Rebecca Mark. Gertrude Stein, *Lifting Belly*, Rebecca Mark, ed. (Tallahassee, FL: The Naiad Press, 1989). *Q.E.D.* is about a love triangle among three women.

19. Radclyffe Hall, *The Well of Loneliness* (New York: Doubleday, 1928), p.430.

20. Ann Bannon's Beebo Brinker series is now published by The Naiad Press: *Odd Girl Out*, 1957; *I Am a Woman*, 1959; *Women in the Shadows*, 1959; *Journey to a Woman*, 1960; *Beebo Brinker*, 1962.

21. Isabel Miller, *Patience and Sarah* (New York: Fawcett Crest, 1973). Originally published in 1969 as *A Place for Us*.

22. Tallahassee, FL: The Naiad Press, 1987 (1964).

23. Originally published by a lesbian press: New York: Daughters Publishing Company, Inc., 1973.

24. "Believing in Literature," in *Skin: Talking about Sex, Class, and Literature* (Ithaca, NY: Firebrand Books, 1994), p. 174. For more on lesbian and gay publishing houses, see chapter 11.

25. *Amateur City* (1984), *Murder at the Nightwood Bar* (1987), *The Beverly Malibu* (1989), *Murder by Tradition* (1991), all published by The Naiad Press.

26. Sarah Schulman, *My American History: Lesbian and Gay Life during the Reagan/Bush Years* (New York: Routledge, 1994); *Empathy* (New York: E.P. Dutton, 1993); *People in Trouble* (New York: E.P. Dutton, 1990); *After Delores* (New York: E.P. Dutton, 1988).

27. New York: Pantheon Books, 1990.

28. Tallahassee, FL: The Naiad Press, 1983.

29. Elly Bulkin and Joan Larkin, eds., *Lesbian Poetry: An Anthology* (Watertown, MA: Persephone Press, 1981).

30. The essay, first published in 1980, is included in *Blood, Bread, and Poetry: Selected Prose 1978–1985* (New York: W.W. Norton and Company, 1986) and also in Henry Abelove, Michèle Aina Barale, and David M. Halperin, eds., *The Lesbian and Gay Studies Reader* (New York and London: Routledge, 1993), pp. 227–254.

31. Adrienne Rich, *The Dream of a Common Language: Poems 1974–1977* (New York: W.W. Norton and Company, 1978); Dorothy Allison, *The Women Who Hate Me* (Ithaca, NY: Firebrand, 1983); Cheryl Clarke, *Living as a Lesbian* (Ithaca, NY: Firebrand, 1986).

32. Katie Brown, "Why We Have Claire Chafee," *Deneuve* 4 (February 1994), p. 34.

33. Television has been more willing to put lesbian characters into episodic shows and some movies of the week. Lesbians are now making shows directed at lesbians, a noted example being "Dyke TV," a weekly half-hour program generated in New York City.

34. Deitch's 1985 *Ms.* interview cited in Vito Russo, *The Celluloid Closet* (New York: Harper and Row, 1981, revised 1987), p. 315. Other lesbians had made lesbian love stories by this time, but not as commercially released and distributed productions.

35. Harmony Hammond, "A Space of Infinite and Pleasurable Possibilities: Lesbian Self-Representation in Visual Art," in Joanna Frueh, Cassandra L. Langer, and Arlene Raven, eds., *New Feminist Criticism: Art, Identity, Action*. (New York: Icon Editions, 1994), p. 105.

36. Ibid., p.102.

37. Many women had been doing this already. The 1980s simply marked a public emergence of these trends, and more open discourse on the various subjects.

38. Pat Califia has been writing about sex since 1979. See her collection of essays, *Public Sex: The Culture of Radical Sex* (Pittsburgh, PA: Cleis Press, 1994).

39. That debate continues with Andrea Dworkin and Catharine A. MacKinnon, both strong antipornography feminists, urging strict antipornography laws and others, including Pat Califia, arguing against such laws, thinking of it as censorship that would result in the banning not just of pornography but of lesbian and gay material as well.

Chapter 18

1. Thomas Mann, *Buddenbrooks: Verfall einer Familie* (Berlin: Fischer-Verlag, 1922), p. 553 (our translation).

2. Marcel Proust, *Remembrance of Things Past*, vol. 1 *(Swann's Way)*, trans. C. K. S. Moncrieff and T. Kilmartin (New York: Random House, 1981), p.122.

3. *The Epic of Gilgamesh*, trans. M. G. Kovacs (Stanford, CA: Stanford University Press, 1989). Reprinted by permission. © 1985, 1989 by the Board of Trustees of the Leland Stanford Junior University.

4. Edmund White, *A Boy's Own Story* (New York: Dutton, 1982).

5. For a somewhat different interpretation of Gilgemesh, see David M. Halperin, *One Hundred Years of Homosexuality and Other Essays on Greek Love* (New York: Routledge, 1990), pp. 75–87. Halperin suggests that, while the friendship between Gilgamesh and Enkidu is explicitly modeled on sexual relationships, this does not justify reading what we call homosexuality into it.

6. We are not aware of any clear evidence about Conrad's sexual orientation. Although his novels seem to be marked by homoerotic themes, they are capable of a variety of interpretations: *The Secret Sharer*, for example, can be read as an entirely intra-psychic drama.

7. Alfred A. Knopf.

8. *The Epic of Gilgamesh*, pp. 69–70.

9. Boy George's version, and a more conventional rendering by Dave Berry, may be compared on a tape issued by SBK Records (4KM-50437).

10. Diane Solway, *A Dance Against Time: The Brief, Brilliant Life of a Joffrey Dancer* (New York: Pocket Books, 1994), p. 3. Stierle died two days after the premiere, aged twenty-three. Dance matriarch Martha Graham, born seventy-three years before Stierle, died in the same month.

11. New York: Crown Publishers, Inc., 1990.

12. New York: Farrar, Straus, and Giroux, 1993.

13. Larry Kramer, *The Normal Heart* (New York: Plume Books, 1985). Reprinted with permission of the author.

14. Oscar Wilde, *Plays* (Harmondsworth: Penguin, 1954), p. 267.

Chapter 19

1. Khalid Duran, "Homosexuality and Islam," in Arlene Swidler, ed., *Homosexuality and World Religions* (Valley Forge, PA: Trinity Press International, 1993), pp. 181–197.

2. Cited in Arvind Sharma, "Homosexuality and Hinduism," in *Homosexuality and World Religions* , pp. 47–80.

3. José I. Cabezón, "Homosexuality and Buddhism," in *Homosexuality and World Religions*.

4. Sacred Congregation for the Doctrine of the Faith, "Declaration on Certain Problems of Sexual Ethics," in Austin Flannery, ed., *Vatican Council II: More Postconciliar Documents* (Grand Rapids, MI: Wm. B. Eerdmans Publishing Co., 1982), p. 486. For a more extensive presentation of the same doctrine, see Sacred Congregation for the Doctrine of the Faith, *On the Pastoral Care of Homosexual Persons* (Rome: Vatican Polyglot Press, 1986).

5. Ron Schow, Wayne Schow, and Marybeth Raynes, eds., *Peculiar People: Mormons and Same-Sex Orientation* (Salt Lake City: Signature Books, 1991).

6. Malcolm Boyd, "Telling a Lie for Christ?" in Mark Thompson, ed., *Gay Spirit: Myth and Meaning* (New York: St. Martin's Press, 1987) pp. 78–87.

7. John Gallagher, "Is God Gay?" *The Advocate* (December 13, 1994), pp. 40–46.

8. For an insightful discussion of these issues, see Marvin M. Ellison, "Homosexuality and Protestantism," in *Homosexuality and World Religions*, pp. 149–179.

9. Judy Grahn, *Another Mother Tongue: Gay Words, Gay Worlds* (Boston: Beacon Press, 1984); Randy P. Conner, *Blossom of Bone: Reclaiming the Connections between Homoeroticism and the Sacred* (San Francisco: HarperSanFrancisco, 1993); Walter L. Williams, *The Spirit and the Flesh: Sexual Diversity in American Indian Culture* (Boston: Beacon Press, 1986). Mark Thompson explores those links in the present day; see *Gay Spirit* as well as *Gay Soul: Finding the Heart of Gay Spirit and Nature* (San Francisco: HarperSanFrancisco, 1994).

10. Starhawk, "Ethics and Justice in Goddess Religion," in Charlene Spretnak, ed., *The Politics of Women's Spirituality: Essays by Founding Mothers of the Movement* (New York: Anchor Books, 1982, 1994), p. 419.

11. Interview, August 24, 1994.

12. Ibid.

13. *The Spirit and the Flesh*, p. 258.

Epilogue

1. *Cherry Grove, Fire Island: Sixty Years in America's First Gay and Lesbian Town* (Boston: Beacon Press, 1993), p. 289.

2. Exit-poll analysis by the *New York Times* (November 13, 1994).

Index